I0805710

# TRANSATLANTIC ROMANTICISM

# TRANSATLANTIC ROMANTICISM

## British and American Art and Literature, 1790–1860

EDITED BY *Andrew Hemingway and Alan Wallach*

University of Massachusetts Press AMHERST AND BOSTON

Copyright © 2015 by University of Massachusetts Press
All rights reserved
Printed in the United States of America

ISBN 978-1-62534-114-3

Designed by Dennis Anderson
Set in Adobe Garamond Pro by House of Equations, Inc.
Printed and bound by Thomson-Shore, Inc.

Library of Congress Cataloging-in-Publication Data

Transatlantic Romanticism : British and American art and literature, 1790/1860 / edited by Andrew Hemingway and Alan Wallach.
pages cm
Includes bibliographical references and index.
ISBN 978-1-62534-114-3 (jacketed hardbound : alk. paper) 1. Romanticism—Great Britain. 2. Romanticism in art—Great Britain. 3. Romanticism—United States. 4. Romanticism in art—United States. 5. Arts, British. 6. Arts, American. I. Hemingway, Andrew. II. Wallach, Alan.
NX452.5.R64T73 2015
700'.4145—dc23
2014026026

British Library Cataloguing-in-Publication Data
A catalogue record for this book is available from the British Library.

The publication of this book was supported by funds from three anonymous donors.

# CONTENTS

# ACKNOWLEDGMENTS

THIS ANTHOLOGY came out of the conference of the same name held at the Paul Mellon Centre for Studies in British Art, the Royal Academy of Arts, and University College London in October 2009. The conference was funded by contributions from these institutions and by the Terra Foundation for American Art. We thank Alison Bracker (Royal Academy) and Martin Postle (Paul Mellon Center) for their support in organizing the event, and Veerle Thielemans (Terra Foundation) for her encouragement and advice. Philippa Kaina played an invaluable role in the management of the conference.

We also want to express our gratitude to the contributors to this volume for their support and forbearance during a long process of gestation, and to Clark Dougan, our editor at University of Massachusetts Press, for his faith in the project. Our thanks as well to Naomi Slipp, who oversaw the myriad details involved in assembling the book.

Finally, we offer heartfelt thanks to Carol Duncan and Phyllis Rosenzweig for their continuing encouragement and critical insights.

# TRANSATLANTIC ROMANTICISM

# Introduction

## Capitalism, Nationalism, and the Romantic *Weltanschauung*

*Andrew Hemingway*

In a well-known essay of 1949, Frederick Antal observed, "Methods of art history, just as pictures, can be dated."[1] Art history has been such a contested and conflicted field in the decades since Antal's remark that this seems something of a commonplace today—even if it did not seem so at the time. I recalled it recently in connection with Hugh Honour's fine book *Romanticism,* which was published in 1979 as one of Penguin's Style and Civilization series, edited by Honour and John Fleming. The series was launched in 1967 and eventually amounted to twelve volumes, of which Honour's was one of the last.[2] An "Editorial Foreword" described the aim of the series as "to discuss each important style in relation to contemporary shifts in emphasis and direction both in the other non-visual arts and in thought and civilization as a whole."[3] The very terms now speak of another time. I suspect that most progressive scholars are uncomfortable with that portentous word "civilization," which reeks of class hierarchies and the demeaning constructions of colonialist and imperialist ideologies. "Style" too is problematic, since, although it still appears in the vernacular of art-historical discourse, art historians generally are little concerned with theoretical reflection on the concept except as a historiographical relic, despite its centrality to the formation of their discipline as a distinct science.

I would hazard a guess that there are three main reasons for the relegation of style to the theoretical shadows. The first is that the category was too much associated with notions of the relative autonomy of art's formal development for the new social history of art that emerged in the 1970s, whose exponents were overwhelmingly concerned to demonstrate the essential connectedness of art with various forms of social power. A second factor is that this new social history of art defined itself against earlier variants largely by its concern with micro-histories of individual works or limited and specific historical episodes: "What exactly were the conditions and relations of artistic production in a specific case?" as T. J. Clark put it in 1974.[4] Correspondingly, it was leery of what seemed the overgeneralizing correlations between style and social outlook that were offered by earlier practitioners such as Antal and Arnold Hauser.[5] The increasing difficulty of making plausible epochal generalizations once art's histories are addressed in this kind of detail has made large-scale style history seem either dubious or obsolete. The third factor was the importation into art history of semiological theory, which to some, at least, promised a more scientific model for establishing the meanings of individual works than style could. Barthesian semiology does not, however, have a precise equivalent to what Meyer Schapiro described as "the constant form—and sometimes the constant elements, qualities, and expression . . . in the art of an individual or group"[6] which makes up style, and often such a concept remains a kind of silent, unspoken or assumed figure in art-historical analysis.

The implications of this neglect of style as an organizing category can be seen, I think, in the most ambitious history of art covering the Romantic period to be published in recent decades, namely, *Nineteenth-Century Art: A Critical History* (1994) by Stephen Eisenman and others, as of 2011 in its fourth edition. Whatever gripes one might have over particular inclusions and exclusions or particular interpretations of works, this is a fine synthesis of much recent scholarship on nineteenth-century art. But it is striking how little attention the authors give to Romanticism as a style category or complex of ideas. I raise this issue not to voice a lament for the good old days when things were simpler, but rather to draw attention to the fact that despite numerous valuable studies produced by the second-wave social history of art, we are still very much in need of fresh work that addresses the relations between artistic forms and the larger history of ideas. "Ideology" and "discourse" are both invaluable concepts, but neither does the work that the now almost unheard-of term *Weltanschauung* used to because they do not fuse ideas with form in the same way or promise the same kind of totalizing synthesis. Part of my argument in this introduction is that we need to refurbish and remobilize the *Weltanschauung* problematic if we are going to develop the kind of synthetic history of arts and ideas that the phenomenon of Romanticism demands.

## *Weltanschauung*

Fundamentally historicist and totalizing, the concept of *Weltanschauung* came to early twentieth-century art history primarily through the philosophical legacy of Wilhelm Dilthey, and reflected his famous distinction between the objects and methods of the *Naturwissenschaften* and *Geisteswissenschaften* (the natural and the cultural sciences).[7] In a brilliantly lucid and ambitious essay of 1923, published in the Vienna *Jahrbuch für Kunstgeschichte,*[8] the Hungarian sociologist Karl Mannheim asserted that cultural products (arts and ideas) were irreducibly part of a totality, the objectification of a *Weltanschauung,* which could not be grasped through conceptual thought or through the cause-and-effect mechanisms central to explanation in the natural sciences. But because a *Weltanschauung* was an experiential object that was a-theoretical and a-logical, this did not mean such objects were irrational;[9] it meant only that atomistic analyses would not deliver their meanings. True understanding of such objects required a kind of "intellectual intuition," capable of approaching them as *Gestalten.*[10] A *Weltanschauung* could be apprehended only through hermeneutic procedures, intuitions of the relationship between whole and part, and part and whole.[11] In fact, Mannheim argued, the history of art offered more promising concepts for the analysis of cultural forms than Dilthey's philosophical typology, exemplifying his point through texts by Alois Riegl and Max Dvořák. Indeed, it was in the correspondences and parallels between phenomena in Dvořák's work that Mannheim found the intuitive method in one of its most sophisticated and persuasive variants. Mannheim's analysis was so attuned to the moment in the development of art history that his essay had a demonstrable influence on Erwin Panofsky's theorization of iconology and on the work of his longtime friend Arnold Hauser.[12]

Mannheim's 1923 formulations are not of a kind that has ever found much of a following in Anglo-American art history. His insistence that the "ultimate object of historical knowledge is . . . the historical process as a whole" is implicitly disparaging of all disciplinary specialisms,[13] while his claims that the cultural analyst is concerned with forms of experience that are by their very nature beyond the compass of reason and conceptual thought and with collective subjects that do not correspond to empirically observable subjects seem paradoxical and the heritage of a discredited and potentially dangerous Hegelian idealism. (One register of this is the comparatively low esteem with which Dvořák's *Kunstgeschichte als Geistesgeschichte* is held within the discipline, compared with the work of, say, Panofsky.)[14] Moreover, Mannheim himself retreated from the extreme historicism of his position in the early 1920s as his career in German academic sociology flourished—although this was a career curtailed by the accession of the National Socialists to power in 1933.

In essays from the early 1930s Mannheim effectively disavowed the claim he had made in 1924 that historicism itself was the *Weltanschauung* of the current epoch.[15] Rather, he argued that ideas should be treated as motivated responses to particular social situations, and resorted to a terminology of "structures" and "functions." In essence, Mannheim sought a middle way between the holistic speculative model of German social thought—epitomized by Hegel and his followers—and the empirical studies of individual social phenomena characteristic of American sociology.[16] In what seems a striking turnaround, he asserted that "ultimate reality . . . attaches only to the individual and only he constitutes the ultimate unit of social action"—although this was qualified by the affirmation that "human relations" were also "real."[17] Given his commitment to a "sociology of the mind," one aspect of the heritage of Hegelianism that Mannheim was bound to repudiate was the notion that ideas had an immanent evolution of their own, a notion he found in its most developed form in art history.[18] Dvořák's work he now presented as only transitional, as leading to a practice in which "discoverable relationships between contemporary works of sculpture, painting, literature, and philosophy" were merely assumed and remained "an intuitive morphology" left undemonstrated.[19] Early social historians of art such as Wilhelm Hausenstein and Richard Hamann had only begun to think the connections between cultural production and social structures. For Mannheim, the "cardinal questions" of an adequate (that is, sociologically grounded) art history would be: "Whose mentality is recorded by given art objects? What is their social identity? What action, situations and what tacit choices furnish the perspectives in which artists perceive and represent some aspect of reality? If works of art reflect points of view, beliefs, affirmations, who are the protagonists and who are the antagonists? Whose reorientation is reflected in changes of style?"[20]

As Mannheim made clear, while such questions could not be answered through concepts such as *Zeitgeist,* neither did they arise within "the fragmentary view of art objects." Indeed, "only society as a structured variable has a history and only in this social continuum can art be understood as a historical entity."[21] Ultimately, causal and interpretative approaches to social phenomena were of equal importance, and indeed complementary; the latter approach, however, was concerned with meaning in the way the former was not. This was the area in which German thought could make its special contribution, "to elaborate the significance of the social processes for the objective creations of culture," though to do so, it needed to be cleansed of "its dead ballast of looseness and falsehood."[22]

Mannheim's "cardinal questions of art history" read like a draft program for the new social history of art that emerged in the 1970s, and there is testimony they had some influence on at least one of its foremost practitioners.[23] But in 1923 Mannheim had been clearer than he was later that the objective of the *Geisteswissenschaften* was interpretative rather than explanatory. A decade or so further on, their work was apportioned between historical (causal) explanation and sociology (structure and functions).[24] Yet while proposing a science that would "study the mechanism by which social thought and action would permeate one another," Mannheim also sought to reassure his reader that this would not reduce the history of art and ideas to "nothing but sociology." On the contrary, "the proposed approach should add a third dimension to the flat and lifeless perspective in which scholastic doctrinaires have presented the creative works of man."[25]

In the end, Mannheim's vision of the "sociology of the mind" left art history a rather unstable compound, since the introduction of social categories inevitably raised questions of social division that threatened to rupture the wholeness of the *Weltanschauung*. Although Dvořák's *Kunstgeschichte als Geistesgeschichte* is almost entirely innocent of sociology, in his fascinating essays on Brueghel and El Greco he defined the "Early Modern" *Weltanschauung* of Mannerism as profoundly contradictory, the product of conflicting impulses in sixteenth-century intellectual culture.[26] For him, the Mannerist style was associated with a reaction against the "widespread spirit of materialism" in the pre-Reformation church, and he compared it with what he understood as the anti-capitalist ethos of contemporary Expressionism.[27] From there it was not a large step to Arnold Hauser's Marxist re-presentation of the Mannerist *Weltanschauung* in his 1964 study of the movement as a response to the forms of alienation produced by the spread of early capitalist social relations.[28] But for all its striking and suggestive homologies between visual forms and ideas, Hauser's argument is notably lacking in analyses of specific works or in that attention to "*facts*—about patronage, about art dealing, about the status of the artist, the structure of artistic production" that Clark saw as an essential component of an adequate social history of art. Put simply, *Weltanschauung* left historians with no obligation to define the specific ideological work that art objects performed and seemed to excuse them from the task of establishing what particular mediations connected ideologies with artistic forms in individual cases.[29]

The reformation of the methodology of *Weltanschauung* as Mannheim had posited it in 1923 in the terms he proposed in the early 1930s was a necessary one, as the limitations of Dvořák's and Hauser's work testifies. Art history needs to encompass causal explanation as well as hermeneutics if its ascriptions of meaning are to have scientific plausibility. The tension between the two is constitutive, not something that can be transcended. But while large generalizations about style and ideas can never substitute for the work of specific interpretation each significant artwork demands, they still have a necessary place in art-historical discourse if we are going to characterize effectively the larger field within which artistic choices are made.

## Romantic Anti-Capitalism as *Weltanschauung*

If the concept of *Weltanschauung* has no currency in present day art-historical scholarship, it has been revived in an exceptionally ambitious and politically charged consideration of Romanticism by Michael Löwy and Robert Sayre, *Romanticism against the Tide of Modernity* (2002), a work that for both authors culminates a long process of reflection on the functions and value of Georg Lukács's concept of "romantic anti-capitalism."[30] Lukács was the leading figure in the Budapest Sunday Circle of 1915–1918, to which Mannheim and the art historians Frederick Antal and Arnold Hauser also belonged. Mannheim and Lukács knew each other from at least 1910 on, and Mannheim was effectively Lukács's follower and disciple to begin with. They would diverge, however, over questions of Marxism and politics in the 1920s, and correspondingly also over philosophy.[31]

Lukács first used the term "romantic anti-capitalism" in print in 1931.[32] It was a term to which he never gave systematic definition, but he deployed it partly to mark a break with his own pre-Marxist writings such as his 1916 book *The Theory of the Novel,* and to designate an "*opposition to capitalism in the name of pre-capitalist values.*"[33] Lukács later described *The Theory of the Novel* as "a reactionary work in every respect,"[34] and for a large part of his later career as a communist he presented "romantic anti-capitalism" as pointing logically toward fascism—inconsistently, since it was precisely such opposition that led him and many other intellectuals of his generation to the left. The novelty of Löwy and Sayre's position lies partly in the way they have turned the category around into a positive term. This does not mean that they give unqualified endorsement to the philosophical position of the pre-Marxist Lukács, but rather that they affirm the "romantic" element that is wedded to Marxism in his early Marxist writings as an appropriate and enriching accompaniment to it—indeed, as effectively the recovery of an element in Marx's own thinking lost within the orthodox Marxism of the Second International. This is notably the case in Lukács's greatest work, *History and Class Consciousness* (1923), a book that he was obliged to renounce in his accommodation with Soviet communism.

So what is "romantic anti-capitalism"? In Löwy's words, it encapsulates the "dominant world view in German and Central European intellectual life" in the early twentieth century, a worldview that entailed a deep hostility to the calculating rationalistic ethos of capitalism which effectively annihilated qualitative values.[35] Or as Löwy and Sayre jointly put it, "romantic anti-capitalism" is an outlook unified by the fact that it "represents the revolt of the repressed, manipulated and deformed subjectivity [that capitalism itself has brought forth] and of the 'magic' of imagination banished from the capitalist world," a revolt that has come in many different forms and political complexions since the eighteenth century and is still a living current in the anti-systemic movements of our own time.[36] Sociologically speaking, it is the outlook of "certain traditional segments of the intelligentsia whose way of life and culture are hostile to bourgeois industrial civilization."[37]

In *Romanticism against the Tide of Modernity,* Löwy and Sayre discard the term "romantic anti-capitalism" on the grounds that it is a pleonasm, since in their view Romanticism—in all its multiple forms—is inherently anti-capitalist. Romanticism is in essence "a specific form of criticism of [capitalist] 'modernity.'" While such critiques may be concerned primarily with the effects of changing technologies on work experience, with the penetration of money and the commodity form into more and more aspects of life, or with the oppressive political and bureaucratic systems that have accompanied these developments, "the most complete and coherent expressions of the Romantic vision" treat these phenomena as all interrelated and forming a totality. Romanticism, so conceived, constitutes modernity's self-criticism, and its particular and distinguishing "tonality" is one of "loss": "The Romantic vision is characterized by the painful and melancholic conviction that in modern reality something precious has been lost, at the level of both individuals and humanity at large; certain essential human values have been alienated." The specificity of Romanticism's critique is thus that it develops "from the standpoint of a value system . . . drawn from the past."[38]

From this perspective, it is possible to see Romanticism as being linked with a diverse range of political stances that Löwy and Sayre characterize through a set of six Weberian ideal types, which are outside my scope here.[39] It encompasses such diverse figures as William Blake, Dickens, Carlyle, Ruskin, William Morris, Charles Peguy, Max Weber, Georg Simmel, Ferdinand Tönnies, Gustav Landauer, Christa Wolf, E. P. Thompson, and Raymond Williams. Chronologically, such Romanticisms can be traced from the eighteenth century down to the present, and the authors' objective is partly to stress the role of Romanticism within all meaningful critique of contemporary capitalism. As Löwy and Sayre put it, "Without nostalgia for the past there can be no dream of an authentic future."[40] While I do not endorse their reconceptualization in all its particulars,[41] it does seem to me that their hypothesis is extremely illuminating in relation to the historical phenomena that are the subject of this volume.

## National Romanticisms

An obvious starting point for reflections on Romanticism as an international phenomenon is Arthur O. Lovejoy's survey of different usages of the term in his provocative 1923 essay "On the Discrimination of Romanticisms," from which he drew the conclusion that "the word 'romantic' has come to mean so many things that, by itself, it means nothing. It has ceased to perform the function of a verbal sign."[42] As a way of re-anchoring it and giving it a more concrete and serviceable content, he urged historians of literature to use the word only in the plural, suggesting that "the 'Romanticism' of one country may have little in common with that of another," and that even within the same national contexts it was important to recognize that the term could apply to "quite distinct thought-complexes."[43] No satisfactory common denominator had been found to unite them all, he opined, and "in any case, each of these so-called Romanticisms was a highly complex and usually an exceedingly unstable intellectual compound; each, in other words, was made up of various unit-ideas linked together, for the most part, not by any indissoluble bonds of logical necessity, but by alogical associative processes."[44]

Lovejoy's position might seem to exemplify precisely the inability of empirical analysis's accumulation of fragmentary observations to apprehend the totality, as Mannheim had posited in 1923. And Lovejoy was criticized for his "extreme nominalism" by René Wellek—a scholar more comfortable with the abstractions of Germanic thought—as part of a general defense of the validity and usefulness of such period terms. Wellek claimed to show (and I agree with him) that "the major romantic movements form a unity of theories, philosophies, and style, and that these, in turn, form a coherent group of ideas each of which implicates the others." As he put it, such period terms should be understood as "regulative concepts," as "a system of norms dominating a specific time," whose rise and decline could be traced, and distinguished clearly from the norms of the preceding and following periods.[45] In other words, they should be understood as something akin to a *Weltanschauung*, although Wellek's claims are not as ambitious or as totalizing as Mannheim's.

Nonetheless, Lovejoy's point about different national Romanticisms is a fruitful one to a degree. That Romanticism was intrinsically linked with the emergence of the modern nationalisms that resulted from the revolutionary anticolonial struggles and European wars of the period circa 1750–1850 is a commonplace. Against the universalizing ambitions of Neoclassicism—although these too could acquire nationalist connotations, as they did in relation to the French Davidian school—Romanticism often vaunted the particularities of what were claimed to be distinctive national cultures and artistic traditions grounded in common language, common histories, and even common racial stock, however mystificatory these claims were. As Roy Porter and Mikuláš Teich have put it, "one common thread to Romanticism across Europe was the forging of historical myths to bolster indigenous national cultures."[46] The mobilization of large numbers of the population for wars conducted by new citizen armies and militias, as well as by older professional armies across a whole range of states with different political formations and ideological requirements, meant that nationalism took a variety of forms and was associated with both radical democratic and reactionary political agendas. Correspondingly, Romanticism had no single political correlate. In Antal's words, "The idea complex, termed romanticism, with its multiple, often contradictory, elements, [signifies] something different in every generation and in each political camp"[47] If nationalism is one of the key factors in explaining the sheer diversity of Romanticism, we should acknowledge its effects in shaping stylistic manifestations but not accept its often patently ideological claims of absolute differences.

## American Nationalism in Washington Irving's *Bracebridge Hall*

In positing the category of Transatlantic Romanticism as the basis for this collection, our conception was not one of a metropolitan English or British Romanticism influencing a postcolonial culture in a condition of dependency but something more dialectical. Yet on the surface, some voices from the period encourage such a view. I am thinking, for instance, of Washington Irving's introduction of "The Author" at the beginning of *Bracebridge Hall* (1822), where he writes, "Having been born and brought up in a new country, yet educated from infancy in the literature of an old one, my mind was filled with historical and poetical associations, connected with places, and manners, and customs of Europe." Indeed, "England is as classic ground to an American, as Italy is to an Englishman; and old London teems with as much historical association as mighty Rome."[48]

Yet one needs to note the tone of irony or burlesque that Paul Giles has pointed up in Irving's style—even though this is arguably more pronounced in *A History of New York* (1809) and *The Sketch-Book* (1819–20) than it is in *Bracebridge Hall*—and also the insistent sense of the author as an observer who is temporally, socially, and politically distanced from his object.[49] Irving describes himself as having "traversed England, a grown-up child" from a "young country," entranced by the novelty of the old, and "delighted by every object, great and small." He not only acknowledges "the whimsical crowd of associations that are apt to beset my mind on mingling about English scenes," but is also clear that the Squire of Bracebridge is "a lingering specimen of the old English country gentleman."[50] There is a constant sense in the book that the squire is a man out of time, the defender of old ways that are not those of the modern world.[51]

Irving clearly marks his own distance by insisting that he is himself "a republican by birth," "brought up in republican principles and habits," and "more confirmed in republican principles by every year's observation and experience."[52] He feels no "servile reverence for titled rank," and Squire Bracebridge represents one of those "families of the ancient gentry, who, though destitute of a titled rank, maintain a high ancestral pride."[53] Although he concedes that when "hereditary distinction . . . falls to the lot of a generous mind" it "may elevate that mind to true nobility," he also implies that there are some with high-sounding titles who do not live up to them and whose loss would not be regretted.[54] One needs to remember that this was published in 1822, only seven years after the end of the so-called War of 1812, which many Americans experienced as a second War of Independence and which boosted American nationalism, although the war also had many opponents in the New England states.

The complex position of a writer such as Irving—who wrote in a style ostensibly associated with English eighteenth-century literature to express a perspective on the contemporary world through the representation of anachronisms—supports, I think, Paul Giles's argument that literature (and art) of the increasingly globalized world system of states that was emerging from the sixteenth century on needs to be studied from a "transnational perspective"[55] if we are to make adequate sense of it. As he claims, "the emergence of autonomous and separate political identities" in the eighteenth and nineteenth centuries "can be seen as intertwined with a play of opposites, a series of reciprocal attractions and repulsions between opposing national situations,"[56] so that "American and British culture comprised disturbing mirror images for each other in the light of their newfound separatism."[57]

In Irving's case this was certainly a mirroring that produced striking tensions and contradictions. For instance, one of Squire Bracebridge's guests is the aged General Harbottle, a fervent royalist who, in the midst of the postwar agricultural depression, refuses to believe there is any "agricultural distress."[58] Yet against the self-interested class blindness of the General needs to be set Irving's deeply unflattering portrayal of the unnamed "village politician" who reads Cobbett and "is a great thorn in the side of the Squire, who is sadly afraid that he will introduce politics into the village, and turn it into an unhappy, thinking community."[59] Yet Irving seems to want to have it both ways here, mocking the appearance of the anonymous newcomer in terms that smack of class distaste—"a long, pale, bilious face; a black beard, so ill-shaven as to leave marks of blood on his shirt-collar [a memory of the guillotine?]; a feverish eye, and a hat sharpened up at the sides into a most pragmatical shape"—at the same time as he gently satirizes the aristocratic blinkers of the General.[60] And while Irving makes the village politician's most intransigent opponent the idealized yeoman farmer "Ready-Money Jack Tibbets," who is characterized as "one of the most loyal men in the country, without being able to reason about the matter," elsewhere he makes it clear that liberty and a thinking, politically engaged people go together.[61] A "thinking community" may be "unhappy," but in the end it is a more just and dignified one. This mix of attitudes may be understood partly as a reflex of Irving's class identification and Federalist politics, but also as the mark of a sense of stadial superiority—the observations of a visitor from a society in a higher stage of social and political development, who condescends to and patronizes the relics of an earlier evolutionary stage.

## The Tonality of Loss in *Bracebridge Hall*

Irving's novel could serve as a paradigmatic instance of Löwy and Sayre's conception of the Romantic *Weltanschauung* in that it repeatedly criticizes the present through a nostalgic roseate vision of an earlier time and is shot through with a sense of loss, however whimsical in expression. These features of the novel emerge most clearly in the contrast between Squire Bracebridge and an old gentleman called symptomatically "Mr. Faddy," who has recently retired to the neighborhood, "having accumulated a large fortune by dint of steam-engines and spinning jennies," and is now "set up for a country gentleman."[62]

Squire Bracebridge's dislike of modern ways is marked in a particularly striking manner in his aversion to "stage coaches, post-chaises, and turnpike roads as serious causes of the corruption of English manners. They have given facilities, he says, to every humdrum citizen to trundle his family about the kingdom, and have sent the follies and fashions of town whirling, in coach-loads, to the remotest part of the island." Irving's observer accepts the logic of the Squire's lament, since later in the book he observes that soon all the quaint objects that distinguish the world of Bracebridge Hall will have disappeared: "Ready-Money Jack will sleep with his fathers; the good Squire, and all his peculiarities, will be buried in the neighboring church. The old Hall will be modernized into a fashionable country-seat, or, peradventure, a manufactory. The park will be cut up into petty farms and kitchen-gardens. A daily coach will run through the village; it will become, like all other commonplace villages, thronged with coachmen, post-boys, tipplers and politicians; and Christmas, May-day, and all the other merry-makings of the 'good old times,' will be forgotten."[63]

Bracebridge's antitype Mr. Faddy has no such sentimentalism, having "brought into the country with him all the practical maxims of the town." He has painted and plastered his old house until it looks "not unlike his own manufactory," and is jealous of his territorial rights being "particularly careful in mending the walls and hedges, and putting up notices of spring-guns and mantraps in every part of his premises." Unlike the Squire, he is "excessively intolerant of everything that is not genteel." But although he seeks to make common cause with the Squire against May Day revels, the Squire—who in fact is deeply concerned to maintain old customs and sponsors the revels—will have nothing of it, and when he is not present rails against the influence of manufactures. "What's to become of merry old England, when its manor-houses are all turned into manufactories, and its sturdy peasantry into pin-makers and stocking-weavers?" Bracebridge asks, and continues, "I have looked in vain for merry Sherwood, and all the greenwood haunts of Robin Hood," but found "the whole country is covered with manufacturing towns." He invokes the view from the ruins of Dudley Castle, which were once the "feudal domains of verdant and beautiful country," but where now he beholds "a mere campus phlegrae; a region of fire; reeking with coal-pits, and furnaces, and smelting-houses, vomiting forth flames and smoke. The pale and ghastly people, toiling among vile exhalation, looked more like demons than human beings . . . What is to become of the country with these evils rankling in its very core? Sir, these manufacturers will be the ruin of our rural manners; they will destroy the national character; they will not leave materials for a single line of poetry."[64]

The Squire believes that trade and the calculating ethos that accompanies it are "destroying the charm of life," and he sees "every new short-hand mode of doing things as an inroad of snug sordid method; and thinks that this will soon become a mere matter-of-fact world, where life will be reduced to a mathematical calculation of conveniences, and everything will be done by steam." Irving's alter ego Geoffrey Crayon, however, does not accept this line of reasoning and is inclined to attribute the passing of that merrier and more leisurely way of life that the Squire mourns, when "the whole nation was a dancing, jovial nation," only partly to "the growing hardship of the times" and the "universal spirit of gain and the calculating habits which commerce has introduced." Chiefly, he thinks, it is down to "the gradual increase of the liberty of the subject, and the growing freedom and activity of opinion," since "a free people are apt to be grave and thoughtful" as "they have high and important matters to occupy their minds."[65]

"They will not leave materials for a single line of poetry." Irving's author laments the passing of a gayer, more leisurely way of life for its aesthetic aspect, but he cannot detach this from the cost of a social order in which deference shades into subservience, and in which inherited rank is open to abuse. Squire Bracebridge has earned the affection of the villagers, but others have not. Irving is caught, however, because through Mr. Faddy he must also acknowledge the increasing dominance of a new order of social relationships in which the social bonds the Squire recognizes play no part. The political order of the American republic puts on the citizenry the responsibility of thinking, which is in the end a more dignified thing.[66] Himself the scion of a mercantile capitalist family, Irving hints at but does not acknowledge a profound tension between the social relations of bourgeois society and the political character of republicanism. The contrast between Squire Bracebridge's Tory paternalism and Mr. Faddy's ruthless exercise of property rights is resolved through the presumed superiority of republican virtue. But there are contradictions here that will not quite jell, and the result is a patched-up job.

To use Löwy and Sayre's terminology, Irving stands for a conservative Romanticism, for which the paradigm is Edmund Burke.[67] That is, he is not a restitutionist who seeks a restoration of an earlier organic hierarchical society—he accepts that the capitalist economic order is an irreversible fact—but he draws on a nostalgic vision of an earlier time to point up the imperfections of the present. I am not suggesting that this is the necessary form of American Romanticism in this period, only that it was a logical and characteristic one for someone of Irving's class and social trajectory. This is confirmed by its commonalities with the outlooks of other Romantic conservatives that feature in this volume, such as Washington Allston and Thomas Cole.

It is partly because of these complex relations between nationalism and the struggles to forge or resist the institutional forms of bourgeois democratic politics that the various theories of Romanticism from the period itself—even if we acknowledge, with Wellek, their basis in a unitary structure of feeling[68]—cannot be made to cohere into a single unitary ideology, despite their common distrust of at least some aspects of Enlightenment universalism and rationalism. Correspondingly, there is no common Romantic style comparable to that of Neoclassical art or Rococo and Baroque; we can only talk about the Romantic styles of particular contexts, and often even of a range of styles that signified Romantic ideas within the same context. In consequence, Antal's aspiration to establish a "precise association of style and outlook" seems a vastly more complex proposition.[69] *Weltanschauung* may be a totality, but the Romantic variant is an internally fractured one that embraces conflicting impulses.[70]

Even so, I hope that my discussion of Irving shows that there is a value in considering American Romanticism from a transatlantic perspective in that the American viewpoint gave a particular character to the Romantic sense of loss.

Irving's revealing observation "My mind was filled with historical and poetical associations, connected with places, and manners, and customs of Europe" suggests that we may need to consider style and iconography in American Romantic painting as being even more infused with connotations of a backward-looking social and political critique than is already commonplace in the historiography of the period.

## The Essays

The arts of the Romantic period, a time frame we roughly designate as circa 1750–1850, were conceived increasingly within and for an urban order of commerce, industry, and capital. This order was inescapably the field of artistic ambition even for artists as much in conservative recoil from modernity as Thomas Cole or Samuel Palmer. It was the cause of that tension between what Raymond Williams described as the period's tendency to view art "as one of a number of specialized kinds of production, subject to much the same conditions as general production," and the characteristic Romantic view that art also embodied some kind of "superior reality" and artists were a very special kind of producer, "the autonomous genius."[71] This tension took shape within the new market conditions in which the artist operated and found expression in his (or more rarely her) frequently voiced sense of distance or estrangement from an uncomprehending audience or public. We find this exemplified in the letters of John Constable, who in 1836 wrote in characteristic vein to a close friend, sounding very much like his American acquaintance Cole: "I now see that I shall never be able to paint down to ignorance. Almost all the world is ignorant and vulgar."[72] Nor was this an opinion Constable reached only in the bitterness and personal disappointment of his later years; back in 1821 he had written to another friend, "I now fear (for my family's sake) I shall never be a popular artist—a Gentleman and Ladies painter."[73]

Such attitudes were hardly unique to Constable. The idea that the public (in the sense of the socially diverse mass of exhibition-goers) was incapable of any profound or discriminating response to serious art is a cliché of early nineteenth-century art criticism; it is paralleled by statements on the reading public by writers as diverse in their political sympathies and social outlook as Coleridge and the young John Stuart Mill. It helps partly to explain the kind of esprit de corps between Romantic writers and artists that we see in their social relations as charted in Wayne Franklin's essay in this volume, and which linked Allston with Cooper, Coleridge, and Irving, and Cole with Cooper and William Cullen Bryant, and so on. One of our motivations for including essays on writers in this volume is that often they gave more developed expositions of Romantic ideology than artists. But another striking feature of the Romantic period is the increasing willingness of artists such as Allston and Cole to enter print to defend their conceptions in the public sphere. They too were in a sense "men of letters."[74] Allston and Cole both wrote poetry, and the former also published a Romantic novel. More important, both aspired to function as moralists to a large audience in need of enlightenment.

We take as a presupposition that London and New York—whatever the differences in their respective ages and cultural histories—were fundamentally similar in their determining character as capitalist metropolises; that Poe might as well have sited his "Man of the Crowd" in Irving's Gotham as in Cobbett's "Great Wen," although he denies it in the story.[75] Matthew Beaumont's essay attends to a key way in which the phenomenology of urban experience was given literary form. In his account, the neurasthenia of the convalescent becomes the signature of a modern consciousness characterized by its distance from quotidian concerns and possessed by a heightened sensitivity that gives it a relentless thirst for the new. It is no accident that the eighteenth century's ideal man of taste was drawn from the landed classes;[76] Beaumont's aesthete in the making is the sick product of a metropolitan milieu governed by fashion and consumption. Yet his fickle feminized sensibility pursues pleasure as an end in itself; in this he too is in reaction against the utilitarian ethos of the capitalist order that has produced him.

In their essays William Vaughan and Dell Upton reflect on general ways in which the metropolis shaped the arts, and in others—notably those by Costello, Grindle, Hemingway, Sayre, and Wallach—we see its specific effects on individual artistic ambitions. Although London would provide the dominant cultural models for American artists in the early nineteenth century, Allston, Catlin, and Cole found that market conditions were broadly similar on both sides of Atlantic, forcing them to contend with the cacophonous displays of the large institutional exhibitions, prompting them to exhibit their works in solo shows they ventured themselves, and putting them in competition with other forms of urban spectacle. Romantic sensibilities may have recoiled in the face of commercialism, but Romantic art was inescapably a commercial phenomenon. As Leo Costello shows, Cole's response to Turner was construed partly through a larger discourse of artistic decline brought about by the corrupting effects of exhibition displays, which were in his eyes a morbid symptom of the inevitable decay of commercial societies. Yet Cole himself could not escape the demands of making a career, as Alan Wallach's account of his calculating moves within the art worlds of New York and London demonstrates. Before the artist made his first return trip to England in 1829, he produced a pair of paintings on spectacular Miltonic themes so close in style to the work of John Martin that he was criticized in the press for plagiarism, and the pull of Martin's inventions did not end there but left traces in some of Cole's most important later pictures. It is striking that Cole should take as a model an artist whose work was almost synonymous with crowd-pleasing exhibition display among British art critics, although Cole may not have understood this initially. As I show in my own essay, while the patrician Washington Allston was equally damning about art that was geared to what he referred to dismissively the "gaze of the multitude," he too was an admirer of Martin and also quite savvy about the showing of his own works.

If Romanticism is best understood, as Löwy and Sayre have argued, as "essentially a reaction against the way of life in capitalist societies,"[77] it was one that proved adaptable to a range of political proclivities. The political tenor of American Romanticism in the early part of the nineteenth century was overwhelmingly "conservative" in the specific sense Löwy and Sayre define. That is, it was infused with a sense of loss for an imaginary ancien régime of stability and organic wholeness, a Europe before the French Revolution. This should not be taken to imply a desire to return to the manners of the pre-Revolutionary French court or the politics of absolutism, but rather something more mythical: an idealized world of chivalry, paternalism, and noblesse oblige grounded in a secure order of ranks, if not in the actual social relations of feudalism. It was not "restitutionist" in Löwy and Sayre's sense—that is, it did not imagine that the pre-Revolutionary order could actually be restored or the advance of capitalism halted—but was closer to Burkean conservatism in the assumption that, while commerce might bring benefits, the leveling forces unleashed by capitalism needed to be constrained by traditional social and political institutions and the forms of deference associated with them.[78] The outlooks of Allston, Cole, Cooper, and Irving can all be seen to match this ideal type, whatever the different stresses within their individual beliefs. That the conservatism of Allston and Cole had stylistic and iconographic correlates is emphasized by the contrasts between their art and that of Martin and Turner drawn out in my essay and Costello's. William Pressly argues that West's shift from a Neoclassical style to what we may see as a Romantic Rubensian mode in his later works was partly what alienated him from his royal patron, already suspicious of the artist's politics.

In the United States there were no radical artisanal artists equivalent to William Blake and Thomas Bewick (discussed in William Vaughan's essay), who exemplify the attitude of what Löwy and Sayre call "Jacobin-Democratic Romanticism," or none who produced an art of any stature, anyway.[79] Neither were there contemporary American equivalents to the more progressive and Promethean visions of Martin and Turner, which, while they register anxieties about the transformations industrial capitalism brought in humanity's relations to nature and within the social order, also manifest a fascination with contemporary technologies and a readiness to treat them as aesthetic matter that matches with a more reformist politics.[80] The implications of these political differences for attitudes toward science are illustrated in Cole's and Martin's respective responses to discoveries in paleontology. As David Bindman shows, Cole did not integrate contemporary discoveries into his images of the early history of the earth in the way Martin conspicuously did. Leo Costello demonstrates that there are equally telling differences in the ways labor figures within the works of Cole and Turner.

Religious experience was one of the main resources for those who sought to resist the increasing dominance of the calculating rationality that accompanied capitalism's penetration of more and more aspects of life. As Max Weber famously (and contentiously) argued, some forms of Protestant belief seem to have been particularly adaptable to this ethos.[81] By contrast, the Romantics tended to be drawn particularly to Catholicism or, in the Protestant countries, to evangelicalism, that is, to versions of Christianity that either were highly ritualized or that placed an emphasis on the individual emotional experience of faith. But faith was not just a personal matter. Christian belief was perceived by the propertied classes as crucial to the maintenance of social order in both European and North American societies of the period, a conviction given added weight by the association between French Jacobinism and atheism and which underlay the major church-building program initiated by the British government in 1818, touched on in Nicholas Grindle's essay. Given the complex relations between the varieties of belief and different social interests, it was inevitable that ideas of religion infused Romantic attitudes toward Enlightenment and politics. Thus the conservatism of Allston and Cole encouraged them to gravitate toward Episcopalianism and Evangelicalism,[82] while Martin's art had associations with radical millenarianism—even if, as David Bindman argues, they were ones he was keen to disavow—and West's apocalyptic themes seem to have had intimations of republicanism in the English context. In his essay, Wayne Franklin points up ways in which the experience of travel on mainland Europe forced American artists and writers to confront Catholic rites and practices that were repugnant to them and most of their fellow citizens. Given the staunch Calvinist orthodoxy of his father, the Reverend Jedidiah Morse, it is not surprising that Samuel Morse found Catholic rituals so distasteful and irrational; doubtless his witnessing them contributed to the anti-Catholic and anti-immigrant pamphlets he published in the 1830s and his role in the Native American Party in the following decade. That Cooper was able to overcome his religious prejudices in a way Morse could not illustrates both the Romantic tendency to valorize poetic experience over calculating reason and to prefer organic hierarchical social relations over atomistic if nominally egalitarian ones.[83]

Questions of capitalist modernity in the United States are inevitably questions about racial difference as well. From the outset, economic growth in the area that became the new polity was linked with the displacement and/or annihilation of native peoples, although this was not a uniform straightforward course in which the original inhabitants and their descendants figure only as passive players. In the long term, however, the kind of exploitative relations with nature and among one another that European settlers brought with them could not coexist with the social arrangements of the tribal societies they encountered. Furthermore, the growth of slavery within the colonies from the early seventeenth century—whatever its economic advantages—introduced an archaic social relationship into an order that was ineluctably modernizing and led to tensions with other expropriative relationships based on "free labor" for both economic and ideological reasons.[84] It also exacerbated differences of interests within the federal structure, further dividing those states in which it was a pivotal economic relationship from those in which it was marginal or nonexistent. These clashes of interests, which were also clashes of cultures, were always reinforced by feelings of otherness that became increasingly racialized. Enlightenment thinking would add to the colonists' ideological armory by giving them a stadial theory of human progress that positioned native peoples and African slaves alike as products of hunting or pastoral cultures that might have particular virtues which accompanied those stages but were destined to be pushed aside in history's inevitable course.[85] At the same time, idealized images of these peoples afforded a vehicle for the primitivist thinking that was one aspect of Romanticism. These tropes are crucial to the various racialized modes of representation analyzed in Robert Sayre's and William Truettner's essays.

Romanticism's valorization of national differences over Enlightenment universalism had the capacity for being racialized. Johann Gottfriend von Herder, however, the leading late eighteenth-century philosopher of cultural relativism, not only refused the idea of polygenesis but also sought to acknowledge national or cultural differences without placing them in some simple hierarchy. For Herder, the differences between the races were effects of environmental conditioning on a single original stock, although this does not take those differences away. Thus for him, black Africans had a peculiarly "sensual disposition" and lacked "finer intellect," whereas Native Americans had a "proud savage love of liberty and war" combined with "goodness of heart, and infantile innocence."[86] These mythologies would increasingly be given "scientific" status.

When considering the role of Romanticism in the ideologies of North American slavery, we should also note that one of its most prominent advocates in the 1850s, the Virginia planter George Fitzhugh, was a precise type of the restitutionist Romantic who, until shortly before the Civil War, argued for slavery not on racial grounds but because, he claimed, the slave was better off, both materially and spiritually, under southern paternalism than the "free laborer" under northern capitalism. Corresponding to this aristocratic social and political vision was Fitzhugh's hostility to the mechanistic Enlightenment philosophies and to modern science.[87]

George M. Fredrickson has argued that by the 1840s, debates about the character of African Americans in the United States generally assumed that "the Negro" was fundamentally different in type from a white race increasingly designated as "Anglo-Saxon." As he puts it, however, "those who ascribed to the priority of feeling over intellect sanctioned by romanticism and evangelical religion" construed "Negro differences" in a way that placed a positive value on them as distinguishing a more virtuous and potentially Christian race, a construction that received its classic literary formulation in Harriet Beecher Stowe's *Uncle Tom's Cabin* (1852), a work that was a powerful weapon in the arsenal of antislavery campaigns on both sides of the Atlantic. The fact that this model of African character, however well intentioned, feminized and de-intellectualized "the Negro," and was usually accompanied by a commitment to repatriation rather than equal citizenship as a long-term solution to race relations in the United States, meant that it was unthreatening to white supremacy and could contribute an ideological bolster to Republican antislavery.[88]

As Janet Koenig argues in her essay, it was the very limits of Stowe's critique of African American subordination—limits that are intrinsic to the particular Romanticism that shapes its imagery—that were crucial to the novel's immense success but also prompted critical responses. As she shows, Richard Hildreth, who had offered a far more radical critique of racial subordination from the perspective of Enlightenment rationalism in his earlier novel *The Slave; or, Memoirs of Archy Moore* (1836), identified one of the key causes of the popularity of *Uncle Tom's Cabin* very acutely in a newspaper article of 1854. Hildreth's own outlook on social and political equality looks limited, however, when set against the ardent democratic Romanticism of Melville's position in his extraordinary *Benito Cereno.*

In organizing this volume we have presumed a unifying outlook that links many of its most substantive works of art and literature with larger perspectives on religion and the organization of social and political life, a particular *Weltanschauung* that is distinct from other possible belief systems in the period. The individual essays touch on this unifying perspective here and there, but like historical essays more generally, they are concerned primarily with positing more limited cause-and-effect relationships. Following Mannheim, we believe that the identification of such causal relationships serves to confirm the existence of the whole and to illuminate the specific ways it was mediated in individual artworks, even if ultimately these essays in part assume what they set out to demonstrate.

## NOTES

1. Frederick Antal, "Remarks on the Method of Art History," in *Classicism and Romanticism with Other Studies in Art History* (London: Routledge & Kegan Paul, 1966), 189.

2. The twelve volumes are John Boardman, *Pre-Classical: From Crete to Archaic Greece* (London: Penguin, 1967); Michael Levey, *Early Renaissance* (London: Penguin, 1967); John Shearman, *Mannerism* (London: Penguin, 1967); Hugh Honour, *Neo-Classicism* (London: Penguin, 1968); Linda Nochlin, *Realism* (London: Penguin, 1971); George Henderson, *Early Medieval* (London: Penguin, 1972); George Henderson, *Gothic* (London: Penguin, 1972); Michael Levey, *High Renaissance* (London: Penguin, 1975); Steven Runciman, *Byzantine Style and Civilization* (London: Penguin, 1975); John Rupert Martin, *Baroque* (London: Penguin, 1977); Hugh Honour, *Romanticism* (London: Penguin, 1979); and Robert Goldwater, *Symbolism* (London: Penguin, 1979).

3. "Editorial Foreword," in Honour, *Neo-Classicism,* 7.

4. T. J. Clark, "The Conditions of Artistic Creation," *Times Literary Supplement* 24 (May 1974): 562. Cf. T. J. Clark, *The Image of the People: Gustave Courbet and the 1848 Revolution* (London: Thames & Hudson, 1973), 10–13.

5. It is worth noting that the single most important conservative voice in British art history in the latter part of the twentieth century, Ernst Gombrich, was also a vociferous opponent of "style and civilization"–type claims and advocated a restrictive Popperian model of "methodological individualism" that seemed to match British art history's penchant for unambitious empiricism before the New Art History came on the scene in the 1970s—although Gombrich's own position was not an empiricist one philosophically speaking.

6. Meyer Schapiro, "Style," in *Theory and Philosophy of Art: Style and Society, Selected Papers,* vol. 4 (New York: George Braziller, 1994), 51. Cf. Barthes's essentially formal concept of "idiolect" in Roland Barthes, *Elements of Semiology,* trans. Annette Lavers and Colin Smith (New York: Hill & Wang, 1968), 21–22.

7. Wilhelm Dilthey, *Dilthey's Philosophy of Existence: Introduction to Weltanschauungslehre,* trans. William Klubach and Martin Weinbaum (New York: Bookman's Associates, 1957); Jürgen Habermas, *Knowledge and Human Interests,* trans. Jeremy J. Schapiro, 2nd ed. (London: Heinemann, 1978), chap. 7.

8. Karl Mannheim, "On the Interpretation of *Weltanschauung,*" chap. 2 of *Essays on the Sociology of Knowledge,* ed. Paul Kecskemeti (London: Routledge & Kegan Paul, 1952).

9. Ibid., 41.

10. Ibid., 69. Cf. "The farther we get away from the world of rigid 'things', the closer we get to the actual historical substratum of psychic and intellectual reality." Karl Mannheim, "Historicism" (1924), ibid., 92. On *Gestalten,* see 121.

11. Ibid., 74, 82.

12. Ibid., 76–80, 56–58. For the interplay between Panofsky and Mannheim, see Joan Hart, "Erwin Panofsky and Karl Mannheim: A Dialogue on Interpretation," *Critical Inquiry* 19, no. 3 (Spring 1993): 534–66. For Hauser and Mannheim, see Arnold Hauser, *Im Gespräch mit Georg Lukács* (Munich: C. H. Beck, 1978).

13. Mannheim, "On the Interpretation of *Weltanschauung,*" 34.

14. Max Dvořák, *Kunstgeschichte als Geistesgeschichte. Studien über abendländischen Kunstentwicklung* (Munich: Piper Verlag, 1924); in English, *The History of Art as the History of Ideas,* trans. John Hardy (London: Routledge & Kegan Paul, 1984). The essay "Idealismus und Naturalismus in der gotischen Skulptur und Malerei," omitted from the 1984 edition, had already appeared as *Idealism and Naturalism in Gothic Art,* trans. Randolph J. Klawiter (Notre Dame: University of Notre Dame Press, 1967). Matthew Rampley's interesting article "Max Dvořák: Art History and the Crisis of Modernity," *Art History* 26, no. 2 (April 2003): 214–37, gives a recent bibliography on Dvořák.

15. Mannheim, "Historicism," 84–85. The later essays appeared as Karl Mannheim, *Essays on the Sociology of Culture,* ed. Ernest Manheim (London: Routledge & Kegan Paul, 1956). For the development of Mannheim's thought in the Weimar years, see Michael Löwy, "Karl Mannheim and Georg Lukács: The Lost Heritage of Heretical Historicism," in *Lukács 2002. Jahrbuch der Internationalen Georg-Lukács-Gesellschaft,* ed. Frank Benseler and Werner Jung (Bielefeld: Aisthesis Verlag, 2002), 61–77.

16. In the lead essay in *Essays on the Sociology of Culture,* "Towards the Sociology of the Mind: An Introduction" (15–89), Mannheim tends to lump Marx with Hegel as both speculative and teleological thinkers, effectively ignoring the monumental empirical aspects of Marx's work and the differences in their epistemologies.

17. Ibid., 53, 68–69.

18. Ibid., 27–28.

19. Ibid., 32–33.

20. Ibid., 33.

21. Ibid., 33. Cf. Mannheim's comments on the limitations of specialist disciplines narrowly conceived: "There is no harm in such constructs . . . so long as they are used as classificatory devices created for convenience," but they were "prone to reification." Ibid., 30.

22. Ibid., 79, 82.

23. T. J. Clark drew my attention to Mannheim's "Digression on Art History" (32–33 in "Towards the Sociology of the Mind") at the conference "L'histoire sociale de l'art: genealogies et enjeux d'une pratique," held at the Institut national d'histoire de l'art, Paris, December, 11–12, 2009, and mentioned its importance for his early thinking on the social history of art.

24. Mannheim, "Towards the Sociology of the Mind," 79.

25. Ibid., 82.

26. Dvořák, *The History of Art as the History of Ideas,* chaps. 5 and 6.

27. Ibid., 103, 108.

28. Arnold Hauser, *Der Manierismus. Die Krise der Renaissance und der Ursprung der modernen Kunst* (Munich: C. H. Beck, 1964); in English, *Mannerism: The Crisis of the Renaissance and the Origin of Modern Art,* trans. Eric Mosbacher (1965; Cambridge: Harvard University Press, 1986), esp. chap. 7. Hauser had already broached this interpretation in *The Social History of Art,* trans. Stanley Goodman, 2 vols. (London: Routledge & Kegan Paul, 1951), 1:353–423.

29. Clark, "The Conditions of Artistic Creation," 562; Clark, *Image of the People,* 13.

30. Michael Löwy and Robert Sayre, *Romanticism against the Tide of Modernity,* trans. Catherine Porter (Durham: Duke University Press, 2001), 7, 4. See also their earlier essay

"Figures of Romantic Anti-Capitalism," *New German Critique,* no. 32 (Spring–Summer 1984): 42–92.

31. On the Lukács-Mannheim relationship, see Löwy, "Karl Mannheim and Georg Lukács." On the Budapest Sunday Circle, see Mary Gluck, *Georg Lukács and His Generation, 1900–1918* (Cambridge: Harvard University Press, 1985).

32. In a 1931 article on Dostoyevsky; see Michael Löwy, "Naphta or Settembrini? Lukács and Romantic Anticapitalism," *New German Critique,* no. 42 (Fall 1987): 27.

33. Georg Lukács, *The Theory of the Novel: A Historico-Philosophical Essay on the Forms of Great Epic Literature,* trans. Anna Bostock (Cambridge: MIT Press, 1971); Löwy and Sayre, "Figures of Romantic Anti-Capitalism," 46.

34. Georg Lukács, "Realism in the Balance," in Ernst Bloch et al., *Aesthetics and Politics* (London: New Left Books, 1977), 49.

35. Löwy, "Naphta or Settembrini?," 23, 16.

36. Löwy and Sayre, "Figures of Romantic Anti-Capitalism," 58.

37. Löwy and Sayre, *Romanticism against the Tide of Modernity,* 85.

38. Ibid., 85, 15, 18, 20, 19, 21, 28.

39. Ibid., 58–83. The six ideal types are denominated by the terms Restitutionist Romanticism, Conservative Romanticism, Fascistic Romanticism, Resigned Romanticism, Reformist Romanticism, and Revolutionary and/or Utopian Romanticism, with the last itself including a number of distinct tendencies.

40. Ibid., 255.

41. I would emphasize more the differences between the character and functions of Romanticism at different moments within this history, along the lines of Lukács's distinction between Romanticism pre- and post-1848 in Georg Lukács, *The Historical Novel,* trans. Hannah Mitchell and Stanley Mitchell (London: Merlin Press, 1962), chap. 3.

42. Arthur O. Lovejoy, "On the Discrimination of Romanticisms," in *Essays in the History of Ideas* (Baltimore: Johns Hopkins University Press, 1948), 232.

43. Ibid., 235.

44. Ibid., 236.

45. René Wellek, "The Concept of Romanticism in Literary Theory," in *Concepts of Criticism,* ed. Stephen G. Nichols Jr. (New Haven: Yale University Press, 1963), 128–29, cf. 156, 195–98; René Wellek, "The Concept of Realism in Literary Scholarship," ibid., 224–25.

46. Roy Porter and Mikuláš Teich, eds., *Romanticism in National Context* (Cambridge: Cambridge University Press, 1988), 5.

47. Frederick Antal, "Reflections on Classicism and Romanticism," in *Classicism and Romanticism,* 26; the essay was published in the *Burlington Magazine* between 1935 and 1941.

48. Washington Irving, *Bracebridge Hall, or The Humourists,* 2 vols. (New York: G. P. Putnam's Sons, 1915?), 1:5. See also the fascinating comparison of English and American trees, in "Forest Trees" (1:113–21). Elsewhere Irving describes England as "my 'fatherland' " (2:319).

49. Paul Giles, *Transatlantic Insurrections: British Culture and the Formation of American Literature* (Philadelphia: University of Pennsylvania Press, 2001), chap. 6. As its subtitle, *The Humourists,* suggests, *Bracebridge Hall* often strikes a comic note and speaks with a kind of storyteller's whimsy, which matches its self-consciously roseate perspective on English

rural and provincial life. "I shall continue on . . . in the course I have hitherto pursued; looking at things poetically rather than politically; describing them as they are, rather than pretending to point out how they should be; and endeavoring to see the world in as pleasant light as circumstances will permit." Irving, *Bracebridge Hall,* 1:11.

50. Irving, *Bracebridge Hall,* 1:8, 10, 14. Bracebridge is partly modeled on Irving's Tory friend Walter Scott, and the estate on the latter's Abbotsford.

51. See, for instance, the chapters titled "Gentility" and "Falconry," ibid., 1:181–87, 150–66.

52. Ibid., 1:119, 9.

53. Ibid., 1:119, 15.

54. Ibid., 1:120–21. On the basis of Irving's literary career as a whole, Allen Guttman argues that Irving and Cooper "were committed *explicitly* to an ordered and hierarchical agrarian society; both were betrayed by their own best works into an implicit celebration of American democrats." Allen Guttman, "Washington Irving and the Conservative Imagination," *American Literature* 36, no. 2 (May 1964): 173. It seems to me that the narrative voice in *Bracebridge Hall* is clear that the political virtues of American republicanism trump the charms of an English rural order that belongs inescapably to the past. This does not alter the rightness of Guttman's judgment overall.

55. Paul Giles, *Atlantic Republic: The American Tradition in English Literature* (Oxford: Oxford University Press, 2006), 5.

56. Giles, *Transatlantic Insurrections,* 1.

57. Ibid., 163.

58. Irving, *Bracebridge Hall,* 1:61.

59. Ibid., 2:67.

60. Ibid., 2:65.

61. Ibid., 2:68, 28–29. Tibbets is introduced in a separate chapter at 1:68–76.

62. Ibid., 2:21.

63. Ibid., 2: 138, 317.

64. Ibid., 2:22, 23, 24–28.

65. Ibid., 2:24–28.

66. "The continual exercise of the mind on political topics gives intenser habits of thinking, and a more serious and earnest demeanor. A nation becomes less gay, but more intellectually active and vigorous. It evinces less play of the fancy, but more power of the imagination; less taste and elegance, but more grandeur of mind; less animated vivacity, but deeper enthusiasm." Ibid., 2:28.

67. Löwy and Sayre, *Romanticism against the Tide of Modernity,* 63–65. Guttman has observed that "the *Sketch-Book* and *Bracebridge Hall* represent a movement from Federalism to a variety of Burkean Conservatism instinctively rather than rationally held" ("Washington Irving and the Conservative Imagination," 170). For another important analysis of Irving's conservatism, focusing on "Rip van Winkle" and "The Legend of Sleepy Hollow," see Donald A. Ringe, "New York and New England: Irving's Criticism of American Society," *American Literature* 38, no. 4 (January 1967): 455–67.

68. Raymond Williams's term aims for something of that deep experiential quality Mannheim associates with *Weltanschauung.* See Raymond Williams, *Marxism and Literature* (Oxford: Oxford University Press, 1977), 128–35.

69. Antal, *Classicism and Romanticism,* 188.

70. In effect, Romanticism's valorization of individualism and its critique of established academic norms served to license criticisms of the hierarchy of genres and to validate new departures in the fields of landscape and genre painting—something that the increasing dependence of many artists on the impersonal mechanisms of the market in bourgeois society made a kind of ideological necessity. While history painting remained the preeminent genre at an institutional level, the rising prestige of landscape and genre ate away at its special claims and at the notion of a common style that was, or should be, the sole *bonne route* in the art of painting.

71. Raymond Williams, *Culture and Society, 1780–1950* (Harmondsworth: Penguin, 1961), 49–50. I have addressed these developments as they bore on the visual arts in Andrew Hemingway, *Landscape Imagery and Urban Culture in Early Nineteenth Century Britain* (Cambridge: Cambridge University Press, 1992), chaps. 1 and 3.

72. John Constable to George Constable, September 16, 1836, in *John Constable's Correspondence,* ed. R. B. Beckett, 6 vols. (Ipswich: Suffolk Records Society, 1962–1968), 5:35.

73. John Constable to John Fisher, n.d. (1821), ibid., 6:63.

74. See Marilyn Butler, "The Rise of the Man of Letters: Coleridge," in *Romantics, Rebels and Reactionaries: English Literature and Its Background, 1760–1830* (Oxford: Oxford University Press, 1981), chap. 3.

75. Edgar Allan Poe, *The Works of Edgar Allan Poe, including the Choicest of his Critical Essays* (London: Chatto & Windus, 1872), 383. Valuable studies of the arts in both metropolises in this period are Celina Fox, ed., *London—World City, 1800–1840* (New Haven: Yale University Press, in association with the Museum of London, 1992); Catherine Hoover Voorsanger and John K. Howat, eds., *Art and the Empire City: New York, 1825–1861* (New York: Metropolitan Museum of Art; New Haven: Yale University Press, 2000).

76. Hemingway, *Landscape Imagery,* chap. 5.

77. Löwy and Sayre, *Romanticism against the Tide of Modernity,* 17.

78. Ibid., 59–65.

79. Ibid., 74–77. The long-term effects of the Anglo-French Wars in stoking nationalism among the British bourgeoisie and middle class as a national popular tradition contributed to the limited appeal of "Jacobin-Democratic Romanticism" for those groups after 1800.

80. For Turner's politics, see John Gage, *"A Wonderful Range of Mind": J. M. W. Turner* (New Haven: Yale University Press, 1987), 212–16; Elizabeth Helsinger, *Rural Scenes and National Representation: Britain, 1815–1850* (Princeton: Princeton University Press, 1997), chap. 5. For Martin's politics, see the essays by Bindman and Hemingway in this volume, which are different in stress. For "reformist Romanticism," see Löwy and Sayre, *Romanticism against the Tide of Modernity,* 71–73.

81. Löwy and Sayre, *Romanticism against the Tide of Modernity,* 30; Max Weber, *The Protestant Ethic and the Spirit of Capitalism,* trans. Talcott Parsons (London: Unwin University Books, 1930).

82. William Truettner and Alan Wallach, eds., *Thomas Cole: Landscape into History* (New Haven: Yale University Press; Washington, D.C.: National Museum of American Art, 1994), 12, 42, 98; David Bjelajac, *Millennial Desire and the Apocalyptic Vision of Washington Allston* (Washington, D.C.: Smithsonian Institution Press, 1988), 197–98n70, 147–53.

83. For Cooper's politics, see Alexander Saxton, *The Rise and Fall of the White Republic: Class Politics and Mass Culture in Nineteenth-Century America* (London: Verso, 1990), 192–93.

84. Eugene D. Genovese, *The World the Slaveholders Made: Two Essays in Interpretation* (Middletown, Conn.: Wesleyan University Press, 1988).

85. Ronald Meek in his study of the theory has shown the centrality of reports of and ideas about Native American cultures in its formulation. See Ronald Meek, *Social Science and the Ignoble Savage* (Cambridge: Cambridge University Press, 1976), chap. 2.

86. Quoted in David Bindman, *Ape to Apollo: Aesthetics and the Idea of Race in the Eighteenth Century* (London: Reaktion Books, 2002), 167–68.

87. Genovese, *The World the Slaveholders Made,* pt. 2; George M. Frederickson, *The Black Image in the White Mind: The Debate on Afro-American Character and Destiny, 1817–1914* (New York: Harper & Row, 1971), 56, 59–60, 68–70. Frederickson contests Genovese's claims for the hegemony of the "aristocratic" theory of slavery in the antebellum South (65).

88. See George M. Frederickson, "Uncle Tom and the Anglo-Saxons: Romantic Racialism in the North," chap. 4 of *The Black Image in the White Mind;* and Alexander Saxton's brilliant analysis in chap. 10 of *The Rise and Fall of the White Republic.*

# I THE CITY

# 1

# "The pit of modern art"

## Practice and Ambition in the London Art World

*William Vaughan*

In 1824, when considering his recent artistic progress, the London-based painter Samuel Palmer wrote in his notebook, "It pleased God to send Mr. Linnell as a good angel from Heaven to pluck me from the pit of modern art."[1]

At the time, Palmer was an ambitious nineteen-year-old. Having first exhibited at the Royal Academy in 1819 at the tender age of fourteen, he was already a seasoned painter of promise who had sold much of his work from exhibition and elsewhere. His decision to turn away from what he saw as a corrupt contemporary practice was spurred not by lack of material success but by an inner turmoil and self-questioning that seem all too evident in the remarkable self-portrait he produced around this time—one of the finest and most evocative self-representations from the period (fig. 1.1). The "Mr. Linnell" he mentioned was John Linnell, a recent acquaintance who had been drawn to Palmer by rumors of the young man's artistic prowess. In recent decades Linnell has been of much interest to art historians for his precocious production of pictures of working landscapes that seem to presage elements of social realism—such as his fine *Gravel Pits at Kensington* (plate 1), in which firmly depicted workmen are shown digging up gravel for use in the West End building trade.[2]

Ironically Linnell's picture of figures toiling in a literal pit could conjure up the metaphorical pit of modern practice that Palmer was protesting about. This was not the side of Linnell, however, that seemed to Palmer to offer him salvation. Rather it was a quite different and apparently contradictory side of Linnell that he was drawn to. This was the side of Linnell that promoted the visionary and the primitive, best remembered in the form of his heroic and generous support

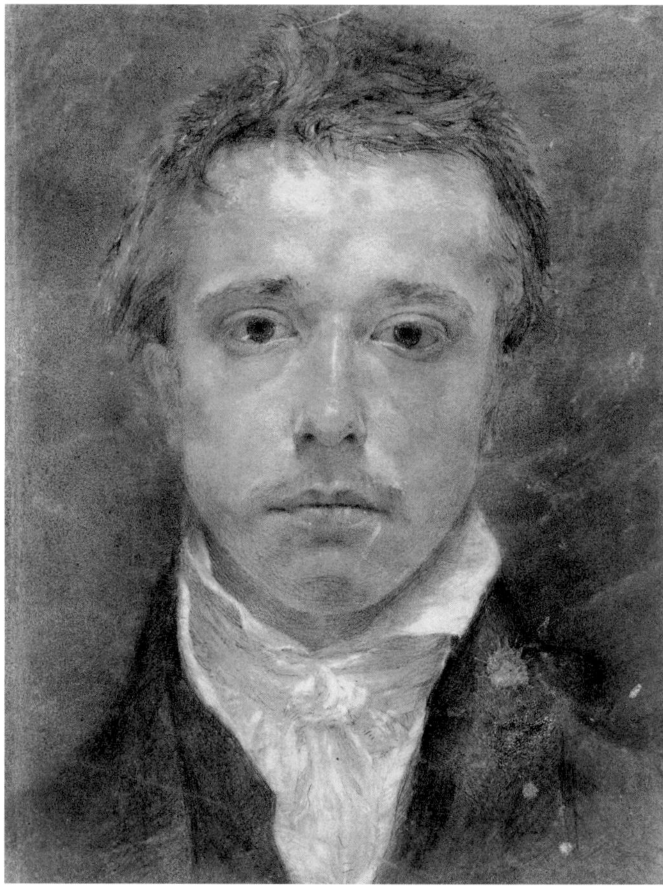

Figure 1.1. Samuel Palmer, *Self-Portrait,* ca. 1824. Black and white chalks on buff paper, 11½ x 9 in. (29.1 x 22.9 cm). Ashmolean Museum, Oxford, 1932.211; purchased (Hope Collection) 1932, © Ashmolean Museum.

of William Blake in the latter's old age. Linnell drew Palmer's attention both to Blake himself and to the art of the later Middle Ages, which seemed to them to be inspired more by spiritual than by materialist concerns. It was such works that opened Palmer's eyes and took him away from the "pit" of modern art.

The outcome in terms of Palmer's work was indisputably to his advantage—artistically if not materially. From being a skilled but unexceptional painter of picturesque sepias and watercolors, he became an innovative explorer of a new kind of spiritualized landscape (fig. 1.2).

The personal gain to Palmer in his journey away from the dominating artistic orthodoxy of the time is indisputable. Yet while this might seem to be one man's protest against the wickedness of the modern world, we should recall that Palmer was far from being alone in his railing against contemporary materialism. Rather one might say that it was the standard complaint. The theme of the fall from grace

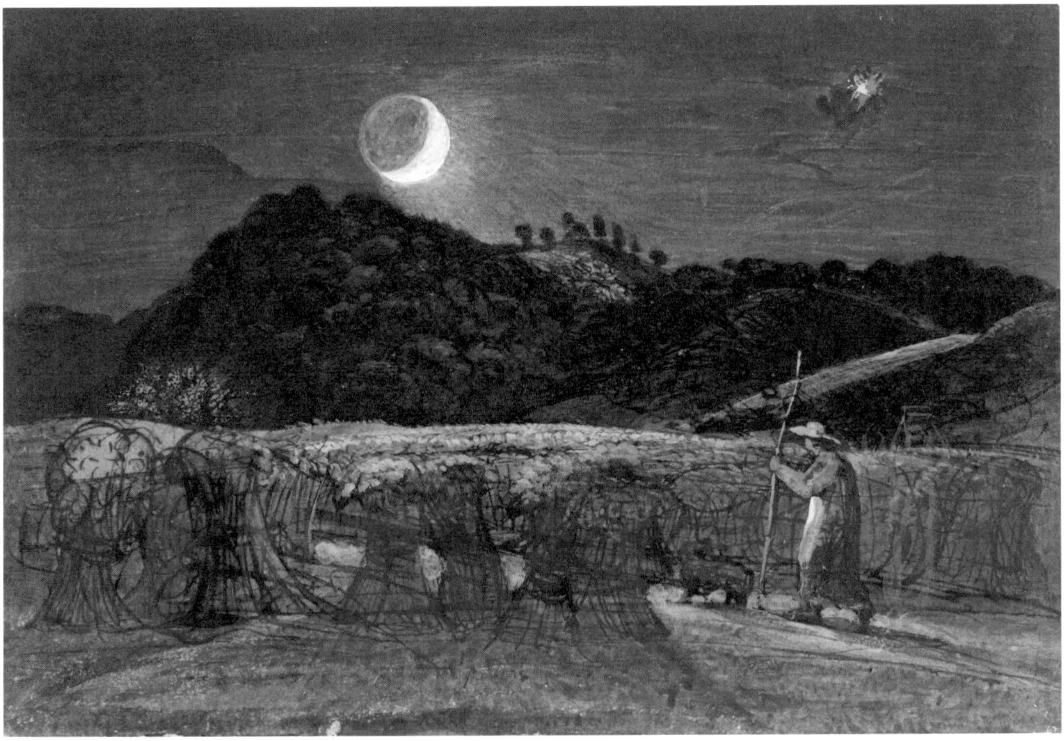

Figure 1.2. Samuel Palmer, *Cornfield by Moonlight, with the Evening Star,* ca. 1828. Watercolor and gouache, with brown ink, varnished, 7¾ x 11¾ in. (19.7 x 29.8 cm). British Museum, London, 1985-5-4-1; purchased with contributions from the National Heritage Memorial Fund, Henry Moore Foundation, British Museum Company, British Museum Friends, and Sir Duncan Oppenheim. © Trustees of the British Museum.

permeated the criticism of the day from the high prose of William Hazlitt to the lowliest of stock-in-trade exhibition reviews.

This tendency in itself brings into play the wider phenomenon that is alluded to in the title of this volume. For one of the central characteristics associated with Romanticism is the expression of a protest against the seemingly irreversible materialistic degradation of the modern world, the Baudelairean "sense of irreparable loss."[3]

Opinion remains divided as ever in historical circles about the usefulness or otherwise of the term "Romanticism." While all would concede that there was a self-conscious "romantic" movement in the period, there is no agreement about whether this signified some fundamental expression of a deep-seated predicament or whether it constituted no more than the posturing of a few escapist reactionaries. Certainly it would be absurd to measure the meaning of all cultural products of the period against some formulaic "romantic" yardstick. Yet it has been noted that the attempt to dismiss the phenomenon altogether leads to a reductive barrenness.[4] Some see the "romantic" protest as a prelude to the more systematic and effective sociopolitical analysis of Marx.[5] While such an interpretation cuts the movement down to size, it does acknowledge the seriousness of the opposition that was being mounted. In *Romanticism against the Tide of Modernity,* Michael Löwy and Robert Sayre have reconsidered the relationship of the movement to an ongoing critique of modern capitalism that has retained its potency to the present day.[6] Their views about its significance are largely shared by the present author.

## British Art and Modernity

Romanticism was an international phenomenon, as evident in the United States as in Britain or in continental Europe. Yet in each country local circumstances stimulated different emphases within the critique. In Britain, where industrialization and entrepreneurial capitalism were already well advanced, the focus was on the dehumanizing and alienating effects of new economic forces. The critique of the modern art world here matched those mounted against aspects of society. To observers both inside and outside Britain, the commercial nature of artistic transactions was never more nakedly evident than it was in London at the time.[7]

This situation is all the more striking because, despite the rampant materialism evident, this seems in retrospect to have been a period of singular artistic achievement. And among those foreign visitors who deplored the commercial nature of the London art world, there were many who nevertheless felt that something new and important had been happening in it. Nowadays we think of 1824, the year in which Palmer anathematized the "pit," as witnessing one of the high spots in British artistic success. For it was in this year that British painting took the Paris Salon by storm, with Constable's famous painting *The Hay Wain* (fig. 1.3) being among the works to receive a gold medal. This success was symptomatic of an enthusiasm for contemporary English art and culture that was sweeping the Continent at that time.[8] As is well known, the great French *romantique* Delacroix is reputed to have repainted the background of his major contribution to the 1824 Salon, *The Massacres of Chios,* after having studied Constable's painting. As Delacroix was later to say, the English opened his eyes to new ways of representing nature. "Their art is so new, Ours is so old," he later wrote to a friend.[9]

The success experienced in British visual arts of the period was strengthened by the international success of contemporary literature, notably the novels of Walter Scott and the poetry of Byron. Behind both was a belief in the presence of an unfettered modernity in British culture.

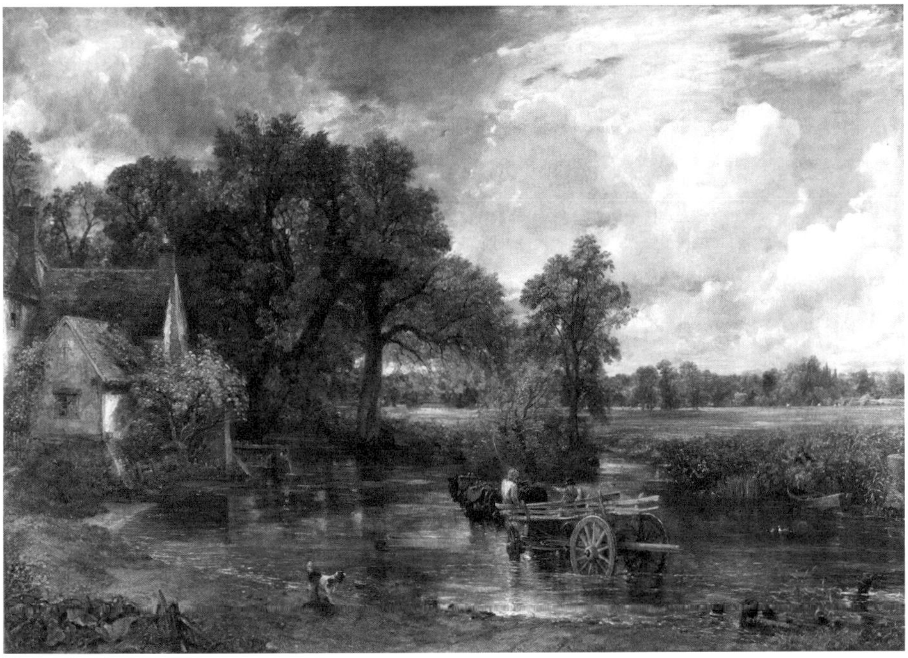

Figure 1.3. John Constable, *The Hay Wain,* 1821. Oil on canvas, 51¼ x 73 in. (130.2 x 185.4 cm). National Gallery, London.

Prowess in landscape was matched, in the eyes of contemporaries at least, by prowess in other forms of modernity. The Scottish artist David Wilkie was at the head of a group who were portraying modern life with a new confidence.[10] Wilkie's patriotic picture *The Chelsea Pensioners Reading the Waterloo Despatch* was so popular that it had to have a bar in front of it when it was shown at the Academy. Yet while evidently appealing to popular nationalistic sentiment, it was also admired by the sophisticated for the freshness of daylight painting in it. It was mentioned with respect by the French painter Géricault, who saw it when he was over in London arranging the exhibition of his celebrated and deeply political masterwork *The Raft of the Medusa.*[11] Géricault's presence in London, incidentally, is a further indication of how important the metropolis was becoming as an international art market at this time.[12]

And as well as landscape and modern life painting, there was also portraiture, the quintessential British skill that had triumphed in the eighteenth century. In the eyes of contemporaries, once again, the undisputed European master of the genre was Sir Thomas Lawrence, who had traveled triumphantly to Rome in 1819 to paint Pope Pius VII and who subsequently became president of the Royal Academy in 1820 on the death of Benjamin West.[13] Lawrence himself had no doubt about the excellence of British art. In his Academy lecture of 1825 he wrote that the contemporary product had no rival in Europe.[14] Doubtless he was influenced by the fact that he was among the artists to be awarded a medal in the Paris Salon of 1824.

Lawrence's confident posture came at the end of a process by which English art seemed to have been gathering in strength over the last half century. His predecessor as president of the Royal Academy, the American Benjamin West, had set the tone for this in many ways with his *Death of Wolfe*—the commemoration of the victor of Quebec who died on the battlefield at his moment of triumph. Despite its clear imperialist message, this celebration of the defeat of the French was celebrated among French artists for introducing the new and relevant genre of modern history painting. The great neoclassical painter David had held a dinner in West's honor when the latter was in Paris in 1802 on account of his innovative opening of this important new genre. And indeed, Géricault, the admirer of Wilkie, could be said to have been following in West's footsteps in the modern treatment of his heroic and tragic historical painting the *Medusa.*

## The Role of the Academy

For many commentators in Britain, including Lawrence himself, much of the growth in the fortunes of British art could be traced back to the establishment of the Royal Academy in London in 1768. Here, for the first time, was an organization with the status of those academies on the Continent—notably that of France—which ensured the production of a high standard of art. In the celebrated picture of the founding members of the Royal Academy by Johan Zoffany, they are shown in conference, a kind of gentlemanly sacra conversazione. The topic that engages them is the positioning of a model—an event that emphasized the correct study of the figure as the linchpin of academic prowess. On the wall behind are plaster casts of antiquity—showing the other great inspiration for academy art, the reverence and emulation of the classical tradition. Though a private institution, the Academy gained authority through royal patronage. Restricted to forty members, it emphasized its status as representing the crème de la crème of the profession. It further cemented its position by running a school for the instruction of young aspirants, and holding an annual exhibition in which the best work of the best contemporary artists could be displayed to the public.

Writing in *The Spirit of the Age* in 1825, Hazlitt commented on how the study of the fine arts "as a polite accomplishment . . . came into fashion about forty years ago."[15] Interestingly, he ascribed to the influence of this fashionable interest the tendency of modern poetry to dwell on minute and exact description of the countryside—whereas we tend to put the influence the other way around. Yet whether Hazlitt's interpretation was accurate, there is no doubt that his assertion of the fashionable status of the fine arts in his time was true, and had as much to do with the impact of the Academy as did the raising of artistic ambition and status. The key factor here was, of course, the annual summer exhibition, which rapidly became a leading event of the social calendar in the later eighteenth century.

The social appeal of the summer exhibition certainly was critical in securing the success of the Academy. This was true not just in terms of social status but also financially. Unlike its counterparts on the Continent, the Royal Academy was—as it remains—a private institution dependent on its own resources for its survival. It charged an entry fee of a shilling to the exhibition. Originally this had been intended as a ploy to keep undesirables—the rabble of the street—out of its polite exhibition space.[16] But the fashionableness of the event meant that it soon made a profit.

I shall return to the matter of the exhibition a little later in this essay. For the moment I want to focus on other implications of the successful establishment of the Academy. The most immediate was that it caused a division in the artistic community. The Academy's creation of an elite of forty members of special status was much resented and soon led to accusations of exclusivity and cronyism. West's *Death of Wolfe* may have been a radically innovative picture that took the Academy by storm when it was exhibited in 1770, two years after the institution's founding. Yet it was not followed by a general policy of support for innovation. In particular, critics felt more and more that the Academy's stated idealism—its support for high-minded historical art—was in conflict with its promotion of commercially saleable works, particularly genre and portraiture. Increasingly there was a body of disappointed idealist artists who felt they had been let down. These included James Barry, the first professor of history painting, who also enjoys the privileged position of being the only academician to be sacked, which happened in 1799 as a result of his open criticism of his fellow academicians.[17]

Early among the dissidents was the visionary painter-poet William Blake. Himself briefly a student at the Academy, Blake was as a young man full of ambition to succeed as a history painter. Yet his manner was too individual for the Academy to contemplate, and he soon found his work being excluded from exhibition. Ultimately this spurred him, in 1809, to stage his own exhibition, in which he showed the works that were receiving so little support, such as the watercolor of the biblical subject *The Angels hovering over the Body of Jesus in the Sepulchre* (plate 2). He also expressed his ambitions for such work in the descriptive catalogue accompanying the show. In the entry for this work he described it as one of the pictures "the artist wishes were in Fresco on an enlarged scale to ornament the altars of Churches, and to make England, like Italy, respected by respectable men of other countries on account of art."[18]

Blake's wish drew attention to a much-felt need for a public display of heroic art that went far beyond the fleeting shows of the Royal Academy. This was felt to be a matter of state importance, something that the Academy—essentially a private gentleman's club—had neither the ability nor the inclination to bring to fruition. Blake's complaint was part of a huge debate that had been going on since the early days of the Academy and that was eventually to lead, in the Victorian period, to the slow and painful involvement of the state in the patronage and support of the arts. In this earlier period, however, despite occasional isolated initiatives, art remained essentially a private matter. The basic attitude of the government is summed up by a remark of one prime minister, Lord Melbourne. When being taxed by the historical painter Benjamin Robert Haydon to initiate state support for monumental patriotic paintings in the 1830s, Melbourne exclaimed, "God help the minister that meddles in art!"[19] The situation seemed all the more urgent at the time when Blake wrote, as the country was in the midst of the Napoleonic Wars, and calls to public duty abounded. There was much patriotic writing up of English art at the time, with particular attention to its "naturalism" set against the artificiality of the French.[20] Such a tendency was good for supporting the naturalistic direction in English art, though it hardly helped Blake's cause.

In fact most of the effective opposition to the Academy was from privately organized pressure groups. These came from two main sources: connoisseurs and dissident artistic practitioners. The most striking instance of the former was the establishment of the British Institution in 1805 by a group of connoisseurs who felt that the Academy—a body exclusively of artists—had failed to provide a high-minded lead in matters of the arts.[21] They organized exhibitions to draw the attention of the public to the high art of the Old Masters. These were interspersed with exhibitions of works by living masters. In general the institution could be seen to have encouraged modern artists to measure their efforts against those of the Old Masters. They even introduced a prize for artists to produce pendants for Old Master works that they showed.

## Art and the Market: Dealing and Exhibition

The events consequent on the French Revolution of 1789 had precipitated an immense influx of Old Masters into London, greatly enhancing the metropolis's position as an international art center. This led, among other things, to the opening of the first public collections in London of Old Master work. Both the earliest of these (the Dulwich picture gallery, founded in 1817) and the most famous (the

National Gallery, established in 1824) were started from collections amassed from the new importations.[22]

The emergence of an international market essentially of Old Masters was a double-edged sword for the British, for while further stimulating the interest in art and providing local artists with new sources for inspiration, the Old Masters also constituted a challenge. It was most keenly felt at the upper end of the market—among ambitious history painters. Elsewhere the matter was different—and there is less sign that local artists suffered. One of the reasons for this was the emergence of a growing middle-class market for art, among people who had little ambition to own murky high-priced pictures of events they'd never heard of but were eager to acquire brightly colored representations of their nearest and dearest, and scenes that evoked recent excursions they had made into the country.

In fact the period saw growing numbers of exhibition opportunities for artists working in these categories. With the exception of the British Institution, these were instigated by the second pressure group mentioned earlier: artists disillusioned by the power and practices of the Academy. The most prominent were the watercolorists, who were legendarily mistreated by the Academy, and who set up their own rival exhibiting society in 1804.[23]After a slightly rocky start, this flourished and was in time joined by other exhibiting societies, such as the Society of British Artists. By 1830 there were five institutions regularly holding exhibitions in London.[24] It has been calculated that these societies raised the number of available annual exhibition spaces from around one thousand in 1800 to around five thousand in 1830.[25] The number of artists who exhibited between these two years rose from 216 to 681 (fig. 1.4). Although none of the new societies had quite the status of the Academy, they were all profitable organizations. Like the Academy itself, these bodies made money through exhibition. This was indeed the only reason why they survived. They bear witness to the growing market for art, and also to the fact that this market was essentially a commercial one, favoring art that entertained rather than elevated.

The growing size of the art market can be seen also in the rise in number of artists practicing—as has been suggested by the fivefold increase in exhibitors just mentioned. The situation is further confirmed by information on artists provided by census returns. By 1841, according to the population figures for that year, there were no fewer than 2,030 painters at work in the London area. Interestingly, London accommodated approximately 60 percent of all artists working in England and Wales.[26] The concentration is made all the more evident by the fact that the metropolis itself accounted for no more than 20 percent of the population of England and Wales. In other words, there were three times as many artists per head of population in London as would be expected from the overall population. To a

ARTISTS IN ENGLAND & WALES — 1841 CENSUS

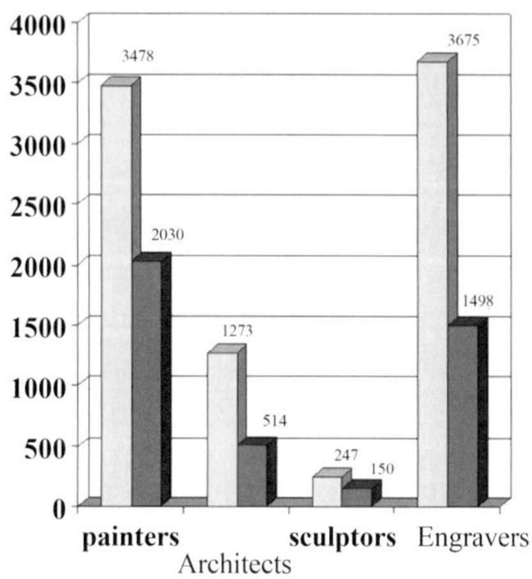


Total Population; 15.9 Million
Total Artists (incl. Architects); 8685

Percentage of Artists in London compared to rest of the Country

| Painters | Architects | Sculptors | Engravers | **Total** |
|---|---|---|---|---|
| 58% | 40% | 61% | 41% | **48%** |

Figure 1.4. Artists in England and Wales, 1841. Figures taken from 1841 Population Census for Great Britain. © William Vaughan.

large extent this artistic community came from outside. According to Christopher Warren, in his dissertation "Professional Pathways for the English Provincial Artist in the Early Nineteenth Century," approximately 80 percent of artists practicing in London came from outside the metropolis.[27] So if you were born outside London at that time and decided to become an artist, you were four times more likely to end up in London than you were to practice elsewhere.

Most of these artists were modest practitioners little regarded by art historians. Yet the evidence is that they were serious professionals earning modest but not disgraceful livings. Their proliferation is a sign of the immense bourgeois market that had grown up as the possession of works of art increasingly became a sign of status in polite society.

Geographically speaking, the artists, like other producers of high-quality luxury goods, were concentrated in specific areas. We are before the days when it had become habitual for the dealer to be the agent of the living artist, and so selling from the studio was still for most artists a highly important outlet. The leading area at this time was what later became known as Fitzrovia—basically the trapezoid network of streets running north of Oxford Street between Regent Street and Tottenham Court Road. What is remarkable, I think, is that all types of artists tended to function here, from the presidents of the Royal Academy (West living in Newman Street, Lawrence in Russell Square, Eastlake in Fitzroy Square) to impecunious students, like the Pre-Raphaelites in their early years.[28]

It was also a center for the service trades—notably the paint makers, such as Rowney's and Winsor & Newton.[29] These serviced professional artists; but they also serviced amateurs, many of whom were significant patrons. Indeed it is probable that the amateur market was more important than the professional in driving technological innovation in this area. Portable premade paints were aimed more at the amateur on tour than the professional studio artist. Yet ultimately the professional gained hugely from the change. It is striking that this area should have seen the birth of one of the most significant advances in paint manufacture—the collapsible tube, so vital in the technical development of *plein air* practices in both Pre-Raphaelitism and Impressionism. The collapsible tube was the brainchild of the American artist J. G. Rand, who was living in Charlotte Street at the time and took out his patent in London in 1840.[30]

Rand's presence is a reminder of the fact that artists from abroad, and perhaps particularly the United States, profited from the great commercial opportunities of the London art world at this time. Individual instances of such connections are examined elsewhere in this book and therefore need not be elaborated here. But I do not want to leave the issue of the wider reach of London without saying a few words about an area not covered elsewhere in this book, namely, its connection with provincial art worlds in Britain.

It may seem paradoxical that the time when artists were so heavily concentrated in London is also the time of a rise of activity in provincial centers—notably Norwich, but also most major ports, such as Liverpool and Bristol.[31] This might seem to be a sign of growing independence and decentralization; and it certainly seems to be the case that by the late nineteenth century, artists were less concentrated in London than they had been. Yet at the same time, this is also a sign of the increasing spread of metropolitan culture through improved communications. Andrew Hemingway has argued that the Norwich school always remained closely connected to the London art world, and this is also true of other regional centers. One could say the rise of provincial centers reinforced the power of London as a market and cultural center.[32]

The apparent failure of art to rise above the marketplace, instead remaining part of the commercial and pleasure-loving side of the expanding metropolis, was much commented on by visitors, and by satirists. The satirical artists Isaac and Cruikshank's picture *A Shilling well laid out* emphasizes this (fig. 1.5). It shows his heroes, two young blades about town, making use of the Academy as a pickup place. In the accompanying text the leading figure, "Corinthian Tom," explains to his follower Jerry how valuable a knowledge of art is to impress the ladies.

The failure of art to rise above such transactions is made even more brutally clear in George Cruikshank's *Monstrosities of 1822* (fig. 1.6). Here he shows young blades strolling in Hyde Park in the ridiculously overblown costume of the day. They come across two young ladies reciprocally garbed. But this is far from a polite encounter. The aggressive display of ankle and petticoat that is going on makes it clear that these are high-class prostitutes plying their trade. Cruikshank spices the joke by placing in the background a famous piece of public "high" art that had recently been erected. This was the statue of Achilles by the academician sculptor Sir Richard Westmacott that had been put up by subscription of the "ladies of England" to honor the Duke of Wellington (whose house was nearby) for his role as the nation's savior at the Battle of Waterloo. Cruikshank has shown the fig leaf put on the statue of this naked Greek warrior to protect its modesty. The warrior is further emasculated by the absence of a sword; a symbol, if ever there was one, of the impotence of high art.

There was something of a personal edge to Cruikshank's satire, for as a caricaturist and illustrator, he was one of those excluded from the ranks of the Academy. This mattered to him. He felt his failure in that direction keenly.[33] But despite its

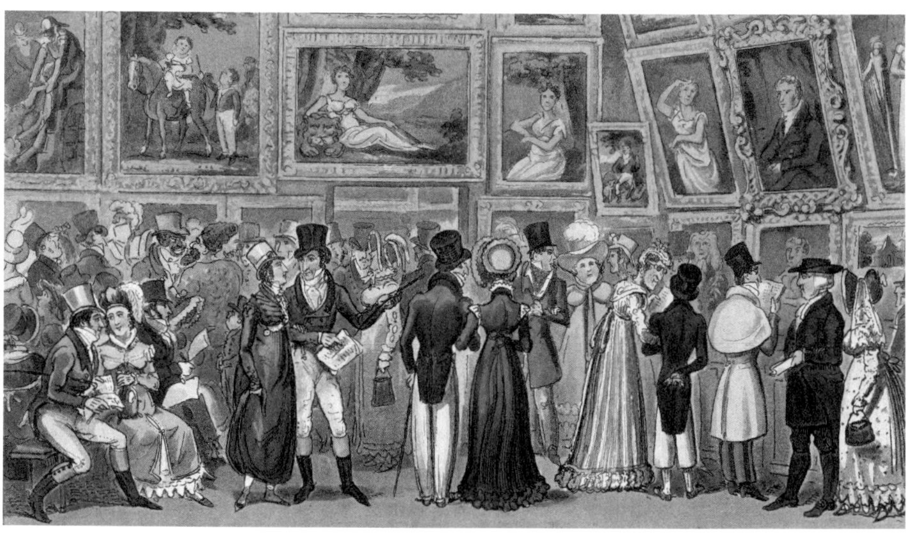

Figure 1.5. Isaac and George Cruikshank, *A Shilling well laid out. Tom and Jerry at the Exhibition of Pictures at the Royal Academy;* from Pierce Egan, *Life in London,* 1821. Etching, 5¾ x 9¼ in. (14.5 x 23.7 cm). © Trustees of the British Museum.

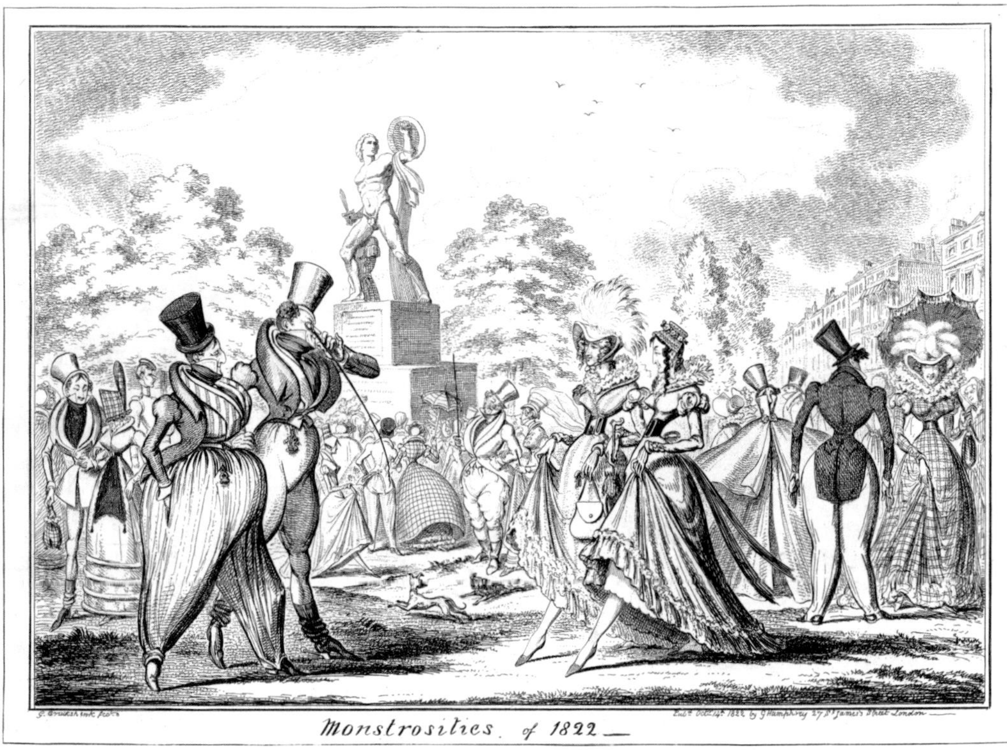


Figure 1.6. George Cruikshank, *Monstrosities of 1822*, 1822. Etching, 10½ x 14½ in. (26 x 37.5 cm). British Museum, London. © Trustees of the British Museum.

lowly status, illustration was becoming more and more the lifeblood of the commercial art world at this time. One of the great developments of the period was the mushrooming of art publications, as well as publications that made use of art illustration. A panoply of new techniques—from the German lithograph to the English aquatint, steel engraving, and enhanced wood engraving—made possible new high-tech and other rapid forms of publication for the growing bourgeois market.[34]

Nothing is more symptomatic of this than the rise of Ackermann's Repository in the Strand, an institution that produced masses of illustrated books on all aspects of fashion, travel, art, and taste. Such activities provided a huge amount of work for the professional engraver but also became a major supplement to the income of a range of artists. Some made fortunes in this way. It is well known that a large part of Turner's wealth came from this market—a wealth that eventually enabled him to adopt a more independent stance in his career as a painter.[35]

## Independence and Opposition

So the art world of London in the early nineteenth century was one of growing economic power and opportunity. But its opportunities came at a price. For while there was much expression of dissatisfaction at the way commercial interest conditioned success, this dissatisfaction did not foment—as it did in contemporary Paris—an active alternative, a determined avant-garde. The small alternative coteries and occasional independent voices did not add up to anything as powerful as this. It was not until the emergence of the Pre-Raphaelites in the late 1840s that such an opposition could be said to have gained any kind of purchase—and even then it was far more mediated than its French counterparts.

The lack of a focused artistic avant-garde in London in the early nineteenth century could well be attributed to structural differences between social and political organization in England and France at the time. In Britain there had been no revolution, no gathering together of dissident forces into an active and alternative opposition. Although radical opposition was maintained and gradually, if painfully, made some headway, it remained throughout this period very much dependent on individual efforts and initiatives.[36] Much the same could be said for artists in Britain who sought to oppose the orthodoxies of the time.

Neither the lack of a cohesive avant-garde nor the overwhelmingly commercial nature of the London art world in the early nineteenth century should permit us to overlook the fact that a certain level of independence remained in artistic practice. While not mounting a consistent communal critique, some artists did at least manage to create some space for themselves. To some degree, such independence could also be seen as symptomatic of the entrepreneurial individualism that flourished as an ideal in the age. Certainly such individuals were as likely to be reactionary as radical in their sympathies. Constable and Samuel Palmer are clear examples of the former, and Blake and Linnell of the latter.

William Blake is perhaps the most striking example of intransigent individualism. Through immense personal sacrifice he managed to maintain an alternative practice with minimal support. Samuel Palmer provided for a time another instance; in his case it was a small legacy that enabled him to pursue his own way for a brief period. It is important to remember that in both these cases, while they were pursuing paths manifestly without economic profit or significant critical acclaim, they were in no sense "private" artists. They had not ceased to address the public. All Blake's prophetic books were for sale, and their tone makes it clear that he is communicating messages of importance to others. "Mark well my words, they are of your eternal salvation" is a much-repeated refrain in his prophetic book *Milton.*

Similarly Palmer, throughout his years of visionary opposition between 1823 and 1835, regularly sent his works for exhibition. And they were largely accepted. He himself expressed surprise that the Academy seemed relatively benign toward what he called his "wonted outrageousness."[37] During his twelve "visionary" years he had thirty works shown at the Academy—not a bad record by anyone's standards. The problem was not that he could not get his work accepted for exhibition. The problem was that he could not sell them.

## The Case of Thomas Bewick

Blake and Palmer are self-evident cases of independent artists seeking to establish their independence. They might seem unique. But I think the occurrence is more extensive than this. There were many other, more covert ways in which artists could maintain integrity toward a personal ambition. I therefore end with a case that might not seem so obvious: that of the Northumbrian wood engraver Thomas Bewick.

Bewick is legendary as the "father" of modern wood engraving, the artist who took a cheap and low-grade form of printmaking and demonstrated that it was capable of the finesse to make it appropriate for high-class printing. Through personal brilliance he was able to reinvent the process—much in the same way that Albrecht Dürer had reinvented the earlier process of the woodcut during the Renaissance. A major outcome was that wood engraving became the standard reproduction method in books until the late Victorian period, when photomechanical processes finally replaced the engraver.

But it is not for this technical revolution alone that Bewick is prized today. It is also for the amazing candor and realism of many of his rural subjects. The son of a Northumbrian farmer, he brought an unsentimental eye to such scenes—much in the same way that Robert Burns and John Clare, both sons of the soil like him, did in their contemporaneous poetry. Bewick's voice is much closer to theirs than it is to that of most of the professional landscape and genre painting of the period, where dominant urban ideologies about rural life prevail. His scenes contrast strongly with those images of rustics in the Royal Academy exhibitions in which the protagonists seem all too often to be suffering from a terminal case of overacting.[38]

I could easily go on praising and citing further instances. But my main question here is, how did he get away with it? He did it, it would seem, by more or less a quirk of fate—or was it by devious and deliberate planning? Coming from an essentially craft background, Bewick—once he had displayed skill at drawing—was trained in the printing trade in Newcastle, much as the artisanal Blake was trained to be an engraver in London. Then, after a few years of developing his prowess, he did what four out of five aspirant provincial artists did at the time. He went to London. Although he was not happy there, his skills were recognized, and within the space of eighteen months he had established himself and clearly had a bright future as a valued engraver in the metropolis. But at this point he did something unusual. He decided to return to his native Northumberland. Retreat was usually the course of those who had not succeeded in the metropolis, but this was not Bewick's case. As Jennifer Uglow has made clear, many of Bewick's friends were at a loss to understand why he would beat a retreat.[39] Yet in fact the move that might have seemed to doom Bewick to obscurity and destruction actually saved him and enabled him to become the artist whose work we admire so much today. Why? Because by returning to Northumberland he was returning to a world that did not have the high degree of specialization—the split between high art and "craft"—so heavily promoted by the Royal Academy in London and so heavily supported by the economic advantages of the division of labor in the new commercial art world. Bewick entered into business with Ralph Beilby, his former master in Newcastle, and became not just the reproducer of other people's designs, as he would undoubtedly have been condemned to be as an engraver in London, but a person who managed, designed, wrote, and illustrated his own publications. These then brought him international fame through that network of commercial relationships that were indeed part of the new capitalist world and that in Britain centered on London. But he maintained his independence by remaining at a distance from London within a more traditional community.

There is more to the matter than this, however. Bewick's fame was based in his own time on his "Natural Histories," works that combined up-to-date knowledge of birds and animals with superlative demonstrations of his skill as a naturalistic engraver of living creatures.

He was at the forefront of knowledge with such works, and no household with claims to politeness and education could be without its Bewicks. But if this were all his art had been, he would now simply be remembered as a great naturalist—a specialist in the history of naturalist illustration. Yet what Bewick is treasured for most of all is those marvelous vignettes he added to the books, in which his rich observation of human life is brought to the fore. These were works that he punningly called his "tale" pieces. And this is more than a simple pun. For these "tale" pieces that sit so incongruously at the foot of his discourse on natural history are indeed "tales," in the sense of stories about his Northumbrian background, his childhood on the farm, and his continued shrewd observation of life around him. They are in no sense sentimental. Nor are they moralizing—except in the earthy sense of a traditional folktale. They are not even politically polemical—though

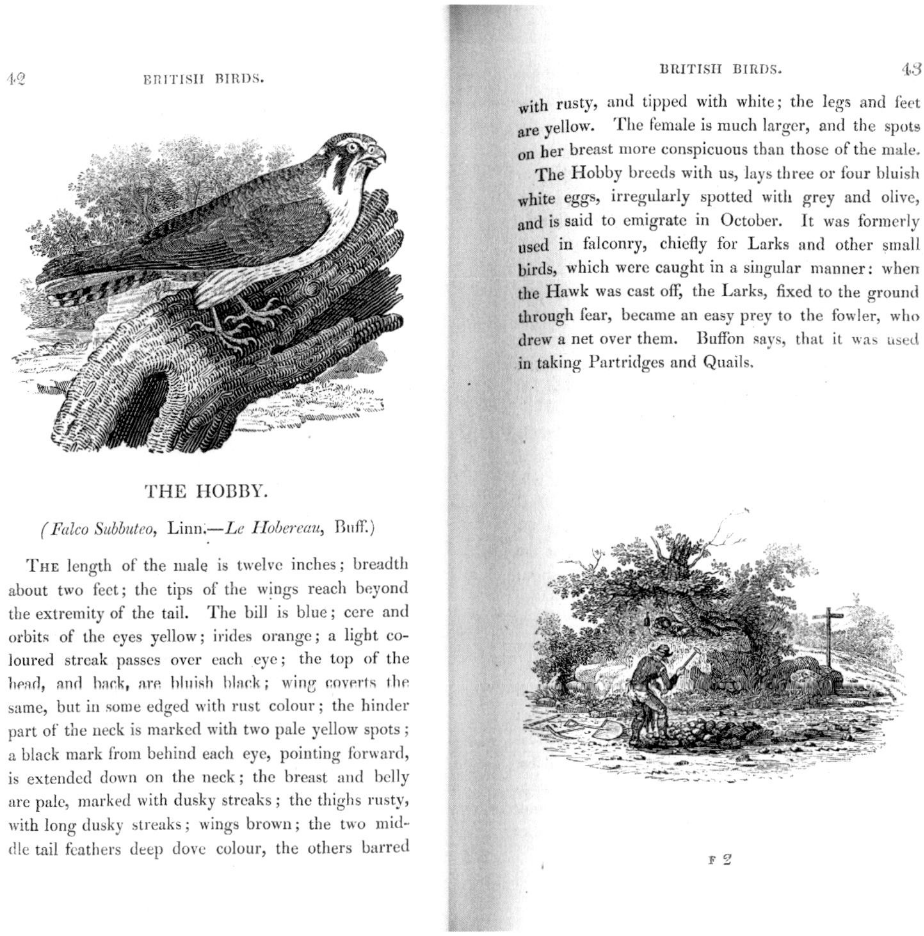
42 BRITISH BIRDS.

THE HOBBY.

(*Falco Subbuteo*, Linn.—*Le Hobereau*, Buff.)

THE length of the male is twelve inches; breadth about two feet; the tips of the wings reach beyond the extremity of the tail. The bill is blue; cere and orbits of the eyes yellow; irides orange; a light coloured streak passes over each eye; the top of the head, and back, are bluish black; wing coverts the same, but in some edged with rust colour; the hinder part of the neck is marked with two pale yellow spots; a black mark from behind each eye, pointing forward, is extended down on the neck; the breast and belly are pale, marked with dusky streaks; the thighs rusty, with long dusky streaks; wings brown; the two middle tail feathers deep dove colour, the others barred

BRITISH BIRDS. 43

with rusty, and tipped with white; the legs and feet are yellow. The female is much larger, and the spots on her breast more conspicuous than those of the male.

The Hobby breeds with us, lays three or four bluish white eggs, irregularly spotted with grey and olive, and is said to emigrate in October. It was formerly used in falconry, chiefly for Larks and other small birds, which were caught in a singular manner: when the Hawk was cast off, the Larks, fixed to the ground through fear, became an easy prey to the fowler, who drew a net over them. Buffon says, that it was used in taking Partridges and Quails.

F 2

Figure 1.7. Thomas Bewick, *Hobby and Stonebreaker*, from *A History of British Birds*, 6th ed., Newcastle, 1826. Private collection.

Bewick was himself a radical in his political sympathies. The point about these "tale" pieces that I want to stress is that they are outside the commercial requirements of the books in which they are contained. They bear no relationship to the project of natural history that the texts and the main illustrations proclaim.

What relationship has a stonebreaker to the bird called a hobby (fig. 1.7)? Or a suicide hanging from a tree to a long-eared owl (fig. 1.8)? These images are there simply because Bewick decided he wanted to put them in. As the director of a successful printing business, he had the power and freedom to put what he liked in his own books. And so—without making them obtrude to the point where they might have compromised the main project of the books and hence their commercial viability—he adds in these extras, which he engraved himself in his own time (and he was an exceedingly busy man). Thus Bewick, by moving against the expected path, by going back to his native environment, and then by adding

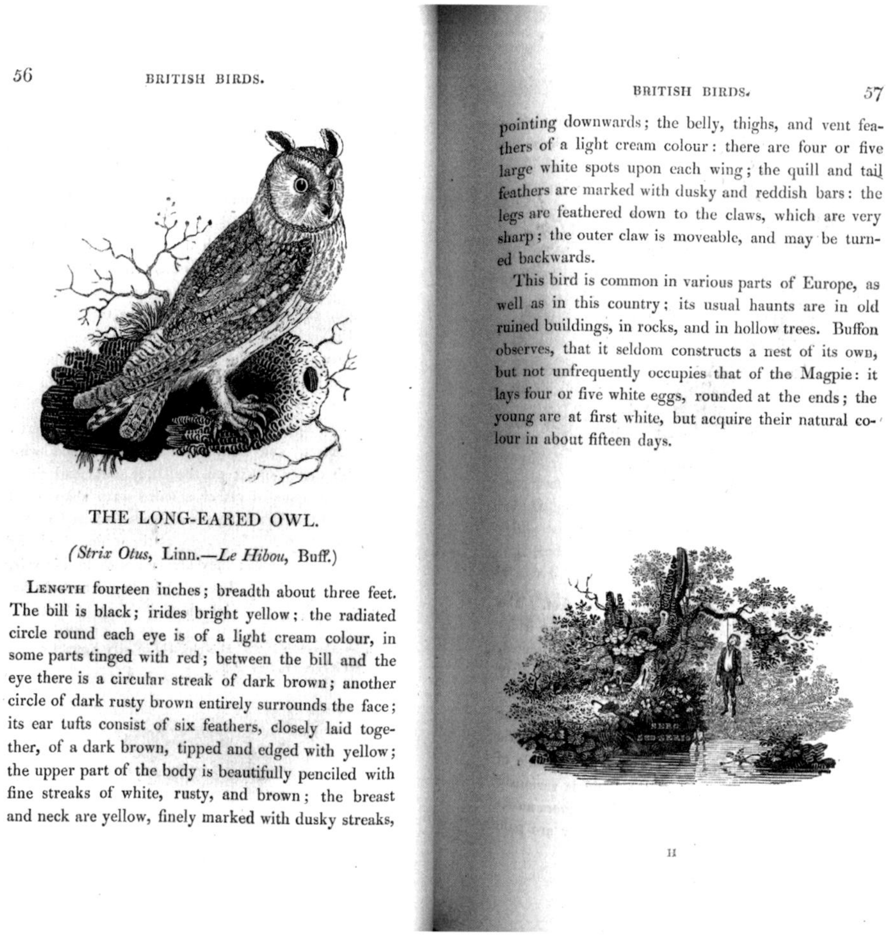

56 BRITISH BIRDS.

THE LONG-EARED OWL.

(*Strix Otus*, Linn.—*Le Hibou*, Buff.)

Length fourteen inches; breadth about three feet. The bill is black; irides bright yellow; the radiated circle round each eye is of a light cream colour, in some parts tinged with red; between the bill and the eye there is a circular streak of dark brown; another circle of dark rusty brown entirely surrounds the face; its ear tufts consist of six feathers, closely laid together, of a dark brown, tipped and edged with yellow; the upper part of the body is beautifully penciled with fine streaks of white, rusty, and brown; the breast and neck are yellow, finely marked with dusky streaks,

BRITISH BIRDS. 57

pointing downwards; the belly, thighs, and vent feathers of a light cream colour: there are four or five large white spots upon each wing; the quill and tail feathers are marked with dusky and reddish bars: the legs are feathered down to the claws, which are very sharp; the outer claw is moveable, and may be turned backwards.

This bird is common in various parts of Europe, as well as in this country; its usual haunts are in old ruined buildings, in rocks, and in hollow trees. Buffon observes, that it seldom constructs a nest of its own, but not unfrequently occupies that of the Magpie: it lays four or five white eggs, rounded at the ends; the young are at first white, but acquire their natural colour in about fifteen days.

II

Figure 1.8. Thomas Bewick, *Long-Eared Owl and Suicide,* from *A History of British Birds,* 6th ed., Newcastle, 1826. Private collection.

his own art when he had the opportunity to do so, was able to make his own independent statement. It was a small one, a covert one almost. Yet it has persisted and now remains one of the most important and moving witnesses of his age. It is striking that he maintained that independence for himself, whereas Linnell failed to persist in his bold representations of working life, apparently through lack of patronal support.

Bewick's example reveals one of the many ways in which independence could be and indeed was maintained within the "pit" of modern art in Britain in the early nineteenth century. It might seem to be an anti-London rather than a London story. And yet, in the end, it was only through the London commercial network that Bewick's remarkable work could reach the wider public that assured his wealth and fame. Perhaps the moral here is that those artists succeeded best who one way or another maintained a certain distance from the London art world while managing to benefit from its advantages. This might be a relevant message to consider in thinking about the relationships between certain American artists and London that feature in this book.

## NOTES

1. A. H. Palmer, *The Life and Letters of Samuel Palmer* (London: Seeley, 1892), 14.

2. Now in Tate Britain (NO5776). See Kathleen Crouan, *John Linnell: A Centennial Exhibition* (Cambridge: Cambridge University Press, 1982), 8–9; ill., 84–85.

3. Anita Brookner, *Genius of the Future; Studies in French Art Criticism: Diderot, Stendhal, Baudelaire, Zola, the Brothers Goncourt, Huysmans* (London: Phaidon, 1971), 86.

4. Michael Löwy and Robert Sayre, *Romanticism against the Tide of Modernity* Durham: Duke University Press, 2001).

5. This position is articulated most clearly in E. P. Thompson, *William Morris: From Romantic to Revolutionary* (London: Merlin Press, 1977), 1, 28–30, 271–74.

6. See note 4. I am most grateful to Andrew Hemingway for having drawn my attention to this work.

7. See, for example, responses by J. V. Adrian and G. Waagen quoted in William Vaughan, "Taste and the Multitude: The Somerset House Exhibitions in Continental Eyes," in *Art on the Line,* ed. David H. Solkin (New Haven: Yale University Press, 2001), 245–47.

8. Judy Egerton, *The British School* (New Haven: Yale University Press, 1998), 47–48; R. B. Beckett, "Constable and France," *Connoisseur* (May 1956): 249–55.

9. Beckett, "Constable and France," 254.

10. This development has recently been explored by David H. Solkin, *Painting Out of the Ordinary: Modernity and the Art of Everyday Life in Early Nineteenth-Century Britain* (New Haven: Yale University Press, 2008).

11. Patrick J. Noon et al., *From Constable to Delacroix: British Art and the French Romantics* (London: Tate, 2003).

12. Vaughan, "Taste and the Multitude," 244.

13. Michael Levey, *Sir Thomas Lawrence* (New Haven: Yale University Press, 2005), 237–39.

14. Ibid., 236.

15. William Hazlitt, *The Spirit of the Age* (London: Henry Colburn, 1825), 367.

16. S. C. Hutchison, *The History of the Royal Academy, 1768–1968* (London: Chapman & Hall, 1968), 55.

17. John Barrell, "Reform and Revolution: James Barry's Writings in the 1790s," in *James Barry, 1741–1806: History Painter,* ed. Tom Dunne and William L. Pressly (Farnham, Surrey: Ashgate, 2010), 127.

18. William Blake, *A Descriptive Catalogue of Pictures* (London: Printed by D. N. Shury for J. Blake, 1809).

19. William Vaughan, "God Help the Minister That Meddles in Art," in *The Houses of Parliament: History, Art, and Architecture,* ed. David Cannadine et al. (London: Merrell, 2000).

20. Kay Dian Kriz, *The Idea of the English Landscape Painter: Genius as Alibi in the Early Nineteenth Century* (New Haven: Yale University Press, 1997), 33–45.

21. Peter Fullerton, "Patronage and Pedagogy: The British Institution in the Early Nineteenth Century," *Art History* 5 (March 1982): 59–72.

22. Francis Haskell, *Rediscoveries in Art: Some Aspects of Taste, Fashion and Collecting in England and France* (Oxford: Phaidon, 1976), 24–29.

23. Greg Smith, *The Emergence of the Professional Watercolorist: Contentions and Alliances in the Artistic Domain, 1760–1824* (Burlington, Vt.: Ashgate, 2002).

24. These were the Royal Academy, the British Institution, the Society of British Artists, the Old Watercolour Society, and the New Watercolour Society.

25. Christopher S. Warren, "Professional Pathways for the English Provincial Artist in the Early Nineteenth Century" (Ph.D. diss., University of Southampton, 2009), 70.

26. British Parliamentary Papers, 1841 population census (GB): P.P. 1841, sess. 2 (52), 2:227.

27. Warren, "Professional Pathways," 284.

28. Kit Wedd, Lucy Peltz, and Cathy Ross, "1770–1850: 'Artists' Street' in Marylebone," in *Artists' London: Holbein to Hirst* (London: Merrell, 2001), 66.

29. Ibid., 78.

30. Jane Turner, ed., *Grove Dictionary of Art,* vol. 23 (New York: Grove, 1996), 787.

31. See Trevor Fawcett, *The Rise of English Provincial Art: Artists, Patrons, and Institutions outside London, 1800–1830* (Oxford: Clarendon Press, 1974).

32. Andrew Hemingway, " 'Norwich School': Myth and Reality," in *Romantic Landscape: The Norwich School of Painters,* ed. David Blayney Brown et al. (London: Tate Gallery Publishing, 2000), 9–23.

33. Jane R. Cohen, *Charles Dickens and His Original Illustrators* (Columbus: Ohio State University Press, 1980), 35.

34. Tim Clayton, *The English Print, 1688–1802* (New Haven: Yale University Press, 1997), 176, 261, 284.

35. Luke Herrmann, *Turner Prints: The Engraved work of J. M. W. Turner* (London: Phaidon, 1990).

36. E. P. Thompson, *The Making of the English Working Class* (London: Penguin, 1980), 9–12.

37. *The Letters of Samuel Palmer,* ed. Raymond Lister (Oxford: Clarendon Press, 1974), 54.

38. For example, in such works as David Wilkie's *Village Politicians* (1806), a satire on proletarian radicalism. See Solkin, *Painting Out of the Ordinary,* 7–19.

39. Jennifer S. Uglow, *Nature's Engraver: A Life of Thomas Bewick* (New York: Farrar, Straus & Giroux, 2007), 105.

# 2

# The Urban Ecology of Art in Antebellum New York

*Dell Upton*

It is worth reminding ourselves that romanticism in art and literature was largely an urban phenomenon, created by men and women who were deeply involved in city life. But this reveals little in itself. In the first half of the nineteenth century, American cities changed in particular ways that colored and occasionally transformed the production and reception of art. I borrow the term *ecology* to describe this process from the psychologist James J. Gibson, who characterized perception as active engagement with physical surroundings of which the perceiver is a part rather than a mere observer. What we call *art* was embedded in, shaped, and was shaped by the urban scene, and thus was inextricable from its premises and its practices.

During the first decades of the nineteenth century, New York became the largest city in North America, rapidly outdistancing its nearest rivals by seizing opportunities offered by the accidents of history and geography. The statistics are simple: a city with a population of 32,000 at the time of the ratification of the Constitution in 1788 had grown to about 150,000 by the time the Erie Canal was opened in 1825, and soared to 813,000 by 1860. The geographical facts are equally straightforward: an island whose urban fabric had just begun to push beyond The Park (now City Hall Park) and the Common in the 1790s was solidly built up to Fourteenth Street by the middle of the nineteenth century, with substantial development as far north as the upper Thirties. All of this was owing to another geographical fact: New York's location at the mouth of the North, or Hudson, River, on a great deep-water port that never froze and that commanded the easiest route to the developing interior of the country. New York's ascendancy was facilitated by the decision of British industrialists to dump excess textile stock accumulated during the War of 1812 at auction in New York. The subsequent construction of the Erie Canal and then the railroads, the selection of New York as the terminus of the first transatlantic steamboat service, the laying of the transatlantic cable, and the development of a financial market underwritten by British capital solidified the city's dominance. Compared to New York, the early nineteenth-century diarist Sidney George Fisher wrote, Philadelphia, the largest city at the time of the Revolution and a rapidly growing industrial metropolis in its own right, seemed "villagelike."[1]

More important than the statistics were the ways that New Yorkers responded to these changes: like adolescents, proud and boastful of newfound strength. Early nineteenth-century New Yorkers already exhibited that charmingly provincial self-involvement that still characterizes the city's residents. But like adolescents as well, they were insecure, unsure of the durability of their power and of their worthiness to hold it, and in need of constant reassurance. Their unease was exacerbated by a pervasive sense of volatility. New Yorkers understood their city as an unsettled, incomplete, and unpredictable place. The pace of construction made New York a "city of perpetual ruin and repair," in which whole districts were left in a raw and half-finished condition, while others were demolished almost as soon as they were built. The consequences of haste were visible everywhere: some new buildings were so shoddily constructed that they collapsed. "We pass many . . . unfinished edifices with an instinctive dread of their falling," wrote one journalist. He reminded his readers of the collapse of Phelps and Peck's wholesale store, one of the first of the new granite-piered buildings that transformed the waterfronts of American cities after the late 1820s. The structure fell on May 4, 1832, crushing several passersby and employees (fig. 2.1).[2]

Some New Yorkers worried more about the constant reconstruction that was erasing the visible record of the city's history. In the 1820s and 1830s, a series of short articles in the *New-York Mirror* lamented the demolition of the last handful of Dutch-style houses in New York. The articles expressed regret at the passing of buildings that recalled momentous events, but acknowledged that "fashion and business care little for antiquarian lumber." Most of these pieces were illustrated with woodcuts drawn by the fledgling architect Alexander Jackson Davis. Shortly after the last of these stepped-gable houses were demolished, Washington Irving evoked their memory in remodeling his suburban farmhouse, Sunnyside.[3]

The economic instability of the new nation added to the sense of foreboding. No one during the boom times of the antebellum years believed that they would last. Architectural writers advised their readers to build to suit themselves, not posterity, because no one could be sure that their children would want or would be able to afford their parents' houses. They understood that prosperity might evapo-

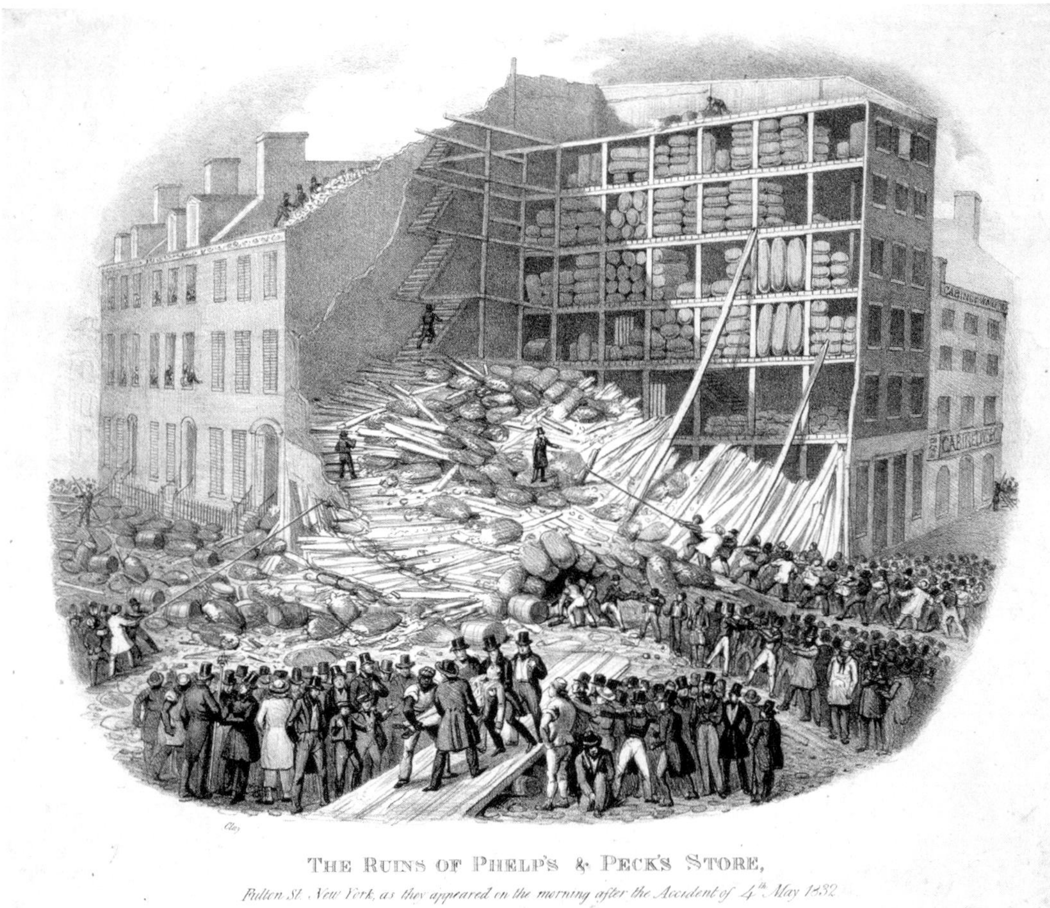


Figure 2.1. Edward W. Clay, *The Ruins of Phelps & Peck's Store, Fulton at Cliff Streets, May 4, 1832,* 1832. Lithograph. Collection of the New-York Historical Society, neg. no. 76193.

rate at any minute, leaving even the wealthiest destitute, as it did most notably in 1837 (fig. 2.2). The diary of Mary Lorrain Peters, a student at a private school in New Haven, recorded the periodic disappearance of her schoolmates, who had been taken away by parents no longer able to afford the tuition.[4]

Several aspects of New Yorkers' response to the new city bore both on urban life and on the art scene within it. Urban elites applied rationalist and neoclassical ideas to urban form, political economy, and social practices. But in cities that were growing larger and more rapidly than any before known in North America, these models were overwhelmed by daily experience. Similarly, didactic republican models of art and its role were swamped by popular commercial culture, although rationalist urbanism and didactic models of art never entirely disappeared.

Elite New Yorkers imagined their city as a node in a great web of transportation, information, and money. They worked to give the urban artifact legibility and an all-encompassing order that would accommodate systems of trade and travel. They also hoped that a properly organized city would mold the behavior of their fellow citizens to the new order, for they, in common with others of their class and education in the new republic, held an abiding materialist faith in the power of embodied experience to shape character. The most ambitious of these projects to "regulate" New York (that is, to order its physical form), though by no means the only one, was the renowned Commissioners' Plan, published in 1811 but not worked out in all its details until the early 1820s. Enamored of eighteenth-century schemes to enumerate and systematize virtually everything, then to make the results visible in tables, graphs, and visual displays (as in Charles Willson Peale's renowned museum in Philadelphia), New York's leaders seized on the age-old grid as a newly meaningful image of transparent and universal order. They imagined New York's streets as a neutral system or network that had the potential to make all private locations equally accessible and equally valuable. Their goals were summarized in phrases widely used in the early nineteenth century, such as "habits of system and order" and "separation and classification."[5]

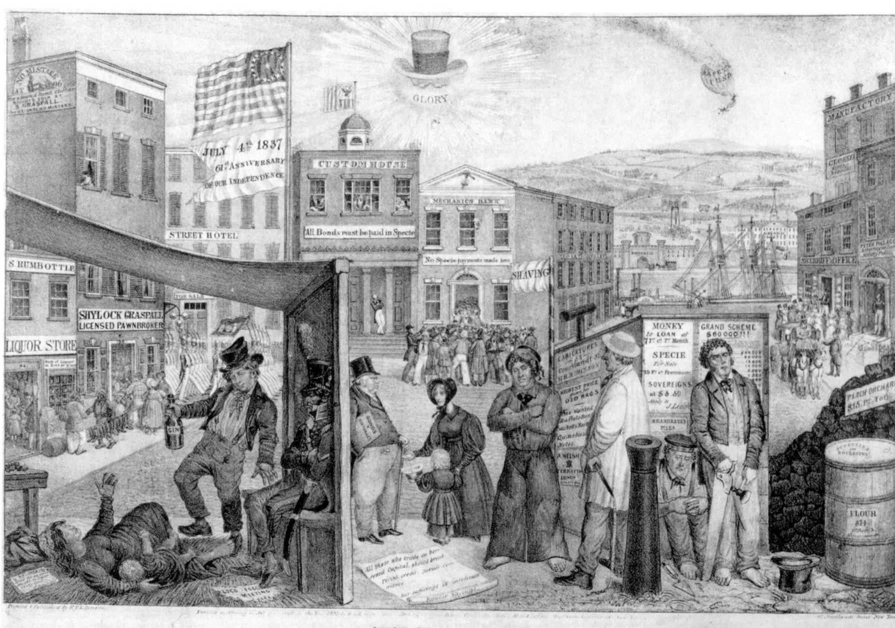


Figure 2.2 Edward W. Clay, *The Times, July 4, 1837*, 1837. Lithograph, 13½ x 19 in. (35 x 49 cm). Library of Congress, PC/US 1837.C619 no. 11.

Regulation entailed the ruthless alteration of urban topography. In New York, regulators cut down hills, filled low places, drained swamps, built levees, widened streets, and reorganized the street network to make Manhattan Island as flat and regular as in the Commissioners' map. According to the Reverend Clement Clark Moore, author of "A Visit from Saint Nicholas," "the great principle which governs these plans is, to reduce the surface of the earth as nearly as possible to dead level. . . . The natural inequities of the ground are destroyed, and the existing water courses disregarded. . . . These are men . . . who would have cut down the seven hills of Rome."[6]

Because the grid was laid out on the ground only as needed, the Commissioners' Plan did not have a tangible effect on New York's physical development until the middle of the nineteenth century, when new residential neighborhoods began to creep up the island. Most antebellum commercial and dense residential development was built on the old patchwork of grids, as well as on the improvised transitional portion of the Commissioners' Plan that stitched the old and new sections together. The real importance of the plan for early nineteenth-century New York was the image it presented of what the city might be, or *would* be. The grid was an emblem of commerce as an impersonal, quantifiable, articulated system, in contrast to the older model of trade as a miscellany of morally or ethically tinged personal relationships. As soon as the grid was built up, its implied equality and interchangeability were lost in the particulars of individually differentiated urban spaces, but it was highly seductive to New York's (and other cities') movers and shakers as an urban topographical and social metaphor.

In three-dimensional reality, the systematic city became a modular city. The street organized individually developed but comparable parcels of space along its margins, while the buildings that occupied these compartments were also conceived and constructed in increasingly modular ways. The introduction in the 1840s of cast-iron façades, which could be assembled in any number of particular ways using prefabricated parts, exemplified a process of standardization that had transformed the American building industry since the seventeenth century. These structures constituted modules in the urban system, and at the same time they were usually systematized inside. The Haughwout Building (fig. 2.3), one of the oldest survivors, housed a firm that sold ceramic and metal household furnishings. It was organized inside like Oliver Evans's rationalized system for grist milling, first published in the late eighteenth century. In both, the goods—raw materials and semi-manufactured ceramic and metal ware in the case of the Haughwout Building—were delivered at the bottom and carried by elevator to the top, then trickled down toward the ground floor as increasing degrees of finish were applied.[7]

The development of individual parcels points to a second aspect of the grid considered as a system of equally accessible spaces: the commodification of urban space that many observers then and since treated as the only rationale for the Commissioners' Plan. In preferring a rectilinear grid to a plan in what Spiro Kostof has called "the grand manner," with diagonals and broad avenues, the commissioners said that "they could not but bear in mind that a city is to be composed principally of the habitations of men, and that strait sided, and right angled houses are the most cheap to build," which implied the commodification of space and housing. But if so, then the urban landscape was less a grand totalizing scheme of knowledge than an array of commodities available, like everything else, to anyone who could pay.[8]

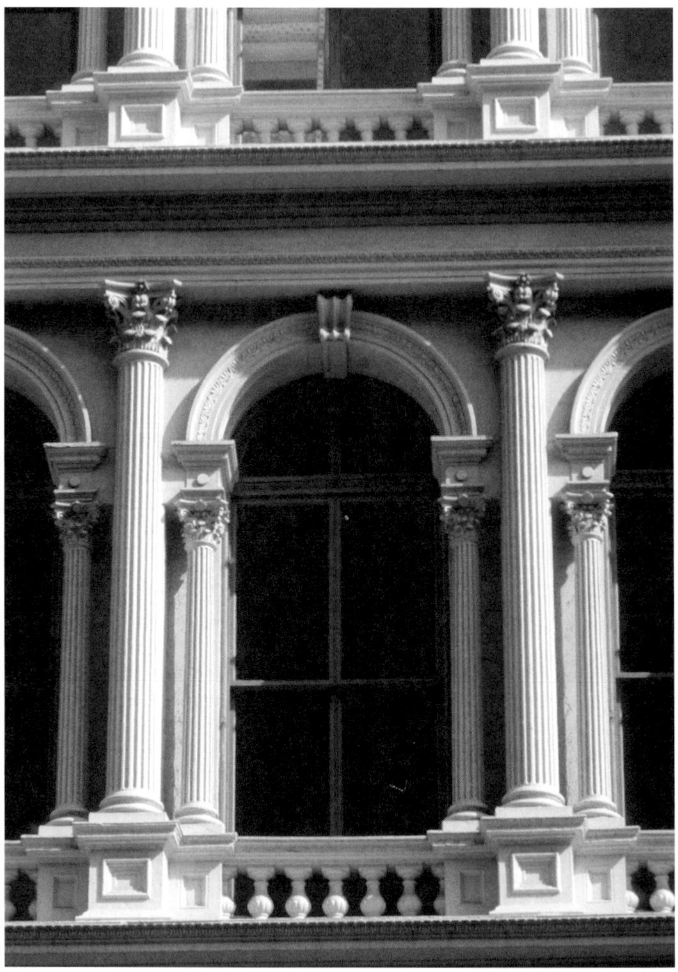

Figure 2.3 John P. Gaynor, Haughwout Building, New York, 1856. Detail of exterior. Photo: Dell Upton.

Metaphors of system and commodity led New Yorkers to imagine their position as that of a spider at the center of an economic web, one that brought them everything they could want and gave some of them the money to buy it. Over the course of the early nineteenth century, though, this profusion overran the structures meant to organize and contain it, so that rationality and visual transparency were overwhelmed by apparent chaos. The historian David Henkin has emphasized the ubiquity both of grids and of texts in burgeoning New York. Like the city itself, newspapers were grids whose modules were filled by individual advertisers. Like newspapers, the modules of the street grid increasingly resembled a kind of classified section, with every free space covered with text. Everything referred to something else. Some signs indexed other parts of the city, while others listed the goods to be found inside. The transparent system of the grid was obscured by layers of texts that refused to be contained or articulated. Inside these structures one often encountered a three-dimensional version of the words outside. For example, in A. T. Stewart's still-standing Marble Palace, a dry-goods store begun in 1844 and quickly enlarged several times, walls were hung with paintings, with goods—"every variety and every available style of fabrics in the market"—piled on every surface and suspended from the ceilings and even from the central dome. The repetition of individually trivial items made the totality appear all-encompassing (plate 3).[9]

By confronting the shopper with more goods than she could easily perceive individually, that is, the display implied that everything she could want or even imagine could be found inside. It alluded to the kind of all-encompassing order that Peale's museum and the urban regulators sought, but the difference is crucial to understanding what happened in early nineteenth-century New York. Like the advertisements that covered the sides of buildings, the system gave way to the list, the compilation, the impressionistic accumulation of sensations (fig. 2.4). The imagined city that was meant to be understood at a glance, the visual and transparent city, became a city of impressions and fragments.

The travel diary of John H. B. Latrobe, a Baltimore physician, captures the impressionistic experience of the city marvelously. In November 1834 Latrobe arrived in New Orleans aboard the *Arkansas* to see the places his late father, the architect Benjamin Henry Latrobe, had described in his journal a decade and a half earlier. Latrobe's ship moored near the vegetable market, and Latrobe set off upriver along the levee toward the meat market, his attention captured by the cries of vendors "shouting forth in French English and the negro patois" and the peals of seven church bells competing to attract worshippers to prayer. As he crossed the Place d'Armes heading toward his boardinghouse on Canal Street, Latrobe was struck by the "full and noisy custom" of the cafés and saloons, whose patrons drank "rum

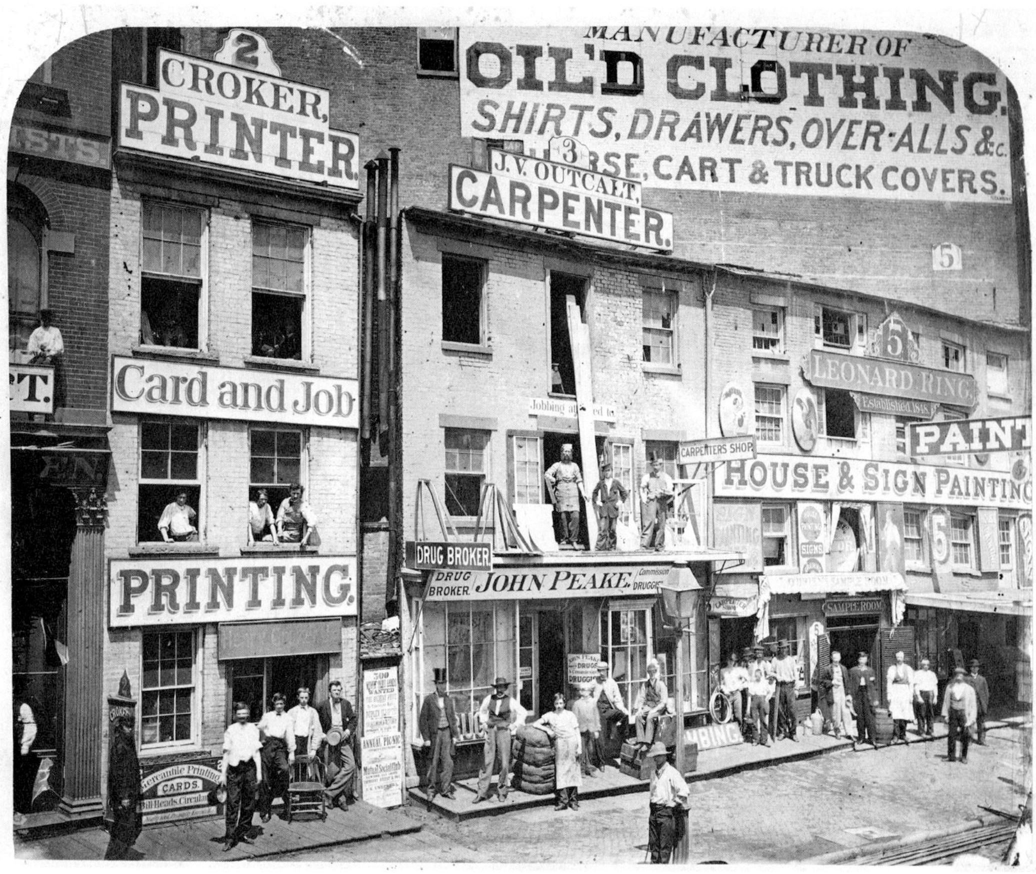


Figure 2.4 Shops and workshops along Lower Hudson Street, New York, ca. 1865. Collection of the New-York Historical Society.

and gin, Monongahela, and Tom and Jerry" prepared from an "army of bottles, with contents of all colors" and served on marble- or mahogany-topped bars fitted with "shining brass works." On the street, soldiers in "gay and tasteful uniform" passed by, as their "sundry thumps upon a bass drum [spoke] martially to the ear." Snatches of inconsequential conversation drifted toward him as he passed the shopkeepers lounging in their doorways, men and older mixed-race women sitting on their balconies smoking cigars, and beautiful young quadroon women.[10]

Latrobe's New Orleans could not be known through the all-encompassing framework of the grid, although New Orleans is a gridded city. It existed for him only as moments of perceptual engagement, as an ephemeral array of sights, sounds, smells, tastes, and textures, a dizzying mixture of immediate sensations and considered interpretations. Latrobe's account was a highly self-conscious effort to catalogue his awareness. As he discovered, the multiple levels of awareness and consciousness through which we experience the city do not always mesh smoothly. He responded positively to a quadroon woman, to signs that we recognize instinctively as human social signals. At the same time, he was also attracted by more limited, culturally defined cues: "a fine figure, a beautiful foot, an ankle like an angel's—an air quite distinqué [*sic*], and then so strange, and characteristic—so Spanish." Latrobe was chastised by his unnamed companion, for he had missed even more subtle, more narrowly defined, local racial signs: "A Quadroon! Well, I'll know better next time."[11]

Early nineteenth-century urbanites sought to *separate* and *classify*, but they were quickly reduced to *listing*. The recitation of lists that were no more analytical or systematic than the signs found on the sides of buildings became a cliché of popular culture. New York's harbor, one journalist wrote, was filled with the "Yorker," the "substantial representative of Old England," the "Dutchman," the "clumsy Dane," the Norwegian polacca, and the "'long-limbed' brigs and schooners that come from 'down east.'" Other journalists chronicled streets lined with a "confused assemblage of high, low, broad, narrow, white, gray, red, brown, yellow, simple and florid," their "glories . . . rather traditional than actual," and teeming with a "river deep & wide of live, perspiring humanity." Former journalist Walt Whitman used lists as building blocks of his "democratic" poetry. In "Starting from Paumanok," he associated his own birth with that of the United States, a nation founded by

> Dead poets, philosophs, priests,
> Martyrs, artists, inventors, governments, long since,
> Language-shapers on other shores,
> Nations once powerful, now reduced, withdrawn, or desolate . . .

He named the

> Okonee, Koosa, Ottawa, Monongahela, Sauk, Natchez, Chattahoochee,
> Kaqueta, Oronoco,
> Wabash, Miami, Saginaw, Chippewa, Oshkosh, Walla-Walla
> who had once peopled the continent, but who were rapidly giving way to
> . . . the wigwam, the trail, the hunter's hut, the flatboat, the maize-leaf,
> the claim, the rude fence, and the backwoods village.[12]

Listers inevitably turned their attention to people. The port brought New York not only goods and money but also non-Anglos and their cultures. New York was "The World in Little," in the words of one benign portrait: "We have Turkish saloons, and Turkish baths, French coffee houses and French theatres, German Gardens, large bier saloons, opera houses, and reading rooms, Spanish hotels,

Italian churches, and Italian newspapers, Chinese boarding houses, inhabited only by the Chinese, and in the lower part of the city, there is a gambling place, we are told, supported principally by natives of Portugal. The Celts, the English, and the natives of 'bonnie Scotia,' have also their especial resorts; so have the descendants of the Africans."[13]

The picturesque variety of the streets was celebrated visually by artists such as the Italian immigrant Nicolino Calyo and verbally by texts such as the *Cries* books, a children's-book genre that described for young readers the cries and wares of street vendors. Both Calyo and the anonymous *Cries* authors tried to capture the fragmented, multisensory experience that John H. B. Latrobe reported. But most of the white, usually comfortable New Yorkers who made prints and drawings, kept diaries, and published newspapers saw themselves surrounded by increasing numbers of uncomfortably different people.

These differences were made all the more conspicuous by the phenomenon of urban sorting. New York was increasingly segregated by ethnicity and social class. More and more middling- and upper-class New Yorkers lived away from their places of business. This meant that there were parts of the city that such people would never see, and that their only contact with people of other classes was on the streets of the commercial districts. None of this had been true in the earlier, smaller, less sorted city. Thus the evenness of the grid was contradicted by development and redefined as a series of picturesquely imagined, often sinister districts such as the notorious Five Points. The Five Points proper was an intersection of five streets along Chatham Street northeast of City Hall, but the name became applied generically to the city's old Sixth Ward.

Nineteenth-century New Yorkers who were not blinded by the Five Points' popular reputation acknowledged that most of its residents were the working poor, not criminals. But social segregation meant that the Five Points could be cast in the popular press as the domain of the criminal and the lazy, an exotic place to which one would travel only heavily guarded. Charles Dickens, for example, noted that on his own visit he was accompanied by two policemen.[14]

In New York, as in Paris and London, this was the era when "lights and shadows" literature proliferated. These books purported to show respectable urbanites parts of the city that they did not know existed. Usually these books were cast as night visits to increase the mystery and the ominous ambience. George G. Foster's *New York by Gas-Light* of 1850 is an early example of such sensationalism. Luc Sante's *Low Life* is a recent one. Such overblown accounts would not have been credible to an earlier generation who were more familiar with their social inferiors. In other words, the increased spatial separation of the city in the mid-nineteenth

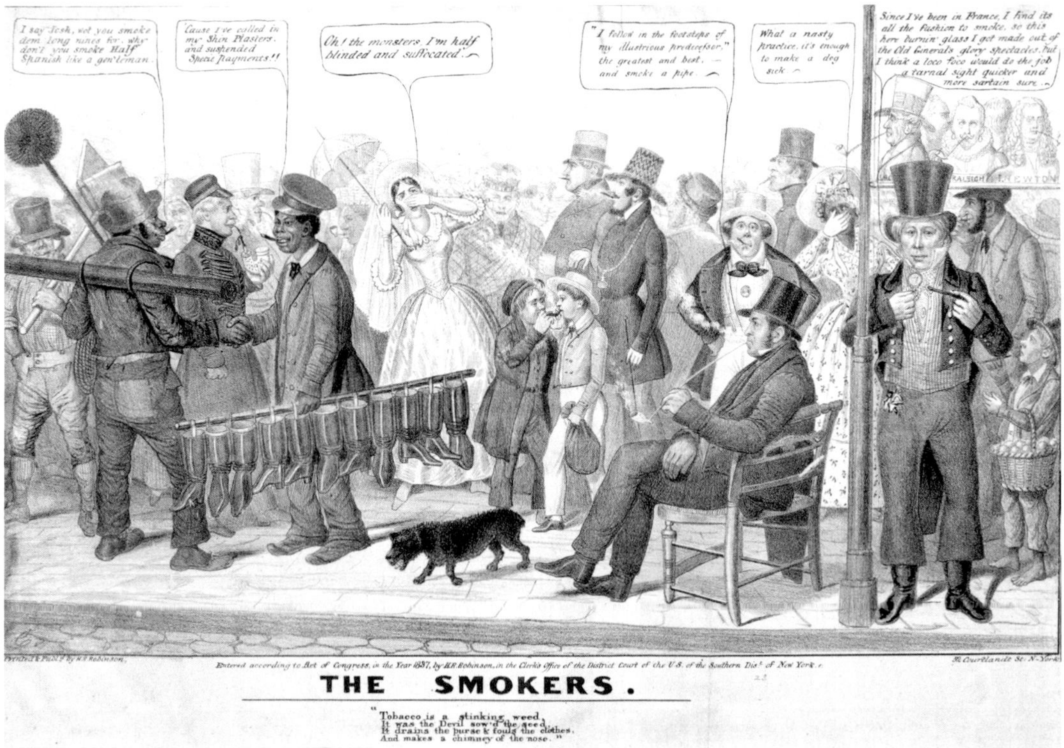


Figure 2.5 Edward W. Clay, *The Smokers,* 1837. Lithograph, 12 x 17¾ in. (32 x 45 cm). Library Company of Philadelphia.

century made the kinds of people who might earlier have seemed different, inferior, even annoying, but unexceptionable now seem exotic and dangerous.[15]

The sheer numbers of people, particularly along Broadway and on the Bowery, also overwhelmed the effort to organize the city rationally. The problem was that, in the context of new codes of respectable behavior that demanded physical and social separation of the genteel from the masses, the streets forced people of all types into contact. The rougher-hewn population—the genteel called them "sovereigns"—grew increasingly assertive of their right to participate in public life. Cigars were emblems of this new social promiscuity—of its cheeky self-confidence, of its oppressive ubiquity, and of its intrusion into genteel preserves (fig. 2.5).[16]

What does this have to do with the arts? The urban changes that I have just outlined, as well as changes in the ways they were imagined and represented, radically transformed the nature and status of art in New York during the first half of the nineteenth century.

First, what we would call *art* was immersed in the Great Emporium. If New Yorkers felt that they had the world of goods at their fingertips, they also believed that they commanded the world of peoples and cultures and experiences. Art became one of those cultural commodities, a consumer good cast onto the counter beside other consumer goods, so naturalized that its ostensible categorical difference from other kinds of artifacts was not always evident to many nineteenth-century New Yorkers. A glance at the columns of any newspaper tells the story: everything was for sale. There, among the corn plasters, the cures for bedbugs, the patent medicines, the foodstuffs, the buildings for rent, and the services for hire, were the textiles, glass, silver, and furniture, the paintings, the sculpture, and the books that art and literary historians study. Whatever their content, they were first of all *objects* to be owned and traded. "When sufficient coin accrues" to the merchant, the jeweler W. L. Tiffany wrote, "then we ascend to the acting of pompous bank-directors, or sublime tuft-hunters in Europe, essaying purchases of elegance, sympathy with art, and admixture with titled company, at a fixed price and quantity, as we have once bought cotton and corn."[17]

Of course, art was long established as a prestige good, but thrown into the marketplace, artists and art were transformed. When art was injected into the heated commodity market of the second quarter of the nineteenth century, artists and architects began to wriggle free of patrons. Samuel F. B. Morse (a frustrated artist who later became a renowned inventor) took the lead in establishing the National Academy of Design in 1826. A decade later, Alexander Jackson Davis, Thomas U. Walter, and others organized the American Institution of Architects, which failed but was revived more successfully as the American Institute of Architects in 1857. These institutions promoted the right of artists and architects to work not to suit the taste of commissioning patrons but for a larger and more anonymous market, and to control their own conditions and modes of production. We might say that artists were transformed from artisans working for patrons to merchants selling to customers.

At the same time, the goal of the public exhibition of works shifted. At the beginning of the nineteenth century, the highest purpose of art was didactic. The political theory of the new republic stressed the need for universal knowledge and common values, to be disseminated by public education. Artists and architects were obliged to use their talents to represent great men and great ideas, thereby instructing and uplifting their fellow citizens. The artist John Trumbull, for example, proposed to hire first-rate artists to paint the great events of American history for public display, while second-rate ones would be employed to make copies of these works to give to the principal actors portrayed in the canvases. The originals would be displayed in the U. S. Capitol as well as in the main public room of the White House.[18]

From this point of view, art should tell a legible story with a high moral content. In the context of the new American republic, this traditional view took on a new urgency, for example, in Morse's portrait of the Revolutionary hero Lafayette or in his monumental painting of the House of Representatives in the newly rebuilt U. S. Capitol (plate 4); in Robert Ball Hughes's statue of Alexander Hamilton (ca. 1831), which stood in New York's first Merchants' Exchange until it was destroyed by fire; or in John Frazee's portrait bust of John Jay (1832), which was displayed in the same building, where it was reputedly seen by four thousand people, before it was installed in the U. S. Supreme Court chamber. Peale's Philadelphia Museum is the most renowned example of the use of art in the service of an educated citizenry, but Barnum's American Museum on Park Row and the new New-York Historical Society, housed behind City Hall in the old almshouse, which had been remodeled to house fledgling cultural institutions, were its New York equivalents.

By the middle of the nineteenth century, art was exhibited as much for artists' profit as for viewers' edification, although lip service continued to be given to the latter. The painter John Vanderlyn built a brick rotunda adjacent to City Hall in 1816 to exhibit his panorama of Versailles (plate 5). It failed, but the exhibition of art for profit became increasingly common over the following decades, so that Hiram Powers reputedly hoped to earn $25,000 by sending his *Greek Slave* on tour in 1847.[19]

Just as the systematic, transparent orders of the grid and the museum were reduced to accumulations of lists, so edifying art, commodified, became spectacle. Edification aimed to inculcate systematic understanding, but spectacle promoted short-term, unexplained, usually visual gratification. Among the most conspicuous examples of popular spectacles presented under the cloak of edifying instruction were the "Aztec children," who were "recently taken from a newly discovered and idolatrous people in Central America, by whom they were kept in superstitious veneration." Were they Aztec deities or, as one correspondent claimed, merely "idiotic dwarves"? Rather than appearing in a carnival sideshow, the children were displayed in the large Exhibition Room of the Society Library on Broadway, a setting that attested to the respectability and high-mindedness of the enterprise.[20] A couple of years later, one could see the "hybrid or Semi-Human Indian from Mexico" at Gothic Hall. "Ladies, unless in a delicate condition," were assured that they would "derive the highest gratification from contemplating the refined taste and amiable disposition of the Hybrid."[21] These were one-offs. Minstrel shows, everyday occurrences from the 1830s, offered white men with blacked faces who lampooned African Americans and American society in general, all the while assuring viewers that the music and skits presented onstage were ethnographic representations of southern African American culture.

My point is that many of the kinds of works that we call *art* were to be found in these spectacles, or "public entertainments." For example, Rubens Peale brought a version of his father's museum to Broadway in 1825. Peale advertised his museum under the obligatory rubric of edification, but it quickly became a species of freak show that competed with the more openly commercial American (later Barnum's) Museum across the street. The artifacts and performances displayed in such museums and in other public entertainments were sorted not as art or non-art but as uplifting or debasing. The Aztec children and other freak shows were "rational amusement," but the drama *Camille* was considered pornographic because it included sickroom scenes that should never be seen in public. So one entrepreneur showed what purported to be Old Master paintings by "Corregio, Poussin, &c." alongside "the genuine Egg-Hatching Machine, in which chicks are seen bursting the shell, in the presence of visiters [*sic*]."[22]

This milieu for the presentation of what we call *art* struck a critic who viewed Edward Brackett's *Shipwrecked Mother and Child* (1859):

> Although the deficiency of vital power and true growth in the public entertainments of New York, is by no means slight or accidental, there is never a lack in variety and numbers, of popular exhibitions. We can always range the scale pretty freely, from the tiny Aztecs up to Mons. Gregoire, the stone-breaking Hercules; from the negro burlesque two minutes and a half long, to the complex opera of three hours; from the amateur farce of the "spout-shop," to the elaborate tragedy of the legitimate "temple of the drama." In the pictorial we are quite as opulent, and find no end to sketches, scratches, and colorings—from the chalk outline on the fence . . . up to a work like this "Shipwrecked Mother and Child," wrought by the finest chisel, from the pure marble, by the patient and well tempered genius of Brackett.[23]

To insist on the narrative and moral function of art in this milieu, as critics and laypeople alike continued to do throughout the process of commodification in the antebellum decades, had the effect of democratizing what we call *art.* Mid-nineteenth-century New York rejected obscure theories and terminologies. Even critics oriented toward high art insisted on legibility in art and its criticism. This meant that anyone could and should enjoy art and might feel free to comment on it. Images from art passed into popular currency and became ways of discussing issues that couldn't be discussed openly.[24]

Hiram Powers's *Greek Slave* exemplified the circulation and reinterpretation of art in popular culture. The sculptor's official, uplifting narrative interpretation of the statue was that it represented a nude Christian woman, enslaved by Turks, who was protected by her faith and modesty from heathen stares. Thus she was not really naked. As the art historian Vivien Green noted, critics in the United States and abroad quickly pointed out the irony that a sculptor from a slaveholding nation should offer such an image for public empathy. "What did the *Greek Slave* say about American ethics and culture?" they asked.[25]

Other public responses undermined the high-minded pretensions of the image from below. While the original was on view in a New York gallery in 1849, visitors to plebeian theaters and saloons could see it presented by what were euphemistically called "model artists." These were nude women who posed in tableaux-vivants as the *Greek Slave* and other renowned works of art. Their reenactment met Powers's statue on the grounds of a commonly articulated standard of mid-century art criticism: verisimilitude. They also undermined the idea of uplift, asserting that artistic images meant what they appeared to represent—a naked woman exposed to male scrutiny in this case—not abstractions, although model artistry was still advertised as an uplifting performance.[26]

Such spectacles reminded cultural arbiters of the volatility of the values they wished art to convey in a democratic society. In response, culture-shapers began to form an interpretation of art and the consumption of art that was very different from the republican version articulated early in the period, and different as well from the democratic version that emerged in the interstices of the society of spectacle. Art remained uplifting, but they rethought the possibility of its universality. Whereas the republican artisan-artist saw his audience as fellow citizens, art mavens of the mid-nineteenth century started to question the ability of most people—of the "sovereigns"—to benefit from it.

Public galleries of art began to charge admission not merely to enrich the exhibitors but to keep out those who did not belong there. Andrew Jackson Downing, the New York landscape gardener turned arbiter of architectural and horticultural taste, wrote ironically of two "sovereigns" viewing Horatio Greenough's *Washington* in the United States Capitol. One was "picking with his fingers, the kernels out of some walnuts which he held it his hand. . . . Stopping short against the statue, he exclaimed, 'I say Bob—if I had a hammer, I'd crack this nut on that old chap's toes!'" In a more serious mood, Downing articulated an architectural theory based on the varying levels of architectural taste that he thought members of each social class were capable of attaining.[27]

All of these changes pointed to a new sense of the role of the *arts* that was closer to what we would call *art.* Cultural authorities began to define *hierarchies* of value and taste. The lower orders could still benefit from the didactic, but the higher realms of sensibility and taste, as opposed to morality, were not available to everyone. The artist was redefined as neither an artisan nor a merchant but by means of a new word. In 1860 the New York diarist George Templeton Strong recorded an encounter with the recently arrived English émigré architect Jacob Wrey Mould, noting that one of Strong's friends "thinks Mould a genius." This is the earliest use in New York that I have encountered of this word in the way we commonly use it, to refer to someone's *being* a genius as opposed to someone's *having* genius.[28]

I don't want to leave the impression that these differences were stark and progressive—that a straight line ran from the first position to the second. Instead, I mean to emphasize the bifurcation of the arts in the commercial culture. Artists such as Powers and Greenough found themselves in a setting where what we call *art* was implicated in the culture of spectacle and commodity. To put it another way, all professions and arts involve both insider and outsider discourses. Insider discourse refers to those aspects of taste, theory, and practice that serve to distinguish professionals in one another's eyes. To outsiders these may seem trivial or even invisible, but to insiders they are subtle indicators of currency, invention, and skill. Outsider discourses are those that connect artists to their audiences—that offer gratification of various sorts to the uninitiated. For example, a popular song may appeal to its audience for its melody or its words, but other musicians may admire it for the inventiveness of its tonalities or the technical mastery required to perform it. Success in any profession requires a balancing of both. This seems to me to be the most significant aspect of the urban ecology of art in early nineteenth-century New York: that successful artists found a way to sustain an insider discourse of aesthetics and taste within a commodified market economy.

## NOTES

1. Sidney George Fisher, *A Philadelphia Perspective: The Diary of Sidney George Fisher Covering the Years 1834–1871,* ed. Nicholas B. Wainwright (Philadelphia: Historical Society of Pennsylvania, 1967), 197.

2. "The City of Modern Ruins," *New-York Mirror* 17 (June 13, 1840): 407; "Modern Buildings," *New-York Mirror* 11 (March 15, 1834): 295; "City Rambles," *New-York Mirror* 9 (May 12, 1832): 358–59.

3. "Buildings of 1646," *New-York Mirror* 5 (December 8, 1827): 174. See also, for example, "Old 76," *New-York Mirror* 8 (March 19, 1831): 289 (with Davis image); "Dutch Architecture. The Old House in Broad-Street," *New-York Mirror* 8 (July 10, 1830): 1; S. Woodworth, "History of the Old Stuyvesant Mansion," *New-York Mirror* 9 (December 31, 1831): 201 (with Davis image).

4. Dell Upton, "Pattern Books and Professionalism: Aspects of the Transformation of American Domestic Architecture, 1800–1860," *Winterthur Portfolio* 19, nos. 2–3 (Summer–

Autumn 1984): 128–29; Mary Lorrain Peters, Diary, 1837–1839, May 1, 1837, MS, New-York Historical Society.

5. Dell Upton, *Another City: Urban Life and Urban Spaces in the New American Republic* (New Haven: Yale University Press, 2008), 113–44.

6. Clement Clark Moore, quoted in Paul E. Cohen and Robert T. Augustyn, *Manhattan in Maps, 1527–1995* (New York: Rizzoli, 1997), 103.

7. "Department of Useful Art. First Article. The Haughwout Establishment," *Cosmopolitan Art Journal* 3, no. 3 (June 1859): 141–47; Eugene S. Ferguson, *Oliver Evans: Inventive Genius of the American Revolution* (Greenville, Del.: Hagley Museum, 1980), 13–32.

8. Spiro Kostof, *The City Shaped: Urban Patterns and Meanings through History* (Boston: Bulfinch Press, 1991), 218–26; Peter Marcuse, "The Grid as City Plan: New York City and Laissez-Faire Planning in the Nineteenth Century," *Planning Perspectives* 2, no. 3 (September 1987): 298.

9. David Henkin, *City Reading: Written Words and Public Spaces in Antebellum New York* (New York: Columbia University Press, 1998), 10–11, 15, 101–4; "The Dry Goods Stores of Broadway," *Home Journal,* October 27, 1849, 3.

10. John H. B. Latrobe, *Southern Travels: Journal of John H. B. Latrobe, 1834,* ed. Samuel Wilson Jr. (New Orleans: Historic New Orleans Collection, 1986), 40–44.

11. Ibid., 43; Ulric Neisser, "Five Kinds of Self-Knowledge," *Philosophical Psychology* 1, no. 1 (1988): 41–45.

12. Northern Star, "The Observer. The City of New-York," *New-York Mirror* 6 (November 15, 1828): 147; George Templeton Strong, Diaries, MS, August 24, 1845, copy at Metropolitan Museum of Art, New York; Walt Whitman, "Starting from Paumanok," in *Complete Poetry and Selected Prose,* ed. James E. Miller Jr. (Boston: Houghton Mifflin, 1959), 16, 23.

13. "The World in Little," *New-York Ledger* 12 (September 27, 1856): 4.

14. Charles Dickens, "American Notes" (1842), in *American Notes and Pictures from Italy* (Oxford: Oxford University Press, 1957), 88–90.

15. George G. Foster, *New York by Gas-Light and Other Urban Sketches* (1850), ed. Stuart G. Blumin (Berkeley: University of California Press, 1990); Luc Sante, *Low Life: Lures and Snares of Old New York* (New York, 1991).

16. On cigars and smoking, see Upton, *Another City,* 306–9, 326–28. The term *sovereign,* alluding as it does to the self-government of independent nations, vividly conveys elite dismay at the independence of New York's ordinary people, and in particular their unwillingness to defer to their betters.

17. W. L. Tiffany, "Art and Its Future Prospects in the United States," *Godey's Lady's Book* 46 (March 1853): 220.

18. John Trumbull, *Letters Proposing a Plan for the Permanent Encouragement of the Fine Arts, by the National Government, Addressed to the President of the United States* (New York: William Davis, 1827), 3, 6.

19. Kevin J. Avery and Peter L. Fodera, *John Vanderlyn's Panoramic View of the Palace and Gardens of Versailles* (New York: Metropolitan Museum of Art, 1988); Fisher, *Philadelphia Perspective,* 198.

20. "Two Living Specimens of the Aztec Race," *The Independent* 4 (January 1, 1852): 4; "The Aztec Children," *The Independent* 4 (January 15, 1852): 10.

21. "The Hybrid or Semi-Human Indian," *New-York Daily Times,* December 8, 1854.

22. "American Museum," *The Ladies Companion* 19 (July 1843): 154; "The Church. All-Soul's Church.—(Unitarian.)," *United States Magazine* 4 (April 1857): 417; "Daniel in the Lion's Den," *New York Herald,* October 31, 1849. *Camille* was also objectionable because it held up "the morals of a courtesan" to youthful admiration. "The Church. All-Soul's Church," 416–17.

23. "The Fine Arts. A 'Brackett' in Public Amusements," *Literary World,* April 10, 1852, 268.

24. For an example of art criticism by an ordinary viewer, see Madaline S. Edwards, *Madaline: Love and Survival in Antebellum New Orleans,* ed. Dell Upton (Athens: University of Georgia Press, 1996), 256–59.

25. Vivien M. Green [Fryd], "Hiram Powers's *Greek Slave:* Emblem of Freedom," *American Art Journal* 14, no. 4 (Autumn 1982): 31–39.

26. "Panorama Saloon" (advertisement), *New-York Herald,* November 1, 1849; "Wallhalla" (advertisement), *New-York Herald,* May 21, 1849; Foster, *New York by Gas-Light,* 77–78, 157; "Franklin Theatre" (advertisement), *New-York Herald,* October 31, 1849; "Wallhalla, 36 Canal Street" (advertisement), *New-York Herald,* October 31, 1849; "Model Artists," *New-York Herald,* December 13, 1849.

27. [Andrew Jackson Downing], "Critique on the February Horticulturist," *The Horticulturist* 7 (April 1852): 174; Upton, "Pattern Books," 124–27.

28. Strong, Diaries, April 26, 1860.

# 3

# Urban Convalescence in Lamb, Poe, and Baudelaire

*Matthew Beaumont*

In this chapter I explore the aesthetic tradition, as I hope to constitute it, of urban convalescence. This tradition is the product of intellectual exchanges, in the first half of the nineteenth century, between the United States, England, and France, exchanges conducted by those celebrated scions of Romanticism, Edgar Allan Poe and Charles Baudelaire. My aim, to put it in Baudelairean terms, is to promote the convalescent to the archetypal status of hero of modernity. In so doing, I hope, among other things, to demote the *flâneur,* who has for a long time occupied this important position.[1] I focus on the figure of the convalescent in Charles Lamb, Poe, and Baudelaire in particular.

Paul de Man grasped the importance of the convalescent for Baudelaire when, in "Literary History and Literary Modernity," he stated: "The human figures that epitomize modernity are defined by experiences such as childhood or convalescence, a freshness of perception that results for a slate wiped clear, from the absence of a past that has not yet had time to tarnish the immediacy of perception (although what is thus freshly discovered prefigures the end of this very freshness), of a past that, in the case of convalescence, is so threatening that it has to be forgotten."[2] The convalescent—particularly the male convalescent, who is, for predictable social reasons, less physically confined than the female convalescent, less domesticated—is not necessarily confined to the sickroom, or to some bucolic refuge, in spite of his infirmity and decrepitude. Indeed, I am especially interested in the moment when, though his nerves are delicate, the urban convalescent takes his first reckless steps in the city from which he has been exiled by illness, and experiences a sense of freedom at once tentative and abrupt. The streets, which he approaches cautiously, still a little feverishly, at first perhaps as an observer who must half-protect himself from the impact of the city, are the site of his fragile reengagement with everyday life. Edgar Allan Poe's "The Man of the Crowd" (1840)—perhaps the most "transatlantic" of his short stories—provides the central myth of the urban convalescent, especially in so far as this myth is then mediated by Baudelaire; and it is on this text that I intend finally to concentrate.[3]

THE IDEA of convalescence as an aesthetic disposition probably originates in Coleridge's *Biographia Literaria.* There the convalescent's experience of his environment is often directly compared to that of the child, because the convalescent's delicate receptiveness to life—a helpless openness to unexpected or half-forgotten sensations—has something of the brittle innocence of a child. For Coleridge, it also has an innate poetic intensity. In the first volume of the *Biographia* (1817), he characterized genius as the capacity "to combine the child's sense of wonder and novelty with the appearances which every day, for, perhaps, forty years, had rendered familiar." The "prime merit" of genius, he continued, and "its most unequivocal mode of manifestation," is "so to represent familiar objects as to awaken in the minds of others a kindred feeling concerning them, and that freshness of sensation which is the constant accompaniment of mental, no less than of bodily convalescence." In convalescence, then, the whole world is made strange. In this state even the most ordinary individual relates to life like a romantic poet. Coleridge—on occasion an almost full-time convalescent himself, especially when living in Highgate, outside London, in the final, drug-addicted decades of his life—captures precisely the state in which I am interested when he refers rhapsodically to "the voluptuous and joy-trembling nerves of convalescence."[4]

So the convalescent, who occupies some indeterminate space between health and illness, even reason and unreason, is at once acutely sensitive to his environment and oddly insulated from it. He is both alive, painfully alive, to the life that continues around him, and dead to it, almost deliciously dead. He is at the same time calm and restless, contemplative and thoughtless. The aesthetics of the city and its anesthetics are for the convalescent inseparable. The convalescent is thus an excellent instance of what Walter Benjamin called "the law of the dialectic at a standstill"—a social being whose immobility itself incarnates the characteristic ambiguities of everyday life in a metropolitan city.[5] As someone cautiously emerging from the state of isolation associated with sickness, and experiencing in consequence a process of more or less reluctant re-socialization, he is a graphic instance of the relationship between individual and society, private and public, in metropolitan society of the early nineteenth century. As an aesthetic archetype, furthermore, the convalescent is precisely situated on the cusp of Romanticism and Modernism, both of which, I am assuming, are politico-cultural responses to capitalist modernity. Convalescence is one of the means by which, in an industrial society and in the increasingly uniform, utilitarian culture associated with it, the subject's body obeys the injunction, characteristic of both Romanticism and Modernism, to "make it new." In this respect, it also represents a revolt, albeit a passive one, that is characteristic of the aesthetics of "romantic anti-capitalism" as defined by Michael Löwy and Robert Sayre; that is, it is a redemptive reaffirmation of "the repressed, manipulated and deformed subjectivity" manufactured by capitalism.[6]

There are of course a number of other, superficially more plausible candidates, throughout the nineteenth and early twentieth centuries, for the Baudelairean role of hero of modernity. The most famous of these, and still the most popular, as I have already implied, is the *flâneur* (whose affinities to the commodity, repeatedly emphasized by Benjamin, are all too often forgotten by those who celebrate him). As a social archetype, the convalescent has a certain amount in common with the *flâneur:* both of them, for example, tend to perambulate the city at a distinctly dilatory pace; and for both of them, as Benjamin puts it, "the joy of watching is triumphant."[7] Like his cousin the *flâneur,* the convalescent inhabits what Fredric Jameson has called "the bereft condition of the anti-hero who has no motivation at all."[8] The convalescent—who does not patrol the marketplace; who, in Benjaminian terms, looks about but does not seek a buyer—is the *flâneur*'s poor relation. More precisely, perhaps, he is his poorly relation. The convalescent is significant, even if he has been invisible to cultural historians of modernity, because he provides an alternative account of the relationship between the metropolis and mental life in the nineteenth century, one in which the immobility of the urban subject is as important as his mobility.

"It is strange that while so much has been written for the invalid in the time of sickness, there are but few books which deal with the special needs of Convalescence."[9] So argued the Reverend S. C. Lowry in *Convalescence: Its Blessings, Trials, Duties and Dangers: A Manual of Comfort and Help for Persons Recovering from Sickness* (1845), a book that explores convalescence as a spiritual, no less than physical, condition. The same statement might be made, *mutatis mutandis,* about contemporary scholarship, and this too has helped to make the convalescent almost invisible in the nineteenth and twentieth centuries and into our own. Sickness, and its role in nineteenth-century literature and culture, has been discussed *ad nauseam,* so to speak. Athena Vrettos, for example, who has devised a "poetics of illness," asserts convincingly enough that "fictions of illness make their appearance in multiple and shifting areas of Victorian thought." Symptomatically, though, her narrative of these "somatic fictions" abruptly shifts "from disease to health," and in so doing completely effaces the importance of convalescence.[10] There is at present no poetics of convalescence, though this indeterminate physical and psychological condition is of relevance both to individuals and to the collective imagination in the epoch of metropolitan modernity.

So how can convalescence be defined, if at all, in a technical sense? In the opening decades of the nineteenth century, when its impact on literature becomes apparent, a number of French medical students seem to have written dissertations on convalescence as part of their final examination.[11] One of these, which I have chosen almost at random, can therefore function as an initial definition. In his thesis on convalescence presented at the Faculty of Medicine in Paris on August 3, 1837, Hyacinthe Dubranle makes this statement: "Convalescence . . . is an intermediary state between the illness that it succeeds and the condition of health that it precedes. It begins at the stage when the symptoms that characterize the illness have disappeared, and finishes at the stage when the free and regular exercise of the functions that constitute health is fully restored."[12] This definition is manifestly problematic because, like all definitions of convalescence, it cannot make sharp distinctions between this transitional phase and the phases that precede and succeed it. Is it possible, it might be asked, to identify the moment when the symptoms of the disease disappear? Or when the free and regular exercise of those functions that constitute a condition of healthiness is "fully restored" (*pleinement rétabli*)? It is, however, useful enough, not least because, in making obvious the difficulty of providing a precise definition at all, it implies that convalescence is a diffusive condition, one that spontaneously undoes an uncomplicated opposition between disease and health. If, on the one hand, convalescence simply occupies the neutral border territory through which the patient must travel in order to escape from disease, then on the other hand the convalescent state stealthily colonizes health itself, sometimes comprehensively. "This flat swamp of convalescence, left by the ebb of sickness, yet far enough from the *terra firma* of established health," as Charles Lamb depicted it in 1825, has a habit of surreptitiously encroaching on terra firma.[13]

The effects of an illness are often especially difficult to eradicate once the patient has resumed ordinary life and resumed his or her labor, even if those effects manifest themselves mainly in the form of psychosomatic anxieties. In the capitalist marketplace of the early nineteenth century, when time became increasingly industrialized and commodified, the labor process was significantly reshaped by emergent forms of temporal discipline associated with the proliferation of clocks and watches. It was not the task that was dominant, as E. P. Thompson has observed, "but the value of time when reduced to money": "Time is now currency: it is not passed but spent."[14] In this context, one in which invalids were invalidated, sickness could not be countenanced. Individuals therefore frequently had to live with illness, accommodating it to everyday life, in order to sustain themselves. Prematurely forced by economic necessity to make regular if not necessarily free use of their physical and mental functions, to appropriate Dubranle's terms, many people are arrested in an almost perpetual state of transition from sickness to health, from health to sickness. These people, more or less forced to participate in an industrial capitalist society to which they do not feel properly fitted, a society in which they feel perpetually unfit, are at once hypochondriac and heroic. Convalescence is in this sense a chronic rather than an acute phenomenon, and it might even be identified as one of those almost existential conditions characteristic of the historical process of industrial modernization. Life in the metropolitan city is itself ineradicably febrile. "The resistance that modernity offers to the natural productive élan of an individual is out of all proportion to his strength," Benjamin writes in "The Paris of the Second Empire in Baudelaire," and "it is understandable if a person becomes exhausted and takes refuge in death." For this reason, he argues, "modernity must stand under the sign of death."[15] It can equally be said to stand under the sign of convalescence, or of some residual state of feverishness equivalent to it.

If convalescence is a state of transition from sickness to health, then in narrative terms, so to speak, this process is not automatically a comic one. To the extent that sickness offers temporary respite from the disciplinary demands of industrial capitalism, convalescence promises not the social reintegration that, like marriage, it signals in the plot of the nineteenth-century novel, but rather a form of disintegration instead.[16] Reintegration and disintegration go together for the convalescent. So in his essay "The Convalescent," which dramatizes the narrative of convalescence as a tragicomic one, Lamb provocatively celebrates sickness. His mischievous claim is that in the "regal solitude" of his sickbed the patient enjoys positively autocratic privileges that he should only reluctantly give up. In the kingdom of the sick, according to Lamb, all citizens are monarchs. "How the patient lords it there! What caprices he acts without controul! How kinglike he sways his pillow," Lamb exclaims. The sick man is thus paradoxically disalienated (in Marx's phrase). "How sickness enlarges the dimensions of a man's self to himself!" continues Lamb in ecstasies of self-afflation. The convalescent, in contrast, is like a despot who has been violently deposed: "From the bed of sickness (throne let me rather call it) to the elbow chair of convalescence, is a fall from dignity, amounting to a deposition."[17]

Specifically, Lamb complains that, as a convalescent, he has once again been made susceptible to the demands of labor. The convalescent therefore feels his or her body, after a delightful interval of enforced unproductivity, being more or less gradually instrumentalized and commodified again. Lamb insists that, because he must divest himself of "the strong armour of sickness," robust health makes him vulnerable. Under capitalism, our bodies are reified, although we are habitually forced to forget this fact. In the ambiguous state of convalescence, however, when we are uncomfortably poised between the health that qualifies us for the production process and the sickness that disqualifies us from it, we are briefly made conscious of the alienation of our physical lives from our mental or spiritual lives. The incontrovertible evidence for the relapse into a state of alienation decried by Lamb is of course his article "The Convalescent" itself, which he offers his editor (who has impatiently requested publishable copy from him) in the deliberately self-reflexive flourish of the final paragraph. Lamb's essay thus reinscribes his convalescence as an abrupt fall back into labor, which in a tone of satirical contempt he calls "the petty businesses of life."[18] It describes a brutal transition from a prelapsarian state, the domain of use-value, to a postlapsarian state, the domain of exchange value. Ironically, however, it is the delicate nerviness of the convalescent, his euphoric sensitivity even, which has made it possible for Lamb to compose this clever, supremely self-conscious effusion for publication in the first place.

Lamb complains that convalescence "shrinks a man back to his pristine stature," using "pristine" in its strict sense to mean original, primitive, or ancient.[19] He employs this adjective to evoke the almost primordial helplessness of the convalescent when, as if in some painfully mundane reenactment of Adam's deposition from Eden, he is violently forced back into the everyday conditions of an advanced civilization. The Reverend S. C. Lowry, whose tract from the mid-1840s I have already mentioned, is interested in convalescence as a spiritual condition, one that is specific to "the transition period between the storm and tempest and the ordinary voyage of life," and, in contrast to Lamb, he identifies it, potentially at least, as a state of redemption.[20] For him, in the accelerated conditions of industrial modernity, it represents the possibility of rebirth. Lowry is conscious nonetheless of the individual's susceptibility, in this uncertain state, to what he calls "the dangers of convalescence," namely, indifference, shallowness, and worldliness. He worries in particular that, once the patient has returned from "the cloistered seclusion" of the sickroom to "the busy duties of life," the repentant attitude he has acquired because of his illness will be fatally lost. "We live at a fast rate these days," he notes, "and sometimes amid all the engrossing occupations and harassing competitions of life, our souls seem to stand a poor chance."[21]

But if convalescence is susceptible to the spiritual perversion that is inseparable from "worldliness," it is also, according to Lowry, "a golden opportunity for *definite conversion* to God."[22] The former, it should be noted, is implicitly associated with urban life, the latter with rural life. In this vision of convalescence, the extent to which it might redeem the patient can be measured by the aesthetic and hence spiritual intensity with which his relationship to nature is reinvented, and made transcendent: "The flowers seem to glow with a lovelier radiance, the fields are clothed with a brighter green. The carol of the birds, the rustle of the leaves, the murmur of the stream, fall upon your ears with a fresh meaning."[23] The ideal convalescent, as Lowry's onomatopoeic diction no doubt unsuccessfully indicates, is as supremely sensitive, and as open to redemptive experience, as a pastoral poet. Lowry's, it might be said, is a reactionary, rural romantic anti-capitalism.

For Charles Baudelaire, the most important proponent of convalescence as an aesthetic disposition in the nineteenth century, the convalescent is in contrast an urban poet, albeit one indebted to the Coleridgean tradition that can be detected in Lowry's book. Convalescence, as he argues, "is like a return towards childhood," for "the convalescent, like the child, is possessed in the highest degree of the faculty of keenly interesting himself in things, be they apparently of the most trivial."[24] Baudelaire primarily derives his interest in convalescence, which to him seems inseparable from a state of rapturous, febrile curiosity, from Edgar Allan Poe, and specifically from "The Man of the Crowd." This is indeed the canonical instance of urban convalescence in literature, so I want to explore it in considerable detail. Poe himself probably derives his theoretical interest in the convalescent from Coleridge, whom he read, of course, with passionate attention, and whose conception of convalescence he deliberately urbanizes and modernizes. It might be added, though, that the prolific American writer Nathaniel Parker Willis, of whom Poe was at this time especially critical, but whose accounts of central London, published in *The Romance of Travel* in early 1840, are a plausible influence on "The Man of the Crowd," subsequently de-urbanized and de-modernized the convalescent, perhaps deliberately, in a collection published in 1855.[25]

Poe's celebrated short narrative, first published in *Graham's Magazine* in December 1840, is set in London, where Poe had lived and been educated between 1815 and 1820. Michael Sheringham has contended that "in Baudelaire's case 'London' provided the code through which he deciphers 'Paris' "; a London, he means, that had been mediated by de Quincey and Poe in particular.[26] Poe's London, it should be stated at the outset, was by the same token mediated as much by the London depicted by Bulwer Lytton, Dickens, and Willis, and indeed by his experiences of other cities like New York and Philadelphia, as by his distant memories of it. In its second paragraph, the narrator recalls the convalescent state he recently inhabited. For it was in the ambiguous condition of the convalescent that he obsessively pursued an enigmatic old man he happened to glimpse in the street; an old man who, in the end, mentally and physically defeated, the narrator, in hopeless or triumphant tones, identifies as "the type and the genius of deep crime." He relates:

> Not long ago, about the closing in of an evening in autumn, I sat at the large bow window of the D—— Coffee-House in London. For some months I had been ill in health, but was now convalescent, and, with returning strength, found myself in one of those happy moods which are so precisely the converse of *ennui*—moods of the keenest appetency, when the film from the mental vision departs . . . and the intellect, electrified, surpasses as greatly its every-day condition, as does the vivid yet candid reason of Leibnitz, the mad and flimsy rhetoric of Gorgias. Merely to breathe was enjoyment; and I derived positive pleasure even from many of the legitimate sources of pain. I felt a calm but inquisitive interest in everything. With a cigar in my mouth and a newspaper in my lap, I had been amusing myself for the greater part of the afternoon, now in poring over advertisements, now in observing the promiscuous company in the room, and now in peering through the smoky panes into the street.[27]

This is an exact description of convalescence as an aesthetic, a state of unpredictable, half-repressed euphoria in which, because he is temporarily exempt from the routine demands of everyday life in an industrial capitalist city, the individual's "electrified" senses are preternaturally attuned to experience. The convalescent is painfully sensitive to his environment and at the same time feels oddly distanced from it. The film has departed from his mental vision, but he nonetheless peers at the life of the city through "smoky panes." His empty, appetitive mood is at once both the opposite of boredom and oddly characteristic of its restless calm: it is "the converse of *ennui,*" or its obverse. His consciousness processes the shocks of urban life, the traffic on the roads and pavements, as concussions that seem almost exquisite because he can remain detached and half-insulated from them.

Poe's urban fable locates his convalescent on the margins of a mass of people. Detached from the "dense and continuous tides of population" that rush past the café as the evening closes in, and from the rhythms of routine production they collectively embody, his convalescent describes his fascination with the people he sees commuting home. He is soon lost in contemplation of them: "At this particular period of the evening I had never before been in a similar situation, and the tumultuous sea of human heads filled me, therefore, with a delicious novelty of emotion."[28] Initially he examines the mass of human forms that pass him in the abstract. He is particularly interested in those who seem unconfident on the street, those who "were restless in their movements, had flushed faces, and talked and gesticulated to themselves, as if feeling in solitude on account of the very denseness of the company around."[29] These are the people for whom everyday life in the city is a kind of sickness or fever. Then Poe's convalescent examines the passersby in more concrete detail, as if they inhabited some grimy aquarium. Sliding down "the scale of what is termed gentility," as the light thickens, he classifies their physiognomies, their clothes and step, carefully sifting through the aristocrats, businessmen, clerks, artisans, "exhausted laborers," pie men, dandies, con men, pickpockets, beggars, and prostitutes. The innumerable drunkards he sees from the café, their countenances pale, eyes a livid red, clutch at passing objects "with quivering fingers" as they stride through the crowd.[30]

It is "thus occupied in scrutinizing the mob," his forehead pressed against the glass beside his seat, that the convalescent glimpses the "decrepit old man" whose *physiologie* he is completely unable to taxonomize. He stumbles into the street, his curiosity heightened by the snatched sight of a diamond and a dagger beneath the old man's cloak, and resolves in a moment of heated decision to follow him. "For my own part I did not much regard the rain," he notes, "the lurking of an old fever in my system rendering the moisture somewhat too dangerously pleasant."[31] He traces the man's mysterious movements, throughout the night and into the day, as he roams the city, in an apparently futile attempt to understand what motivates him; but he finally only tracks him back, on the evening of the second day, to the coffeehouse from which he had first set out. The old man, who appears completely unconscious of the narrator, seems to be more than human—as if his labyrinthine path through the streets had traced not the arbitrary trajectory of an individual but the secret form or logic of the corrupt, decrepit metropolitan city. So the convalescent abandons his pursuit: "*He is the man of the crowd.* It will be in vain to follow; for I shall learn no more of him, nor of his deeds."[32]

The old man incarnates the industrial capitalist city in its antiheroic rather than heroic form. In "On Some Motifs in Baudelaire," composed exactly one hundred years after this short story was first published, Benjamin decides that he cannot ultimately identify Poe's "man of the crowd" as a *flâneur,* mainly because in him "composure has given way to manic behavior." Instead, according to Benjamin, he exemplifies the destiny of the *flâneur* once this intrinsically urbane figure has been "deprived of the milieu to which he belonged" (a milieu, he implies, that London probably never provided).[33] The same might be said of Poe's convalescent, in whom composure must compete with a positively monomaniacal mood. Indeed, it might be argued that "The Man of the Crowd" allegorizes the process by which, in the hectic conditions of a metropolis like London in the mid-nineteenth century, the *flâneur* splits apart and produces two further metropolitan archetypes, one almost pathologically peripatetic, the other static to the point of being a sort of cripple. The former is the nightwalker, a disreputable, indeterminately criminal type who hypostasizes that half of the *flâneur* characterized by a state of restless mobility; the latter is the convalescent, who hypostasizes the half of him characterized by a state of immobile curiosity. For Poe, these characters are spectral doubles.

Baudelaire's discussion of "The Man of the Crowd" is contained in the opening chapter of *The Painter of Modern Life* (1863), his encomium to the artist Constantin Guys, "a passionate lover of crowds and incognitos." He portrays Guys there as someone whose genius resides in a childlike curiosity, which he characterizes in terms of "the fixed and animally ecstatic gaze of a child confronted with something new, whatever it be." Like the child, who actually "sees everything in a state of newness," and who is consequently "always drunk," Guys is exquisitely susceptible to impressions. For him, "sensibility is almost the whole being." Ordinarily, Baudelaire emphasizes, adults can recover this spontaneously poetic disposition only when they are in a state of convalescence. Guys, however, positively personifies this disposition, because he is "an eternal convalescent." If you "imagine an artist who was always, spiritually, in the condition of that convalescent," Baudelaire concludes, "you will have the key to the nature of Monsieur G."[34]

Baudelaire identifies Poe's convalescent as his inspiration for this claim:

> Do you remember a picture (it really is a picture!), painted—or rather written—by the most powerful pen of our age, and entitled "The Man of the Crowd"? In the window of a coffee house there sits a convalescent, pleasurably absorbed in gazing at the crowd, and mingling, through the medium of thought, in the turmoil of thought that surrounds him. But lately returned from the valley of the shadow of death, he is rapturously breathing all the odors and essences of life; as he has been on the brink of total oblivion, he remembers, and fervently desires to remember, everything. Finally he hurls himself headlong into the midst of the throng, in pursuit of an unknown, half-glimpsed countenance, that has, on an instant, bewitched him. Curiosity had become a fatal, irresistible passion![35]

It is immediately apparent from this paragraph that Baudelaire's principal interest does not lie in the drama described by Poe's narrative, that is, the convalescent's pursuit, through the tortuous, sometimes tedious streets of London at night, of the abstracted, evil old man with whom he has become obsessed. Instead, he seems more interested in the scene in which the story is initially set. He insists on representing Poe's narrative, in fact, as a relatively static picture, as if he were himself examining the convalescent through a frame. Perhaps it is most accurate to state that he reconstructs the story as a diptych. In the first panel, the convalescent is passively seated in the coffeehouse. As he observes the street life through the pane of glass, he simultaneously introjects the scenes outside, assimilating them to his consciousness, and projects his consciousness onto the scenes outside, assimilating his consciousness to them. He is "pleasurably absorbed in gazing at the crowd, and mingling, through the medium of thought, in the turmoil of thought that surrounds him." The convalescent "rapturously breath[es] in all the odors and essences of life," making the surface of his body seem absolutely porous, even as the solid pane of glass that he sits beside has apparently been rendered completely permeable. In the second panel, Baudelaire's description captures Poe's protagonist, as if in a photograph, in the act of flinging himself into the street—like the Baudelairean protagonist who, according to Benjamin, "plunges into the crowd as into a reservoir of energy."[36] He is freeze-framed, so to speak, as he "hurls himself headlong into the midst of the throng." The convalescent thus metamorphoses into a noctambulist.

The second of these portraits is in effect an image of the convalescent as hero, actively seeking to satisfy his feverish curiosity, even if it is finally fatal to do so (as if Baudelaire had resolved to stalk the seductive widow he wistfully describes in "À une passante"). Baudelaire's convalescent is thus saved from the humiliating defeat that Poe visits on his convalescent at the end of "The Man of the Crowd," when he is forced to admit that he has failed to identify the man he has so assiduously pursued through the metropolis, at least as an individual. Poe's spectral convalescent, more spiritually decrepit than Baudelaire's, and less rapturous, is not so deeply indebted to the Coleridgean tradition, in spite of the fact that Baudelaire probably encountered this tradition through the mediation of Poe. But like Poe's convalescent, Baudelaire's convalescent remains terminally peripheral to the life of the street, in contrast to the *flâneur.* The *flâneur,* according to Baudelaire, in the same section of "The Painter of Modern Life," is situated "at the center of the world," even though he also "remain[s] hidden from the world."[37] In this respect, as in others, he is like the commodity, which is so pervasive as to be invisible. The convalescent, Baudelaire implies, by contrast resists the performative aspect of the *flâneur*'s life in the streets and refuses the spectacular logic of the marketplace.

It is implicitly Poe, however, and not Constantin Guys, who embodies the spirit of convalescence for Baudelaire. Baudelaire had first referred to what he so evocatively describes as "convalescence, with its fevers of curiosity" in "Edgar Poe, sa vie et ses ouvrages" (1853).[38] In this piece, which subsequently reappeared as the introduction to his translations in the *Histoires extraordinaires* (1856), Baudelaire locates the "single character" that populates Poe's numerous narratives as "the man of razor-sharp perceptions and slackened nerves." He concludes that "this man is Poe himself."[39] This description, I want to contend in conclusion, perfectly captures the constitution of the convalescent, who is acutely sensitive to the life of the streets but at the same time oddly anesthetized to it. The poetics of convalescence that is perceptible in Poe, and that Baudelaire elaborated, makes him absolutely central to the process by which Romanticism, in nineteenth- and twentieth-century literature, became urbanized and transatlanticized. Poe is for Baudelaire one of the patron saints of metropolitan modernity because, as "the writer of the nerves," he too is a perpetual convalescent.[40] In the urban sensorium described by Poe and Baudelaire, the sick are too sensitive to cope with the shocks of everyday life, and the healthy are constitutionally insensitive to its secret aesthetics. The convalescent is thus the perfect metropolitan subject.

## NOTES

A previous version of this chapter appeared as "Convalescing," in *Restless Cities,* ed. Matthew Beaumont and Gregory Dart (London: Verso, 2010), 59–77. I am grateful to Andrew Hemingway and Helen Rogers for their comments on the draft of this version.

1. Like Tom Gretton, for whose comments on the thesis of this chapter I am extremely grateful, I am convinced that "for Baudelaire other figures were as good as or better than even the perfect *flâneur.*" See Tom Gretton, "Not the *Flâneur* Again: Reading Magazines and Living the Metropolis around 1880," in *The Invisible Flâneuse? Gender, Public Space, and Visual Culture in Nineteenth-Century Paris,* ed. Arun D'Souza and Tom McDonough (Manchester: Manchester University Press, 2006), 95. In this essay, Gretton proposes other figures instead, including the "incognito prince" and the philosophe, but he too neglects Baudelaire's interest in the convalescent. See also Gregory Shaya, "The *Flâneur,* the *Badaud,* and the Making of a Mass Public in France, circa 1860–1910," *American Historical Review* 109 (2004): 41–77.

2. Paul de Man, *Blindness and Insight: Essays in the Rhetoric of Contemporary Criticism,* rev. ed. (Minneapolis: University of Minnesota Press, 1983), 157.

3. Contending that, in his fiction, Poe positions himself "on an eerie dividing line between British convention and American independence," Paul Giles has noted that "in 'William Wilson' (1839), this fissure is located specifically within a transatlantic context, as Poe's narrator tells the story of his youth and upbringing in England, where he found himself always haunted by a shadow self." See Paul Giles, *Transatlantic Insurrections: British Culture and the Formation of American Literature, 1730–1860* (Philadelphia: University of Pennsylvania Press, 2001), 189. It can be added that "The Man of the Crowd," set in the center of London, also mines this fissure. "William Wilson" and "The Man of the Crowd" are the only short stories in which Poe draws directly on his experiences of England as a child, when he attended schools in Chelsea and Stoke Newington in the late 1810s.

4. Samuel Taylor Coleridge, *Biographia Literaria, or Biographical Sketches of My Literary Life and Opinions,* vol. 1, ed. James Engell and W. Jackson Bate, in *The Collected Works of Samuel Taylor Coleridge,* vol. 7 (London: Routledge & Kegan Paul, 1983), 81. Note that William Morris subsequently transmutes the romantic tradition initiated by Coleridge, lending the idea of convalescence a utopian, anti-capitalist impetus in his lecture "The Society of the Future" (1887): "I remember, after having been ill once, how pleasant it was to lie on my bed without pain or fever, doing nothing but watching the sunbeams and listening to the sounds of life outside; and might not the great world of men, if it once deliver itself from the struggle for life amidst dishonesty, rest for a little while after the long fever and be none the worse for it?" William Morris, "The Society of the Future," in *Political Writings of William Morris,* ed. A. L. Morton (London: Lawrence & Wishart, 1973), 203.

5. See, for example, Walter Benjamin, *Understanding Brecht,* trans. Anna Bostock (London: Verso, 1983), 12.

6. Michael Löwy and Robert Sayre, "Figures of Romantic Anti-Capitalism," *New German Critique* 32 (Spring–Summer 1984): 58. See also Michael Löwy and Robert Sayre, *Romanticism against the Tide of Modernity,* trans. Catherine Porter (Durham: Duke University Press, 2001).

7. Walter Benjamin, *Charles Baudelaire: A Lyric Poet in the Era of High Capitalism,* trans. Harry Zohn (London: Verso, 1983), 69.

8. Fredric Jameson, *The Modernist Papers* (London: Verso, 2007), 76.

9. S. C. Lowry, *Convalescence: Its Blessings, Trials, Duties and Dangers: A Manual of Comfort and Help for Persons Recovering from Sickness* (London: Skeffington, 1845), 1.

10. Athena Vrettos, *Somatic Fictions: Imagining Illness in Victorian Culture* (Stanford: Stanford University Press, 1995), 1, 19.

11. These studies might be seen as related to the pervasive interest in intermediate states of being, such as somnambulism and mesmeric trance, which Tony James has identified in France in the early nineteenth century; see Tony James, *Dream, Creativity, and Madness in Nineteenth-Century France* (Oxford: Clarendon Press, 1995).

12. "La convalescence . . . est un état intermédiaire à la maladie à laquelle il succède et à la santé à laquelle il conduit. Elle commence à l'époque où les symptômes qui caractérisent la maladie ont disparu, et fini à l'époque où l'exercise libre et régulier des fonctions qui constituent la santé est pleinement rétabli." Hyacinthe Dubranle, *Essai sur la convalescence: Thèse* (Paris: Rignoux, 1837), 5.

13. Charles Lamb, "The Convalescent," in "Elia and the Last Essays of Elia," in *The Works of Charles and Mary Lamb,* ed. E. V. Lucas, 7 vols. (London: Methuen, 1903), 2:186.

14. E. P. Thompson, "Time, Work-Discipline and Industrial Capitalism," in *Essays in Social History,* ed. Michael W. Flinn and T. C. Smout (Oxford: Clarendon Press, 1974), 43.

15. Walter Benjamin, "The Paris of the Second Empire in Baudelaire," in *The Writer of Modern Life: Essays on Charles Baudelaire,* ed. Michael W. Jennings (Cambridge: Belknap Press of Harvard University Press, 2006), 104.

16. See Natalie Bell Cole, "Attached to Life Again: The 'Queer Beauty' of Convalescence in *Bleak House,*" *Victorian Newsletter* 103 (Spring 2003): 17–19.

17. Lamb, "The Convalescent," 185.

18. Ibid., 186.

19. Ibid., 185.

20. Lowry, *Convalescence,* 3.

21. Ibid., 33, 42–43.

22. Ibid., 33.

23. Ibid., 11.

24. Charles Baudelaire, "The Painter of Modern Life," in *The Painter of Modern Life and Other Essays,* trans. Jonathan Mayne (London: Phaidon, 1995), 7–8.

25. See Nathaniel Parker Willis, *Romance of Travel, Comprising Tales of Five Lands* (New York: Colman, 1840); and *The Convalescent* (New York: Scribner, 1859).

26. Michael Sheringham, "Archiving," in *Restless Cities,* ed. Matthew Beaumont and Gregory Dart (London: Verso, 2010), 4.

27. Edgar Allan Poe, "The Man of the Crowd," in *Selected Tales,* ed. David Van Leer (Oxford: Oxford World's Classics, 1998), 84.

28. Ibid., 84.

29. Ibid., 85.

30. Ibid., 86–87.

31. Ibid., 87–88.

32. Ibid., 91.

33. Walter Benjamin, "On Some Motifs in Baudelaire," in *The Writer of Modern Life,* 188.

34. Baudelaire, "The Painter of Modern Life," 7–8.

35. Ibid.

36. Benjamin, "On Some Motifs in Baudelaire," 191.

37. Baudelaire, "The Painter of Modern Life," 9.

38. Charles Baudelaire, "Edgar Allan Poe: His Life and Works," in *The Painter of Modern Life,* 90.

39. Ibid., 91.

40. Ibid., 90.

# II HISTORY

# 4

# Sublime and Fall

## Benjamin West and the Politics of the Sublime in Early Nineteenth-Century Marylebone

*Nicholas Grindle*

A KEY characteristic of recent writing on British art by Anglophone historians is a drive to see the conflicts of the present in the art of the past. Thus three decades in which the public good was increasingly identified with the pursuit of private interest has seen historians' interest turn away from government patronage of art and toward the workings of a private market.[1] This has been especially the case for the period covered by this volume. There are signs that the tide is turning, with books published more recently on the government's sponsorship of art in a time of increased bureaucracy needed to maintain a fiscal-military state (an early instance of what David Egerton has called the "warfare state").[2] But one area in which historians have been especially reticent is altarpieces. Even where historians have acknowledged that the Royal Academy exhibitions witnessed a constant trickle of altarpieces, a widely held assumption that a society is more modern in proportion to the degree it is secular has meant that these works have been held as exceptional cases, oddities and quirks that belong with drawings made from human hair and the like.

A corollary of the assumption that modern societies are necessarily more secular has been to associate representations of Apocalypse with radical politics. Apocalypse, meaning "revelation," describes the vision recorded by the disciple and apostle John in the Book of Revelation, foretelling the final battle between God the Father and Satan, and the vindication of believers and martyrs when Christ returns. Historians have argued that a belief in the literal imminence of these events was the resort of those whose political aspirations were frustrated.[3] If this is true of antinomian sects in the mid-seventeenth and late eighteenth centuries, it is also true of a number of significant artists, most notably James Barry, for whom the promise of moral revival through the visual arts in the form of the Royal Academy under the patronage of the king had disappeared. Critics have seen in Barry's work an exemplary and incoherent amalgamation of brute masculinity and socialized virtue that exemplifies the contradictory aims of moral reform in the context of capitalist society.[4] Historians have suggested that if James Barry, Henry Fuseli, John Flaxman, William Blake, and others, who all produced apocalyptic subjects, held beliefs deemed esoteric relative to the doctrines of the Church of England, it only confirms the fact that the church established by law was incapable of being an agent of the radical reform sought by those whose aims necessitated the overthrow of existing structures.[5]

One outcome of a loss of interest in the public patronage of art, combined with a reading of apocalyptic imagery as political critique, is that the continued sponsorship of painting for churches in the Romantic period, and the Apocalypse as a quintessentially Romantic subject, are topics kept far apart from each other in the historiography of British art. The singular exception, leaving aside William Beckford's commissions for Benjamin West to decorate his chapel at Fonthill, is West's commission for George III's projected Royal Chapel at Windsor. The designs for the chapel, often referred to as the Chapel of Revealed Religion, included five scenes from Revelation, only two of which were exhibited (*The Opening of the Four Seals, vide Revelation, a sketch* and *The Destruction of the Beast and the False Prophet,* shown at the Royal Academy in 1796 and 1804 as numbers 246 and 30, respectively). The commission was abandoned definitively in 1804, a decision that has been attributed by historians to the king's sensitivity to Revelation as a subject that appealed to "democrats," among whose number he was thought to count West.[6] The fact that it was never completed, but that West continued as president of the Royal Academy for the next sixteen years, has tended to be cited as the exception that proves the rule.

Controversy about a commission for a religious history painting arose once more in the final decade of West's life. In the first initiative of its kind for more than a century, the government voted a grant of £1 million to build new churches. The decision was set against a chorus of warnings about the effects of overpopulation and the chaos that would result from a populace starved of religious instruction, a subject that readily lent itself to being cast in apocalyptic terms. Marylebone parish in London was cited as the exemplary instance of a lack of church provision, and its select vestry was held up to ridicule for its dithering attitude toward church building. Yet this same parish was the focus for West's largest commission in this decade, a design for a transparency that would stand seventeen feet high when finished. The sublime scale of the piece, and the principal figures, not to mention West's charge to the parish officials, who thought they were getting the design gratis from an eminent parishioner, were frequently cited by contemporaries, yet they sat in sharp contrast to the polished manners of West himself. It is evident that West was able to achieve this commission because he was known as a painter of sublime subjects, yet he himself was the very antithesis of the excessive masculinity that historians have suggested was characteristic of his contemporaries such as Fuseli and younger artists such as Blake. It is almost as if his own person recuperated the destructive excess inherent in the sublimity of his paintings in a way that had evidently not been the case in 1804, when he was suspected of democratic sympathies.

In this essay I show that a Whiggish discourse of the sublime served to govern the reception of both West's subjects and his ambition, but that Tory speakers used the same discourse to frame a different cultural politics after 1815, one that highlighted the imminence of Apocalypse and undermined the security of West's discursive position. The discourse about sublime painting for churches was one of a number of discourses that, as Peter de Bolla has shown with the discourse on debt in mid-eighteenth-century England, not only are about excess but also are themselves characterized by excessive language.[7] Other examples included the discourse on population and the discourse on church building. For de Bolla, whose focus is on the embodiment and practice of the sublime as a discourse, as well as its theorization, William Pitt the Elder is the exemplar of the subject as a "functional effect," that is, not as an individual but as a subject position who embodies the discourse and at the same time renders it as a public text, not as the destroying specter of private ambition. I argue that West was an exemplary subject who "worked his socially legitimating magic in proportion as the transitions from text to public are smooth and uninterrupted."[8] That is to say, West's mastery of the technical demands made on him by very large altarpieces issued in a recognition of his own exemplary sublimity, that is, his public constitution as someone who is himself sublime. Yet his exemplary nature proved to be insecure, and I suggest that as a discursive specter or function-effect of discourse, West failed to contain the contradictions between private ambition and public interest. In this sense, he offers an interesting view of other exemplary public bodies associated so closely with Marylebone, especially the Prince Regent, and the parish vestry.

Historians writing about West and history painting, particularly in view of his relationship to the Crown, have tended to look to the personality and politics of West and his patron, King George III, and to how the artist's sympathies were perceived to clash with the king's in light of the Revolutionary war with France, in order to explain the significance of apocalyptic subject matter in West's painting.[9]

But rather than conceiving of painting in terms of personalities and subject matter, I instead think of it as a mode of discourse that takes the artist and patron not as coherent personalities, but as subjects whose words and actions are not substantial but have a signifying function within the discourse; or, in other words, whose words and actions serve to embody the discourse. For example, if the specter of rampant unbridled power as visualized in West's second version of *Death on a Pale Horse* had discomforted George III when it was exhibited at the Royal Academy in 1796, and even more so when admired by Napoleon in 1802, it is important to note that as far as West's contemporaries were concerned, all his paintings of religious subjects were sublime, not only in their subject matter but also in their physical scale, and in what they revealed about the scope of West's ambition.

## The "Elegance and Pathos" of Mr. West

Joseph Farington's diaries are littered with comments about the enormity of West's undertakings. Farington notes in some detail the objections raised at court against West in November and December 1804, recording gossip that "the King's great prejudice was against *West,* & that He considered those who acted with Him to be *Democrats,*" and that the king's influence in the Academy was declining in the face of "the Democratic disposition that prevailed in it."[10] This talk focused in the immediate instance on West's desire to get the architect Robert Smirke elected a member.[11] (Smirke would later be a key player in the improvements effected in Marylebone.) "The King had considered Smirke to be a *Democrat,*" Farington recorded, and in the same entry also noted the king's decision "that the pictures which West had painted for the Chapel at Windsor should not be put up, except the Altar piece, *that* should *not be a Bedlamite scene from the Revelations.*"[12] Historians have seen in the king's supposed reference to Bedlam a sensitivity both to the chaos wrought by revolution and to his own bouts of mental illness.[13] Farington, however, barely mentions the subject matter, referring only to *Death on a Pale Horse* to note Joseph Nollekens's displeasure that it sat in the midst of his pictures at the Academy show in 1796, and that West was allowed to choose its position on the Salon walls when it was exhibited in Paris in 1802.[14] What attracted his interest at this time was what concerned West himself about his work: "He talked of what had been said respecting His account given to the King for pictures painted, and asked what we thought of the charges He had made, when for the *large picture of the Crucifixion,* intended for one end of the Chapel at Windsor, the size 36 feet high by 28 feet wide, & containing near 70 figures, many of them Colossal in size, He had charged only 2000 guineas."[15]

West was evidently trying to persuade Farington and Smirke's father, the painter Robert Smirke, that his charges were reasonable, given the scale of the work itself. Earlier in the year he had discussed the size and price of a comparable commission, the altarpiece for the chapel at Greenwich Hospital. The context for this discussion is worth explaining. John Singleton Copley had demanded unpaid fees from Sir Edward Knatchbull, who claimed Copley had overcharged for a large family portrait. The plaintiff had subpoenaed West and other artists to speak in his defense. Discussing this with the Smirke family, Farington, and Thomas Daniell, West said "that He had £1200 for the Altar Piece which He painted for Greenwich Hospital Chapel which is 27 feet high."[16] At the hearing itself, he later told Farington, J. M. W. Turner, and the sculptor J. C. F. Rossi, "he was asked what the size of the Greenwich Chapel picture was? & the price?—He said 27 feet high by 16 or 18 wide and contained abt. 50 figures, the largest of which were 8 feet high. For that picture He had 1200 pounds and thought himself well paid." West did not disparage Copley in as many words, saying that although Copley's original fee was a "handsome price," he believed that "some circumstances which had come out in evidence might render it proper to go beyond that."[17] Even so, he still managed to cast his compatriot in a poor light by painting himself as a public servant who did not haggle over a fee but was, by contrast, pleased to be paid the sum he received. Whereas the scale of Copley's painting only served to draw attention to the scope of his personal ambition, which revealed itself in a bitter fight to claim enormous fees from a client, West, in his own representation as recorded by Farington, was careful to offer himself as the model of socialized virtue whose public-spirited conduct made safe the ambition revealed by the epic dimensions of his paintings.

Matters were slightly different when West discussed the success of his enormous painting *Christ Healing the Sick,* which he exhibited at the British Institution in 1811. The painter told Farington that "after paying Him 3000 guineas and all other expenses, they [the British Institution] wd. be £2000 in pocket by it." But even here, West moved comfortably between the axiom that a successful artist tackles significant subjects on an ambitious scale for huge profit, and the public interest, because having "spoke of the success attending the Exhibition of His picture," he went on to say "that it had happily proved that He had not overcharged the *King* when for painting His design of the Crucifixion, for a painted window to be executed from it, which picture was 28 feet high, and for the smaller picture, the *study* of the subject only 8 feet high He asked only £1500, yet that sum was thought by those abt. the King to be a very high price."[18] It is therefore not surprising that when West was asked to paint a design for the new chapel (soon to be the parish church) in Marylebone, he should let Farington know. "He told me," the diarist wrote in 1815, "he was at present employed in painting a picture for Marybone [*sic*] church." In 1817, however, Farington heard from the painter Henry Thomson that West had charged large fees: "Thomson sd. West had 800 guineas for the transparency at Marybone [*sic*] new Church."[19] This is almost as much as Farington says about the major public commission of West's final decade (as we shall see, the elder Smirke has a bit more to say), but the two isolated sentences are revealing. I want to consider the Marylebone commission in more detail in order to see the fine grain of the politics of the sublime.

West was approached to design an altarpiece for the new church in Marylebone in March 1815. "Resolved, that Mr Hardwick do Consult B[enjamin] West, Esquire of Newman Street as to a design for the Windows at the back of the Altar in the New Church, and Report thereon to this Board."[20] In this way the select vestry of St. Marylebone parish recorded in its *Proceedings for New Churches and Chapels* its decision to approach one of its most eminently suitable parishioners about the question of decoration for the new parish church then being erected to the designs of Thomas Hardwick.[21] The vestry had only recently decided to upgrade the building from a chapel into the parish church, and it soon became clear that the unusual organ design for the new church would leave a large space in the window behind the altar. Unusually for a church, the nave ran on a north-south axis, with the altar at the south. West was almost certainly approached not only because he was a parishioner—for as Kit Wedd and others have shown, there were plenty of artists living in Marylebone, though West as president of the Royal Academy was preeminent—but also because of his work for George III. Robert Southey's dig that "for thirty years [the king] employed Mr West when that admirable artist had no commission from any other person" may not be entirely true—he worked for William Beckford—but it shows how the public perception was shaped by West's twenty years of exhibiting at the Royal Academy designs for paintings to hang in George III's projected scheme for the Royal Chapel at Windsor Castle.[22] West had also painted altarpieces for a number of churches in the capital such as St. Stephen Walbrook and Greenwich Hospital Chapel, and had been involved in projects to produce windows for large churches in the capital, namely, St. Anne Limehouse and St. James Piccadilly. He offered the vestry a design that Gerald Carr has shown was very similar to a window in the ensemble completed by West in St. George's Chapel, Windsor, which, in Carr's words, "was praised unstintingly by many and criticized by few."[23] The subject was the Annunciation of the birth of Jesus to the shepherds outside Bethlehem. In West's own words, the transparency was sublime. "That Picture is in height 17 feet by 8 in Width," he wrote to the vestry, in terms that should be familiar by now,

> and its subject, demanding the principal Angel to maintain its preeminence in Character, could not be less than 7 feet in height: this height has been considered the sublime, or standard for Visionary Figures, or beings supernatural, such as the Apollo, St Michael and other celestial characters and, under this elevation of a 7 feet figure, I thought proper to delineate the principal Angel in that Picture; that all those persons, who might be seated in distant parts of the church, should see the energy with which he announced good tidings and great joy he brought to all people.[24]

West's design was also close to a frontispiece he drew for Jacob Duché's *Discourses on Various Subjects,* the main difference being that in the window at St. George's chapel and in the transparency there was only one figure. William Paley and David Bindman have shown that Duché and his engraver William Sharp, both millenarians, had close relations with West over a number of years, yet as Martin Myrone has pointed out, West's work was never characterized by the kind of radical dissociation between artistic value and socialized virtue that characterized the hypermasculinity of figures by Barry, Fuseli, and Blake, and the character of those artists themselves.[25]

West's St. Marylebone commission is very well documented in the parish records, and is notorious, in a minor way, for two reasons. First, as Smirke senior gossiped to Farington, "from the manner in which he undertook this business the Trustees concluded that what He was to do wd. be gratuitous, but He surprised them by making a charge of 800 guineas, which was paid Him."[26] Smirke's comments echo what Thomson had told Farington a year earlier, and what had already been said at court about West: that he charged high prices. The more serious insinuation here, moreover, was that West charged a fee when the patron had understood the work, a public commission, to be a gratuity. It was, as Smirke told Farington, who recorded it all in great detail, identical to what had happened at Greenwich Hospital: "The Governors of the Hospital considered [a design for a pediment sculpture] to be *gratuitous* from Him, but judged it proper to present Him a *piece of plate* as an acknowledgement for what He had done. A person was deputed to wait upon to signify this to Him, but Mr. West said, that He was not a man in rich circumstances & that money would be more acceptable than plate; and being requested to mention a sum, He said, one thousand pounds, which when reported to the Governors astonished them, but the money was paid Him."[27] Second, the transparency was dismantled only ten years later, in 1827, and while the vestry minutes suggest that plans were made to auction it through Christie's straightaway, it did not come up for sale until 1840, and was sold for only £10. A contemporary newspaper reported that "the picture was originally removed from the church of St Marylebone, at the instigation of the then rector and several of the congregation, as giving the church a Popish appearance."[28] Explanations for why it was removed have rehearsed the view that it was "too popish." This may be true. A new rector had in fact replaced the previous incumbent just a year earlier, and as Claire Haynes has observed, there were "no consistent rules, laws, doctrines, or legal precedents to distinguish acceptable from unacceptable images" within the Church of England, and that "at times of political uncertainty, practices previously tolerated could suddenly appear Popish or schismatical."[29] But rather than trying to trace the politics of individuals, I want to focus a bit more on the politics of the sublime as revealed in the vestry's relations with West in 1815–1817.

The vestry minutes record two occasions on which West attended meetings of the committee, and in two instances special mention is made of his manners. On February 1, 1817, "Mr West attended and informed the Board, that he had executed the design for a glass window, agreeably to their request; and that the same was now fixed in the New Church in the place appropriated to receive it, and that the subject was the annunciation of the Birth of our Saviour." He also offered them, "as a gratuitous mark of his great esteem for the parish of Saint Marylebone in which he had resided with such satisfaction and happiness for a period of near 40 years," a picture to be placed "in the centre of the screen at the back of the altar," whose subject was yet to be decided but which would correspond to the Annunciation. The vestry minutes record that "this memorable and impressive speech of Mr West was delivered with such elegance and pathos" that a committee was formed to prepare a vote of thanks to West, and allocated him tickets for the consecration.[30] I want to focus on the way the minutes take the trouble to note the character of West's speech, because the minutes reveal an interest in how well West performed, as it were, the role of a figure able to stir the feelings of the vestry in a way that was fitting for a painter of sublime subjects. If West's design was sublime, on a scale large enough for "the principal Angel to maintain its preeminence in Character," it was fitting that he himself knowingly embodied those very values, in order to function as a means by which the public (here taken as the vestry) might share in them, and therefore find their own collective identity. In other words, the minutes find the vestry's own justification in the figure of West and the legibility of his conduct.

It is worth noting, at this point, that the vestry itself had been select since 1768, meaning that vestrymen were co-opted by existing members rather than being elected by ratepayers, a move instigated by Lord Foley, a relative of the Duke of Portland, who wished to develop forty acres of land northwest of Cavendish Square.[31] West, it hardly needs to be said, was president of another self-selecting body, founded in the same year for the same purpose, namely, the interests of its members. These are important points to note because they help explain what happened next.

Two weeks after West had attended the vestry, a report was made on a meeting with West regarding the subject of the picture, about which the explanatory letter from West quoted earlier was read out. A further letter was also read, in which West wrote, "Mr Collins and other Gentlemen of the Vestry are solicitous of a letter from me, addressed to the Vestry, what the Parish was indebted to me for the picture."[32] He was not independently wealthy, he wrote; otherwise he would donate his work. And given the size of the design, he suggested £800 would be a reasonable fee. An emergency meeting of the vestry was called, and a motion was proposed and passed by a vote of thirty to ten to pay West what he charged.[33]

If the vestrymen were pleased by West's initial appearance, and if their feelings were stirred by his speech, any suggestion that he was acting on mercenary principles risked undermining their own claims to taste, that is to say, their own awareness of being transported by the power of his eloquence, and their own self-consciousness as a body of gentlemen, since it would remove West as the exemplary instance of taste which they had fleetingly, but significantly, identified with themselves as a corporate body, and would lead people to think that they themselves were mercenary, since they were effectively putting a price on taste. Therefore they decided to pay him, and they took the trouble to invite him to vestry again and thanked him for his "very handsome present" of a small canvas to be placed behind the altar.[34]

The position of the vestrymen was essentially a conservative one, assuming the integrity of private feeling and the reconciling effects of custom to a body of private gentlemen (which is how West and the vestry described themselves). For them, West offered the specter of a subject who in his capacity to stir feelings through oratory and painting was both entirely private and entirely public. He gave figure to their own incorporation. This is why they had no choice but to retain that fiction when its contradictions began to appear.

## The "Incapable" Mr. West

The altarpiece at St. Marylebone was a transparency, that is, a painting on paper that would be lit by the sun shining through the windows behind the altar, which faces south. There is contemporary evidence that this was in fact what happened. Many years later a writer for the *Art-Union* recalled, "The effect was so transcendent, that on the second Sunday after the opening of the church, the picture was suddenly strongly illuminated by the sun, and attracted the attention of the whole congregation, and called forth spontaneous expressions of admiration."[35] The principal subject of admiration was presumably the angel, which West had painted over seven feet in height, explaining to the vestry, in the letter quoted earlier, that "this height has been considered the sublime, or standard for Visionary Figures, or beings supernatural, such as the Apollo, St Michael and other celestial characters." The effect on the congregation recalls the poses struck by leading actors such as Sarah Siddons and her brother John Philip Kemble, which would be held onstage to great applause from the audience. This is probably more than simply coincidence, since West meant the figure to be seen by people "in the distant parts of the church." Hardwick's church, for its part, was not unlike a theater. Prior to rebuilding in 1885, it had two balconies and, like all other churches and theaters, was built "to the full extent of the human voice," and for preachers to be "impressive, articulate, and audible," like actors. Moreover, as F. H. W. Sheppard points out in his magisterial study of local government in Marylebone, "at the sides of the organ were private galleries, fitted with chairs and fireplaces, which 'so exactly resembled the private boxes which look upon the proscenium of our theatres, that the spectator might almost suppose he was in a building that originally had that destination.' "[36]

"Indeed the theatre is a better school of moral sentiments than churches," wrote Edmund Burke in 1790, "where the feelings of humanity are . . . outraged."[37] Asking why pitiful scenes moved him, he said:

> Because it is *natural* I should [be moved]; because we are so made as to be affected at such spectacles with melancholy sentiments upon the unstable condition of mortal prosperity, and the tremendous uncertainty of human greatness; because in those natural feelings we learn great lessons; because in events like these our passions instruct our reason; because when kings are hurl'd from their thrones by the Supreme Director of this great drama, and become the objects of insult to the base, and of pity to the good, we behold such disasters in the moral, as we should behold a miracle in the physical order of things.[38]

Plays in theaters, Burke wrote, appeal to our feelings. He allowed for the possibility that a viewer can pretend to be moved by something she or he sees onstage, but argued that just as moral sentiments are *natural* (his emphasis), so a natural sense of shame will prevent such "hypocrisy" and "folly," adding: "I should be truly ashamed of finding in myself that superficial, theatric sense of painted distress, whilst I could exult over it in real life. With such a perverted mind, I could never venture to shew my face at a tragedy. People would think that the tears that Garrick formerly, or that Siddons not long since, have extorted from me, were the tears of hypocrisy; I should know them to be the tears of folly."[39] Burke was taking up a Whig position which reconciled human understanding and moral conduct, and following Richard Steele and Joseph Addison in *The Spectator* some eighty years earlier, he appealed to the theater as a case to prove his point. St. Marylebone was itself a thoroughly Whig parish, being closely associated with two aristocratic Whig dynasties, the Cavendish and Bentinck families. The parish patrons were the Dukes of Portland, and the third duke (d. 1809) was a former prime minister from the same Rockinghamite faction of the party as Burke, which may help explain why the vestrymen were so keen to play the part of gentlemen ready to be moved by West's performance both on canvas and in person.

By the time St. Marylebone was consecrated in 1816 and the congregation "called forth spontaneous expressions of admiration" at West's altarpiece, Burke's Whiggish theory of moral sentiments was under attack from conservative and radical critics alike. Debates on altarpieces and on West's work in particular helped crystallize the issues. This was due in part to West's prominence as an artist whose ambitions were situated precisely at a point where church and theater could be said to meet, that is, in large-scale paintings of biblical history presented at public exhibition in London.

For contemporaries such as Benjamin Robert Haydon, West's painting *Christ Healing the Sick,* which was shown at the British Institution in 1811 and bought by it for the record-breaking sum of three thousand guineas, was an exemplary instance of how these lines were blurred. Haydon, who had a complex relationship with the president of the Royal Academy, was sickened by the sum spent by the British Institution on a single painting when artists such as himself were struggling to win commissions for the kind of public history painting to which he aspired. His frustrations are borne out by the vestry minutes. Before West approached the Marylebone vestrymen with an offer of a painting for their new church, Sir Thomas Barnard offered them a choice of biblical paintings by Henry James Richter, William Hilton, and Richard Westall, promising, "Should either [*sic*] of them prove a desirable possession, and an Ornament for the Altar of the new Church, I will endeavour to obtain the Offer of it as a Donation from the Institution."[40] The vestrymen sought the opinion of Hardwick, who replied that the pictures were too large for the church (it turned out they were not); yet when the painter John James Halls proposed that they *buy* one of his pictures for the new chapel of St. Mary, Bryanston Square, they silently ignored his request.[41] When Richard Westall's large painting *Ecce Homo* was donated to the new Marylebone church of All Souls, Langham Place, its recent display at the Royal Academy "in a very conspicuous situation in the principal room" did not stop a writer for the *London Magazine* from declaring that the artist "is known so well as a profit-making artist in the *trade,*" and a writer for *The Examiner* drawled, "His elegant mind supplies the Public in many of their best book embellishments."[42]

Residual doubts about the moral character of artists help explain the anxieties felt about how painters might threaten to introduce the church to commerce. Writing in the conservative *Blackwood's Edinburgh Review* in July 1823, John Wilson doubted that most artists were inclined to adopt the kind of solemn attitude with which the vestry members liked to think of themselves approaching the matter of public worship: "As for the future world, I strongly suspect it is far from occupying anything like a due proportion of their attention. [Artists] seldom go to church at all, the more is the shame to them; and, when they do so, it really is not much better, for instead of attending to the divine truths which the eloquent preacher is uttering, they are generally studying some *effect* about the chandeliers or the window-curtains, or scratching down the heads of the church-warden and his lady on the fly-leaf of the little red Prayer-book."[43]

Haydon was foremost among those who had something to say on the matter. "It was a disgrace to Mr West to have charged 800," he wrote, consoling himself by noting that West "was as incapable of conceiving or executing the character of Christ as he was of performing his miracles."[44] Haydon took the view that it was artists like himself, and not the church, who were threatened by the spread of what was called "the *trade.*" Publishing his views in 1818 in a pamphlet titled *New churches considered with respect to the opportunities they afford to encourage Painting,* he urged that the Church of England, now in receipt of £1 million to build new churches, had a duty to preserve art from commerce by spending 3 percent of the Chancellor of the Exchequer's grant on altarpieces:

> As a matter of art it would correct the great fundamental and pernicious effects of exhibitions. Where a picture is bought or sold, as it happens, and then hurried into obscurity, no opportunity is ever given for candid examination, nothing is left to time; its errors or its beauties are pressed on the people according to the interests or enmities of those who conduct, or of those who oppose, the society where it is exhibited; parties puff or censure, ridicule or praise, just as it suits; the whole town is in a whirl of feeling, and before any one has time to estimate with perspicuity, the exhibition closes, and the picture and the painter are remembered or forgotten till a new season and a new subject obliterate the recollection of both.[45]

The chancellor, Nicholas Vansittart, rejected Haydon's proposals, reportedly saying, "Let us build churches first and think about decorating them afterwards," although the painter continued to lobby MPs for some time.[46] An additional problem for Haydon, as his subsequent career showed, was that large-scale paintings were sensational both in the impact they made on the viewer's senses and in the impact they made on the public imagination. By the second decade of the nineteenth century, large-scale paintings could be seen at a number of venues, mainly clustered around Piccadilly, which included sites such as Bullock's "Egyptian Hall," where Haydon was to exhibit *The Raising of Lazarus* in 1823. Rosie Dias has noted how many reviewers made a point of favorably comparing these shows to those at the Royal Academy, and drawing the conclusion that the former institutions were meritocracies that fostered native talent, while the latter was badly in need of reform, which may explain why Haydon hoped that the church, and not the Academy, would save painting.[47]

By the 1810s the character of urban improvement in Marylebone threatened to make the experience of viewing art in churches very similar to the experience of visiting new venues of popular entertainment. St. Marylebone was one of five new churches erected in the decade following 1815. (The others were Holy Trinity, New Road, by John Soane; All Souls, Langham Place, by John Nash; Robert Smirke's St. Marys, Bryanston Square; and Christ Church, Cosway Street, by Hardwick.) For contemporaries these churches quickly became part of the repertoire of significant public buildings, as they were all planned to be seen at the end of the long new streets which characterized the improvements in Marylebone, and which in turn gave an additional cachet to the new estates as they were being built.[48] Indeed the whole of the "New Street" project provided spectacular new vistas, such as the view from Carlton House Terrace to Piccadilly, or Marylebone (that is, Regent's) Park to St. John's burial chapel, St. John's Wood, as well as its reworking of older prospects obscured by the urban sprawl in the interim period, such as the view of James Gibbs's St. Martin in the Fields from St. James's Palace.

Like churches, theaters and buildings for popular entertainment also served as picturesque *ronds-points* and terminations to new vistas. John Britton's 1833 map "Topographical Survey of the Borough of St Marylebone" shows quite clearly the crescent at the top of Portland Place, with All Souls at one end, and the Diorama and Colosseum at the other; and at the other end of the New Street was the Quadrant leading into Piccadilly. Marylebone Park itself was organized around a large circus in the southwest corner, and Nash even toyed with the idea of a huge circus encompassing the entire width of the park on its south side.[49] As well as being good for carriages, circular roads and walks also provided pedestrians with a constantly changing view as they walked, and avoided the monotony of a straight road like Portland Place, thereby conforming to a key tenet of picturesque beauty, as was appropriate for a road connecting two newly landscaped parks. Britton's map also reveals that some of the new churches were similar in plan and appearance to theaters and buildings for popular entertainment, such as the two structures erected on the southeast corner of Marylebone Park, the Diorama and the Colosseum. While the function of the circular plan differs in each—the Diorama's circle meant the seats could be moved from facing one screen to facing another, whereas the Colosseum used the wall of the circle as a vast canvas, as in Robert Barker's famous Panorama in Leicester Square—they are forms unique to buildings devoted to a single visual spectacle. When Haydon exhibited his giant *Lazarus* in the "Egyptian Hall," the work was shown alongside other curiosities, including a living display of Laplanders. Contemporary illustrations give a sense of the way that works and visitors were crammed together. But visitors to the Diorama, Colosseum, or Cosmorama, in Regent Street and Regent's Park, were invited to contemplate a single large artwork in conditions that resembled the display of West's painting in St. Marylebone Church.

The moral parity of theaters, churches, and entertainments alluded to by Burke therefore enjoyed architectural expression in the development of Marylebone. It is hardly surprising that conservatives such as Haydon fretted about how the church could wash its hands of the taint of commerce which came from handling art that was so closely associated with exhibition and entertainment.

There have been many suggestions that public "improvements" to the metropolitan fabric in the years after Waterloo were the response of a reactionary government which aimed to contain popular unrest. John Summerson's perceptive insight that Regent Street was planned as a "social barrier" that separated the light industry and third-rate streets to the east from the first-rate squares to the west remains very persuasive.[50] More recently, Rodney Mace and Dana Arnold have suggested that social unrest was contained through "improving" the environment by reshaping it physically to ensure that order could be kept, and by erecting imposing symbols of state power.[51] Lisa Keller has argued that in this regard, New York and London provide comparable case studies in urban planning and control.[52] James Anderson, by contrast, has suggested that postwar government policy was not confined to the introduction of repressive measures; the government, he argues, sought to create jobs in order to relieve the pressure for reform, a policy in which the "Million Act" played an important part, as did the New Street Act of 1813.[53] This policy was interventionist, not reactionary, and it raised the specter of further inflation, at a time when 80 percent of government spending went toward servicing a wartime national debt of almost £1 billion.

Among conservatives, the discourses of inflation, of both debt and population growth, were conducted in inflationary language. Thomas Malthus's influential work *An Essay on the Principle of Population,* first printed in 1798 and appearing in its fifth edition by 1820, opened with the stark warning that if the population of England continued to grow at its present rate, by 1900 it would be 176 million, but that the nation would have the means to support only 55 million, "leaving a population of a hundred and twenty-one millions totally unprovided for."[54] In reality, however, Malthus wrote, preventative and positive checks served to keep the population at a level more or less proportionate to the means of subsistence. These constraints, he repeatedly wrote, are all resolvable into moral restraint, vice, or misery. Both the specter and the solution were, to a degree, sublime. Malthus impressed on the reader the urgency of his findings. "The truth is," he wrote, "that, if the view of the argument given in this essay be just, the difficulty, so far from being remote, is imminent and immediate."[55]

The sublime visions of vice and misery raised by Malthus worried conservatives such as Robert Southey, but the language of inflation was not lost on him either. In a long essay for the *Quarterly Review* in 1820, he energetically supported calls for more churches to be built to encourage moral restraint. He showed that Marylebone had the same population as Manchester (75,000), but whereas Manchester had enough churches to cater to 19,000 inhabitants, Marylebone had only half that number. As Southey was writing a year after Manchester witnessed the Peterloo Massacre, the point would not be lost on his readers. He noted that in America there was no established church, and because "the general government has no power to interfere with or regulate the religion of the Union," chaos must ensue. He quoted the American preacher Lyman Beecher in order to make his point: "Let that tide of population roll on for seventy years as it has done for the seventy that are past, and let no extraordinary exertion be made to meet the vastly increasing demand for ministers, but let them increase only in the slow proportion that they have done, and what will be the result? There will be within the United States seventy million souls, and sixty-four million out of that society will be wholly destitute of religious instruction."[56] This prospect was not itself a problem for Southey, since, as a conservative, he believed that it would see the Americans repaid "for the evils which their political lessons have brought upon Europe." Indeed, democracy was the problem, because, combined with atheism, it brought destruction. He agreed with Beecher that "the right of suffrage in the hands of an ignorant and vicious population . . . will be a sword in the hand of a maniac, to make desolate around him, and finally to destroy himself."[57]

This image recalls West's *Death on a Pale Horse,* which the painter had recently exhibited as an enormous canvas in 1817. For Southey's readers it may have recalled the charges of democratic sympathies leveled at West, who was American, in 1802–1804, and signals the potential to disturb that such imagery still presented. Southey agreed with Richard Yates's influential argument in *The Church in Danger* (1815) that building new churches would strengthen both religion and the law, and since the church in question was the church established by law (specifically the Acts of Supremacy), the two were synonymous. Pictures had a part to play, since they were the conduits through which "[the people] are . . . made familiar with the great and leading facts of Gospel history." To this end Southey enthusiastically reviewed Haydon's proposal for funding the purchase of altarpieces, taking the conservative view that people had long been reconciled to the appearance of pictures in churches.[58] He clothed his suggestions in patriotic bombast. Paintings that excite devotion, he argued, "would do for London, by national generosity and the force of native genius, what Buonaparte attempted to do for Paris, by national robbery and force of arms; it would make it what Athens has been in the old, and Rome in the modern world, the acknowledged and unrivalled school of arts."[59] The overpowering images and inflationary language of Southey's essay, which culminated in the specter of Napoleon, seek in vain for a figure to contain or recuperate the excess. The new king, George IV, was one candidate, who through his purchase of the Elgin marbles had aligned himself with the cause of personal reformation which art can effect by speaking to the eye and impressing young imaginations. Likewise, his recently deceased father, George III, had set a similar precedent, as "for thirty years he employed Mr West when that admirable artist had no commission from any other person."[60]

Southey used his remark about West to conclude his essay, and he left his point hanging in the air for the reader to ponder what discursive function West might serve in the conservative cause. West was closely associated with George III, but less in the cause of personal reformation and more in relation to "Bedlamite scenes," and both West's works for his royal patron and that patron himself were associated with the madness that Southey spent much of his essay describing in vivid detail. West was also associated with America, which Southey points to as an example of the apocalyptic scenes that would soon overwhelm Britain in general if action were not quickly taken. West was also closely associated with exhibitions, which Haydon had railed against in his pamphlet, an attack quoted approvingly at length by Southey. Finally, and perhaps most important, the accumulation of all these signifiers has the effect of rendering West a figure associated with exorbitant power—unparalleled royal patronage, apocalyptic scenes, democratic sympathies, immense commercial success which did not stop with his death—whose eloquence or conduct cannot be justified as exemplary passion for a public transported by the kind of art called for by Haydon and Southey.

## NOTES

1. A notable exception is Jules Lubbock, *The Tyranny of Taste* (New Haven: Yale University Press, 1995).

2. See, for example, Douglas Fordham, *British Art and the Seven Years' War: Allegiance and Autonomy* (Philadelphia: University of Pennsylvania Press, 2010). For Egerton, see David Egerton, *Warfare State: Britain, 1920–1970* (Cambridge: Cambridge University Press, 2006).

3. For example, see David Bindman, "The English Apocalypse," in *The Apocalypse and the Shape of Things to Come,* ed. Frances Carey (London: British Museum Press, 1999).

4. See Martin Myrone, *Bodybuilding: Reforming Masculinities in British Art, 1750–1810* (New Haven: Yale University Press, 2005).

5. See Bindman, "The English Apocalypse."

6. On West's commission, see Helmut von Erffa and Allen Staley, *The Paintings of Benjamin West* (New Haven: Yale University Press, 1986); Morton Paley, *The Apocalyptic Sublime* (New Haven: Yale University Press, 1986); Bindman, "The English Apocalypse"; Annette Wickham, *Death on the Pale Horse and Other Works by Benjamin West* (London: Royal Academy of Arts, 2009); Ann Bermingham, "*Death on the Pale Horse* and the Revelation of Benjamin West," in *Living with the Royal Academy: Artistic Ideals and Experiences in England, 1768–1848* (Farnham, Surrey: Ashgate, 2013).

7. Peter de Bolla, *The Discourse of the Sublime: Readings in Discourse, Aesthetics and the Subject* (Oxford: Basil Blackwell, 1989).

8. Jonathan Lamb, "The Subject of the Subject and the Sublimities of Self-reference," *Huntington Library Quarterly* 56, no. 2 (1993): 203.

9. See, for example, von Erffa and Staley, *The Paintings of Benjamin West;* Paley, *The Apocalyptic Sublime;* Bindman, "The English Apocalypse"; Wickham, *Death on the Pale Horse.*

10. Joseph Farington, *The Diary of Joseph Farington,* ed. Kenneth Garlick et al. (New Haven: Yale University Press, 1978–[1984]), 2454 (entry for November 27, 1804), 2469 (entry for December 14, 1804).

11. See Bermingham, "*Death on the Pale Horse* and the Revelation of Benjamin West," 157–62, for a short and detailed discussion of democratical opinions within the Royal Academy.

12. Farington, *Diary,* 2461 (December 1, 1804).

13. See, for example Bindman, "The English Apocalypse," 212. Bedlam was the popular name for the Bethlem Royal Hospital, an asylum for the mentally ill.

14. Farington, *Diary,* 528 (April 23, 1796), 1820 (September 1, 1802).

15. Ibid., 2468 (December 11, 1804).

16. Ibid., 2251 (February 22, 1804).

17. Ibid., 2259 (March 3, 1804).

18. Ibid., 3970 (July 15, 1811).

19. Ibid., 4898 (September 6, 1815), 5000 (April 11, 1817).

20. St. Marylebone Vestry, *Vestry Proceedings for New Churches and Chapels* (hereafter *VPNC*), Westminster Record Office, 3:35 (March 31, 1815).

21. A detailed account of West's commission can be found in Gerald L. Carr, "Benjamin West's Altar Paintings for St Marylebone Church," *Art Bulletin* 62, no. 2 (1980): 11. A broader discussion of the decoration of the Commissioners' churches after 1818 is in Gerald Lawrence Carr, "The Commissioners' Churches of London, 1818–1837: A Study of Religious Art, Architecture, and Patronage in Britain from the Formation of the Commission to the Accession of Victoria" (Ph.D. diss., University of Michigan, 1976). A slightly older study is M. H. Port, *Six Hundred New Churches: A Study of the Church Building Commission and Its Church Building Activities* (London: SPCK, 1961).

22. Robert Southey, "Review," *Quarterly Review* 46 (July 1820): 549–91.

23. Carr, "Benjamin West's Altar Paintings," 296.

24. *VPNC,* 4:6–7 (February 15, 1817).

25. See Myrone, *Body Building,* 14.

26. Farington, *Diary,* 5173 (March 13, 1818).

27. Ibid.

28. The unidentified paper was inserted in Benjamin Robert Haydon's diary and published in *The Autobiography and Memoirs of Benjamin Robert Haydon,* ed. T. Taylor (London: Peter Davies, 1926), 677–78.

29. Claire Haynes, *Pictures and Popery: Art and Religion in England, 1660–1760* (Aldershot: Ashgate, 2006), 135.

30. *VPNC,* 3:356 (February 1, 1817).

31. See F. H. W. Sheppard, *Local Government in St Marylebone, 1688–1835* (London: Athlone, 1958), 125–27.

32. *VPNC,* 4:6–7 (February 15, 1817).

33. *VPNC,* 4:10–11 (February 22, 1817).

34. *VPNC,* 4:195 (October 10, 1818).

35. *Art-Union* (August 1840), 129; quoted in Carr, "Benjamin West's Altar Paintings."

36. Sheppard, *Local Government,* 267, quoting Thomas Smith, *A Topographical and Historical Account of the Parish of St Marylebone* (London: John Smith, 1833), 89–92.

37. Edmund Burke, *Reflections on the Revolution in France,* ed. L. G. Mitchell (Oxford: Oxford University Press, 1993), 81. Burke was referring to the storming of Versailles and the alleged mistreatment of Louis XVI and his family.

38. Ibid., 80.

39. Ibid., 81.

40. *VPNC,* 2:335–36 (November 26, 1814).

41. *VPNC,* 6:263 (May 3, 1823). Halls was a frequent contributor of reviews to *Blackwood's Edinburgh Magazine;* see Alan Lang Strout, *A Bibliography of Articles in Blackwood's Edinburgh Magazine, 1817–1825* (Lubbock: Texas Technological College, 1959).

42. "Exhibition of the Royal Academy," *London Magazine* 7 (1823): 700–705; *The Examiner,* no. 880 (1824): 786.

43. John Wilson, "Lectures on the Fine Arts I: George Cruickshank," *Blackwood's Edinburgh Review* (1823): 19.

44. Haydon, *Autobiography,* 678.

45. Benjamin Robert Haydon, *New Churches Considered* (London, 1818), 14–16, quoted in Southey, "Review." 587. On the government's attitude toward expenditure on decoration in churches, see Port, *Six Hundred New Churches.*

46. On Vansittart, see Carr, *The Commissioners' Churches,* 107; on Haydon, see Paul O'Keeffe, *A Genius for Failure: The Life of Benjamin Robert Haydon* (London: Bodley Head, 2009), 187, 231–32.

47. Rosie Dias, "A World of Pictures: Pall Mall and the Topography of Display, 1780–99," in *Georgian Geographies: Essays in Space, Place and Landscape,* ed. Miles Ogborn and Charles W. J. Withers (Manchester: Manchester University Press, 2004), 93.

48. For illustrations of the churches in contemporary topography, see Bernard Adams, *London Illustrated, 1604–1851: A Survey and Index of Topographical Books and Their Plates* (London: Library Association, 1983).

49. For the different plans put forward for the New Street and park by John White, James Wyatt, Thomas Leverton, Thomas Chawner, and John Nash, see James Anderson, "Marylebone Park and the New Street: A Study of the Development of Regent's Park and the Building of Regent Street, London, in the First Quarter of the Nineteenth Century" (Ph.D. diss., University of London, 1998).

50. See John Summerson, *Georgian London* (1946; New Haven: Yale University Press, 2004); and John Summerson, *The Life and Work of John Nash, Architect* (London: Allen & Unwin, 1935).

51. See Rodney Mace, *Trafalgar Square: Emblem of Empire* (London: Lawrence & Wishart, 2005); Dana Arnold, "Rationality, Safety and Power: The Street Planning of Later Georgian London," *Georgian Group Journal* 5 (1995): 37–50.

52. Lisa Keller, *The Triumph of Order: Democracy and Public Space in London and New York* (New York: Columbia University Press, 2009).

53. See the introduction to Anderson, "Marylebone Park and the New Street."

54. T. R. Malthus, *An Essay on the Principle of Population* (London: J. Johnson, 1798), 24. See also the introduction to Anderson, "Marylebone Park and the New Street."

55. Malthus, *Essay,* 143.

56. Southey, "Review," 551.

57. Ibid.

58. Ibid. In the event, Southey proposed an annual grant for this purpose instead of taking a percentage of the "Million Act."

59. Ibid., 587, 589.

60. Ibid., 591.

# 5

# Benjamin West's Royal Chapel at Windsor

## Who's in Charge, the Patron or the Painter?

*William Pressly*

Benjamin West was born on October 10, 1738, in the small town of Springfield, Pennsylvania, ten miles west of Philadelphia. From an early age he was enthralled with the idea of becoming a painter, but his environment offered few resources for artistic training, a lack that proved more of a stimulus than a deterrent. The dream of what constituted artistic excellence was more potent than immersion in the reality. Although the accounts of West's struggles to become an artist, which include his appropriation of fur from the family cat to make brushes, fall more into the realm of myth than reality, there is no doubt that, given his humble beginnings, he was largely self-taught. Artists such as the English-born portraitist John Wollaston, who was active in Philadelphia when West was a teenager, provided limited opportunities for emulation. West, however, was able to enjoy the intellectual stimulation of engaged patrons, such as the Lancaster gunsmith and inventor William Henry, who commissioned his first historical painting, *The Death of Socrates,* and the learned Reverend William Smith, the first provost of the newly formed College of Philadelphia (later the University of Pennsylvania). Subsequently Smith was instrumental in enabling the young man, at age twenty-one, to sail for Rome. West was only too happy to seize this opportunity to study the Old Masters, becoming the first American artist to cross the Atlantic for that purpose. Departing from Delaware on April 12, 1760, he arrived in Rome via Leghorn on July 10. After studying in Italy for three years, he landed in England on August 20, 1763, in order to visit London before returning to America. Finding unexpected opportunities for a history painter, he decided to remain, enjoying a distinguished career that stretched over almost six decades.

In London, West exhibited paintings at the earliest opportunity, showing three works at the Society of Artists' spring exhibition of 1764. Soon he came to the attention of King George III, who admired his large canvas *Agrippina Landing at Brundisium with the Ashes of Germanicus,* painted in 1768 for Robert Hay Drummond, the archbishop of York. In that same year West was also one of the founding members of the Royal Academy of Arts, and he exhibited his first picture painted for the king, *The Departure of Regulus for Rome,* at the Academy's inaugural exhibition of 1769. His 1770 painting *The Death of General Wolfe,* which he exhibited the following year, was a milestone in the creation of the new genre of history paintings of contemporary subjects.[1] His having been born in America, on the fringes of European culture, had helped give him the needed perspective to adapt long-entrenched academic theory to new criteria. Although the patronage of George III seems to have been motivated more by a dutiful desire to promote the arts in Britain than by any intrinsic love of painting, the king was apparently on comfortable terms with the artist; the two of them were the same age, having been born only four months apart. George bestowed exclusively on West all of his commissions for history paintings, and from 1772, the artist proudly identified himself in the Royal Academy exhibition catalogues as "Historical Painter to the King." Although the king was inclined to commission paintings only for specific spaces rather than acquiring works for their own sake, his decision in the late 1770s to restore and refurbish Windsor Castle as the chief royal residence opened up an exciting range of possibilities for his historical painter. Among those commissions was the most promising opportunity afforded an artist of the English school in the eighteenth century: the decoration of the Royal Chapel at Windsor.

## The Romantic Period's Greatest Religious Commission

West first mentions his commission "to paint the Royal Chapel at Windsor Castle" in a letter of October 15, 1779.[2] Beginning in 1780, he was to draw an annuity of £1,000, primarily to underwrite this major project, which in 1811 he called "the great work of my life."[3] Although John Galt's hagiographic biography of West, written when the artist was an old man with a self-aggrandizing memory, cannot always be trusted, it offers a detailed accounting of how the king worked with the painter to create a magnificent edifice embellished with an encyclopedic series of sacred pictures. Galt writes:

> When he [the king] had resolved to adorn Windsor-Castle with the achievements and great events of the reign of Edward the Third, he began to think that the tolerant temper of the age was favourable to the introduction of pictures into the churches: at the same time, his scrupulous respect for what was understood to be the usage, if not the law, relative to the case, prevented him for some time from taking any decisive step. In the course of different conversations with Mr. West, on this subject, he formed the design of erecting a magnificent oratory, or private chapel, in the Horns' Court of Windsor-Castle, for the purpose of displaying a pictorial illustration of the history of revealed religion.[4]

Although, according to Galt's account, the king initiated this "superb project," he felt the necessity of consulting distinguished members of the clergy about "the propriety of the design." Galt continues:

> Accordingly, he desired Mr. West to draw up a list of subjects from the Bible, susceptible of pictorial representation, which Christians, of all denominations, might contemplate without offence to their tenets; and he invited Dr. Hurd, afterwards Bishop of Worcester, Dr. Douglas, Bishop of Salisbury, the Dean of Windsor, and several other dignitaries, along with the Artist, to consider the business. He explained to the meeting his scruples, declaring that he did not, in a matter of this kind, owing to his high station in the state, feel himself a free agent; that he was certainly desirous of seeing the churches adorned with the endeavours of art, and would deem it the greatest glory of his reign to be distinguished, above all others in the annals of the kingdom, for the progress and successful cultivation of the arts of peace. "But, when I reflect," said His Majesty, "how the ornaments of art in the churches were condemned at the Reformation, and still more recently in the unhappy times of Charles the First, I am anxious to govern my own wishes not only by what is right, but by what is prudent, in this matter. If it is conceived that I am tacitly bound, as Head of the Church of England, to prevent any such ornaments from being introduced into places of worship; or if it be considered as at all savouring in any degree of a popish practice, however decidedly I may myself think it innocent, I will proceed no farther in the business. But, if the church may be adorned with pictures, illustrative of great events in the history of religion, as the Bible itself often is with engravings, I will gladly proceed with the execution of this design."[5]

Along with their charge, the clergymen received "a paper, containing a list of thirty-five subjects which he [the king] had formed with the Artist, for the decorations of the intended chapel."[6] After due consultation, the members of the committee met again with the king and West in order to report that "they were unanimously of opinion, that the introduction of paintings into the chapel, which His Majesty intended to erect, would, in no respect whatever, violate the laws or usages of the Church of England; and that, having examined the list of subjects, which he proposed should constitute the decorations, there was not one of them, but, which properly treated, even a Quaker might contemplate with edification."[7] West began immediately on designs for the paintings, with Galt noting: "Afterwards with the King himself, he assisted to form an architectural plan of the chapel, which it was proposed should be ninety feet in length by fifty in breadth. When some progress had been made in the paintings, Mr Wyat[t], who had succeeded Sir William Chambers as the royal architect, received orders to carry this plan into execution; and the grand flight of steps in the great staircase, executed by that architect, was designed to lead immediately to a door which should open into the royal closet, in the new chapel of REVEALED RELIGION."[8]

The project outlined by Galt was never achieved. Indeed it seems never to have come to a final resolution, as the exact number of paintings and their distribution remained in flux, each of the six surviving inventories differing from the others.[9] The project was halted on August 15, 1801, when James Wyatt, who, unlike Chambers, was no supporter of the artist, told West that the king desired its suspension.[10] West, who kept hoping for a reversal in his fortunes, wrote a letter to the king dated September 26, 1801, in which his characterization of the chapel accords with Galt's later summary and obviously with the king's expectations: "Since that period [1797, when West submitted to the king a list of paintings completed up to that time] I have finished three pictures, begun several others, and composed the remainder of the subjects for the chapel, on the progress of Revealed Religion, from its commencement to its completion; and the whole arranged with that circumspection, from the Four Dispensations, into five-and-thirty compositions, that the most scrupulous amongst the various religious sects in this country, about admitting pictures into churches, must acknowledge them as truths, or the Scriptures fabulous."[11] The most logical identifications of the four dispensations are the Antediluvian and Patriarchal, the Mosaical, the Gospel, and Revelation; but however characterized, the intention was an ambitious one—to outline "the progress of Revealed Religion, from its commencement to its completion." As related by Galt, the mutual respect of the English king and the American painter gave, at least for a time, the promise of achieving a religious monument for all mankind. The committee of clergymen had performed only as a rubber stamp, thereby setting the artist free, with the monarch's blessing, to undertake this major work.

West's commission, as we have seen, dates to no later than 1779. Just two years earlier, his colleague at the Royal Academy, James Barry, had embarked on another important series of history paintings, this time in central London for the Society of Arts (since 1908 the Royal Society of Arts). The similarities and differences in the commissions are instructive. In 1774, after having recently moved into its new building designed by Robert Adam and eager to see its Great Room appropriately decorated with paintings, the Society had approached six artists, Barry and West among them, to execute one painting each on a subject drawn from British history, with two additional painters to create less ambitious allegorical pieces. The artists, however, rejected the offer, because they were to receive only the proceeds from an exhibition to be held on the completion of their work. Then, in 1777, Barry approached the Society on his own. Although the Society again provided only limited financial support, what made the arrangement remarkable is that Barry insisted on, and received, complete freedom in his choice of subject matter. This is perhaps the first time, at least in Western art, that a patron granted an artist unsupervised control over his work in a prominent public interior. Seven years later, Barry completed his *Series of Paintings on Human Culture,* which focused primarily on the civilization of classical Greece.[12]

As recounted in Galt's biography, West's commission was similar in nature. Although in West's case there was a committee of advisers, this group was content to let the artist proceed free of interference as long as he remained within the framework of biblical subject matter. With these two major projects, begun in the late 1770s, one witnesses a changing ethos that, more and more, granted greater autonomy to painters. Artists, of course, were more enthusiastic than their patrons in embracing a newfound reverence for the creative genius's unfettered imagination,[13] but even so, patrons apparently were willing to make major concessions. West's account places him, alongside Barry, in the forefront of those who championed an artist's claims to free expression, even within prominent venues representing a private patron to the public at large. But as I demonstrate in the next section, West's characterization of his role in the chapel's conception was more fiction than fact. Close examination of the earliest surviving drawings for the "new" chapel suggests a different scenario, one in which the clergymen played the traditional role of conceiving a plan for the artist to follow—a plan, however, that the artist did attempt, with some success, to subvert. Ultimately, however, West's alterations to the original scheme would prove his undoing.

## Paul's Sermon at Antioch as Prelude to the British Becoming God's Chosen People

Although the plans for the chapel evolved into a highly ambitious program, the earliest surviving designs show a different, more limited format, one that was presumably conceived, because of its sophistication, not by the artist but by the Anglican clergymen who served on the king's committee, among whose number Galt had named Richard Hurd, later bishop of Worcester, and John Douglas, later bishop of Salisbury and dean of Windsor. Initially, then, West's arrangement

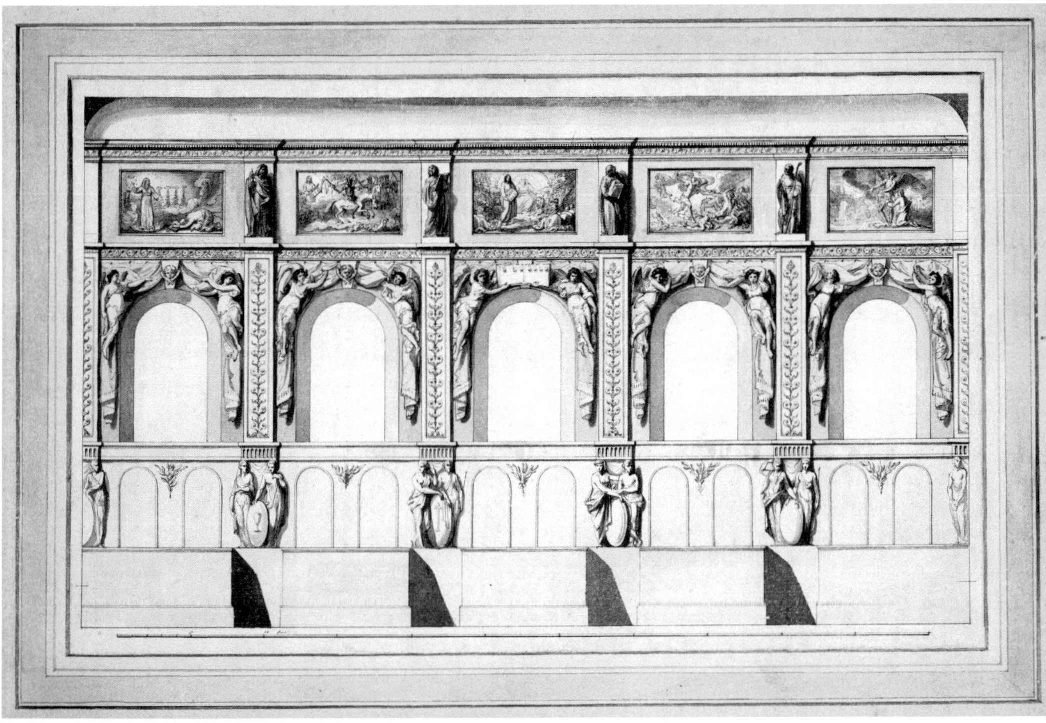

Figure 5.1. Benjamin West and Sir William Chambers (?), *Design for a Wall of the Royal Chapel at Windsor*, ca. 1779–80. Pen and ink, wash, watercolor, 11½ x 18⅞ in. (29.2 x 48 cm). Royal Collection Trust / © Her Majesty Queen Elizabeth II 2013.

followed the traditional model, with the king and his advisers closely controlling the subject matter.

As first pointed out by Nancy Pressly, the surviving sketches for the first scheme (plates 6–7 and fig. 5.1) demonstrate that the original venue was not Horn Court but rather a reconfiguring, under the direction of the king's architect Sir William Chambers, of the existing Royal Chapel at Windsor, which had last been remodeled in the late seventeenth century in the reign of Charles II with paintings by Antonio Verrio (fig. 5.2).[14] This chapel reversed the usual orientation, having its entrance at the east end of St. George's Hall and its altar wall with a painting of the Last Supper on the west end.[15] The north wall, decorated with an extensive scene of Christ healing the sick that included Verrio's self-portrait along with portraits of two of his contemporaries,[16] had no fenestration, while the south wall was punctuated with five large windows topped by a clerestory.[17] Verrio, whose iconography had also presumably been determined by advisers, conceived the chapel as an organic whole. The spiraling columns, which referred to those of the

Temple of Solomon in Jerusalem, provided an Old Testament frame for all three walls. The north wall illustrated Jesus' miraculous healing powers, which were appropriately echoed in modern times by "the king's touch," and the grand crescendo of Christ's Resurrection and Ascension into heaven literally sprang up from the west wall, where the Savior instituted the ritual of the Eucharist.

The three walls depicted in West's designs conform to this overall layout. It should be noted, however, that the draftsman who sketched the architectural frame of the three walls was perfunctory in fulfilling this assignment (Sir William Chambers may have sketched the architectural frame, for which West provided the images): in each instance the light source falls from the upper left, a standard convention; but all natural light in the chapel would have come from the

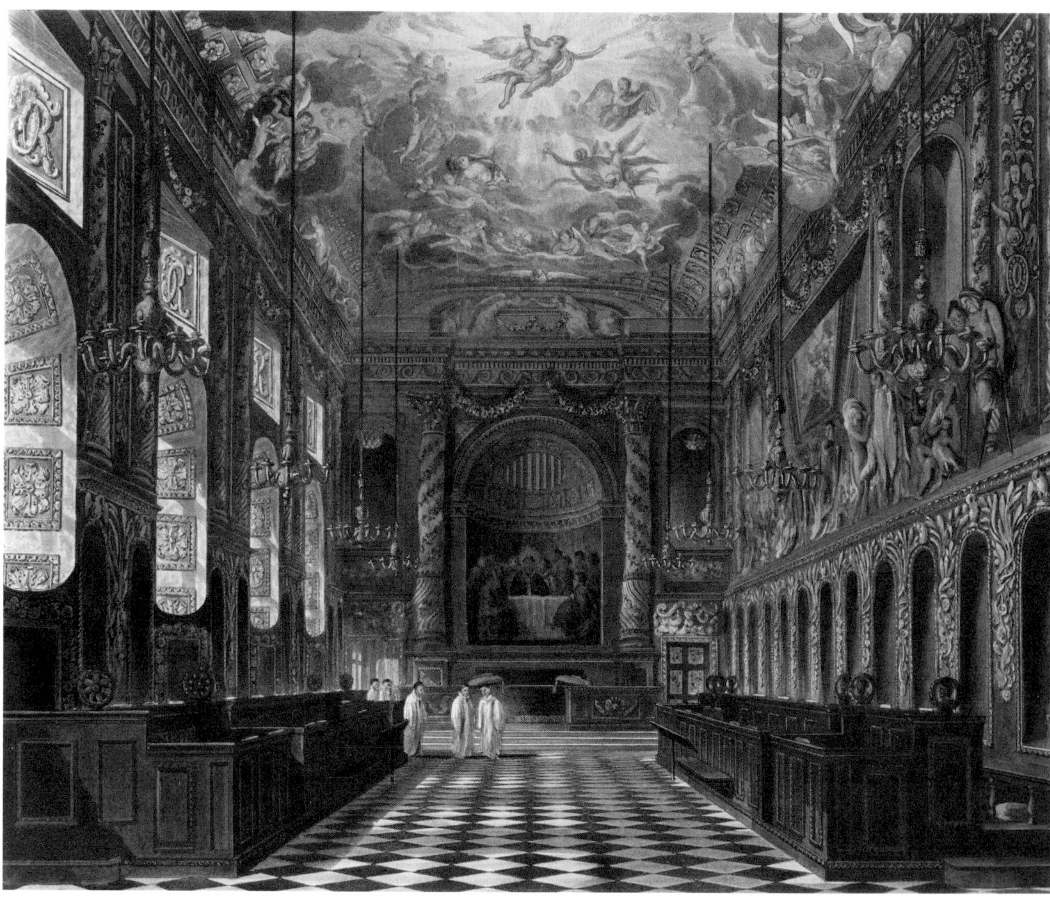

Figure 5.2. *The Royal Chapel, Windsor Castle,* June 1, 1818. Engraving by T. Sutherland after C. Wild, 10⅛ x 12½ in. (25.8 x 31.9 cm). From W. H. Pyne's *History of the Royal Residences,* vol. 1. Yale Center for British Art, Paul Mellon Collection.

windows on the south wall, a source that symbolizes the divine light that blazes throughout the chapel's compositions. Finally, the fact that no drawing survives depicting the entrance wall also agrees with the old chapel's design, as its entrance wall contained no pictures. Above the entrance along the width of the wall was a gallery for the royal family "beautifully embellish'd with carv'd Work" by Grinling Gibbons with two small rooms beneath, flanking the entrance, which furnished space for "Sacerdotal Vestments, Books, and other necessary Materials belonging to the Chappel."[18] To have tampered with Gibbons's carvings would perhaps have been unthinkable.

In the proposed reconfiguration, one entered to be drawn in by the impressive altar wall (see plate 6), where a large vertical painting of Moses receiving the law was situated directly above a horizontal canvas showing the Last Supper, which was placed over the Communion table.[19] The Last Supper is, of course, appropriately associated with Communion, and its alignment with the image of Moses is traditional as well. Moses established the law by which mankind is judged, and Christ offers forgiveness for transgressions of this law, of which all fall short, thereby making salvation possible. In the upper register at the left and right, profile portraits of the king and queen witness, and are associated with, the lighted opening to God himself behind and above Moses.

After having been drawn into the chapel, the visitor turned to face the north wall (see plate 7), where the history of God's involvement in the affairs of mankind would have begun at the upper left.[20] Moses plays a prominent role in the unfolding drama, being featured in the first two subjects: *Moses and Aaron before Pharaoh* and *The Triumph of Moses over Pharaoh and His Host.*[21] On the right-hand side beyond the arched frame of the wall's central painting are two more Old Testament scenes showing later developments: *The Twelve Tribes Drawing Lots for the Lands of Their Inheritance* and *David Anointed King.* These four paintings, which set the stage for the large New Testament subjects in the lower register, are appropriate to a royal chapel as they all depict strong leaders who, under divine guidance and even divine intervention, direct a nation's progress. In the first scene, Moses and his brother Aaron, as instructed by God, appear before Pharaoh to perform a miracle meant to persuade the Egyptian ruler to let the children of Israel go. At Moses' command, Aaron cast down his rod, which became a serpent. At Pharaoh's command, his wise men and sorcerers did likewise, only to have Aaron's serpent swallow up their own, the moment depicted in the projected painting. After more proofs, Pharaoh was finally persuaded to release the Israelites from bondage but then reneged on their departure. Pursuing them at the head of his army, he trapped the Israelites at the banks of the Red Sea. Following God's command, Moses raised his rod and the sea parted to allow the Israelites to cross. The second scene shows Moses with his followers on the other side of the Red Sea, as he again lifts up his rod to cause the waters to roll back on the Egyptians, drowning Pharaoh and his host. Moses receiving the tablets on the altar wall depicts a moment in the following forty-year period, during which he led the children of Israel through the desert, and the final two Old Testament scenes on the north wall are concerned with the establishment of the Israelites in the Promised Land. Joshua, Moses' successor, sits at the left to oversee the parceling out of the conquered lands to the twelve tribes.[22] The last scene depicts Samuel, again directed by God, visiting the family of Jesse during the reign of Saul under the pretense of sacrificing a heifer but in reality to anoint one of Jesse's sons as God's chosen king for Israel. After God told Samuel to reject the seven sons who had passed before him, Jesse sent for David, his youngest, who had been tending sheep. The scene depicts Samuel anointing the young shepherd with oil from his horn, as Jesse and his other sons look on.

Moses is one of the principal prefigurements of Christ, and the two images in the lower register beneath his scenes feature important moments in the Savior's life. The first scene, *The Holy Spirit Descending upon Christ after His Baptism at the River Jordan,* shows the moment when Jesus acknowledges his mission.[23] Even John the Baptist, who holds in his right hand the bowl of water that he had used in the baptism, is astonished as the Holy Spirit in the form of the dove descends from the blazing light of heaven. His entire attention turns to the heavens, away from the bowl of water, with which he appears to be absentmindedly baptizing another attendee. Next is *Christ Healing the Sick,* an image of tender mercy that contrasts with the sublime scene of Old Testament destruction depicted above it. After these two paintings, augmented by *The Last Supper* on the altar wall, the subjects of Christ's life climax in the central arched canvas, *The Ascension,* where two angels announce both the Savior's departure and his return (Acts 1:10–11), setting the stage for the Second Coming and the end times depicted on the wall opposite.

The next two paintings, which depict the dispensing of the Gospel after Christ's departure, close out the bottom register of the north wall. The first painting, *St. Peter's First Sermon after Being Filled with the Holy Ghost,* shows the cloven tongue as of fire (see Acts 2:3), a sign of divine inspiration that here singles out Peter at the Pentecost, inspiring him in his address to the crowd. Because of Peter's close association with the Roman Catholic Church, this picture is then supplanted by the final scene, *Paul and Barnabas Rejecting the Jews and Receiving the Gentiles.*[24] When speaking in Antioch, Paul had asserted Christianity's mission to the world, and if the Catholics could identify closely with Peter, the English held Paul in particular regard, with St. Paul's Cathedral being the English equivalent of St. Peter's in Rome.

In light of the more encyclopedic approach of the later plans for the chapel, the original conception outlined here seems even more eccentric in its range and choice of subject matter. When you have only four Old Testament scenes, outside of Moses receiving the commandments, why these four? Why begin with Moses and not Adam and Eve or Abraham? Given the limited number of pictures, would not just one of Moses' demonstrations of God's power over Pharaoh have sufficed? And why focus on the tribes drawing lots, hardly a dramatic episode when the entire Old Testament is available? The reason for these choices becomes clear when one realizes that this early program is intended as a visualization of Paul's sermon at Antioch (Acts 13:16–41). In his sermon, Paul began with the account of how God brought the Israelites safely out of Egypt, and how, after destroying their enemies, he divided their new land by lots. Then, during a long period, the Israelites were ruled by judges, of whom Joshua was the first, even if he was not mentioned by name in the abbreviated summary of the sermon recorded in Acts. This time was followed by the prophet Samuel and the reign of King Saul, who was replaced by David, from whose seed sprang Jesus. Next Paul told of how Jesus superseded John the Baptist as the way to salvation; how Christ was unjustly slain but raised from the dead and ascended into heaven. He concluded with how Christ's offer of the forgiveness of sins justifies the believer, who could not otherwise be justified by the law of Moses. Thus Paul is the shaper of the vision preached in this version of the Royal Chapel, with only the scenes of Christ healing the sick and Peter preaching being added to enhance and expand on his history. This decision to base the primary part of the chapel on a visual unfolding of Paul's sermon is surely the work of the learned clergymen and not of the artist, who soon expanded the number and scope of the paintings.

To the right as one entered the chapel, *Paul and Barnabas Rejecting the Jews and Receiving the Gentiles* is fittingly the first painting one would have encountered, as it sets the stage for the larger program. The painting, however, actually shows the events of the Sabbath following Paul's delivery of his sermon. At that time, the Jews denounced his message because they were envious of the multitudes that had assembled to hear him. The picture shows that moment in which Paul rejects the Jews, who are portrayed as a group consisting entirely of adult males in the lower-left corner, a reminder of the High Priest and his male companion who are less than enthusiastic witnesses at the left of the picture *Christ Healing the Sick.* Paul is in the process of turning to the eager cluster of Gentiles at the right, a group consisting of all ages and both genders, to whom he proclaims, "For so hath the Lord commanded us, *saying,* I have set thee to be a light of the Gentiles, that thou shouldest be for salvation unto the ends of the earth" (Acts 13:47). At this point the chapel's divine history concludes with Paul reaching out to the larger world as Christianity becomes a world religion. The pitcher behind his left hand is filled either with water for baptism or with wine for communion, an indication that the sacraments now belong to all believers. One is reminded as well of the opening of Paul's earlier sermon: "The God of this people of Israel chose our fathers, and exalted the people when they dwelt as strangers in the land of Egypt" (Acts 13:17). Now that God has embraced the larger world, he can be seen also to have chosen Great Britain's fathers, thereby sanctifying the right of George III to reign and making explicit what had been implicit in these scenes of divinely anointed leaders.

From the time of Paul's ministry, God was thought to have continued to intervene in human affairs, but certainly nothing in the modern world can compare with such miracles as the parting of the Red Sea or the sending of his only Son. Yet there is a written "history," still to be performed, when God and his Son will again participate robustly on an earthly stage: the spectacular events foretold in the Book of Revelation marking the end of time. Five scenes of the Apocalypse unfold from left to right across the upper zone of the south wall (see fig. 5.1), eventually leading one back to the altar wall. From left to right they are as follows: *John Called to Write the Revelation, Death on a Pale Horse, Saints Prostrating Themselves before the Throne of God, The Destruction of the Beast and False Prophet,* and *An Angel Showing John the New Jerusalem.* The book with the Seven Seals appears twice in the center of the wall—in the rectangular painting at the top and held by the two angels over the window arch beneath.[25]

West's drawing of a ceiling is presumably also intended for the Royal Chapel (fig. 5.3).[26] One presumes as well that the artist (and the architect) would have chosen not to extend the imagery into the coved ceiling's sharply angled sides. Even Verrio, when depicting the Ascension in his ceiling, had filled out these steep edges with painted rosettes, although, in Baroque fashion, he also added figures, some of which spilled over into the architectural decoration. In West's design, the central oval displays the Last Judgment, in which the artist reassuringly emphasizes the saved over the damned. This traditional subject matter illustrating Christ's Second Coming, drawn from passages such as the Book of Matthew 25:31–46, supplements the account of the last days as envisioned in the Book of Revelation. In the four corners, filled out by rosettes, are dynamic square images of the four Evangelists. Again the artist emphasizes the importance of scriptural authority, literally the Word of God, by showing all of the Evangelists in the act of composing or meditating on their manuscripts, while an angel, seated next to Christ in *The Last Judgment,* holds open another sacred text, possibly the Book of Life or the lines from Matthew.

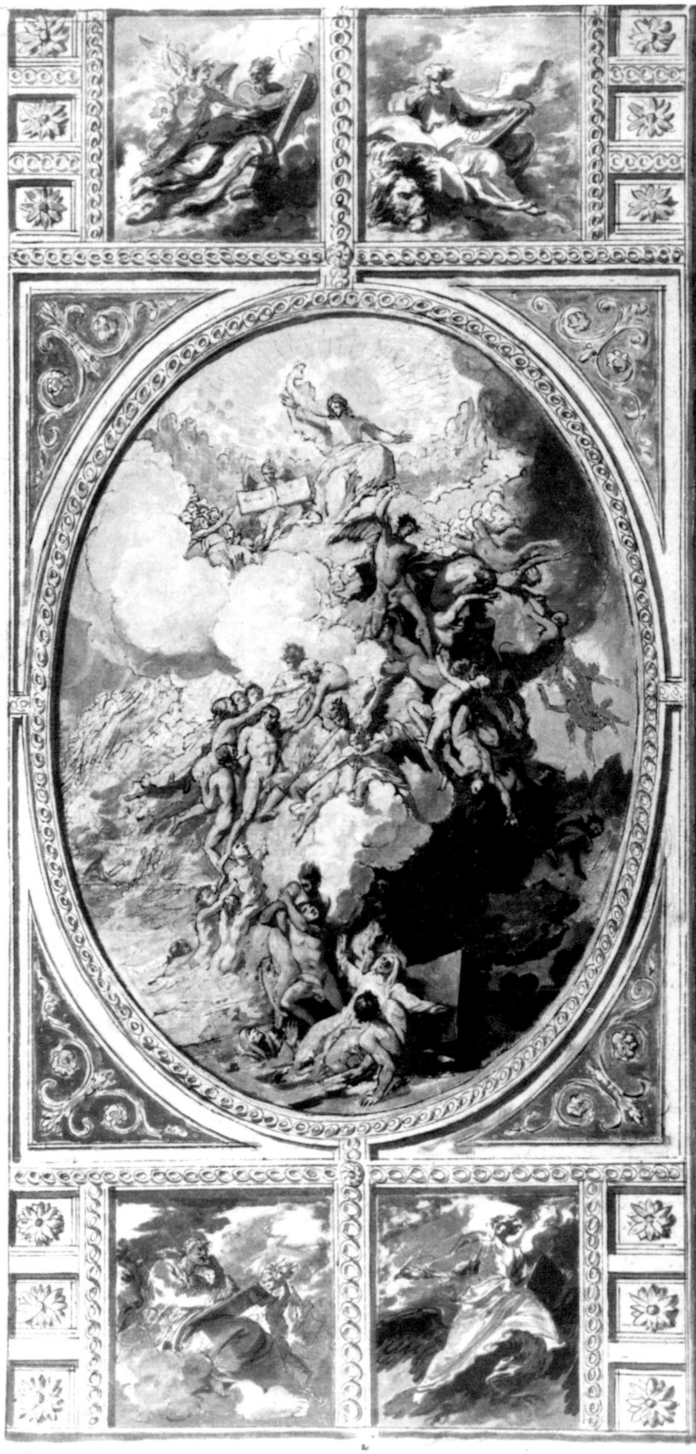

Figure 5.3. Benjamin West and Sir William Chambers (?), *Design for the Ceiling of the Royal Chapel at Windsor,* ca. 1779–80. Pen and ink, wash, watercolor heightened with white, 20¾ x 13 in. (52.7 x 33 cm). Location unknown (formerly in the collection of Mr. and Mrs. Erving Wolf).

## Changes in Style and Scope

According to Galt's account, which is derived from West, the king assembled the ecclesiastical committee merely to approve the project, but not to participate in it. The committee was to establish whether or not religious pictures violated Anglican practice and if any of the subjects chosen by West in consultation with the king might offend a good Christian, a category that included Anglicans and Quakers but not Catholics. But, as we have seen, the sophisticated focus of the chapel as first articulated points to the committee itself as having formulated the plan. Its potent ideological specificity, illuminating a complex theological argument, would have been beyond the artist's scope or interests. As West finished pictures for the chapel, he displayed them in the Royal Academy's annual exhibitions, and these works demonstrate that he was soon altering the original conception in an effort to expand on the chapel's meaning and purpose, a departure that underscores his lack of enthusiasm for, and commitment to, the original proposal. His earliest exhibited works, *An Historical Picture, Representing the Sick, Possessed, etc., Brought to Our Saviour to Be Healed* of 1781 and *The Ascension of Our Saviour* of 1782, are in accordance with the original layout. But in 1784 he exhibited six works, three of which went beyond the original program. In addition to *Moses Receiving the Law on Mt. Sinai* and designs for *The Last Supper* and *The Triumph of Death, from the Revelation* (i.e., *Death on a Pale Horse*), he exhibited *The Call of the Prophet Isaiah* and *The Call of the Prophet Jeremiah.* These last two were to flank *Moses.* Thus, while they were unrelated to the content of Saint Paul's sermon, the early configuration could still have accommodated them by substituting them for the recessed balconies on the west wall. But the design of *Moses Striking the Rock* means either that the plan had to be expanded or a substitution made. By the time of the Royal Academy's presentation of the exhibited paintings, *Moses Showing the Brazen Serpent to the Israelites* (1790) and *The Expulsion of Adam and Eve from Paradise* (1791), the original plan could no longer have been in effect.

The number of subjects grew to thirty-five or thirty-six paintings, a far cry from the sixteen images in the early program (twenty-one images if one counts the five ceiling pictures). With this expansion in its subject matter, the Royal Chapel's focus as a confirmation of the English having become God's chosen people changed to a history of revealed religion, beginning with Adam and Eve.[27] Once the scope outgrew the space available in the existing Royal Chapel, the neighboring Horn Court then became the venue for an entirely new chapel. At this point the ambitious artist must have seen himself as playing a role similar to Saint Paul's: he was addressing his pictures to all peoples, the same global audience that Paul also had had in mind. As West wrote on May 25, 1811, "Had it [the chapel] been completed, it would have marked itself as worthy of His Majesty's protection as a Christian, and a Patriot King, and all Christendom would have received it with affection and piety."[28] Thus the content of the revised chapel was fit for the king, for the nation's welfare, and for all Christendom's delight and edification, this last a bold expansion of the initial aspirations. In expanding the chapel's program, West must have come to see its decoration, executed for the head of the Anglican Church, as having achieved parity with the Sistine Chapel, whose decoration had been executed for the head of the Roman Catholic Church. In effect, this was his opportunity to become the English Michelangelo and the Anglican Church's opportunity to rival and surpass Catholic dominance in the portrayal of Christian subjects.

West had been born into that part of the Atlantic world dominated by a dynamic Great Britain. Although the American colonies were soon to win their independence, in the artist's lifetime the British Empire was to extend broadly its power and dominion. Not only did Britain exert ever-greater influence over the political and economic life of far-flung nations, but also cultural dominance and exchange formed part of this imperial expansion. West's conception, far more than that of the committee of clergymen, which focused more on the relationship of the monarch and the nation to divinity, imparted a global perspective. Through his art, a Christianity in keeping with Anglican orthodoxy would be exported to the four corners of the world, opening up a new cultural front in the multifaceted wars then being waged by imperial European powers. As conceived by the artist, the chapel's scope and purpose swelled to extravagant proportions.

Numerous factors contributed to the chapel's failure. First of all, West took too long to complete his task. During the more than two decades that he was employed on this ambitious project, the king experienced bouts of his illness that eventually forced the creation of a regency. If the king had more pressing concerns, those around him were even less sympathetic to West's plan. James Wyatt, who did not hold West in high regard, replaced Chambers as the king's architect, and, as we have seen, it was he who conveyed the news to the artist that the king had suspended his plans. The quality of some of the paintings West had completed and had exhibited at the Royal Academy was also suspect. His sketches are often sublime, whereas the more labored finished canvases are not. In addition, the response to the apocalyptic scenes in particular became politicized in ways that could not have been imagined when these subjects were first introduced into the original plan. The French Revolution, with its public manifestations of violence toward royalty and aristocracy and promise of systemic changes in the social, political, and religious spheres, could be viewed as portending the final days, a possibility that did not appeal to King George, even as republicans welcomed the prospect of radical change. The king, who was aware that some members of his own Royal Academy harbored seditious sentiments, balked at attending the exhibition of 1794, when West was its president, because the Academy was "under the Stigma of having many Democrats in it."[29] West's developing fascination with apocalyptic subject matter depicting violent change could only have added to the king's increasing unease with the artist's evolving perspective.[30] In 1804, when deciding what to do with the paintings already executed for the abandoned chapel project, Joseph Farington recorded the king as remarking, "The pictures which West had painted for the Chapel at Windsor should not be put up, except the Altar piece, & *that* should *not be a Bedlamite scene from the Revelations,*"[31] an acknowledgment of his detestation for such scenes and their radical associations.

The stylistic development of one of West's subjects, that of the triumph of Moses over Pharaoh and his host, gives some idea of how his approach changed in terms of form as well as content over the ensuing years. In the small sketch appearing in the drawing of the north wall (see plate 7), the emphasis is on the salvation of the Israelites. At the left, Moses turns with his upraised rod to cause the waters to roll back together, thereby engulfing the entrapped Egyptians. In the center are clusters of grateful Israelites with the pillar of cloud and fire behind and with Aaron, as a second Moses, continuing the nation's advance into the desert. The composition evokes the stately progress of a classical frieze, befitting an artist who drew inspiration from Poussin, particularly his *Crossing of the Red Sea.*

West's later painting of this subject, exhibited at the Royal Academy in 1792, has not survived, but a sketch for this work (plate 8) shows how much his conception had changed.[32] In this vertical rendition, he places the viewer amidst the chaos experienced by Pharaoh and his flailing army, a detail that had been kept at a distance in the more serene earlier interpretation. As in the biblical account, the wheels have come off the chariots, and the horses and horsemen all perish in the ensuing catastrophe. A black boy holds with both hands the reins of the horse at the far right, recalling the appearance of numerous black servants in British portraiture. In this instance, the black attendant is being wiped out with the elite whom he serves. The Israelites stretch across the entire upper background, beginning with a cluster beneath Moses' right hand, with another group seen in the distance above his left heel. While the Egyptians are equipped with horses, both groups of Israelites have camels in preparation for the long desert trek. Above, divine light bursts forth from the cloud of darkness as an angel points the way to salvation. Beneath the angel is a foreground cluster of women giving thanks to God, while the most prominent of the women is embraced by her two children. Behind them, carried by the men, is a box that foreshadows the Ark of the Covenant. A steep embankment closes the right-hand side.

Towering above the Egyptians is the heroic figure of Moses, behind whom is his brother Aaron praising the Lord. Moses is no passive witness but rather the dynamic instigator of God's fury, his hair and beard blowing in the wind much like contemporary depictions of Shakespeare's King Lear.[33] From his elevated vantage point, he too recalls images of Thomas Gray's Bard calling down curses and casting confusion on Edward III and his army, a poem that West also illustrated.[34] As with the Bard, Moses symbolizes the inspired creative genius imposing his will on human history. At its core, this image is not just a biblical scene but also a sublime celebration of the triumphant power of genius that was so much a part of the Romantic psyche. No wonder the king might recoil from a sensibility so unlike his own. The controlled Poussinesque version has turned into a horrific Rubensian fantasy, in which the subject has become the artist himself who has power over even the rulers of this world.

West's brilliance is best seen in preparatory sketches such as *The Triumph of Moses over Pharaoh and His Host,* which taken individually are indeed remarkable creations. But given the pedestrian quality of so many of his large finished canvases, one cannot be too upset at the failure of the project. Yet, despite West's training and abilities not having been up to the task, he had dared to dream bigger dreams than his English-born contemporaries. In the end his downfall was not so much the result of his artistic deficiencies as it was the result of his hubristic belief in his own genius, a belief that impelled him to soar above the constraints of patronage. What had begun as a thematic ensemble demonstrating how Paul's sermon initiated a divinely sanctioned history that led to the glorification of the British nation in general, and to its political and spiritual leader, George III, in particular, ended by representing a far grander agenda. Given its erudite sophistication and its focused program, the original conception presumably had been planned by the king's advisers, but in a breathtaking example of artistic hubris, West expanded on this plan to encompass a more grandiose history of Revealed Religion that would offer a message for the entire world. Instead of creating images that would serve the needs of a royal chapel, he determined to use the chapel to serve his desire to portray the entire Bible in a series of paintings. In the process he outgrew the original space. As the number of proposed paintings increased in order to accommodate the enlarged program, the existing Royal Chapel proved inadequate, requiring instead the building of a new one in the neighboring Horn Court. Obviously the king had to approve this departure, but the fact that the surviving lists of the chapel's paintings vary in their content suggests that West never did arrive at a final solution before the plan was canceled. The challenge of creating on his own a cohesive intellectual program proved daunting. The more freedom he assumed, the more indecisive he became in bringing the project to closure. Over time, the king's enthusiasm for this seemingly never-ending undertaking must have waned. Eventually the unbridled ambition underlying the grandiosity of West's personal vision became unacceptable to the only audience that mattered—the king himself.

## NOTES

1. For a recent study on how artists, such as West in *The Death of General Wolfe,* capitalized on the English public's enthusiasm for imperial conquest, see Douglas Fordham, *British Art and the Seven Years' War: Allegiance and Autonomy* (Philadelphia: University of Pennsylvania Press, 2010).

2. Letter of October 15, 1779, from West to Daniel Daulby, quoted in Nancy L. Pressly, *Revealed Religion: Benjamin West's Commissions for Windsor Castle and Fonthill Abbey* (San Antonio, Tex.: San Antonio Museum of Art, 1983), 15.

3. Draft of letter of May 25, 1811, from West to H. Rowland interleaved in folio edition of John Galt, *The Life, Studies and Works of Benjamin West,* vol. 5 (London, 1820), 43, in the collection of the Historical Society of Pennsylvania, quoted in Pressly, *Revealed Religion,* 15.

4. John Galt, *The Life, Studies, and Works of Benjamin West, Esq. President of the Royal Academy of London, Composed from Materials furnished by Himself,* pt. 2 (London, 1820), 52–53; hereafter cited as Galt 2. Part 1 had first been published independently of this edition in 1816 under the title *The Life and Studies of Benjamin West, Esq. . . . Prior to his Arrival in England.* Galt's remarks to the contrary, the commission for the seven subjects illustrating the reign of King Edward III postdates the commission for the chapel. West painted these pictures for the Audience Chamber at Windsor from 1786 to 1789, but from the vantage point of 1820, they may have seemed to have preceded the religious commission, because the latter had never been completed.

5. Galt 2:53–54.

6. Ibid., 55.

7. Ibid.

8. Ibid., 56.

9. For the six lists, see John Dillenberger, *Benjamin West: The Content of His Life's Work with Particular Attention to Paintings with Religious Subject Matter* (San Antonio: Trinity University Press, 1977).

10. West gives the date as August 15, 1801, in his letter of September 26 of that same year; see Galt 2:193.

11. West's letter is printed ibid., 194.

12. Why Barry was so intent on having complete control over his content is discussed in my forthcoming book *James Barry's Murals at the Royal Society of Arts: Envisioning a New Public Art,* to be published by Cork University Press.

13. For an examination of how the first generation of important history painters in Great Britain seized on the discourse of original genius as a core element in identity formation, see my book *The Artist as Original Genius: Shakespeare's "Fine Frenzy" in Late-Eighteenth-Century British Art* (Newark: University of Delaware Press, 2007). Barry and West are both

treated in this context, as are John Hamilton Mortimer, Henry Fuseli, Alexander and John Runciman, James Jefferys, George Romney, John Flaxman, and William Blake. In their embrace of Shakespeare's legacy, at least as they chose to interpret it, they helped to usher in the Romantic movement. In addition, for an early study on the tensions between the traditional paternal relationship of patron to painter and the more independent possibilities opened up by new market forces, particularly those provided by the exhibition room, see Josephine Gear, *Masters or Servants? A Study of Selected English Painters and Their Patrons of the Late Eighteenth and Early Nineteenth Centuries* (New York: Garland Publishing, 1977).

14. See Pressly, *Revealed Religion,* 15. 17–18.

15. W. H. St. John Hope offers further clarification: "The Room, which our Lord and the Apostles are suppos'd to be in, has a Dome, thro' which is seen the Real Organ belonging to the Chappel." W. H. St. John Hope, *Windsor Castle: An Architectural History,* 2 vols. (London: Published at the Offices of *Country Life,* 1913), 1:337.

16. See William Henry Pyne, *The History of the Royal Residences of Windsor Castle, St. James's Palace, Carleton House, Kensington Palace, Hampton Court, Buckingham House, and Frogmore,* 3 vols. (London, 1819), 1:179.

17. According to "Appendix I: West's Paintings for the Royal Chapel in Windsor Castle," there were five windows along the south wall of the seventeenth-century chapel designed by Hugh May, although only four are shown in the illustration. See Helmut von Erffa and Allen Staley, *The Paintings of Benjamin West* (New Haven: Yale University Press, 1986), 578.

18. St. John Hope, *Windsor Castle,* 1:338.

19. West exhibited the Royal Chapel's *Moses Receiving the Law on Mt. Sinai* at the Royal Academy in 1784, along with a design for the Last Supper. He exhibited the completed painting *The Last Supper* the following year.

20. For other versions of the north wall and one of the south wall, see Jerry D. Meyer, "Benjamin West's Chapel of Revealed Religion: A Study in Eighteenth-Century Protestant Religious Art," *Art Bulletin* 57 (June 1975): 250–51, figs. 1, 2, and 6.

21. This subject is catalogued in von Erffa and Staley, *Paintings of Benjamin West,* as *Pharaoh and His Host Lost in the Red Sea* (see cat. nos. 254 and 255), which is one of the names provided in various lists of the chapel's inventories. (See Dillenberger, *Benjamin West,* 145, no. 76, for its name as used in six such lists.) I, however, have adopted the title West used when exhibiting his now missing painting of this subject at the Royal Academy in 1796, which rightly emphasizes Moses' supremacy.

22. Joshua, again following God's dictates, oversees the drawing of lots for nine of the tribes and the half tribe of Manasseh (see Joshua 13:7). Two of the tribes, the Reubenites and the Gadites, had already received their inheritance from Moses. In addition, the Levites, as the priestly caste, received no land. West correctly shows nine men standing to the right of the boys picking out the lots.

23. This title is the one used when the painting was exhibited at the Royal Academy in 1794. Alternate titles are listed in the various inventories; see Dillenberger, *Benjamin West,* 147, no. 98.

24. West completed and exhibited at the Royal Academy versions of all five of the large New Testament scenes shown along the north wall: *The Holy Spirit Descending upon Christ after His Baptism at the River Jordan* (1794), *An Historical Picture, Representing the*

*Sick, Possessed, etc., Brought to Our Saviour to Be Healed* (1781), *The Ascension of Our Saviour* (1782), *St. Peter's First Sermon after Being Filled with the Holy Ghost* (1785), and *St. Paul and Barnabas Rejecting the Jews and Receiving the Gentiles* (1793).

25. Each of the side walls exhibits four male figures in the upper tier standing on the tops of the decorated pilasters. On the north wall, all of the figures seem to be patriarchs. Perhaps Abraham is at the left; Moses and David, who both prefigure Christ, perhaps flank *The Ascension;* and the last figure is possibly King Solomon. The four figures on the south wall are presumably disciples and apostles, since the Four Evangelists, as we shall see, appear in what is surely the ceiling (see fig. 5.3). Twin caryatids accompanied by shields support the pilasters. On the north wall, the shields are adorned with abstract virtues: from left to right, the olive branch of peace; a smoking censer symbolizing the ascending prayers of the faithful; the anchor of Hope; and the broken column of fortitude. The angel with the two infants to the right of the anchor of Hope is of course Charity, and the trinity of Faith, Hope, and Charity is intended either by combining these images with that of the smoking censer or by additions to be made to the angel accompanying Charity. On the south wall, only two shields are decorated, one with the chalice and the other with the cross.

26. Figure 5.3 is reproduced from a photograph taken of West's drawing when it was in the collection of Erving and Joyce Wolf. This work has previously been reproduced in von Erffa and Staley, *Paintings of Benjamin West,* 579. A drawing of this same subject appeared in the sale at Christie's, London, November 21, 2007, lot 36. This may in fact be the Wolfs' drawing, which is, in any case, no longer in their collection. Although the measurements of the Christie's drawing (20¼ x 12½ in.) differ slightly, it is by a uniform half inch for each dimension. In addition, the thumbnail reproduction in Christie's online catalogue entry, so far as can be ascertained, corresponds to the photograph of the Wolfs' drawing. The verso of the Christie's drawing shows sketches for another ceiling painting—the decoration of the Royal Academy Council Chamber at Somerset House, which West was contemplating at this same time. I thank Franklin Kelly, John Hagood, and D. Dodge Thompson at the National Gallery of Art, Washington, D. C., for their invaluable help in sorting out questions of provenance and the identity of the present owner of the drawing formerly in the Wolf collection.

27. The subject of the creation of Adam and Eve was listed in only one of the early inventories, but all six lists record *The Expulsion of Adam and Eve from Paradise;* see Dillenberger, *Benjamin West,* 143, nos. 62 and 63.

28. Draft of letter of May 25, 1811, from West to H. Rowland, quoted in Pressly, *Revealed Religion,* 23.

29. Joseph Farington, *The Diary of Joseph Farington,* ed. Kenneth Garlick et al. (New Haven: Yale University Press, 1978–[1984]), 1334 (December 28, 1799).

30. For two helpful overviews, see Pressly, *Revealed Religion;* and David Bindman, "The English Apocalypse," in *The Apocalypse and the Shape of Things to Come,* ed. Frances Carey (London: British Museum Press, 1999), 208–69.

31. Farington, *Diary,* 2461 (December 1, 1804).

32. A preparatory drawing for this same subject has recently resurfaced and is discussed in an article that appeared as this essay was going to press: Elizabeth Jacklin, "A Rubensian Drawing for a Lost Painting: Benjamin West's Study for *Pharaoh and His Host Lost in the Red Sea,*" *British Art Journal* 14 (Autumn 2013): 39–44.

33. John Hamilton Mortimer's etching *Lear* of 1776 and James Barry's 1774 painting *King Lear Weeping over the Body of Cordelia* are reproduced in Pressly, *The Artist as Original Genius,* figs. 24 and 89. Fittingly, as West would have known, the head of Lear, in its turn, harks back to Parmigianino's celebrated Moses in Santa Maria della Steccata in Parma.

34. Reproduced in von Erffa and Staley, *Paintings of Benjamin West,* no. 198. While West's *Bard* is more often related to *Moses and the Law,* thematically it is more closely aligned with *The Triumph of Moses over Pharaoh and His Host.*

# 6

# The Politics of Style

## Allston's and Martin's *Belshazzars* Compared

*Andrew Hemingway*

The contemporaneity of Washington Allston's *Belshazzar's Feast* with the painting of the same theme by the English artist John Martin is a commonplace of scholarship on both men (plates 9–10).[1] Allston's picture was begun in 1817 and left unfinished at his death in 1843; Martin's was painted in 1820 and exhibited at the British Institution in London to great acclaim the following year.[2] The two men had met in 1814 and became friends.[3] According to the recollection of Martin himself, looking back from 1834, the germ of his own painting was an argument with Allston seventeen years before: "He was himself going to paint the subject, and was explaining his ideas, which appeared to me altogether wrong, and I gave him my conception." Allston's pupil and intimate Charles Robert Leslie, who had introduced the pair, also "entirely differed" from Martin in his "notions of the treatment," so much so, according to Martin, that "he called on purpose and spent part of a morning in the vain endeavour of preventing my committing myself and so injuring the reputation I was obtaining."[4] These differences, I will argue, were more than just differences of personal opinion; they were grounded in a politics of style of which the artists themselves were only partially conscious: in effect, their contrasting choices represent the contrasting *Weltanschauungen* of different class perspectives. The theme of the collapse of empire had an obvious contemporary pertinence because of the recent defeat of Napoleon and the imperial ambitions of the British state, which were symbolized in the ostentatious court rituals of the Prince Regent, who had acceded to the throne as George IV by the time Martin's picture was produced. The politics of style, however, were certainly of equal moment.[5]

When Martin's *Belshazzar* was first displayed, Leslie described it to Allston as "Martin's picture of *your subject*" and reported that it had "made more noise among the *mass of people* than any picture that has been exhibited since I have been here. The artists however & connoisseurs did not like it much. It was first exhibited at the gallery & drew such crowds that they kept it open a fortnight longer than usual solely on account of that picture. The directors gave him 200 guineas as a premium & the picture was bought for *eight hundred* by a speculator who immediately opened an exhibition of it himself & has made a great deal of money by it."[6] I shall have more to say about the implicit condescension of Leslie's report later. But Allston himself—who had read a favorable review of the painting in *Blackwood's Magazine* before he received Leslie's letter—responded to the news of the exhibition with characteristic generosity: "It is delightful to hear of such success of those who really deserve it, and especially when they happen to be those we also esteem as men. Tell Martin I would have got up before sun rise, and walked twenty miles to have seen his picture: which is saying a great deal for me."[7] The joke here depends, of course, on the fact that Allston was physically indolent and a notoriously late riser.

Not only did Allston display great professional camaraderie with other artists, but also he detested personal rivalries as unworthy of the artist's high calling and as bringing the taint of the marketplace into the profession. "There is an essential meanness in the wish to *get the better* of anyone," he wrote on the wall of his Cambridge studio. Correspondingly, "if an Artist love his Art for its own sake, he will delight in excellence wherever he meets it, as well in the work of another as in his own."[8] Indeed, "the very word *rival* grates upon my nature," he wrote in 1840 in a letter to the *North American Review* to contradict an earlier report in the magazine that asserted Martin had taken from him the idea of making the "writing on the wall" function as the principal lighting of his *Belshazzar.* This, Allston insisted, was not the case, and he proceeded to affirm his admiration for "my friend, Mr. Martin," declaring: "I feel it a duty which I owe to an honorable man and distinguished artist, to state distinctly, *that Mr. Martin has never borrowed from me either thought or hint in a single instance.* He has too much genius to borrow from anyone." In any case, Martin's art did not "depend on such subordinate accessories as this; in my opinion a more original mind than his was never impressed on canvass." Elaborating the kind of Romantic aesthetic he was arguing in his *Lectures on Art* in the 1830s, Allston insisted that his conception of the theme and Martin's were in fact different not just in degree but in "*kind*" because they were conceived by different minds and reflected their unique constitution as such: "Between Mr. Martin's Belshazzar and mine, *there is not a single point of resemblance;* nor could there well be, since each was conceived according to the character of our individual minds."[9]

Allston's claim that the paintings are different in "*kind*" was, I think, correct, even if the way he accounted for this was inadequate. At a basic level the paintings belong to different genres and were scaled accordingly. Martin's picture is essentially a historical landscape, approximately five by eight feet, while Allston's is a grand manner history painting a little over twelve by sixteen feet. But the differences in their styles go deeper than this.

While Allston enunciated a paradigmatic Romantic conception of aesthetic value,[10] his conception of artistic processes was that of the eighteenth-century British Royal Academy, and particularly that of Reynolds—an artist for whom he repeatedly expressed the highest respect. In a letter of 1824 he referred to "*my* Sir Joshua," and then continued, "I call him mine, for I feel as if I had a property in his mind; quoad the *painter,* he has laid the foundation of my own, most of my speculations are built on it, and it is mine by right of settlement."[11] Consonant with the model of academic theory, Allston understood that the stylistic patterns of earlier art, "the Old Masters," effectively represented the language of expression on which the history painter must draw.[12] The "Old masters . . . are the only Masters to make a great Artist—I mean an original one," he wrote to Leslie in 1822. Artists who neglected them merely imitated their contemporaries under the delusion that they were imitating nature.[13] What gave this theory a particularly Reynoldsian and indeed English cast was the emphasis Allston put on chiaroscuro as the primary expressive medium of art, and the priority he gave it over drawing. In a letter to John Vanderlyn he wrote:

> Art will do a great deal; but nature *has done* more. The first may teach a man to draw a correct outline; I mean after a model: may teach him to put figures together, so that they appear neither awkward nor embarrassed; to dispose of light & shadow, so as to correspond with common reason: But to the last alone is reserved the province of feeling & expressing the beauty of form; of painting the soul, of giving life & motion to a group; & expression, & harmony, & magic to the mystery of the chiaro'scuro.[14]

In his *Lectures on Art,* Allston gave this quality the technical term used by British artists of the period, namely, "breadth," and associated it with what he denoted "Harmony," that production of "a Whole" in painting which signifies "the complete expression, by means of form, color, light and shadow, of one thought, or series of thoughts."[15] It is important to note, however, that Allston, like some British contemporary painters—notably Benjamin Robert Haydon—had corrected Reynolds, in that he thought the qualities of chiaroscuro and color needed to be wedded to an accuracy and a level of detail in drawing in which Reynolds's art was notoriously lacking.[16]

Corresponding with this position, Allston's models of artistic perfection were conventional ones from antiquity and the sixteenth-century Roman school, particularly Michelangelo and Raphael. For Allston, "the genius of Michael Angelo was essentially *Imaginative,*" while "the mind of Raffaelle was an ever-flowing fountain of human sympathies. . . . His Apostles, his philosophers, and most ordinary subordinates, are all to us as living beings."[17] In his *Lectures* Allston defines "Invention" as "the new combination of known forms" according to "*what is,* or *has been,* or, when limited by the *probable,* to what strictly may be." To demonstrate that this is a feature of all schools, he analyzes an unspecified interior with a slaughtered pig by Isaac van Ostade,[18] together with Raphael's cartoon of *The Death of Ananias.* Whereas Allston's analysis of *The Slaughtered Pig* is all about how light, color, and shape lead the eye through the picture "till the scientific explorer loses the analyst in the unresisting passiveness of a poetic dream," that of the *Ananias* is entirely concerned with expression and narrative. Raphael, he concludes, has "invented the chain which we have followed, link by link, through every emotion, assimilating many into one."[19] Appropriately, then, the Raphael cartoons were the primary reference point for *Belshazzar's Feast.*

Allston would have had access to James Thornhill's copies of the cartoons at the Royal Academy on his first residence in Britain, and he also almost certainly saw the originals on a trip to Windsor Castle with John Blake White in April 1803.[20] A decade later, during his second trip, he made a ten-day excursion with Samuel F. B. Morse and C. R. Leslie that took in Hampton Court—where the cartoons had been moved in 1804—along with Windsor, Oxford and Blenheim.[21] I think that both the written and visual evidence suggests that Raphael's *Death of Ananias* and *Conversion of the Proconsul* (figs. 6.1 and 6.2) were the key models for Allston's conception—a relationship that is somewhat clearer from a comparison between the cartoons and the grisaille version of the composition (fig. 6.3). This is both because the statuesque quality of the figures and the linear structure of the design are more clearly defined in this version, but also because the changes Allston made to the perspective of the large canvas in 1820–21, by lowering the viewpoint and increasing the distance between the foreground figures and the viewer's space, diminished the resemblance somewhat.[22]

Thematic parallels made these cartoons particularly pertinent. All three compositions are concerned with divine retribution occasioned by disrespect to God. Belshazzar will be slain and his kingdom pass to Darius the Median because he and his "princes, his wives, and his concubines" drank wine to the old gods out of the holy vessels taken from the Temple at Jerusalem (Daniel 5:1–4 and 30–31). Ananias and his wife, Sapphira, sell land to raise money for the apostles, but hold

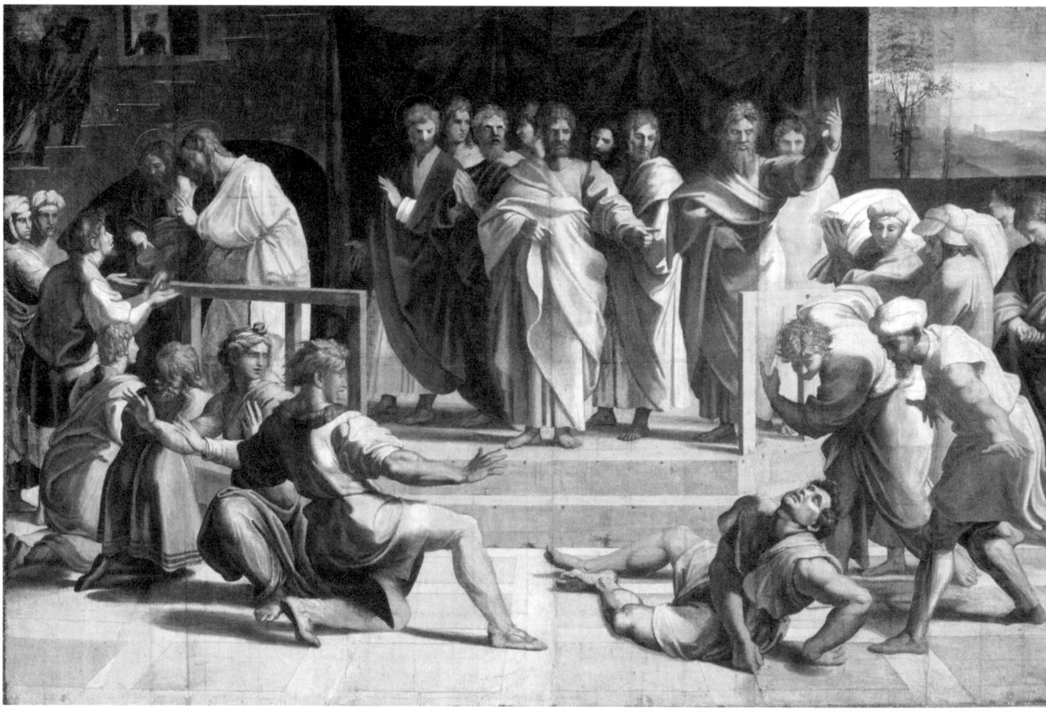

Figure 6.1. Raphael, *Death of Ananias,* 1515–16. Bodycolor on paper mounted on canvas, 12 ft. x 17 ft. 4⅔ in. (3.4 x 5.3 m). V&A Images / The Royal Collection, on loan from H.M. the Queen, Victoria and Albert Museum. Photo: V&A Images, London, Art Resource, New York.

part of it back and thus lie to the Holy Ghost, with the result that both die (Acts 5:1–10). The sorcerer Elymas seeks "to turn away . . . from the faith" the deputy Sergius Paulus, who wanted to hear the preaching of Barnabas and Paul, and as a punishment he was temporarily blinded (Acts 13:1–12). In each case we have a shallow compositional box like a stage (which was of course commonplace in history paintings) with a tripartite division of side groups centralized around a key character, a group of observers enacting significant responses to the main action. All three have a similar floor patterning. *The Conversion of the Proconsul* is closer to Allston's composition in its relative simplicity and in the placing of the reactive figures in a position similar to that of his Chaldean astrologers and soothsayers. (Allston's friend Haydon had drawn on the composition for his own *Judgment of Solomon,* which Allston would have seen on its exhibition at the Society of Painters in Oil and Water-Colours in 1814; see plate 11).[23] But the messenger of divine retribution, Saint Paul, is to the left, and the center is taken by the astonished figure of Sergius Paulus. In the *Ananias,* Saint Peter, who bears the divine message, has the central position, similar to Allston's Daniel, but the narrative is rendered more complex by the apostle to his right, who stares menacingly at Sapphira as she enters, absorbed with counting money. (Although positioned differently, Belshazzar's defiant-looking queen could stand as her equivalent). We might also find in the heathen deity in the far distance of Allston's image an echo of the statue of Mercury in the background of Raphael's *Sacrifice at Lystra.*

The other clear source for the *Belshazzar*—though only for the background of the composition—was Veronese's *Wedding at Cana* (fig. 6.4). Allston would have seen the painting in the Musée Napoléon when he was in Paris in 1803–4. In line with Reynoldsian theory, he was already an enthusiast of Venetian coloring by this time, and adopted Venetian techniques after studying pictures by Titian, Tintoretto, and Veronese in that collection.[24] Writing to William Dunlap in 1833, he recalled his response to works by all three, which "absolutely enchanted" him

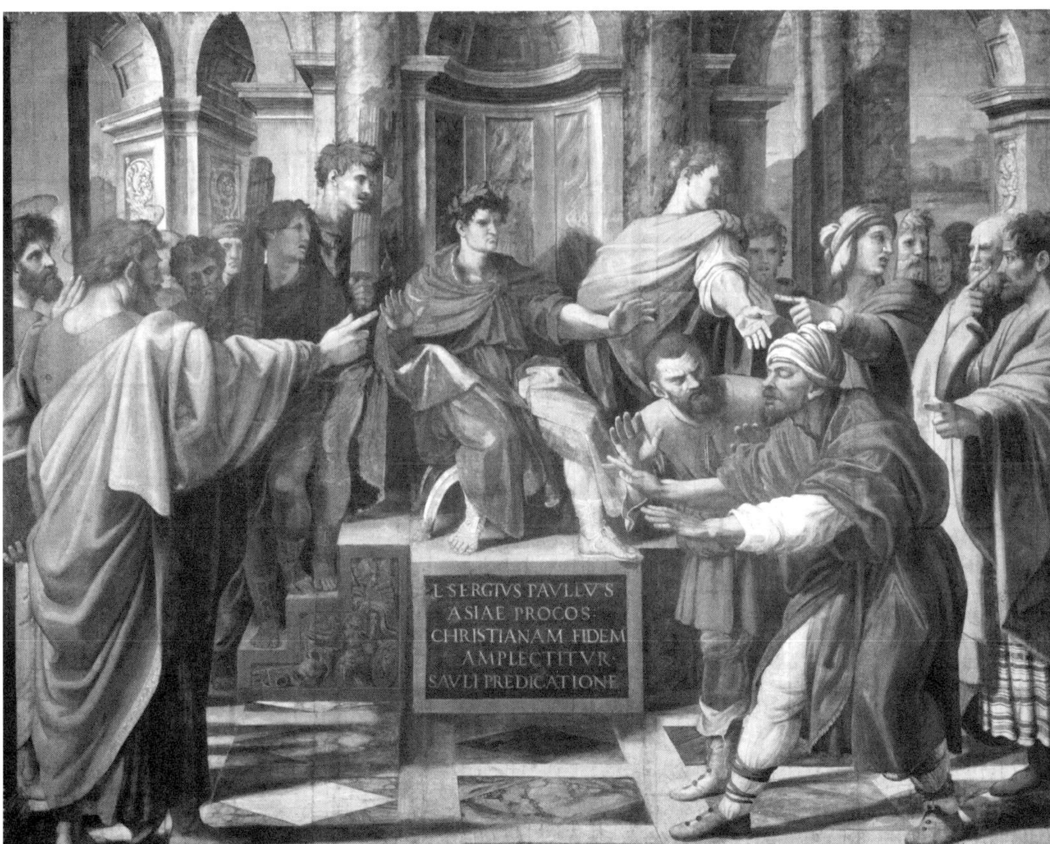


Figure 6.2. Raphael, *Conversion of the Proconsul,* 1515–16. Bodycolor on paper mounted on canvas, 11 ft. 1⅝ in. x 14 ft. 5¼ in. (3.4 x 4.4 m). V&A Images/The Royal Collection, on loan from H.M. the Queen, Victoria and Albert Museum. Photo: V&A Images, London, Art Resource, New York.

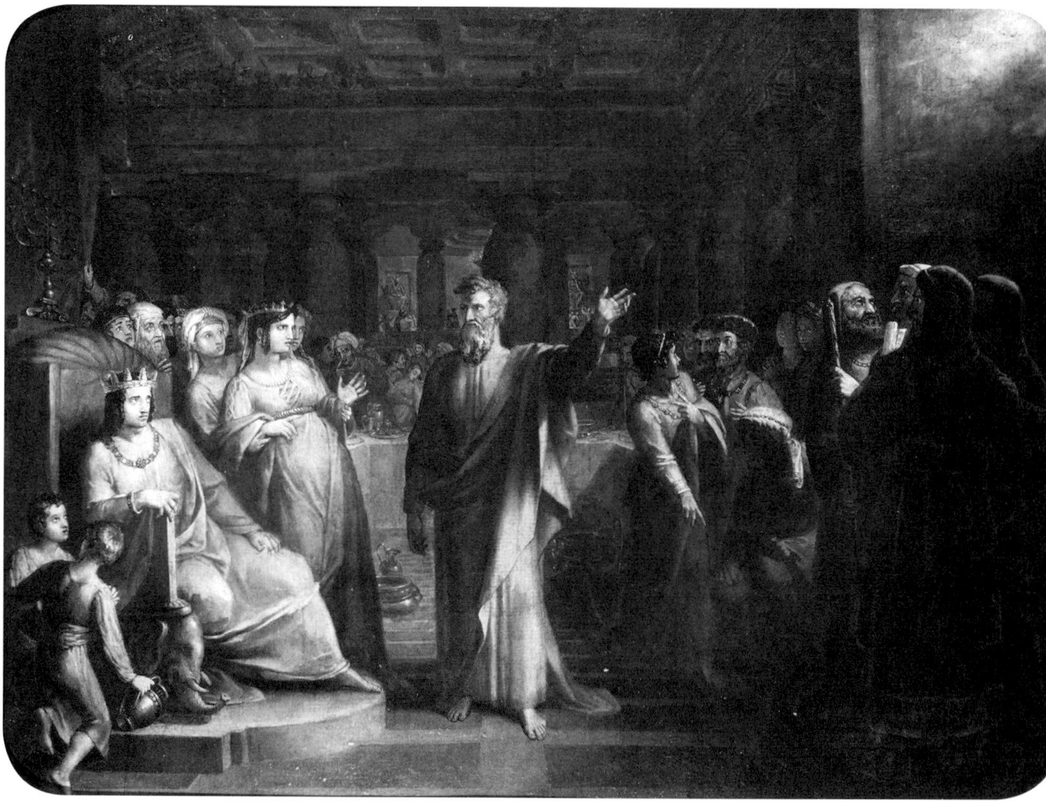

Figure 6.3. Washington Allston, *Belshazzar's Feast,* 1817. Oil on composition board, 25½ x 34 in. (64.2 x 86.4 cm). Harvard Art Museums / Fogg Museum, Loan from the Washington Allston Trust, 122.1942.

because "they took away all sense of the subject." Standing before them, he wrote, "I thought of nothing but the *gorgeous concert of colours,* or rather of the indefinite forms . . . of pleasure with which they filled the imagination. It was the poetry of colour which I felt; procreative in its nature, giving birth to a thousand things which the eye cannot see, and distinct from their cause." Of these works the *Wedding at Cana* impressed him especially in the way it produced a poetical effect without any "*ostensible*" story—something he likened to the effect of music.[25] When he made his second visit to Paris in 1817—by which time he was already working on the *Belshazzar*—he made a copy after the picture.[26] Veronese's composition, I want to suggest, contributed to the idea of a two-tiered feast with a balcony, and Venetian coloring would have seemed appropriate to that part of the picture and the grouping of Belshazzar and his wife and the adjacent temple objects.

But Reynolds associated Venetian color with the "*ornamental*" not the "*grand*" style,[27] and Allston's theme demanded the latter. That Allston registered the distinction is evident from the passage in his *Lectures* concerning the *Wedding at Cana,* where he uses the picture to exemplify the principle of "variety" as a cause of pleasure, arguing that the appropriate "*degree*" of variety depends on "the kind of the subject treated." Veronese's *Wedding* carried variety "perhaps, to its utmost limits," he wrote, "for literally the eye may be said to *dance* through the picture, scarcely lighting on one part before it is drawn to another, and another, and another, as by a kind of witchery." But this is appropriate only to a subject of "a gay and light character," such as the "gorgeous *pageant*" Veronese depicted.[28] By Reynolds's criteria, Allston's subject required less variety and a much more somber chiaroscuro, something that brought the conception closer to the dark tonalities of Reynolds's own history paintings, such as *The Death of Dido* (1781), or the works of Haydon that Allston so admired, the *Judgment of Solomon* (see plate 11) and *Christ's Entry into Jerusalem* (1814–1820).[29]

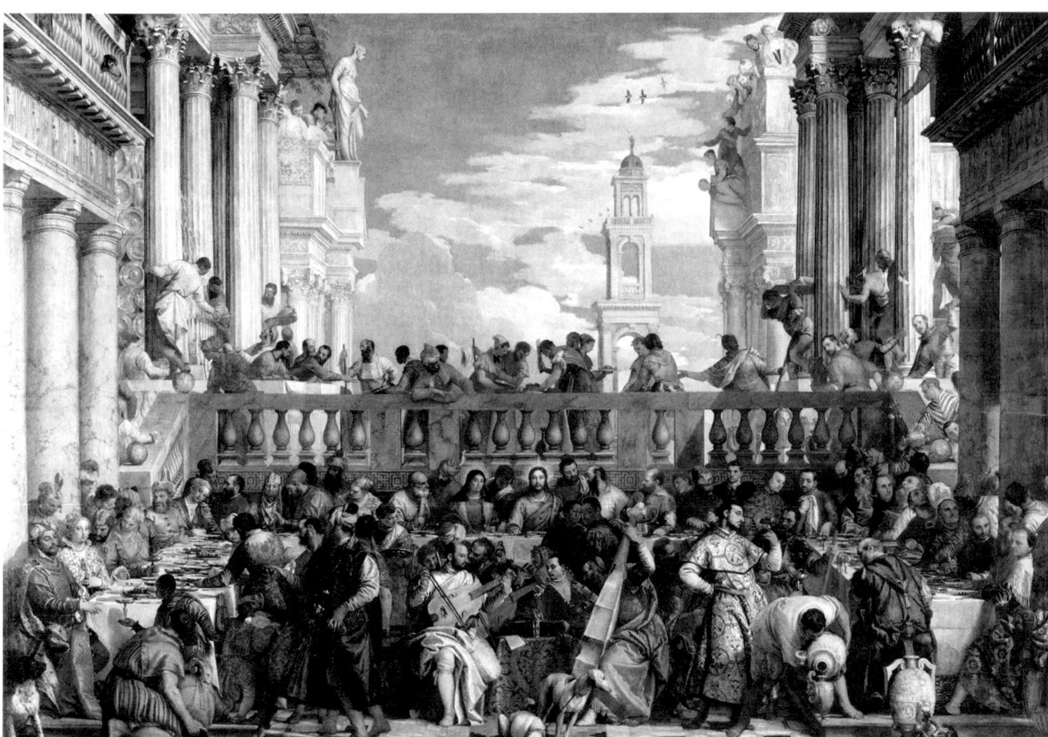

Figure 6.4. Paolo Veronese, *Wedding at Cana,* 1562–63. Oil on canvas, 21 ft. 10¼ in. x 32 ft. 5⅔ in. (6.66 x 9.90 m). Louvre Museum. Photo: © RMN—Grand Palais/Art Resource, New York.

If Allston's *Belshazzar* was a thoroughly academic concoction within the scheme of English school ideology, Martin's was emphatically not. As I observed earlier, his *Belshazzar* was, loosely speaking, a historical landscape, but it was far removed from the approved models of that genre as represented by Claude and Poussin, which Allston drew on in works such as *Diana and her Nymphs in the Chase* (1805) and *Elijah in the Desert* (1817–18). Martin's conception is more like a *vedute* or architectural capriccio in its linear perspective of temples and palaces, while in using a colossal architectural vista to produce an impression of overpowering scale it resembles the compositions of Piranesi, Panini, and Joseph Gandy (fig. 6.5).[30] Its sensational effect was modeled partly on that of contemporary panoramas and partly on illuminations. It was only fitting that Martin reverted to his craft training as a painter on china and glass and produced a glass version that was illuminated in the window of William Collins's shop on the Strand as an advertisement for the painting after it moved there.[31] A painting of vast hordes that resembled a battle scene, it did not offer the truth to emotions that Allston found epitomized in Raphael, although Martin made some claims of that kind; rather its distinguishing characteristic was a kind of pseudo-antiquarian accuracy that was amplified in the explanatory pamphlet its author produced to accompany its second showing, which included a numbered diagram and key. From this we learn that the scale of the figures meant that the length of the halls must be one mile, while the "costume of remote ages," insofar as it could be known or guessed at, "has been adhered to with the strictest accuracy."[32] For all its extravagant effects, Martin's conception was imprinted with the literal mentality of the architectural topographer.[33] Significantly, his *Description* claimed to show "the intellectual mechanism" by which light and shadow operated in his work "to produce harmony";[34] to Allston, such effects were ultimately ineffable.

It was the peculiarly literal aspect of Martin's work that Charles Lamb faulted in his essay for the *London Magazine,* "Barrenness of the Imaginative Faculty in the Productions of Modern Art." Martin's architectural fantasies, Lamb conceded, were "of the highest order of the material sublime," and they satisfied "our most stretched and craving conceptions of the glories of the antique world." But he wished they had been left unpeopled. "By a wise falsification," Lamb observed, "the great masters of painting" had not sought to depict "actual appearances . . . all that was to be seen at any given moment by an indifferent eye, but only what the eye might be supposed to see in the doing or suffering of some portentous action." Without any biblical authority, Martin had assumed that the writing on the wall had been seen by a multitude of others besides Belshazzar and thus presented a "needless multiplication of the miracle." Moreover, rather than depicting the stupor of fear appropriate to "a supernatural terror," he had suggested only "vulgar

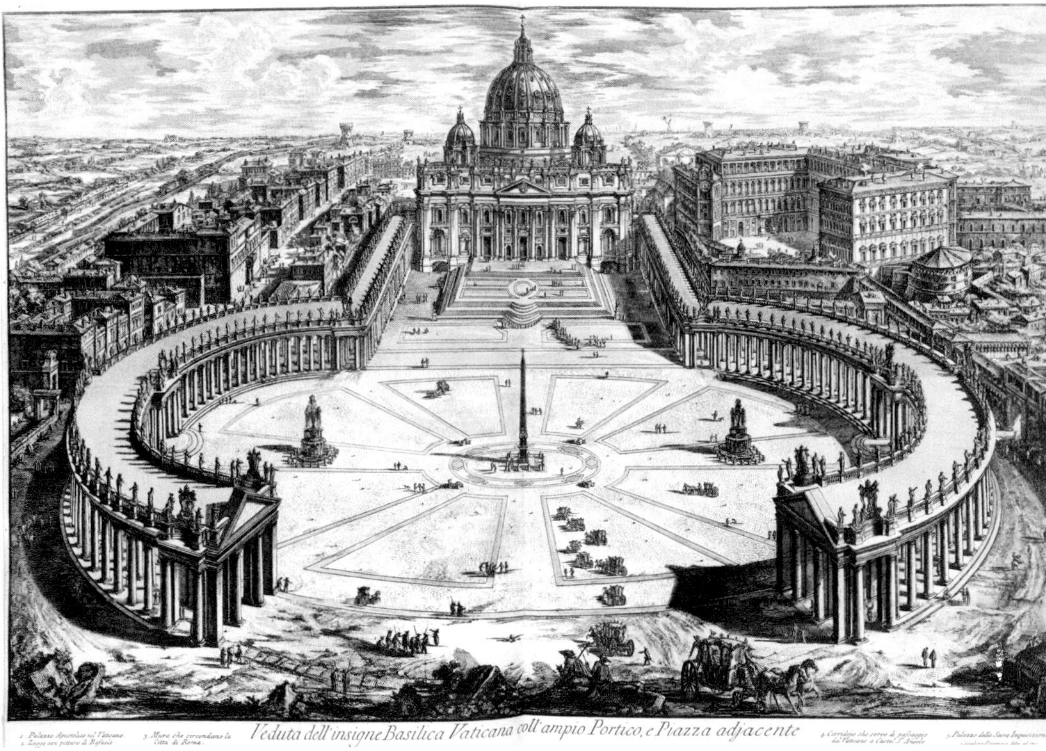


Figure 6.5. Giovanni Battista Piranesi, *St. Peter's Basilica and Square with Colonnades,* ca. 1750. Engraving, 17¾ x 28¾ in. (45.0 x 70.5 cm). Kunstbibliothek, Staatliche Museen, Berlin. Photo: Knud Petersen/Art Resource, New York.

fright," the "mere animal anxiety for the preservation of . . . persons—such as we have witnessed at a theatre, when a slight alarm of fire has been given." Artists such as Martin confused "*poetic* with *pictorial subjects*" and focused on "exterior accidents," thus missing the "unseen qualities" of their themes.[35]

We might gloss on this response by saying that Martin's paintings were the conceptions of an artisan autodidact unconcerned with academic principles—hence in part their originality, which so impressed Allston and other contemporaries. But there was also a vulgar literalness about them that betrayed his limited artistic training and apparent ignorance of Old Master techniques and the language of style they encoded.

The import of these differences between the formal conceptions of the two works was registered in the social character of those to whom they appealed, or interpellated as subjects.[36] While Allston's experience of British aristocratic patronage was ultimately a discouraging one, he had been awarded premiums by the British Institution for his paintings *Elisha* in 1814 and *Uriel* in 1818, and he had sold works to several of the leading patrons of the period in Sir George Beaumont, Lord Egremont, and the Marquess of Stafford.[37] His friendship with Beaumont and his wife is particularly noteworthy, since Beaumont was not just a prominent patron and collector but an amateur painter himself with aspirations to play the role of a conservative arbiter of taste—at least until the furor around the publication of the satirical *Catalogue raisonnées* [*sic*] in 1815 and 1816 dampened his enthusiasm for that part.[38] In a letter to Wordsworth of 1825, Allston referred to the Beaumonts as "my excellent friends" and asked him to tell them "I still retain a grateful remembrance of their many kindnesses."[39] Surviving letters from Beaumont to Allston confirm their friendship, and the former sought to dissuade the artist from returning to Boston at a point when, he argued, he was near a career breakthrough in England.[40]

In contrast with his approbation of Allston's style, Beaumont's recorded judgment on Martin's was a symptomatically condescending piece of dinner table small talk. In April 1821 John Constable—who had none of Allston's generosity toward potential rivals and who described Martin's painting disparagingly as a "pantomime"—reported to his friend John Fisher: "I dined, last week, at Sir George Beaumont's. Met Wilkie, Jackson, and Collins. [William Collins was one of Allston's closest English friends.] It was amusing to hear them talk of Martin's picture. Sir George said some clever things about it, but added, 'even allowing the composition, its only merit, to be something, still if the finest composition of Handel's were played entirely out of tune, what would it be?' "[41]

This judgment stands in marked contrast to the overwhelming tenor of the critical response, which was extensive and predominantly favorable.[42] Many reviews confirm the reports of contemporary letters that Martin's *Belshazzar* drew unprecedented crowds. But whatever the divisions over Beaumont's influence among artists, many shared his view that Martin, for all his success, suffered from a disabling ignorance of technical knowledge. Haydon, who, when he was commenting on the work of others, was often perceptive, noted in his diary in 1828: "Martin & Danby are men of extraordinary imaginations, but infants in *painting*. Their pictures always seem to Artists as if a child of extraordinary fancy had taken up a brush to express its inventions. The Public, who are no judges of the Art, as an *Art*, over praise their inventions, & the Artists, who are always professional, see only the errors of the brush. Thus neither are just."[43] Part of the issue here was that most artists, in private at least, did not regard the socially diverse crowds who attended exhibitions as an appropriate public for their work, merely as an audience.

This distinction is particularly clear in the literary remains of Allston, who believed it a "solemn" fact that "thousands die whose minds have never been born," and frequently used locutions such as "the promiscuous multitude."[44] Allston believed that the most profitable career in painting was to be achieved by exhibiting large history paintings in private exhibitions to fee-paying visitors, on the model of Benjamin West.[45] But he made a radical distinction between the small number who were qualified to judge such works—and who inevitably came from the highest social rank—and "the lower classes," the "mass of the town," who attended such exhibitions as "places of public amusement" out of mere "curiosity" or for "entertainment."[46] Although the profitability of this type of exhibition depended on such visitors, in fact Allston believed that "every successive exhibition of a picture lessens its chance of selling" and that those who might buy one from an artist's room "are apt to look at it with indifference, or at least with diminished interest, when it becomes the gaze of the multitude."[47]

By contrast with Allston's highly elitist conception of the artist's audience, Martin framed the presentation of his *Belshazzar's Feast* within a discourse of public access and democratic entitlement. "Everyone possesses, more or less, a sense of discrimination; a certain share of taste, and of judgment," he wrote in his *Description.*[48] Hence the painting was presented not just as entertainment but as a work of original genius that the pamphlet would elucidate for precisely those whose opinions Allston disdained.

My claim that the styles of the paintings represent divergent class perspectives might seem to founder on the fact of Allston and Martin's friendship and mutual respect. But beyond the obvious response that personal relations can and often do transcend political and social differences, my argument is about objective meanings and does not require that the artists themselves be fully conscious of the significance of their works—a requirement that no artist can reach, or any other social agent for that matter. In any case, it is a claim that does match with their social identities and political values in what are at least suggestive ways, and in this respect they could hardly have been more different.

Allston was the eldest surviving son of a South Carolina slave-holding family. He was schooled in Charleston and Newport, Rhode Island, and attended Harvard from 1796 to 1800. As William H. Gerdts has observed, he was "certainly the best educated American artist of his time"—although we should understand "educated" here in a particular class conception of the term.[49] When Allston came of age in 1800, he inherited a considerable property by his father's will, a property he sold in two installments in 1800 and 1804 to finance his artistic education and the beginnings of his career.[50] Although by 1814 Allston was beginning to have the financial difficulties that would dog him for the rest of his life,[51] his whole formation had given him the character of a "gentleman"—an identity that he himself was at pains to project and that was remarked as the salient feature of his persona by many who encountered him. At Harvard, where his classmates referred to him as "the count,"[52] he had acquired social connections that established him as part of elite Boston society. But his class style and assumptions must also have helped him in his dealings with British aristocratic patrons.

Martin was the child of impecunious lower-middle-class parents and left Haydon Bridge Grammar School in Northumberland at fourteen.[53] After an abbreviated apprenticeship to a Newcastle coachbuilder, and another to a jobbing Piedmontese artist, he moved in 1806 to London, where he supported himself through a range of artistic skills until he drew attention as an oil painter with his *Sadak in Search of the Waters of Oblivion* at the Royal Academy exhibition of 1812.[54] Martin was thus a model of the entrepreneurial striver; in 1812 his workmates at William Collins's shop went on strike against him because he had served no apprenticeship. He in turn felt no kinship with them.[55] But he was nevertheless, politically speaking, a reformer, who alarmed C. R. Leslie by hissing when the national anthem was played at a concert in 1821 to express his support for George IV's estranged wife, Queen Caroline, who was the improbable focus of radical sentiments at the time.[56] He was an ardent supporter of the 1832 Parliamentary Reform Act, and was reportedly a deist and a rationalist in religious matters, a close friend of the political philosopher William Godwin.[57]

By contrast, according to his close friend and executor Richard Henry Dana Jr., Allston's political principles were "highly conservative," while a Harvard friend recalled that he "always belonged to the Federal party," probably because the Federalists were "more gentlemanly" than their Republican rivals.[58] In his *Lectures* he refers to the French Revolution as the consummation of all human evil since "the first Fratricide," while in a sonnet on the theme he likened it to "the King of Hell" and declared that there had been nothing equal to it since the Flood.[59] This is entirely consonant with the conservative outlook of the intellectual circles in which Allston mixed in Britain; these included the Romantic poets Coleridge, Southey, and Wordsworth, all three disenchanted radicals by the time he met them.[60] It is notable that his friendship with Coleridge—which was particularly close—came at a time when the latter was projecting himself as the foremost public intellectual of British conservatism and that his key texts the *Lay Sermons* (1816–17) and *Biographia Literaria* (1817) appeared around the time of *Belshazzar's* gestation.[61] As with Coleridge, Allston's belief in social hierarchy was linked with religious conservatism, and after he returned to the United States in 1818 he joined the Episcopal Church, despite the fact that he had close friendships among the Unitarians, whose liberal doctrines were the subject of heated debate among the New England clerisy in these years.[62]

The Anglicanism of Allston's religion precisely matches the Anglicism of his politics and his art. Although Allston espoused a conventional patriotism, even referring in a letter of 1816 to "our highly favoured country,"[63] he could be disdainful of the materialism and lack of culture of his compatriots, whom he found immodest with regard to their opinions in matters of taste "where they have no means of information."[64] England was the standard by which he measured contemporary culture, and he described it to his English friend Collins as "the land I love next to my own" and to an American friend as "kind, hospitable old England (for such, even while a foe of my country, such she ever was to me)."[65] Not only did he maintain that "the present English School comprises a great body of excellent artists, and many eminent in every branch,"[66] but also he regarded himself as belonging to it and hoped to found a branch of it in the United States. In 1819, after his election as an associate of the Royal Academy in absentia, he wrote to Collins that although it might be his lot "never to revisit England, I still hope to preserve my claim as one of the British School, by occasionally sending my pictures to London for exhibition; a claim I should be most unwilling to forego—my first studies having been commenced at the Royal Academy & the greater part of my professional life passed in England & among English artists." That this was more than just a display of personal friendship is confirmed by the sentences that follow: "At any rate, I may have the satisfaction of founding an English School here. I may well stickle for it when I think of the other Schools in Europe."[67] The implicit contrast here was surely with the contemporary French school, of which Allston, like most of his English contemporaries had a low opinion.[68] This was a judgment heavily loaded with political implications, since French art of the Davidian school was understood to be deeply invested with the values of French Revolutionary politics.[69] In brief, I am claiming that the self-conscious Anglicism of Allston's style was effectively anti-French and all of a piece with his conservative *Weltanschauung.*

Confirmation of this can be found in the representation of England in the writings of Allston's friend Washington Irving. In the essay on Lamb and Irving that concludes *The Spirit of the Age,* Hazlitt writes of the latter's *Sketch-Book* and *Bracebridge Hall* that they are "literary *anachronisms*" based on eighteenth-century precedents: "Mr. Irving's language is with great taste and felicity modeled on that of Addison, Goldsmith, Sterne, or Mackenzie: but the thoughts and sentiments are taken at the rebound." The author had come to England and fancied himself "in the midst of those characters and manners which he had read of in the *Spectator* and other approved authors," and "instead of looking around to see what *we are,* he sets out to describe us as *we were*—at second hand." Instead of marking the changes in English society since Addison or Fielding, "he transcribes their account in a different hand-writing, and thus keeps us stationary, at least in our most attractive and praiseworthy qualities of simplicity, honesty, hospitality, modesty, and good nature." This was the key to Irving's popularity, since it complimented the "national and Tory prejudices" of his English readers.[70]

Allston's pictorial style, I would argue, did something rather similar.[71] In the practices and ideology of the English school of painting, he found a model of aesthetic conservatism suitable for export to a society in which the same kind of challenges to the established prerogatives of rank and wealth by the "promiscuous multitude" were ubiquitous. The contrast between the style of his *Belshazzar's Feast* and Martin's helps to point that up. But while contemporaries felt the need to comment on the plebeian pretensions of Martin's work, the style of Allston's work was so much part of the hegemonic culture that its class claims needed no direct articulation. To borrow from Burke, they were simply part of the "entailed inheritance" of the dominant order.

## NOTES

1. E.g., William H. Gerdts and Theodore Stebbins Jr., *"A Man of Genius": The Art of Washington Allston (1779–1843)* (Boston: Boston Museum of Fine Arts, 1979), 107–8; David Bjelajac, *Millennial Desire and the Apocalyptic Vision of Washington Allston* (Washington, D.C.: Smithsonian Institution Press, 1988), 5–7; Thomas Balston, *John Martin, 1789–1854: His Life and Works* (London: Gerald Duckworth & Co., 1947), 53–54; William Feaver, *The Art of John Martin* (Oxford: Clarendon Press, 1975), 49–51.

2. It is very likely that Martin saw the two sketches Allston made for his composition in 1817 and also the final canvas in the seemingly advanced form it was in before the latter's departure for Boston; Allston cannot have seen Martin's painting in the original, although he certainly knew one or more of the prints made after it that circulated widely in the United States. The sketches are numbers 101 and 102 in the catalogue of E. P. Richardson and H. W. L. Dana; see Edgar P. Richardson, *Washington Allston: The Biography of a Pioneer of American Art and a Study of Romantic Art in America* (Chicago: University of Chicago Press, 1948), 202. Richardson's surmise that that the composition of the painting itself "must have been well blocked in when he rolled it up for transportation to America" (201) seems confirmed by Washington Allston to James McMurtie, November 7, 1818: "All the laborious part is over, but there still remains about six or eight months more work to do on it." *The Correspondence of Washington Allston,* ed. Nathalia Wright (Lexington: University Press of Kentucky, 1993), 128. Allston mentioned that Martin's picture was well known in the United States through prints in Washington Allston to the Editor of the *North American Review,* [June 1840], in *Correspondence of Washington Allston,* 445. For the later history of Martin's *Belshazzar's Feast* and copies after it, see Balston, *John Martin,* 59–61.

3. To the extent that, after Allston returned to the United States in 1818, he asked to be remembered to Martin (along with other friends) in several of his letters to Charles Robert Leslie, who in turn reported reciprocal greetings from Martin. See Washington Allston to C. R. Leslie, November 15, 1819, May 20, 1821, May 8, 1822, February 7, 1823, and C. R. Leslie to Washington Allston, August 30, 1821, in *Correspondence of Washington Allston,*

169, 184, 199, 204, 189. For Allston and Leslie, see ibid., 562–63, and Charles Robert Leslie, *Autobiographical Reflections* (1860), ed. Tom Taylor, 2 vols. (repr., Wakefield, Yorks.: E. P. Publishing, 1978), 1:29, 30, 32; 2:24–25, 329, and passim.

4. John Martin, "Autobiographical Notes," *The Athenaeum* (1834): 459, quoted in Feaver, *Art of John Martin,* 49.

5. Both Allston and Martin referred to the theme as one of the downfall of empire. In a letter to Washington Irving of May 9, 1817, Allston described his conception as depending on "the solemn contrast" between "a mighty sovereign, surrounded by his whole court, intoxicated with his own state" and "the Prophet [Daniel], standing like an animated pillar in the midst, breathing forth the oracular destruction of the empire!" *Correspondence of Washington Allston,* 100, 101. In a pamphlet of 1821 explaining his picture, Martin described its theme as "the overthrow of the Assyrian Empire." Balston, *John Martin,* 262. The political connotations of Allston's iconography are charted comprehensively in Bjelajac, *Millennial Desire.*

6. C. R. Leslie to Washington Allston, August 30, 1821, in *Correspondence of Washington Allston,* 189; all emphasis is original except "*your subject.*" The speculator was Martin's former employer William Collins—not to be confused with Allston's friend the landscape painter of the same name—who had a china and glass painting business on the Strand. See Feaver, *Art of John Martin,* 52, 13.

7. Washington Allston to C. R. Leslie, September 7, 1821, in *Correspondence of Washington Allston,* 190. Allston was referring to "The British Gallery," *Blackwood's Magazine* 8, no. 48 (March 1821): 684–86. Although the author, who signed himself A CONNOISSEUR, praised Martin's *Belshazzar* above all other works in the exhibition, it was not truly a historical painting or "an attempt at the highest styles of art." Rather, it belonged in the "ornamental" class, and he recommended that the artist mend his use of color through studying Tintoretto and Veronese. One can imagine that Allston would have agreed with such a judgment of Martin's work.

8. From "Aphorisms," "Sentences Written by Mr. Allston on the Walls of His Studio," in Washington Allston, *Lectures on Art* (Dodo Press, n.d.), 111.

9. Washington Allston, "Note to Article III of Number 107," *North American Review* 51, no. 109 (October 1840): 518–20, reprinted in *Correspondence of Washington Allston,* 444–45. The *Lectures on Art* were never completed or delivered, and were only published posthumously in 1850. The theme of genuine originality as distinguished from competitive distinction is also developed in Washington Allston to Gulian Crommelin Verplanck, March 26, 1830, in *Correspondence of Washington Allston,* 286. Cf. "by Originality we mean that thing (admitted by the mind as *true*) which is peculiar to the Author, and which distinguishes his work from that of all others." Allston, *Lectures on Art,* 50. Cf. William Dunlap, *The History of the Rise and Progress of the Arts of Design in the United States,* ed. Frank W. Wright and Charles E. Godspeed, 3 vols. (Boston: C. E. Godspeed & Co., 1918), 2:313–14.

10. The classic account of this theory is Meyer Howard Abrams, *The Mirror and the Lamp: Romantic Theory and the Critical Tradition* (Oxford: Oxford University Press, 1953).

11. Washington Allston to Gulian Crommelin Verplanck, July 2, 1824, in *Correspondence of Washington Allston,* 217. "Quoad" stands for *quoad hoc,* meaning "as far as this" or "to this extent." In 1819 Allston told Leslie that he was so familiar with Reynolds's image, "his manners, habits, modes of thinking and even of speaking," that he felt almost persuaded at times

that he had known him. See Washington Allston to C. R. Leslie, November 15, 1819, ibid., 168. This familiarity probably came from reading James Northcote's *Life of Reynolds* (1813), which he seems to have borrowed a few months earlier. See Washington Allston to Henry Sargent, [August 20, 1819?], ibid., 162. See also Dunlap, *History of the Rise and Progress,* 2:304–5.

12. Allston observed that "the greatest geniuses . . . are generally found to be the widest likers." In Allston, *Lectures on Art,* 104. Cf. Washington Allston to William Dunlap, November 4, 1833, in *Correspondence of Washington Allston,* 343: "I am by nature, as it respects the arts, a *wide liker.*" The principle is that enunciated by Reynolds in a famous passage in "Discourse Six": "The mind is but a barren soil; a soil which is soon exhausted, and will produce no crop, or only one, unless it be continually fertilized and enriched with foreign matter." Joshua Reynolds, *Discourses on Art,* ed. Robert R. Wark (New Haven: Yale University Press, 1975), 99. Cf. Reynolds's defense of Raphael's borrowings from Masaccio in the cartoons in "Discourse Twelve" (*Discourses on Art,* 219–21), which Allston did not accept (Allston, *Lectures on Art,* 104).

13. Washington Allston to C. R. Leslie, May 8, 1822, in *Correspondence of Washington Allston,* 198–99.

14. Washington Allston to John Vanderlyn, April 23, 1808, ibid., 54. This was perhaps intended as a defense of the English school to counter Vanderlyn's more Francophile predilections.

15. Allston, *Lectures on Art,* 103, 102.

16. Washington Allston to John Greenough, August 12, 1827, in *Correspondence of Washington Allston,* 244. In this letter—in contrast to the 1808 letter to Vanderlyn—Allston does acknowledge that in addition to accuracy in drawing, which can be learned, there is "a grace and beauty" to some drawing that requires "genius" and not just skill. Allston admired Haydon, whom he knew, and considered him as "ranking among the very first of living artists." See Washington Allston to James McMurtie, May 27, 1831, ibid., 299. On the friendship of Allston, Leslie, Morse, and Haydon, see Leslie, *Autobiographical Recollections,* 1:220–21. Allston's critique of the idea that "some parts of a picture should be left *unfinished*" (Washington Allston to William Dunlap, November 4, 1833, in *Correspondence of Washington Allston,* 344) runs counter to Reynolds's practice. See Andrew Hemingway, *Landscape Imagery and Urban Culture in Early Nineteenth-Century Britain* (Cambridge: Cambridge University Press, 1992), 88–89, for "breadth," and 94–95 for Haydon's critique of Reynolds.

17. Allston, *Lectures on Art,* 93. Cf. Reynolds's comparison of the two in "Discourse Five."

18. Perhaps a copy or variant of *The Slaughtered Pig* (1639) by Isaac van Ostade in the Maximilian Museum der Stadt Augsburg.

19. Allston, *Lectures on Art,* 59–61. Cf. Coleridge's description of Allston's *Elisha* in "Essay Third" of "On the Principles of Genial Criticism Concerning the Fine Arts," in Samuel Taylor Coleridge, *Biographia Literaria with His Aesthetical Essays,* ed. J. Shawcross, 2 vols. (London: Oxford University Press, 1907), 2:234.

20. "The Journal of John Blake White," ed. Paul R. Weidner, *South Carolina Historical and Genealogical Magazine* 43, no. 1 (January 1942): 35–36.

21. Leslie, *Autobiographical Recollections,* 1:190–91, 193.

22. Allston describes the changes in Washington Allston to C. R. Leslie, May 20, 1821, in *Correspondence of Washington Allston,* 184. Leslie replied: "I am sure the alterations you have made in your 'Belshazzar' must have improved it. A low point of sight is certainly essential to a large picture which must necessarily be hung above the eye of the spectator; the reverse is very injurious to the effect of Raphael's cartoons." C. R. Leslie to Washington Allston, August 30, 1821, ibid., 187. Elizabeth Johns has argued that Allston was already drawing on the *Death of Ananias* in *The Dead Man Restored to Life by Touching the Bones of the Prophet Elisha* (1811–1814) in "Washington Allston's *Dead Man Revived,*" *Art Bulletin* 61, no. 1 (March 1979): 88.

23. See Frederick Cummings, "Poussin, Haydon, and the *Judgement of Solomon,*" *Burlington Magazine* 104, no. 709 (April 1962): 141–52.

24. Gerdts and Stebbins, *"A Man of Genius,"* 32; *Correspondence of Washington Allston,* 38–40. He also bought a copy of *Il Disignanno* by Veronese during his sojourn in Italy. See *Correspondence of Washington Allston,* 81–82.

25. Washington Allston to William Dunlap, November 4, 1833, in *Correspondence of Washington Allston,* 343.

26. Richardson and Dana catalogue no. 103, in Richardson, *Washington Allston,* 203; Gerdts and Stebbins, *"A Man of Genius,"* 100.

27. See especially "Discourse Four," in Reynolds, *Discourses on Art,* 57–73.

28. Allston, *Lectures on Art,* 97.

29. Allston saw *Christ's Entry into Jerusalem* "in a very unfinished state" before he left England and "thought very highly of it." He saw the finished painting when it was exhibited in Boston in 1833 and judged it "a magnificent work of art." Washington Allston to James McMurtie, May 27, 1831, and Washington Allston to Thomas Sully, April 8, 1833, in *Correspondence of Washington Allston,* 299, 324. On the question of Rembrandt's possible influence on the conception, see Gerdts and Stebbins, *"A Man of Genius,"* 107.

30. Some critics at least—William Hazlitt among them—recognized the priority of Gandy's conception in his *Pandemonium, or Part of the High Capital of Satan and his Peers* (1805), which had made an impact at the Royal Academy's 1805 exhibition. See Brian Lukacher, *Joseph Gandy: An Architectural Visionary in Georgian London* (London: Thames & Hudson, 2006), 111–15, 131.

31. Feaver, *Art of John Martin,* 52.

32. *A Description of the Picture BELSHAZZAR'S FEAST Painted by Mr. Martin . . . ,* (1821), reprinted in Balston, *John Martin,* 261–65. Leslie had reported to Allston in 1820 that Martin conceived "the writing on the wall to be about *a mile long.*" C. R. Leslie to Washington Allston, March 3, 1820, in *Correspondence of Washington Allston,* 172.

33. The *Morning Herald*'s reviewer captured the incongruity: "The picture by Mr. MARTIN is an extraordinary example of patience and perseverance in the tedious details of perspective, a mechanical department of art. This is so rarely met with in unison with that impetuosity of genius which . . . characterizes the work." "British Institution, Pall Mall, No. III," *Morning Herald,* February 8, 1821.

34. Balston, *John Martin,* 262.

35. Charles Lamb, "Barrenness of the Imaginative Faculty in the Productions of Modern Art," in *The Essays of Elia* (London: Grant Richards, 1901), 310–11, 314, 312–13,

317. Significantly, given the implicit comment on empire the theme invoked, Lamb also likens the effect depicted to that of a dinner given by the Prince Regent at the Brighton Pavilion, at which a huge transparency was suddenly shown with the words "BRIGHTON—EARTHQUAKE—SWALLOWED-UP-ALIVE!" to the consternation of the guests (311). Lamb's critique parallels that of his fellow *London Magazine* contributor T. G. Wainewright, who at the end of an extensive review observed, "Better still would it be for him if he could make up his mind to paint out all his little abortions, and renounce the ambition of becoming an historical painter; for which his professional education has in no way qualified him, as his futile attempts at the human figure lamentably show." Janus Weathercock [Thomas Griffiths Wainewright], "The British Institution," *London Magazine* 3 (April 1821): 442.

36. Althusser's conception of ideological interpellation seems particularly apt here. See Louis Althusser, "Ideology and Ideological State Apparatuses," in *Lenin and Philosophy and Other Essays* (London: New Left Books, 1971), 162–70.

37. Johns lays out a persuasive case for seeing Allston's experience of British patronage as discouraging in "Washington Allston's *Dead Man Revived,*" 92–99.

38. Anon. [Robert Smirke], *A Catalogue raisonnée of the pictures now exhibiting at the British Institution. Printed with a sincere desire to assist . . . the directors in turning the public attention to those pieces which they have . . . selected with the . . . intention of affording the most favourable contrast to modern art, etc.* (London, 1815, 1816). Beaumont is represented under the pseudonym "FIGGITY," and described as "A man of some taste, and a tolerable Painter; but uncertain, capricious, cowardly, and treacherous as a Hyena, who entices little children into his den, and then devours them" (part 2, p. v; see also 46). This is almost certainly a reference to his treatment of Haydon over the commissioning of a painting of *Macbeth.* For a sharply critical response to this publication—which rightly positions it as an assertion of academic interests—see William Hazlitt, "On the Catalogue Raisonné of the British Institution," in *Complete Works of William Hazlitt,* ed. Percival Presland Howe, 21 vols. (London: J. M. Dent & Sons, 1933), 18:104–11, originally published in the *Examiner,* November 3, 1816. For Beaumont, see Felicity Owen and David Blayney Brown, *Collector of Genius: A Life of Sir George Beaumont* (New Haven: Yale University Press, 1988).

39. Washington Allston to William Wordsworth, June 6, 1825, in *Correspondence of Washington Allston,* 222.

40. Sir George Beaumont to Washington Allston, June 29, 1818, ibid., 118.

41. Charles Robert Leslie, *Memoirs of the Life of John Constable, Composed Chiefly of His Letters,* repr. of second edition (London: Phaidon, 1951), 79, 81. Cf. David Wilkie to Sir George Beaumont, February 16, 1821, in Allan Cunningham, *The Life of Sir David Wilkie,* 3 vols. (London: John Murray), 2:56.

42. Reviews of Martin's *Belshazzar's Feast* appeared in "British Institution, Pall Mall," *Morning Herald,* January 29, 1821; "British Institution, Pall Mall, No. 3," *Morning Herald,* February 8, 1821 (more critical); *Morning Post,* May 7, 1821 (on crowds around the picture on the exhibition's final day); "British Institution," *The Times,* January 30, 1821 (enthusiastic, uncritical); *Guardian,* February 18, 1821 (long and favorable); "British Institution," *Sun,* January 27, 1821; "British Institution," *Champion,* no. 421, January 27, 1821 (high praise: "With some faults of style and manner, it is still one of the most extraordinary and effective pictures we have ever seen from the British pencil"); R. H. [Robert Hunt], "Fine Arts. British Institution," *Examiner,* February 5, 1821 (long and enthusiastic); Janus Weath-

ercock [Thomas Griffiths Wainewright], "The British Institution," *London Magazine* 3 (April 1821): 437–42 (detailed and brilliantly caustic); "British Gallery," *European Magazine and London Review* 79 (February 1821): 146–47 (favorable but cursory); Z, "Belshazzar's Feast," *Literary Gazette,* no. 216 (March 10, 1821): 153–55 (a letter: says the effect is impressive from afar, but the details are weak; crowds make it difficult to see the work from a proper distance); M.M., "Belshazzar's Feast," *Literary Gazette,* no. 218 (March 24, 1821): 185 (a letter: acknowledges correctness of Z's critique but emphasizes the work's merits); W. H. Parry, "British Gallery, No. II," *Literary Chronicle and Weekly Review,* no. 93 (February 24, 1821) (full page, highly favorable); "Fine Arts, British Institution Gallery," *New Monthly Magazine* 1 (March 1821): 109 (gushing enthusiasm, no criticism); "Exhibition of the Works of the British Artists, placed in the Gallery of the British Institution, Pall Mall," *Monthly Magazine* 51, no. 351 (March 1821) (mixed); "The British Institution," *Repository of Arts* 11, no. 63 (March 1, 1821): 163 (long and enthusiastic; only slight queries about drawing and color).

43. Entry for May 9, 1828, in *The Diary of Benjamin Robert Haydon,* ed. Willard Bissell Pope, 5 vols. (Cambridge: Harvard University Press, 1963), 3:276.

44. Allston, *Lectures on Art,* 105, 10.

45. Washington Allston to Henry Pickering, May 18, 1820, in *Correspondence of Washington Allston,* 175.

46. Washington Allston to Samuel Morse, April 15, 1823, in connection with the exhibition of Morse's *Hall of Congress* (1821) in Boston, ibid., 207–8.

47. Washington Allston to James McMurtie, October 30, 1819, ibid., 165. Correspondingly, Allston asserted that "Reputation," having its source in "the popular voice," was "essentially contemporaneous . . . always at the mercy of the envious and ignorant," whereas "Fame" was necessarily "*posthumous.*" "Aphorisms," in Allston, *Lectures on Art,* 115. His poem "Eccentricity," which David Bjelajac has dated to 1810, refers to "the mob's applauding stare." Bjelajac, *Millennial Desire,* 82.

48. John Martin, *A Description of the Picture BELSHAZZAR'S FEAST Painted by Mr. Martin, Lately exhibited at the British Institution . . .* (London: J. Robins & Co., 1821), reprinted in Balston, *John Martin,* 262. On the extent of Martin's popular appeal, see Martin Myrone, "John Martin: Art, Taste, and the Spectacle of Culture," in *John Martin: Apocalypse,* ed. Martin Myrone (London: Tate, 2011), 11–21.

49. Gerdts and Stebbins, *"A Man of Genius,"* 14. For Allston's early life, see ibid., 10–12, and Bjelajac, *Millennial Desire,* 49–65.

50. For Allston's property, see *Correspondence of Washington Allston,* 36–37n1. Sarah Burns has argued that the early experience of slavery inflected Allston's aesthetic throughout his career. Although she raises an important issue, I find the argument overly speculative. See Sarah Burns, *Painting the Dark Side: Art and the Gothic Imagination in Nineteenth-Century America* (Berkeley: University of California Press, 2004), chap. 3.

51. Washington Allston to Samuel Finley Breese Morse, January 2, 1814, in *Correspondence of Washington Allston,* 65.

52. Gerdts and Stebbins, *"A Man of Genius,"* 20. In his 1805 *Self-Portrait,* Allston's gold Phi Beta Kappa key dangles from his watch chain. Cf. C. R. Leslie's judgment in 1812 that he was "a most accomplished scholar and in his manners a finished gentleman." Leslie, *Autobiographical Recollections,* 2:329.

53. Myrone's description of him as from a "working-class background" is misleading ("John Martin," 14). Although Martin was born in a one-room cottage outside the village of Haydon Bridge in Northumberland, his mother came from a family of petty landowners and his father worked at a variety of occupations, including tanner, soldier, publican, fencing master, woodman, and drover. Unlike most working-class children, Martin attended grammar school, leaving at fourteen literate and with some knowledge of history and literature. He did not come from a proletarian family.

54. Feaver, *Art of John Martin,* 1–15.

55. Ibid., 13.

56. Balston, *John Martin,* 82–83. Martin attributed the later decline of his friendship with Leslie to their differences over the Royal Academy.

57. Ibid., 159–60, 162–65. As Myrone points out ("John Martin," 15), Martin was not a republican and regularly made displays of deference to royal and aristocratic patrons in the interest of extending his market.

58. Richard Henry Dana Jr., preface to Allston, *Lectures on Art,* n.p.; Jared B. Flagg, *The Life and Letters of Washington Allston* (New York: Benjamin Blom, 1969), 29.

59. Allston, *Lectures on Art,* 25.

60. Allston's Harvard friend Leonard Jarvis recorded that his admiration for Southey predated the poet's conservative turn. See Flagg, *Life and Letters,* 27–28.

61. For Allston and Coleridge, see ibid., 61–66; Gerdts and Stebbins, *"A Man of Genius,"* 50–51, 63, 87; *Correspondence of Washington Allston,* 538–41; Bjelajac, *Millennial Desire,* 69–71, 88–91, 104–5, and passim. For Coleridge's stature as the intellectual spokesperson of British conservatism at this time, see Marilyn Butler, *Romantics, Rebels and Reactionaries: English Literature and Its Background, 1760–1830* (Oxford: Oxford University Press, 1981), 87–93.

62. The leading spokesman of Unitarian theology in Boston, the Reverend William Ellery Channing, had been a friend of Allston's since his Newport schooldays and was also the brother of Allston's first wife, Ann, who died in 1815. On Allston and the Unitarian-orthodox controversy, see Bjelajac, *Millennial Desire,* 76–88. On his joining the Episcopal Church, see ibid., 197–98n70.

63. Washington Allston to Myndert van Schaick, November 13, 1816, in *Correspondence of Washington Allston,* 96.

64. Washington Allston to Gulian Crommelin Verplanck, July 2, 1824, ibid., 217. Allston had arrived at his Anglicism even before he left the United States, to judge from a witty letter to his friend John Knapp of October 23, 1800, written partly in a vein of self-mockery: "Our country is at present so young that few of our towns bear an[y] traits of originality. . . . Sometime, to be sure, we may light on a connoisseur, or something of that kind to laugh at; but for your buildings, your paintings, your music, give me old England '*for my money!*' To be sure this country of ours is '*in the main*' a very good one; in no other place must it be confessed are there better citizens, or better *men,* but I am still of the opinion that the best coat of arms for America would be a pudding for her body, a bag of cotton for her head, and a bag of dollars for her heart." Ibid., 17–18.

65. Washington Allston to William Collins, August 23, 1818; Washington Allston to Gulian Crommelin Verplanck, March 1, 1830, in *Correspondence of Washington Allston,* 123, 283.

66. Washington Allston to Henry Pickering, November 23, 1827, ibid., 245. In this letter Allston declared that the English school of landscape painting was superior to all the other contemporary schools, and its preeminent figure, Turner, had "no superiour [*sic*] of any age." Cf. the comments on contemporary British art in Washington Allston to William Collins, May 18, 1821, and Washington Allston to C. R. Leslie, May 20, 1821, ibid., 180–81, 183–84. Allston had arrived at his view of Turner's preeminence by the time he saw the artist's *Snow Storm: Hannibal and his Army Crossing the Alps* at the Royal Academy exhibition in 1812. See Leslie, *Autobiographical Recollections,* 2:13.

67. Washington Allston to William Collins, April 16, 1819, in *Correspondence of Washington Allston,* 146.

68. On Allston's low opinion of French art, see Gerdts and Stebbins, *"A Man of Genius,"* 102; Bjelajac, *Millennial Desire,* 68. As these authors have pointed out, Allston's friendship with German artists in Rome is linked with his anti-French aesthetic.

69. A good instance of the near-hysterical anti-French nationalism of British artists in this period is Haydon's account of his trip to France in 1814. See *The Autobiography and Journals of Benjamin Robert Haydon* (London: Macdonald, 1950), chap. 13. Cf. "French Pretensions," *London Magazine* 6 (October 1822): 293–304; Y, "French School of Painting," *London Magazine* 10 (December 1824): 611–17. On the political functions of this position, see Gerald Newman, "Anti-French Propaganda and British Liberal Nationalism in the Early Nineteenth Century," *Victorian Studies* 18, no. 4 (June 1975): 385–418.

70. William Hazlitt, *The Spirit of the Age* (London: Grant Richards, 1904), 269, 270. Hazlitt knew Allston, whom he met in Paris in 1803 or 1804. *Correspondence of Washington Allston,* 38, 39.

71. Allston and Irving met in Rome in 1805 and became intimate friends, being particularly close during the years 1815–1818, when both were in England. Their contacts are sketched in *Correspondence of Washington Allston,* 559–60. The earliest of Allston's surviving letters to describe *Belshazzar's Feast* was written to Irving on May 9 of the year before. See Washington Allston to Washington Irving, May 9, 1817, and Irving's reply of May 21, 1817, ibid., 100–101, 108–9. (Irving wrote an essay on Allston, which is now in the New York Public Library.) In 1822 Allston wrote to Leslie that "the public" in Boston were "all agog" for *Bracebridge Hall,* and that "Irving well deserves all his popularity." After reading the first volume, he asked the same correspondent to tell the author he was "delighted" with the work, continuing, "Every individual of the family is as well drawn as . . . could be, and I felt as if I had been reading of real people." Washington Allston to C. R. Leslie, May 8, 1822, July 23, 1822, ibid., 199, 201. That Allston was also predisposed to interpret English society through the image conjured up by eighteenth-century literature is suggested by his first surviving letter from England in 1801, in which he contrasted London, which disappointed his expectations of "every species of grandeur" by its stark juxtapositions of "luxury" and abject poverty, and the servile deference of the middle class to persons of "rank," with the countryside, which was "beyond my expectation beautiful and picturesque; and the appearance of the people that of . . . health and contentment; in short every leaf seemed to embody a sentiment, and every cottage to contain a venus." Washington Allston to Charles Fraser, August 25, [1801], ibid., 25.

# 7

# James Fenimore Cooper and American Artists in Europe

## Art, Religion, Politics

*Wayne Franklin*

Early in February 1828, the popular American novelist James Fenimore Cooper, author of such international Romantic successes as *The Pilot* (1822) and *The Last of the Mohicans* (1826), went to London from Paris with the intention of finishing and seeing through the press a new book, *Notions of the Americans,* that was not intended to be kind to his British hosts. This fictional travelogue, supposedly written as a series of letters back home by an enlightened European visiting the United States, had as its main purpose the correction of European, and more specifically English, mistakes—worse, prejudices—about republican society and institutions in the United States. Yet in his also contentious narrative of his English experiences, called *Gleanings in Europe: England* (1837), Cooper would often go out of his way to specify how well he had been treated by particular Englishmen and Englishwomen in 1828, including an array of other writers and artists. Probably he did so partly because he had genuinely enjoyed himself in London even as he kept a secret account of English failings. Besides, most of those whom he praised were, like the famous Whig poet and banker Samuel Rogers, already sympathetic to Cooper and his country. Such British writers had much in common with Cooper not only politically but also with regard to their aesthetic tastes and values.

They had been warmed up for Cooper by letters of introduction supplied by the English expatriate William Spencer, a friend of Cooper's in Paris. Spencer was tardy in getting his letters ready, but once they had been deployed, visitors started calling on Cooper in such numbers and were so gracious that their demands on his time soon presented the novelist with something of a problem. The Scots poet Thomas Campbell, especially famous in America for his often recited and reprinted *Gertrude of Wyoming* (1809), knocked on Cooper's door early in his stay, about the same time as Rogers (who lived around the corner from Cooper's lodgings and showed up there within days of Cooper's arrival). Cooper liked Campbell's poetry; he already had drawn three epigraphs apiece from *Gertrude of Wyoming* for *The Spy* (1821) and *The Pioneers* (1823), and one more for *The Pilot.* That Campbell was as much of a Whig as Rogers gave Cooper even more reason to appreciate the former's company, although little seems to have come of the opening.[1]

Much more consequential was Cooper's socializing with the minor London-born poet and translator William Sotheby, who first contacted him on or before March 27. The relations between the two took some time to establish themselves, but Sotheby was persistent and offered powerful inducements. When he sent Cooper a note inviting him to a May 9 dinner with Lord and Lady Dacre, Cooper had to decline because he and his wife were planning to visit Oxford and Cambridge at that time. But in the same note, Sotheby offered to take the American novelist on a "tour of Hampstead and Highgate," with calls at the homes of the Scots poet and dramatist Joanna Baillie and of Sotheby's close friend Samuel Taylor Coleridge. The prospect of such a trip sparked Cooper's "great pleasure," causing him to throw open his calendar after the Oxbridge visit. This was not an obligation but rather a chance to extend his cultural reach.[2]

Cooper in fact had already met Coleridge at Sotheby's dinner table on April 22, when Sir Walter Scott (whom Cooper had met and socialized with in Paris in 1826) and his son-in-law John G. Lockhart also were there, along with several others. On that occasion, Cooper thought Coleridge, now in his mid-fifties, "a picture of green old age; ruddy, solid, and with a head as white as snow." The novelist had every reason to be grateful for the chance to engage in conversation with the great poet, with whom he shared a mutual friend, Washington Allston.[3] As Cooper soon learned, however, "conversation" was not quite the right word for what took place in the presence of Coleridge, who in this instance as in most others held forth in what amounted to a series of brilliant monologues. In his journal Scott thus noted that "the orator" of that particular evening was "that extraordinary man Coleridge," who, though perfectly silent until the table had been cleared, then began "a most learned harangue" on the mystery cult of the Cabiri (chthonic Samothracian gods), then "diverged to Homer, whose *Iliad* he considered as a collection of poems by different authors" rather than by the single blind poet to whom it was customarily attributed, at the time a controversial view. "Zounds!" Scott quoted Shakespeare's *King John.* "I never was so bethumped with words."[4]

Cooper admitted that he "knew too little" of the overt topic of Coleridge's "dissertation" to judge the cogency of his arguments. In any event, he was more interested in the verbal and psychological drama of the whole performance than in the dogma per se. He detected, from the deliberateness of Coleridge's voice and the exactness of his pronunciation, a constant struggle "between an affluence of words and an affluence of ideas." Even Coleridge, that is, had trouble keeping up with Coleridge. Yet Cooper admired "the beauty of the language, and the poetry of the images." Finding Coleridge's performance "much more wonderful than convincing," he concluded his 1837 account of it by comparing Coleridge to "a barrel to which every other man's tongue acted as a spigot; for no sooner did the latter move, than it set his own comments in a flow."[5]

Cooper's second encounter with Coleridge took place in Highgate, then a genteel village just off Hampstead Heath north of the city. Coleridge occupied an attic apartment at number 3 The Grove, the family home of his physician and friend Dr. James Gillman, though he also had a parlor downstairs for receiving guests such as Cooper. Seriously addicted to opium, Coleridge had moved in with Dr. Gillman and his family in 1816 and was to die in his quarters on The Grove in 1834. Like Scott or Cooper himself, most literary figures who visited Coleridge there in these years or saw him elsewhere found themselves overwhelmed by the verbal assaults pouring forth from him. He was less a sage whose ideas about poetry and the arts in general could provide guidance to the rising generation than a performer who bodied forth older (and now somewhat tattered) notions of Romantic inspiration. Boston minister William Ellery Channing had thoroughly enjoyed listening to Coleridge at Highgate in 1823, but was amused to learn that the poet, writing enthusiastically about the visit in a letter to Allston, Channing's brother-in-law, praised Channing's gifts for conversation. "My part was simply interrogative," Channing responded in his memorandum book. "I made not a single remark!"[6] When Ralph Waldo Emerson called during his first visit to England in 1833, he managed to work a few comments and questions into their conversation, but in the end wrote that it was "impossible to recall the largest part of his discourse, which was often like so many printed paragraphs in his book,—perhaps the same, so readily did he fall into commonplaces. As I might have foreseen, the visit was rather a spectacle than a conversation, of no use beyond the satisfaction of my curiosity." Channing, one of the most generous men of his generation, was finally more blunt. "Coleridge, I believe, loved truth," he wrote to an English correspondent, the author Lucy Aikin, shortly after the poet's death, "but I fear, he loved more that subtle, refined action of mind, by which he was authorized in his own judgment to look down with contempt on the common judgments of men."[7]

Cooper was not so direct, but his view was similar. He had less veneration for Coleridge as a thinker than did Channing, yet at the same time he seemingly had more luck breaking Coleridge's conversational spell. His closeness to Allston made him very welcome at Highgate, for there was a ritual of appreciation for the painter in which all Americans seemed bound to participate. When Cooper arrived there, he noticed "a beautifully painted little picture" in one of the outer rooms and went over to it to take a closer look. Coleridge quickly informed him that the work, based on a detail in Titian's *Adoration of the Magi,* had been painted in Italy by Allston, and he proceeded to tell Cooper a story connected with the work that was one of the poet's favorite anecdotes. Five years after Cooper's visit, when Emerson called, the story was again trotted out.[8]

In a very real sense, Cooper's visit to Highgate had been about Allston as much as Coleridge: Cooper's seven-year stay in Europe was to teach him more about art and artists than about literary topics or personalities. He had met Allston in Boston in 1824, when the novelist went there to research a book set in New England during the Revolution. The two were already great admirers of each other's work. Allston had read Cooper avidly, liking his Romantic tales so well that he encouraged his Boston friend (and future brother-in-law) Richard Henry Dana Sr., also an admirer of the novelist's works, to send Cooper a fan letter. When Dana did so, informing Cooper of Allston's encouragement, Cooper replied with his own praise for the painter, promising that he would seek him out once he came to Boston. By that time Allston was among the most cosmopolitan not only of American artists but also of American writers, having published a collection of poems in 1813 and having completed his novel *Monaldi* in 1819, although it was not published until 1841. Allston had been to Europe twice since graduating from Harvard in 1800, and had socialized closely with Coleridge in Rome in 1805–6 and again in England from 1811 to 1817. Among his paintings from the earlier period is an unfinished portrait of the poet, now in the Fogg Art Museum at Harvard University. A second, more formal portrait, completed during Allston's second European trip, is in the National Portrait Gallery in London.[9]

## Greenough in Florence, 1829

Meeting Coleridge had been a high point in Cooper's London visit because the white-haired British poet vividly represented the wider Romantic movement of which the thirty-eight-year-old American novelist was already a postcolonial exemplar. The two writers' remembrance of Allston underscored the same point, but also prepared Cooper for fresh artistic discoveries on the Continent, for which he departed late in May 1828. He had brought his family to Paris in July 1826, and before the London visit had spent all his time in and about the French capital. His contacts there had been varied, consisting largely of the figures in the circle of the great republican—and American hero—Lafayette. But in at least one instance, Cooper had formed a close friendship with an artist, the young sculptor Pierre Jean David d'Angers. In fact, David had finished a bust of Cooper during the novelist's absence in London and presented it to him on his return.

Cooper was not back in Paris for long. He quickly sent the David bust to New York for safekeeping and then, packing up his whole family (his four daughters had remained in school in Paris), departed for Switzerland.[10] The Americans toured much of that country from their base in Bern, but once the cold weather began settling in that fall, they headed over the Simplon into Italy. It was in the latter country that Cooper's artistic education, partly through gallery-walking and partly through further personal associations and cultural experiences, was to become especially rich.

The novelist and his family took up lodgings in a palazzo in Florence. Soon at work in the city was the aspiring Yankee sculptor Horatio Greenough. Greenough, who had visited Florence briefly during his first European trip in 1825–1827, planned to winter there in 1828, and in future years would make it his more or less permanent home. When exactly the artist met Cooper is not known. Greenough passed the fall of 1828 in nearby Carrara, where his marble was quarried and the preliminary work on his statuary was done by hired boasters, craftsmen who roughed in the stone blocks, a common practice then. In mid-October, just before Cooper's arrival, Greenough went to Florence from Carrara for the yearly exhibition at the Academy of Fine Arts. That short trip may have lasted long enough for him to cross paths with the novelist, or at least to learn of his pending arrival. In a letter written the next February, he certainly would claim that his relocation to Florence toward the end of 1828 was "hastened by the arrival in that city of Mr. Cooper." Undoubtedly he had been urged to meet Cooper by his very close friend Allston, with whom he had socialized while visiting Boston in 1827–28.[11]

Arriving back in Florence in late November or early December 1828, Greenough began to draw close to Cooper around the third week of January 1829. The friendship between the two would become very deep, but it seems to have developed slowly at first. It was not until April 18 that Greenough, writing to Allston, would open up his mind about Cooper, saying at last that the novelist was "a man who understands perfectly what my aim is and who seems to have gradually become thoroughly interested in my success."[12] By early in 1829 Greenough was at work modeling the head of the novelist at the suggestion of another mutual friend, James Ombrosi, the American consul in Florence. Greenough produced the initial clay head over the first three weeks in January and set his boaster working on the marble in February. Then when Cooper, happy with the project, decided to commission a larger work from Greenough, the portrait bust was put aside, to be resumed later.[13] Cooper picked the subject of the second work from a detail in a painting at the Pitti Palace—the *Madonna del Baldacchino* (Madonna of the Canopy), by Raphael. The novelist's eldest daughter recalled in 1870 that her father, particularly attracted to a pair of cherubs occupying the lower border of Raphael's canvas, pointed them out to Greenough when the two men visited the gallery together.[14] These "chanting cherubs," sharing a musical scroll between them, sing in adoration of the Christ child and Mary, who sit on a throne over which the canopy is being held open by angels. When Greenough had just begun his labors on the group, he acknowledged that "the suggestion was Mr Cooper's," but he took to it with such enthusiasm that by May 1829 he considered his work on the clay model for the group "finished." Early the month before, Cooper had taken a visiting American to Greenough's studio, where that man saw "a very pretty cast of two little Angels—singing from a book of music," so it must have been nearly complete even then.[15]

Cooper claimed that the relatively limited scope of *The Chanting Cherubs,* which stood under three feet high, was owing to what he described to William Dunlap in 1834 as a "due regard to my purse." But he was also trying to lay out a plausible path for Greenough, who in 1829 was full of grand plans but had in fact produced little finished work. Very much taken with "Michael Angelo or the heroic school," Greenough harbored ambitions that were "averse to success in his art." Eventually, of course, Greenough would sculpt both his colossal bare-chested Washington as a Roman hero on a commission from the U.S. Congress and his *Rescue* group for the Capitol. But at a time when no such commissions were foreseeable, Cooper was convinced that Greenough would make his way in the market only if he followed "the popular taste." Doing so would produce immediate income and perhaps prepare the way for further, better commissions. "It was my wish," Cooper continued to Dunlap in 1834, "that [Greenough] should do something to win favour from those who are accustomed to admire Venuses and Cupids, more than the Laocöon and the Dying Gladiator. Thousands would be sensible of the beauty of a cherub who would have no feeling for the sublimity and mystery of the Moses of Buonarotti. With this view the subject was selected." The group commissioned by Cooper was to be sent to the United States and put on exhibition to bring Greenough the attention that would, Cooper hoped, stimulate further commissions. Cooper had experienced stunning popular and commercial success since the publication of his second novel, *The Spy,* in 1821. Like Scott, whose example he closely followed, he enjoyed the benefits of the relatively recent establishment of a literary market that, through mass reproduction, allowed writers profits of which painters and sculptors could only dream. His motives for coming to Europe had been multiple, but among them had been the wish to extract from the markets there (in England, France, and Germany in particular) even more profit from his writing. Here again he succeeded. At the same time, knowing how accomplished Greenough was, he saw how different the sculptor's financial situation was from his own. The insight thus gained surely led Cooper to become Greenough's patron himself and to seek out other sources of support for hm.[16]

In addition to buying his work, Cooper gave Greenough direct financial aid. Although the sculptor's father, Boston builder and real estate developer David Greenough, had once been considered wealthy, the family endured serious difficulties as a result of the 1819 panic. The artist's return to Europe in 1828 was financed by loans from several Boston merchants, and he had accepted free passage on a vessel belonging to Thomas Handasyd Perkins that stopped in Spain on its way to Canton.[17] Cooper must have known a good deal about Greenough's impoverished personal situation from the beginning, since he not only paid him for *The Chanting Cherubs* but also insisted that the proceeds of its U.S. showings go to the sculptor.[18] Furthermore, when the costs associated with getting the group safely to the United States proved too much for Greenough to assume, in February and March 1831 Cooper agreed to pay for crating and shipping and to indemnify the artist for any losses en route. Cooper also gave Greenough more general financial support in this period: by the fall of 1832 he had lent him some eleven hundred francs.[19] That August, Greenough, sheepishly admitting he had failed to repay this amount, was upset that he might not see his friend and set things right before the Coopers left Europe for home. But Cooper replied graciously: "You are unnecessarily punctilious about our little money transactions. Return me what you have borrowed at your entire convenience." Within a month, prompted by Cooper's supportive generosity, and now expecting large payments from the U.S. government for the *Washington,* Greenough drew on the novelist in Florence for another five hundred francs, thereby increasing his debt by nearly 50 percent.[20] In addition to cash, Cooper also gave the artist considerable emotional support. That fall Greenough wrote Allston, "Cooper is the noblest patron I have yet found—has the broadest ideas on the subject of art and wishes me well personally I've reason to think." Even later, Greenough famously declared that the novelist's intervention had been not just helpful but crucial: "Fenimore Cooper saved me from despair, after my second return to Italy. He employed me as I wished to be employed; and has, up to this moment, been a father to me in kindness."[21]

So strong were Greenough's feelings for his mentor that, after Cooper's death in September 1851, he wrote from Boston to William Cullen Bryant in especially warm terms: "The death of my dear friend & early patron Mr Cooper has afflicted me with the greater grief, as I had promised myself . . . to look once more into that blue eye where I never saw [aught] less than goodness and nobleness." Shortly after that, Greenough was being considered as the right choice to undertake a memorial statue of Cooper, and was very interested in the project. Although the project came to nothing, Greenough retained his own interest in creating a memorial to the novelist. A few months before his own death in December 1852, Greenough wrote Cooper's daughter Susan, "The colossal model of your father's portrait is finished"—adding that it was to be cast in bronze "in a few weeks." That was fitting in many ways, not least because the friendship had begun with Cooper taking a lively interest in Greenough's talent, which he first glimpsed in the clay model of himself. Cooper had not been able singlehandedly to change Greenough's commercial prospects, but with his own literary earnings he had been able to mitigate the problem.[22]

## Morse in Rome, 1830

The name of Washington Allston runs like a thread through the later tapestry of Cooper's artistic friendships. The second major American figure with whom the novelist established close ties while in Europe, Samuel F. B. Morse, had been known to Cooper for some years by the time they met again in Italy in 1830 and then later in France. But Allston, through whom Cooper had gained closer access to Coleridge and Greenough, must also have deepened his interest in Morse, both directly and, again, via Greenough. For Morse had been one of the people with whom Greenough had socialized when back in America in 1827–28, along with Allston and the New York polymath William Dunlap, likewise a close friend of Cooper's. Here again the circles of affiliation closed and reclosed among these Americans who were to find so much of their artistic inspiration while abroad.[23]

Cooper had not met Morse until the two of them attended an open house at the presidential residence in Washington, D.C., early in 1825.[24] They associated closely in New York later that year and up to the point of Cooper's departure for Europe. The artist was, for instance, an active member of Cooper's famous club, the Bread and Cheese Club, the body to which Cooper nominated Allston in 1826. It is likely that Cooper attended Morse's four "Lectures on the Affinity of Painting with the Other Fine Arts" at the Columbia College chapel in March and April 1826; certainly Cooper was in New York City at the time, and Morse was already a member of the Bread and Cheese Club by then.[25] Morse was taking the artistic and cultural circles of the city by storm just at this moment. Not only was he chosen to give those lectures under the auspices of the New York Athenaeum, for which Morse served as secretary; he also became the first president of the newly founded National Academy of Design some months prior to the lectures, a position he was to retain until 1845.[26] After Cooper left New York, Morse remained deeply embedded in the city's cultural life, a fact that would give him special value for Cooper once the two were reunited—for Morse could update Cooper on what had been taking place at home. The Coopers had arrived in Rome from Sorrento (where they stayed for three months after departing Florence) at the start of December 1829 and settled into rented lodgings on Via Ripetta, near the Tiber below the Piazza del Popolo. Once Morse arrived in the city on February 20 with the architect (and fellow founder of the National Academy) Ithiel Town, he took lodgings not far from the Coopers, on Via Prefetti between the Tiber and the Corso, and his presence was known immediately: on the very day of his arrival, he received an invitation to a celebration of Washington's Birthday from its five organizers, including Cooper. Morse not only attended that fête but also rose to give a toast to "Americans Abroad." As soon as Monday, February 29, he went with the Coopers to view the moonlit Coliseum. On March 6, again in the evening, he visited with the novelist, and two nights later was also "at Mr. Cooper[']s." On the afternoon of March 15, a Monday, he went with Cooper to the Vatican Library and Museum, tarrying to observe a brightly lighted ceremony during which three new cardinals were created. Again that evening Morse was at the Coopers' lodgings. Doubtless they socialized further, although Morse's diary does not indicate precisely when or how.[27]

Of all the fellow artists with whom Cooper fraternized while in Europe, he probably became closest to Morse. They clearly spent a good deal of time exploring Roman paintings and sculpture, and especially the sacred architecture of the city and the Vatican. But they did not experience what they saw with anything like the same sympathies. In fact, between Cooper and Morse there opened up a diagnostic contrast on the subject of how Americans responded to the Catholic culture of the Continent. The two had relatively similar political views, as would become apparent once they reunited in Paris in 1830. But on religious issues they differed widely. Both men had been born into families that owed their spiritual dues to churches on the left wing of the Protestant movement—Morse to New England Puritanism, Cooper to Delaware Valley Quakerism. And each had a healthy degree of secular skepticism about religion in both institutional and doctrinal terms. For the remainder of this essay, however, I trace out the differences in their response to European Catholicism in both biographical and aesthetic terms.

I begin with a humorous anecdote in Cooper's Italian travel book that I am tempted to think may just refer to the two men. Speaking of changes that had made it safer for predominantly Protestant Americans to wander the Continent,

Cooper relates how he and a friend, walking the streets of Rome one day, were almost done in by their innocent rationality. "Strangers are no longer expected to kneel at the appearance of the Host in the streets," he comments, "or even in the churches. The people understand the prejudices of Protestants, and, unless offensively obtruded, seem disposed to let them enjoy them in peace." Then he inserts his anecdote: "I saw a strong proof of this lately:—A friend of mine, walking with myself, stepped aside in a narrow street, for a purpose that often induces men to get into corners." Unfortunately, with a peculiar brand of American insouciance, the unnamed friend chose to urinate against an out-of-the-way wall directly over which a figure of the Madonna had been set into the masonry. Although the spot seemed "quite retired," no sooner had he finished than, sensing the possible danger to himself as people started gathering, the offender hastily departed. Cooper, however, stayed behind, curious as to what the upshot might be. A priest showed up with some holy water, with which the defiled spot was sprinkled as the milling crowd stood in complete silence, alternately staring at Cooper and at the wall. "Thirty years ago," Cooper concluded, "such a blunder might have cost us both our lives." But now, in the growing daylight of post-Napoleonic secularism, the dire sin had become a tourist gaffe.[28]

But not completely. Whether or not the public defiler was Morse, the inadvertent disrespect of the act comports well with his avowed attitude toward Catholic Rome during his residence there with Cooper, and his poisonous anti-Catholic activism later on in the United States. Paul Staiti, in his study of Morse's art and ideas, points out, for instance, that the group of paintings Morse produced in 1830 on the theme of the Chapel of the Virgin at Subiaco, in the Sabine Hills east of Rome, displays a curious disjunction between "splendid scenery" and the stiff, tiny devotional figures uneasily occupying it. Morse's deep suspicion of what he saw as the mental thralldom imposed on Catholics by their faith left him unable to portray with anything like empathy the faith of the young woman kneeling before the shrine in either version of *The Chapel of the Virgin at Subiaco.* She kneels in a wooden posture before the shrine, the size of which Morse consciously or unconsciously exaggerated as if to suggest the enormous burden of the church on the individual.[29]

Morse's unease with regard to Catholic subject matter expresses a more general problem that American artists and writers faced in confronting continental life. Even Allston, although he had been brought up as an Episcopalian, had Huguenot roots and thus shared a good deal in common with the Quaker Cooper and Puritan Morse. Moreover, his long residence in Newport (whence his stepfather hailed), his intermarriage with the Unitarian Channing clan, and his education at Harvard had surely familiarized him with typical Yankee values and views, including both traditional and radical ones. When he married Richard H. Dana Sr.'s sister Martha in 1830, he moreover "converted" to Congregationalism.[30] He certainly did not eschew religious themes in his painting, although the vast majority of his religious canvases took their inspiration from Old Testament texts. This fact suggests both his quasi-Puritan roots and his avoidance of the more troubling Catholic subjects. In this light, his Titianesque *Adoration of the Magi* is notable for the conversion of the Magi themselves into what a later owner among the Gillman family (which inherited the work from Coleridge) seems to have regarded as hangers-on at a Spanish horse market.[31] Mary is conspicuously omitted by virtue of Allston's halving of the picture—as, of course, are Joseph and the infant Jesus. If Jesus enters any of Allston's work, he tends to be an adult, not a child.[32]

When Samuel Morse came face-to-face with Catholic art, particularly that featuring themes and figures deeply imbued with doctrinal significance, he became notably uneasy, too. Among the works he studied in France and Italy, many had overtly religious subjects, although his interest in them often was focused on matters of color and lighting rather than those subjects. A notebook sketch based on Titian's *Virgin and Child with Saints Étienne, Ambrose, and Maurice* represents what Staiti calls "the gross figural masses" only, without facial detail; Morse coded different areas of the sketch with numbers representing the tones—"bright flesh," "naples yellow," and the like. The Titian was instructive, but not in a doctrinal sense.[33] Morse certainly did not avoid looking at religious works. Among the surviving records of this period, however, there is scant indication that he copied any major religious canvases. Moreover, in his personal experience he displayed similar avoidance. Watching the procession of the Corpus Domini in Rome on June 6, 1830, a very important part of church ritual, Morse responded in his notebook with a flood of dismissive details:

> Next came monks of the Franciscan and Capuchin order, with their brown dresses, and heads shaved, and such a set of human faces I never beheld[.] [T]hey seemed many of them, like disinterred corpses for a moment reanimated to go through this ceremony and then to sink back again into their profound sleep, pale and haggard and unearthly, the wild eye of the visionary and the stupid stare of the idiot [were] seen among them and it needed no stretch of the imagination to find in most the expression of the worst passions of our nature.

There clearly was a connection between this deep sense of revulsion and Morse's defiant posture later the same day, when he stood along the street with his hat atop his head, writing down more details, as another procession passed. Without warning, a soldier ("or rather a poltroon in a soldier's costume") violently knocked the hat off Morse's head, using his gun with bayonet affixed. Reading the record of this episode, one wonders whether the incident involving the Madonna in the wall—if Morse was indeed the defiler—did not entail something more than inadvertence or innocence. Certainly the Corpus Domini diary account provides a corrective to Cooper's blithe note that the Roman authorities now understood the habits of Protestants and tolerated them.[34]

## Art/Religion/Politics: Cooper and the Catholic Faith

By the time Cooper wrote his Italian travel book in 1838, he had come to view such things from a more latitudinarian perspective than he had adopted at first. While one might be tempted to view his warming to Catholic practice as a sign of some Romantic desire to retreat into the past, in fact it reflected instead his modern republican values. He was moving forward, not back. To be sure, he understood religion in contemporary Europe as fraught with conflicting political impulses. In France, where Napoleon's secularist program had produced profound effects, Cooper found scant trace of the old devotional attitudes and practices. Neither Catholicism nor any other creed seemed to matter to the public at large. Only when, on his way back from the London stay in 1828, he passed through the Catholic parts of the Lowlands did he begin to appreciate the still deep attachment of the ordinary population of the Continent to traditions of the Roman faith.

That was a brief but eye-opening experience on which it may be useful to pause for a moment. In particular, Antwerp gave Cooper important instruction on Roman Catholic practice. He visited the spectacular Onze-Lieve-Vrouwe Kathedraal (Cathedral of Our Lady) in the marketplace a few blocks from his hotel. In 1828 this was "one of the noblest Gothic structures on the continent," at least for the author of the guidebook Cooper used, the Englishman Edmund Boyce, who devoted one of his few plates to it; and in 1832, when Cooper returned to Antwerp, he made a point of going back to see this "beautiful edifice."[35] The cathedral, begun under the direction of Jan Appelmans in 1352, garnered particular comment from visitors for its stunning single tower on the front, soaring on the north corner to four hundred feet. But Cooper was particularly impressed by a pair of altarpieces by Peter Paul Rubens, *The Elevation of the Cross* (1610) and *The Descent from the Cross* (1611–1612), which had wide fame.[36] These triptychs, completed as part of a Catholic resurgence in the southern Lowlands after the Spanish Reconquest in 1585, were focused on the crucifixion—and thus reinforced, for a population that had been catechized in Dutch Calvinism over the previous generation, the central importance of the Eucharist to the Roman church. Later in 1828 Cooper would open his mind and feelings to Catholic ritual, which he found seductive. That opening up may well have begun as he stood before these magnificent works of devotional genius in Antwerp. His warm description, in another of his travel books, of what he had seen of Catholicism in Liège, in the heart of Walloon country, in 1831 probably indicates that he recovered there what he had already begun to feel in Antwerp and Brussels three years earlier. It was what one might call the Protestant sense of regret or foreclosure. "I sometimes wish I had been educated as a Catholic," Cooper disarmingly wrote, "in order to unite the poetry of religion with its higher principles." The Episcopal Church was to supply some of that poetry for Cooper after the family's return to the United States.[37]

On Thursday, June 5, when the family was due to leave Antwerp, the religious theme somewhat unexpectedly sounded again—for, as Cooper noted in his journal, that was indeed the date in 1828 for the celebration of the "Fête Dieu," the moveable feast of Corpus Christi, the very festival Morse was to take notes on in Rome two years later. Apparently the Coopers witnessed this celebration while at another of the city's churches, the late Gothic St. Paul's, located to the north of the Hôtel de Ville. Perhaps the Coopers went there to honor their son Paul's name, then chanced upon not only the feast, and possibly some street processions, but also the "remarkable Calvaire" in the courtyard of the church.[38] This artificial mount or grotto, a "representation of Mount Calvary, exhibiting in a rude, but spirited style, the wild and rocky grandeur of the place," was, to continue quoting Edmund Boyce, "thronged with innumerable figures of patriarchs, prophets, and apostles. On descending some steps under the rock," Boyce added, "the traveller enters the tomb of Christ. The Saviour, shrouded in beautiful and costly silk, tranquilly sleeps in death, while around him are represented all the horrors of purgatory. The red flames strongly glare on the walls, and amidst them are delineated the pale and agonized features of those who are suffering the ordeal of that dreadful fire." Boyce reported that "the catholic devoutly crosses himself as he gazes on this frightful scene, and the protestant is not always unaffected."[39] Cooper was certainly moved. Here was another means by which the softening of his radical Protestant attitude toward Catholic practices was probably effected. And it was art that drove in the wedge.

The change in view would be extended and enriched later that year, when the Cooper family relocated to Switzerland on its way to Florence. Although, to the common American understanding, the Swiss were the champions of both republicanism and Protestantism, once in the country Cooper quickly discovered its actual array of institutional practices, both political and religious. As he passed north through Soleure (Solothurn) on a tour a month or so after settling into rented quarters in Bern, he noted with interest how abruptly a traveler passed back and forth across boundaries between Catholic and Protestant areas. Bern was a predominantly Protestant canton, Soleure "rigidly Catholic." The Americans "constantly saw crosses" in Soleure, as a result, but when they entered a sliver of Bern that projected farther west near Attiswyl, those symbols suddenly disappeared, only to reappear when they once more went back into Soleure. Nor was it a matter of mere symbolism. Church buildings and convents abounded in the Catholic parts of the country, and Cooper also registered secular cultural markers: the villages and farms on the Franco-Catholic side of the cultural border appeared "much less neat than" those in Bern. Or, as he would put the idea more self-reflexively in his Swiss *Gleanings* (written eight years later, after his return to the United States), in Soleure "our Protestant eyes began to imagine there was a change for the worse in neatness and comfort." Class differences might be adduced to explain such contrasts—except that, "Soleure being almost as aristocratic as Berne," Cooper fell back on that other value cluster. The Americans had had something of a similar experience, in reverse, on passing out of the less interesting and less tidy Franche-Comté into French-speaking but predominantly Protestant (and to their eyes more orderly) Neuchâtel the month before. At this point Cooper's attitudes toward Catholicism remained relatively unsubtle, not unlike those of Morse.[40]

One can confirm this initial conclusion by examining Cooper's first response to one of the most intensely Catholic sites he would visit in all of Switzerland, the abbey of Einsiedeln in Schwyz. As he approached that site, he encountered masses of Catholic pilgrims converging on the abbey to worship before its famous shrine, the Lady of the Hermits, and was more than usually skeptical about them. "Great air of faith in something," he wrote acerbically in his journal, "though in most cases every appearance of excessive ignorance." Cooper and his Swiss guide, a "dogged protestant," had a lively conversation about the failings of the Catholic Church, but after dinner the American went back into the church, which was thronged with the faithful. Some things touched him, such as hearing the prayers of the pilgrims once they entered, or just the look of them with their packs on their backs as they lay down to pray for an hour without stop, "some with outstretched arms and some in silence." But the memory of his Protestant upbringing steeled him against the emerging empathy. "I was the only human being," he wrote in his journal, "who did not seem to pray." In his Swiss *Gleanings,* written soon after the violent anti-Catholic attack on the Ursuline Convent in Charlestown, Massachusetts, in 1834, he cast a more conciliatory light on the experience. Whereas Morse was alarmed like other nativists by the threat he saw in immigrant hordes, especially Catholic ones, Cooper saw no threat worth mentioning in immigrants, be they Catholic or not.[41]

Cooper returned to the Einsiedeln church the next morning to find "priests saying mass and a crowd of pilgrims." Even after he left, walking north on foot with his guide, he found more groups of pilgrims "carrying on their backs and heads heavy burthens, praying aloud." Coming from the Tyrol and even Germany, not just Schwyz, they were all pushing on to the shrine past the stations of the cross that punctuated this route and the others leading to Einsiedeln. Cooper, despite his initially warm response to Catholic ritual and especially Catholic art earlier that year in the Lowlands, was here confronting a kind of peasant culture he had not met before, and it took him time to adjust to it. Throughout Switzerland, he associated prosperity and the idea of the modern with Protestantism, and all he saw in this stretch of Catholic Switzerland deepened his prior conclusions. He was therefore happy to leave religion behind him, at least temporarily, and return to what he then might have called "genuine" Swiss scenery.

Cooper's experience of Italy brought his attitudes toward Catholicism to a higher, more complex level. He would famously admit to Greenough in 1833, "Italy . . . haunts my dreams and clings to my ribs like another wife," calling it three years later "the only region of the earth that I truly love."[42] The love began with the landscape, but it extended to the people and their culture, including their religion as well as their art. Take a simple example. Whereas Morse, with his sturdy self-reliance, excoriated the beggars whom he encountered throughout Italy, Cooper developed a notable rapport with them. On arriving at Sorrento in the fall of 1829, he exhibited the same dismissive, superior attitude as Morse, noting, "The great number of beggars that torment one like gnats was at first a drawback to our pleasures." During the family's walks, it was not uncommon to find a dozen mendicants dogging their heels. Usually the Coopers gave them small coins, but if they had no change, they would be harassed by the beggars going and coming back. The family's habits became so well known that beggars would sit outside the gate of their rented house waiting for the family to emerge. One day, looking over the railing from the terrace, Cooper saw a stalwart seated on a bench there, a lame old man who was "as fine a mendicant as one shall see in a thousand." When the beggar noticed the novelist, he stood up and doffed his cap. Cooper called for his servant Roberto to bring out some small change and then tossed the old man a *grano,* a copper coin worth less than half an English penny. "This little ceremony," Cooper noted, "established a sort of intercourse between us." The man came again the next day, and soon he was sure to be punctually present just when Cooper took his usual morning break from writing and adjourned to the terrace. For ten days or so the ceremony went on, till Cooper found two men on the bench at the gate. He gave each man a *grano,* only to find "three pensioners" there the next day, and by the time a month was out, a dozen were showing up every day at the same time. Cooper dutifully paid his pittance to each of them, day after day. One result was that he and his family found themselves completely unbothered on their walks in Sorrento and the surrounding country. Beggars still appeared, wrote Cooper, "but they invariably drew modestly aside, permitting us to pass without question." The crowd at the gate simultaneously swelled, until (as Roberto learned) people were coming from five or six miles away because they had learned that they would all be "accommodated with a *grano* apiece by the *American admiral*"—for as such the novelist, a sometime navy man, was regarded. Eventually he would pass out coins to forty or fifty mendicants each day, although he began to screen the applicants once he learned that some of them (fishermen's wives, for instance) were not really poverty-stricken. When the family finally left Sorrento for Rome, a corps of ninety-six beggars, some from as far as ten miles away, gathered to wish Cooper well.[43]

## "Fair Play"

That anecdote of course hinges on a kind of easy though tolerant condescension. But it suggests as well how Cooper, releasing his prior views, became fully accepting of the reality of Italian life. He announced it as a principle, given Italian habits and the large numbers of visitors in Rome, that few foreigners "see much of Italian society." And he admitted that he personally knew "too little of Italian society to say anything new about it, or even to speak very confidently on any of the old usages." For the most part, he sketched a series of random, mostly superficial observations. Yet he certainly had seen enough to form strong opinions about Italy and Italians. Almost twenty years later he would unabashedly write: "I like the people of Italy. . . . They are full of feeling, and grace, and poetry, and a vast number are filled with a piety that their maligners would do well to imitate"[44] As to that last point, the question of faith, he was speaking not just about personal piety but of course about the Roman church. He made no bones about his impartiality on the issue, frontally stating that, far from having unreasonable suspicion or fear of Roman Catholicism in Europe or in America (as Samuel F. B. Morse assuredly did), he thought that a kind of market system ought to be followed in faith as in other matters. Thus far he was Jeffersonian in his political outlook. He had learned that the Roman church wished to make converts in the United States: "If this can be done, let it, for I am for giving all sects fair play."[45] To be sure, he thought the Roman church would actually make little progress converting American Calvinists. But he also had learned, from his firsthand experience in Italy, that the church of 1830 was not the church of the pre-Napoleonic era. And he urged mutual tolerance and respect.[46]

His openness on matters of faith carried over into his experience of Roman art and music. He had rushed to see St. Peter's Basilica on his very first evening in the city, and throughout his stay he kept going back there. He liked visiting it when vespers were performed in the Chapel of the Choir, off to the left as one faces the main altar. Since there was no organ in St. Peter's, the voices alone created the effect Cooper came to relish: "Sometimes I withdraw to a distance, and the sounds reach me like the swells of airs in another world; and at times I go near the door of the chapel, and receive the full bursts of its harmony."[47] The whole family went there on Christmas, causing Susan Cooper to write her sister Caroline, "I can hardly conceive any thing finer, than this exquisite music, in this Magnificent Building."[48] Her husband, to be sure, did not care for everything he saw or heard in St. Peter's. People lingering around the doorway of the Chapel of the Choir, for instance, often carried on worldly conversations that no American, he protested, would engage in or tolerate. He even witnessed a young cardinal, obviously a man of some great family, enter St. Peter's with a quartet of followers, including two other clerics and two secular servants. The cardinal comported himself in a "subdued, gentle, and devout" manner, while the other men in black followed suit. The servants to their rear, however, laughed and grimaced at each other, mocking the other three.[49]

Despite such firsthand evidence of moral corruption—or was it bad breeding?—Cooper found his interest in "the poetry of Roman worship" deepened by his stay in Rome. He explained, "The odour of the incense, the vaulted roofs, attenuated aisles and naves, the painted windows, and the grand harmonies of the chants, are untiring sources of delight to me." He missed the Gothic architecture that had accompanied and increased his discovery of this fascination in northern Europe. But the artistic wonders of the churches of Rome for the most part strengthened his appreciation of the Roman faith. It was not just the grandeur of St. Peter's that he meant. All over he found public sanctuaries and especially private chapels that he counted as "architectural gems," the best of them to his mind being the private chapel of the Corsini family in St. John Lateran, which Mariano Vasi, one of Cooper's sources on Italy, called "very magnificent."[50] Cooper repeated from Vasi the count of Roman churches—"one hundred and thirty-three," a figure that excluded the chapels that had been made out of ancient temples. The number was impressive, but even more notable to Cooper, who never tired of measuring Europe's wonders with an American ruler, was their individual and collective size. Not only was the *smallest* of the Roman churches (excluding those converted temples) as "large as the largest of our own," but also he thought each of the six basilicas in Rome was probably as large in cubic volume "as all the churches of New York united," much as he concluded that St. Peter's Square might contain all of New York's short, modest churches.[51]

It is by no means easy to separate Cooper's response to the religious elements of European life from his growing interest in European art, much of it experienced in churches or other religious sites. In common with other American Protestants abroad at the time, he had left home with a certain skepticism about the Roman Catholic Church. In his case, however, the comparatively longer period of time he spent in Europe provided him with many occasions on which to test his prior ideas against his present perceptions. Morse owed his rigid ideas in part to the greater severity of his upbringing—but in part, too, to the relative brevity of his experience on the Continent. As Cooper lingered in Europe, and particularly in the Catholic landscapes of Italy, he had increasing opportunities to modify his own views.

Nowhere are the results of that process more visible than in a novel called *The Heidenmauer* (1832), written in France following Cooper's Italian sojourn. In this book, which is based on a violent uprising against a German monastery in the period of Luther, Cooper would controvert many of the notions that he—and his fellow American Protestants—routinely shared about the supposed glories of the Reformation. In the book's action, he thus showed virtue and vice on both sides of that historic split. Catholic clerics and German princes and burghers are seen to be equally flawed, but at the same time, genuine piety exists among priests and laity as well. Most interesting is the novel's dénouement, in which the local nobleman and burghers who have sacked the monastery are ordered to do penance by undertaking a pilgrimage to the shrine of Einsiedeln. Drawing on, but significantly altering, his own impressions of that site, Cooper concluded the book's fictional pilgrimage with a scene rarely witnessed, at least with the equanimity Cooper displays, in American literature of the period—that is, a performance of the Catholic mass. Gone from the characters' visit to the shrine are the doubts Cooper had experienced there in 1828. Those doubts have been displaced by the aesthetic awe he gradually had come to feel in the presence of Roman art, an awe whose absence from Protestant culture he now regretted. Borrowing artistic details from the churches of Rome that had no real counterpart at Einsiedeln, Cooper made the sanctuary there into a summary of all the wonder he had experienced in Italy and other Catholic countries. Although he thus parted company with the likes of Morse, without Morse and Greenough and indeed Allston, Cooper never could have come to the personal and artistic conclusions he reached as his seven-year visit drew to its end in 1832. If he transcended Morse in particular, it was because Morse and the other American artists discussed here had helped Cooper become both a patron of the arts and a connoisseur of the ideas and values they expressed.

## NOTES

1. Campbell's socializing was severely restricted at the time owing to the illness and then death of his wife. See *The Life and Letters of Thomas Campbell,* ed. William Beattie,

2 vols. (New York: Harper & Brothers, 1850), 2:204. On Spencer's assistance to Cooper and Rogers's visit, see James Fenimore Cooper, *Gleanings in Europe: England,* ed. Donald A. Ringe, James P. Elliott et al. (Albany: State University of New York Press, 1982), 24–25, 27–30.

2. *The Letters and Journals of James Fenimore Cooper,* ed. James Franklin Beard, 6 vols. (Cambridge: Harvard University Press, 1960–1968), 6:299, 1:261.

3. Cooper, *Gleanings in Europe: England,* 124. It is worth noting that Cooper drew none of the epigraphs for his novels from Coleridge prior to 1840; nonetheless, one assumes that he must have read at least "The Rime of the Ancient Mariner" years before his European sojourn.

4. *The Journal of Sir Walter Scott, from the Original Manuscript at Abbotsford,* ed. David Douglas, 2 vols. (New York: Harper & Brothers, 1890), 2:164.

5. Cooper, *Gleanings in Europe: England,* 127–28. Cooper contrasted Coleridge in this regard to Sir James Mackintosh, the liberal polymath famous for his ethical and historical writings.

6. Quoted in John Beer, "William Ellery Channing Visits the Lake Poets," *Review of English Studies,* n.s., 42 (1991): 219–20.

7. Ralph Waldo Emerson, *English Traits,* in *Essays and Lectures* (New York: Library of America, 1983), 770–73; William Ellery Channing to Lucy Aikin, quoted in Beer, "Channing and the Lake Poets," 222.

8. See Cooper, *Gleanings in Europe: England,* 260. The Allston canvas, although it does not include the left side of the Titian original, where Jesus, Joseph, and Mary rest under a primitive arbor, is nonetheless also called *Adoration of the Magi;* it is reproduced from a private collection in William H. Gerdts and Theodore E. Stebbins Jr., *"A Man of Genius": The Art of Washington Allston (1779–1843)* (Charlottesville: University Press of Virginia for the Museum of Fine Arts, Boston, 1979), 101. Coleridge liked telling visitors about a "famous picture-dealer, of great skill in his calling," who took the partial Allston copy for "a real Titian!" Only when he felt the paint with his fingers did he realize his mistake. Cooper, *Gleanings in Europe: England,* 260. Emerson, *English Traits,* 772; Samuel Taylor Coleridge, *Collected Letters,* ed. Earl Leslie Griggs, 6 vols. (New York: Oxford University Press, 1956–1971), 4:794–95. Writing his nephew John Taylor Coleridge in 1825, the poet called Allston, who by then had been back in the United States for seven years, his "very dear friend," 5:422.

9. On Cooper's Boston visit, see Wayne Franklin, *James Fenimore Cooper: The Early Years* (New Haven: Yale University Press, 2007), 416–17.

10. *Correspondence of James Fenimore Cooper,* ed. James Fenimore Cooper [1858–1938], 2 vols. (New Haven: Yale University Press, 1922), 1:147–49.

11. *Letters of Horatio Greenough,* ed. Nathalia Wright (Madison: University of Wisconsin Press, 1972), 24.

12. Ibid., 28.

13. Susan Cooper, speaking of her husband in a letter to her sister Martha from Leghorn in August 1829, commented that "a very promising American Artist, has taken a bust of him in Marble, while we were at Florence"; Susan DeLancey Cooper to Martha DeLancey, August 4, 1829, James Fenimore Cooper Papers, box 2, American Antiquarian Society, Worcester, Mass. Once Greenough returned to the project, the fact that Cooper had since gained weight led him to remodel the head. When completed in 1831, it represented the

novelist not during his months in Florence but rather after his 1830 return to Paris, where Greenough visited that fall. The roughed-in marble block of the original bust was converted to a new project, and a new marble version of the second model was not begun until the summer and fall of 1832, after Greenough had once more returned to Florence. Nathalia Wright, *Horatio Greenough: The First American Sculptor* (Philadelphia: University of Pennsylvania Press, 1963), 67, 83.

14. Susan Fenimore Cooper, "The Chanting Cherubs," *Putnam's Magazine* 15 (1870): 241–42.

15. *Letters of Greenough,* 24, 32. William Dunlap, who knew both Greenough and Cooper, asserted that the sculptor worked from a print of the Raphael, a print that several of the Coopers' daughters were at the time copying. Given the presence of the original in the Pitti Palace, however, that seems unlikely. See William Dunlap, *A History of the Rise and Progress of the Arts of Design in the United States,* ed. Rita Weiss, 3 vols. in 2 (New York: Dover Publications, 1969), 2:419; Thomas B. Johnson, diary, December 16, 1828–April 28, 1829, Adams Papers, Massachusetts Historical Society, Boston.

16. *Letters and Journals of Cooper,* 3:53. When writing to Dunlap, Cooper was of course aware of Greenough's having received the congressional commission for his monumental *Washington* in 1832. Indeed, in 1829 Cooper indicated that Greenough's private plan for a sculpture of the first president had taken a decidedly "heroic" turn; ibid., 1:390. Although *The Chanting Cherubs* when at last finished and put on exhibition in the United States garnered some good critical comment, the broad public response Cooper hoped for did not materialize. Nor were the profits large enough to give Greenough much tangible support. After its tour, *The Chanting Cherubs* went into storage in New York City. Cooper is reported to have sold the work late in his life, perhaps to the wife of the yachtsman John Cox Stephens. Its present whereabouts is unknown. Nathalia Wright, "The Chanting Cherubs," *New York History* 38 (1957): 193.

17. Perkins had been urged to help by one of the artist's few patrons, the wealthy Baltimore collector Robert Gilmor Jr., who had commissioned Greenough to do a bust of his wife. But Greenough brought few other commissions with him to Italy, and as of 1828 he had not yet acquired enough to support himself fully. Wright, *Horatio Greenough,* 37, 56.

18. Cooper and Greenough agreed to a price of $200 for the group, $50 paid down and the rest due on its completion. Greenough was soon skeptical that this amount would "cover the expences [*sic*]." At the same time, though, he thought that Cooper did not "suspect this," and he neither informed him of his views nor pressured him for more money. Greenough's reluctance on this occasion reflected the personal closeness of the two men, but also the fact that Greenough expected that he might gain from the work's public exhibition in America. Greenough to Allston, September 19, 1829, in *The Correspondence of Washington Allston,* ed. Nathalia Wright (Lexington: University Press of Kentucky, 1993), 273. Cooper formalized the understanding about the group's U.S. showings in an April 6, 1830, letter to Greenough; see *Letters and Journals of Cooper,* 1:407.

19. Wright, *Horatio Greenough,* 70, 90. *Letters and Journals of Cooper,* 2:53, 2:335n2; *Letters of Greenough,* 70–71, 100. The details of the financial dealings are not completely clear, in part because various portions of the Greenough–Cooper correspondence in this period do not survive, but one can conclude that Cooper acted as Greenough's main source of financial support during this time.

20. *Letters and Journals of Cooper,* 2:335; *Letters of Greenough,* 145, 147.

21. *Letters of Greenough,* 28, 36, 47; Dunlap, *Arts of Design,* 2:422.

22. *Letters of Greenough,* 265–66, 270–72, 392, 422. The casting of Greenough's statue of Cooper did not take place, and the model appears to have been lost.

23. Wright, *Horatio Greenough,* 48–56.

24. See Franklin, *James Fenimore Cooper,* 455.

25. On Allston and Irving, see ibid., 519. Morse informed his parents in a November 18, 1825, letter that he had been elected to Cooper's club; see *Samuel F. B. Morse: Letters and Journals,* ed. Edward Linn Morse, 2 vols. (Boston: Houghton Mifflin, 1914), 1:272. Morse is also included in a nearly contemporary membership list ("Lunch | A. Bleecker's | Report," copy of unlocated ca. March 1826 original in James F. Beard Papers, box 5, American Antiquarian Society). *Lectures on the Affinity of Painting with the Other Fine Arts, by Samuel F. B. Morse,* ed. Nicolai Cikovsky Jr. (Columbia: University of Missouri Press, 1983), 13.

26. *Morse: Letters and Journals,* 1:276–80.

27. Clare Benedict, *Voices Out of the Past* (London: Ellis, 1929), 36; Samuel F. B. Morse, diaries, December 12, 1829–May 3, 1830, Samuel F. B. Morse Papers, Library of Congress. Sometimes it is evident that both men attended the same events. See, for instance, their accounts of the fireworks show Morse described in his diary and Cooper recalled in his Italian *Gleanings:* Morse, diary, April 12, 1830; James Fenimore Cooper, *Gleanings in Europe: Italy,* ed. John Conron and Constance Ayers Denne (Albany: State University of New York Press, 1981), 255–56. But in that and other cases there is no overt indication from either of them that they attended together. The Washington's Birthday invitation is found in General Correspondence and Related Documents, bound vol. 11, Morse Papers. For Morse's toast, see *Daily National Journal,* June 9, 1830. Morse's fellow traveler Ithiel Town also attended; see R. W. Liscombe, "A 'New Era in My Life': Ithiel Town Abroad," *Journal of the Society of Architectural Historians* 50 (1991): 11. The second American artist with whom Cooper spent some time in Rome, John Gadsby Chapman, was friends with Greenough in Florence prior to Cooper's arrival there. Once in Sorrento, Cooper learned from Greenough that Chapman had relocated to Rome to copy Old Master paintings. Greenough urged the novelist to make contact with Chapman once the Cooper family itself relocated there. Cooper replied: "I shall be glad to see your friend Mr. Chapman at Rome. He will do me the pleasure to come and see me without ceremony"; *Letters and Journals of Cooper,* 1:389–90; see also *Letters of Greenough,* 435. By the middle of February, just before Washington's Birthday, Cooper informed Greenough that he had "set young Chapman to copying the Aurora of Guido" (a fresco in a building on the grounds of the Palazzo Pallavicini) as a kind of test of his abilities; *Letters and Journals of Cooper,* 1:404. By that summer, when the copy had been finished (and in fact shipped by Chapman to New York without, apparently, Cooper's having seen it in its final form), the novelist was writing Mary Jay, whose husband, Peter, was ultimately to receive the shipment, that Chapman "promises very well as a painter"; *Letters and Journals of Cooper,* 1:430–31; see also Chapman to Cooper, May 3, 1830, James Fenimore Cooper Collection, box 2, Yale Collection of American Literature, Beinecke Library. Soon Cooper wrote New York newspaper editor Charles King urging him to see the picture once it arrived and, if he liked it, to "remember the artist," that is, by publicizing him and perhaps giving him a commission; *Letters and Journals of Cooper,* 1:433. What pleased Cooper in the original painting is suggested by his proprietary reference to it in describing a wintry Swiss landscape in *The Headsman* (1833): "The day was among the peaks, . . . while the

shades of night still lay upon the valleys, . . . like that exquisite and poetical picture of the lower world, which Guido has given to the celebrated al-fresco painting of Aurora"; James Fenimore Cooper, *The Headsman; or, the Abbaye des Vignerons* (Philadelphia: Carey, Lea & Blanchard, 1833), 2:131. I have not located the whereabouts of the Chapman "Aurora."

28. Cooper, *Gleanings in Europe: Italy,* 233.

29. Paul J. Staiti, *Samuel F. B. Morse* (Cambridge: Cambridge University Press, 1989), 181–86.

30. Jared B. Flagg, *The Life and Letters of Washington Allston* (New York: Charles Scribner's Sons, 1892), 292.

31. The Gillmans' son knew the painting as "the picture of the Horse Fair in Spain." Alexander William Gillman, *The Gillmans of Highgate* (London: E. Stock, 1895), 20c. His mother's description, quoted by Flagg, *Life and Letters,* 128, likewise divulges no knowledge of the Titian connection.

32. It is worth noting that Cooper's *Cherubs* were themselves likewise detached from the religious context of the original painting. In Greenough's version, they must have looked more like children than putti, their meaning sentimental rather than devotional.

33. Staiti, *Morse,* 177–80.

34. Morse, diaries, May 4, 1830–March 3, 1831, Morse Papers (compare *Morse: Letters and Journals,* 1:352–53); Cooper, *Gleanings in Europe: Italy,* 233.

35. Edmund Boyce, *The Belgian Traveller, being a Complete Guide through Belgium and Holland, or the Kingdom of the United Netherlands* (London: Samuel Leigh, 1827), 229; James Fenimore Cooper, *Gleanings in Europe: The Rhine,* ed. Ernst Redekop et al. (Albany: State University of New York Press, 1986), 95.

36. In writing of his 1832 return to the city, Cooper spoke of "the two Ruben's [*sic*]" as being "cased up, and . . . literally bomb proof, in preparation for an attack"; *Letters and Journals of Cooper,* 2:279. These must have been the same two that had especially affected him in 1828; presumably his strong initial response led to his inquiry after them in 1832. See Karl Baedeker, *Belgium and Holland. Including the Grand-Duchy of Luxembourg,* 14th ed. (Leipzig: Baedeker, 1905), 168–69. In 1828 Cooper also went to a "Picture gallery," by which he certainly referred to the museum that was then located in an old convent, where, as Boyce indicates, what Cooper in his journal called the "study of the descent from the cross" (*Letters and Journals of Cooper,* 1:267) could have been seen; see Boyce, *Belgian Traveller,* 236–37.

37. Cooper, *Gleanings in Europe: The Rhine,* 106. In the Antwerp cathedral, Cooper also appreciated what in his journal he called "Sculpture in wood"; *Letters and Journals of Cooper,* 1:267. This category would include the early eighteenth-century pulpit carved by Michiel van der Voort (see Baedeker, *Belgium and Holland,* 171), but Cooper was referring to the wide array of wood decorative elements in the building. Thus, in his *Gleanings,* he asserted that in general it was the pulpits of the Belgian churches that contained "the most elaborate designs" (*Gleanings in Europe: The Rhine,* 96–97), though he made it clear that he also was fond of the altars. See James Fenimore Cooper, *Gleanings in Europe: Switzerland,* ed. Robert E. Spiller et al. (Albany: State University of New York Press, 1980), 95, where he compared the carved wood altar of the abbey church of St. Gall favorably with those he had seen in Belgium, even as he acknowledged that St. Gall lacked the altarpieces by Rubens. Elsewhere in that same book he declared, "If Italy be the land of marbles, Belgium is, or rather has

been, the very paradise of those who carved in wood." Here he singled out the "oak confessionals," which he found to be "highly and allegorically ornamented"; Cooper, *Gleanings in Europe: Switzerland,* 96–97. Actually, Cooper's best example of Lowlands carved wood decoration came from Gorinchem, where he took special note of a few stunning "figures over the door of a hospital"; Cooper, *Gleanings in Europe: The Rhine,* 97.

38. *Letters and Journals of Cooper,* 1:267.

39. Boyce, *Belgian Traveller,* 232.

40. *Letters and Journals of Cooper,* 1:293–94; Cooper, *Gleanings in Europe: Switzerland,* 71–73, 91. Cooper later described Soleure as "a walled town, with a monastic look, very Catholic, and not very Swiss" in annotating his copy of the guidebook he used for this trip; see *Letters and Journals of Cooper,* 1:294n1.

41. *Letters and Journals of Cooper,* 1:323–26; Cooper, *Gleanings in Europe: Switzerland,* 163–72. For Morse's vituperations in the wake of the Ursuline attack, see his anonymous screed *Foreign Conspiracy against the Liberties of the United States* (New York: Leavitt, Lord, & Co., 1835).

42. *Letters and Journals of Cooper,* 2:371, 3:233.

43. Cooper, *Gleanings in Europe: Italy,* 123–25. On Morse's attitude, see *Morse: Letters and Journals,* 1:330.

44. Cooper, *Gleanings in Europe: Italy,* 230–31; *Letters and Journals of Cooper,* 5:179. When writing Brantz Meyer in 1848, Cooper would compare Italy to Mexico. Both countries, he opined, evinced "a fine nature in the hands of a fallen people—amiable, and in a certain sense polished, but indolent and inefficient"; *Letters and Journals of Cooper,* 5:367.

45. One source for Cooper's knowledge of this effort may well have been the Right Reverend John Dubois, Catholic bishop of New York, who sat to one side of Cooper at a celebration Cooper chaired on Washington's Birthday; see *Daily National Journal,* June 9, 1830. Dubois was certainly very interested at this time in expanding the role of the Catholic Church in North America. See a letter from him on this topic, written in Rome, March 16, 1830, in United States Catholic Historical Society, *Historical Records and Studies* 5 (1909): 216–30.

46. In his account of Holy Week in 1830, during which he attended two ceremonies led by Pope Pius VIII, Cooper wrote: "The voice of the Pope [could not] be heard, but his gestures were graceful and pleasing. The Catholics kneeled, but the Protestants did not; to my surprise, for the blessing of no good man is to be despised. . . . [We] Protestants . . . seem often to think there is a merit in intolerance and irreverence, provided the liberality and respect are to be paid to Catholics. He who comes voluntarily into a Catholic ceremony is bound to pay it suitable deference; and then, God is omnipresent. I never saw anything wrong in kneeling to the Host; for, while we may not believe in the real presence as to the wafer itself, we are certain that a homage to God himself can never be out of place or out of season. All men would be of the same way of thinking, had not politics become so much mixed up with religion." Cooper, *Gleanings in Europe: Italy,* 255.

47. Ibid., 233–34. Cooper wrote Greenough on January 28, 1830, "I have been to St. Peter's often to hear vespers, for it is one of the great things of Rome" *Letters and Journals of Cooper,* 1:403.

48. Susan DeLancey Cooper to Caroline DeLancey, January 1–11, 1830, James Fenimore Cooper Collection, box 3, Yale Collection of American Literature.

49. Cooper, *Gleanings in Europe: Italy,* 234–35.

50. Ibid., 235. A bilingual English-Italian edition of Mariano Vasi's *Nuova Guida di Napoli* had recently been issued in Naples; see J. B. De Ferrari, *A New Guide of Naples, Its Environs, Procida, Ischia and Capri. Compiled from Vasi's Guide, Several More Recent Publications, and the Personal Visits of the Compiler . . .* (Naples: Printed for George Glass, 1826), 97. As John Conron and Constance Ayers Denne point out (Cooper, *Gleanings in Europe: Italy,* xlv–xlvi), Cooper openly cited Vasi's guide to Rome and obviously made broad use of it. In making a comment about the size of the Vatican, Cooper himself notes (241) that while writing the book he consulted Mariana Starke's *Travels in Europe between the Years 1824 and 1828* (London: John Murray, 1828).

51. Cooper, *Gleanings in Europe: Italy,* 236. In this book Cooper did not completely ignore the various works of art he saw during visits to the Vatican. He professed that he was "not going the rounds of the galleries and museums" with his reader, and referred those with deeper interests to "the regular books for . . . detailed accounts of the treasures . . . with which all Rome abounds" (238; 242). The most he ventured were a few fugitive comments. He thus confessed that he found much to admire in Raphael's frescoes, but took exception to how the artist portrayed the Creator as an "old sprawling man, casting his body, with open palms and extended arms, into a chaotic confusion of gloomy colours" (238). And he called Michelangelo's *Last Judgment* "one of the most extraordinary blendings of the grand and the monstrous in art" (242). Cooper also must have spent considerable time looking at the easel paintings on display in the Vatican Palace, as well as the statuary there, on both of which he likewise offered a few comments. His most unequivocal comment concerned the *Laocöon,* which he called "the noblest piece of statuary that the world possesses" (240).

# III LANDSCAPE

# 8

# John Martin, Thomas Cole, and Deep Time

*David Bindman*

John Martin (1789–1854) was born in Northumberland and by the 1820s had a huge reputation in London based not only on his paintings of apocalyptic subjects but also on his mezzotints on steel, which were generally admired and circulated widely as soon as they were published in Europe and in the United States.[1] Thomas Cole (1801–1848) also came from the north of England, from Bolton in Lancashire, but he immigrated with his family to the United States in his teens in 1818, ending up in New York in 1825. He came back to England for the first time in 1829 as an established painter, from which point on he became familiar not only with Martin's paintings (he met Martin in London) but also with those of other landscape painters such as J. M. W. Turner. My concern here is with Cole before his first return to England, and his relationship with Martin's art based on his knowledge of it in the 1820s in the United States.

There can be no doubt that Cole knew some of Martin's small- and large-scale mezzotints of biblical, Miltonic, and other subjects in New York before he returned to England in 1829. Nor is there any doubt that Martin was a decisive influence on Cole's turn, in the later 1820s, toward what the artist called "composition," or "a higher style of landscape."[2] The fact that Cole was forced to defend himself against the public accusation that he had plagiarized Martin in his 1828 paintings *The Garden of Eden* (plate 12) and *Expulsion from the Garden* (plate 13) is proof of Martin's currency in the United States, and Martin's art certainly influenced both works.[3] During his English visit beginning in 1829, he was able to become familiar with the work of Turner, Constable, and others, all of whom left their mark on his later epic series, *The Course of Empire* (1836) and *The Voyage of Life* (1840), though Martin's influence remains the strongest.

Simply tracing this influence (which, it hardly needs saying, went only from Martin to Cole and not in the other direction) would bring out little that we do not know already from the painstaking work of Ellwood C. Parry III. Instead I want to broaden out the relationship between the two artists by looking at their common interest in geology in a period when the subject was undergoing momentous changes, of which both artists were intensely aware.[4] They both appear to have taken on board the overwhelming evidence that the world was of an unfathomable age going back into "deep time," in contradiction to the temporal account of the Creation in the Bible, which suggested that the physical world was only a few thousand years old. But they still clung, as did most clergymen and thinkers in the pre-Darwinian age, to the belief that the new geology only reinforced the Christian doctrine that the forms of the earth and of mankind were a deliberate and integral part of God's creation and design.

The main issue raised by the new geology was, then, to reconcile two quite different conceptions of *time,* but this cannot be reduced to a simple opposition of biblical and geological time. Biblical time, according to eighteenth-century calculations by Isaac Newton and others, made the world approximately six thousand years old, dating from the Creation described in Genesis. By the early nineteenth century, the evidence of geology and fossil remains made it clear not only that the world was infinitely older but also that it must have preceded the creation of man by a huge stretch of time. But biblical time is also concerned about the *future,* when the world would, according to the prophecies of the Old Testament and especially the Book of Revelation, ultimately be destroyed by God. Mankind would then be redeemed eternally following the thousand-year rule of the saints, the destruction of Satan, the Last Judgment, and the establishment of the heavenly city of Jerusalem. The fate of mankind was just as much a subject of speculation as the age of the earth, and equally a source of disagreement between those who took the Bible literally and saw the end of the world as imminent, and those who thought the end would come in the indefinite and unknowable future.

Geologists of the early nineteenth century, though united in their belief in the great age of the earth, were divided over the process of change. On one side were the "uniformitarians," like James Hutton and then Charles Lyell, who believed that the earth was of an immense age but that most change had come about gradually, by an infinitely slow development. The other school of thought, the "cataclysmic" school, was that of William Buckland, who also accepted that the world was of a great age before the advent of man, but, following Georges Cuvier, believed that it was formed by a series of cataclysms, the last of which was the most dramatic and extensive, the biblical Deluge or Flood, which encompassed the whole world.[5] It should be made clear that these distinctions were not absolute; uniformitarians accepted that such phenomena as earthquakes also affected the earth, just as the cataclysmic school accepted the earth's great age. Buckland and his followers tended to be clergymen of the Church of England, and were often known as "Mosaic geologists." Unlike the Huttonians, they were passionately interested not only in mineralogy but also in fossil remains as evidence of extinct creatures and of the phases of the cataclysms that had formed the earth, especially Noah's Flood.[6] The cataclysmic theory saw evidence of massive changes and eruptions of the earth's crust in the formed and re-formed valleys and mountains, the changing relationship between land and sea, in fossils of crustaceans on land, and in the presence of displaced boulders known as erratics. Buckland and his followers were also pioneers in the discovery and picturing of prehistoric creatures, an interest that drew them toward John Martin in the late 1830s and 1840s.

The cataclysmic theory was compatible with a biblical orthodoxy that saw the destruction of cities and multitudes as a demonstrable consequence of God's wrath toward sinful humanity, described in the Old Testament and Book of Revelation. But what had happened many times, from the age of Noah to Sodom and Gomorrah, Babylon, Nineveh, Pompeii, and Herculaneum (all subjects painted by John Martin), was bound to happen again. The only question was when: Was it imminent, as William Blake believed, with the French Revolution as a sign of the unleashing of the Four Horsemen of the Apocalypse, or was it to take place at some unspecified time in the future, beyond the present epoch?[7]

John Martin, as I have argued elsewhere, is right in the thick of this debate, as he was about the age of the earth.[8] On the face of it, he would seem to be among the biblical literalists, who were, like Blake, from nonconformist and lower-class backgrounds. His own background was that of an artisan; he began as an apprentice to a coach painter. Many of his most prominent paintings seem to demonstrate an apocalyptic analogy between the present-day luxury of upper-class and big city life in the 1820s in the reign of George IV, and the luxurious Old Testament cities that brought down God's destructive wrath. It is notable that most of Martin's *grandes machines* of the 1820s were of such subjects as Belshazzar's Feast, the destruction of Sodom and Gomorrah, and the Deluge, all of which showed the destruction of sinful humanity by a vengeful God. If one reads near-contemporary writings by millenarians such as Blake, Richard Brothers the pamphleteer, and William Sharp the engraver, it seems inconceivable that *Belshazzar's Feast,* for instance, was not aimed at the sybaritic and extravagant court life of King George IV. One might also note that Martin's brother Jonathan, to whom he remained loyal, took his own millenarian beliefs strongly enough actually to burn down York Minster as a warning to the bishops of the Church of England to give up their luxurious lives.[9] But one also has to be aware that Martin's paintings of destruction visited upon humanity were loved especially by royal and aristocratic patrons, to whom the artist paid public obeisance in flowery dedications to his prints after them; the mezzotint of *Belshazzar's Feast* was, remarkably, dedicated "to his most gracious majesty William Fourth King of Great Britain, &c. &c. &c . . . with permission, by his Majesty's Most faithful and devoted subject John Martin." *The Fall of Nineveh,* another scene of retribution for urban luxury, was dedicated effusively to Charles X of France, *The Deluge* to the czar of Russia, and *The Fall of Babylon* to the purchaser of the painting, Henry Philip Hope of the Dutch banking family.[10]

How did John Martin get away with painting and selling subjects seemingly so threatening to the very people to whom he dedicated the prints after them? This may be the wrong question, because it appears that nobody at the time saw him as a millenarian, though it seems probable in hindsight that he was. His late great series of three paintings in the Tate Britain from the late 1840s, *The Great Day of His Wrath, The Last Judgement,* and *The Plains of Heaven,* are explicitly of the last days as prophesied in the Book of Revelation, and show the destruction of the Powers of the World and of the new railways.[11] He seems in fact to have been perceived by his contemporaries as a Deist or mainstream Anglican believer in Natural Religion. He was also polite, sociable, well dressed to the point of dandyism, respectful to persons of rank—he was even on friendly terms with the very bishops his brother Jonathan had warned to repent as he burned down York Minster—and his paintings were attractive to those not invested in strict academic standards. It is also likely that the literary learning he expressed in his pamphlets accompanying the paintings, his scientific interest in the improvement of London, and his knowledge of geology contributed to his respectable standing; but there were also persistent complaints about his flashy technique and even the vulgarity of his art by Hazlitt and others. I would argue that his public commitment to geology as a bulwark of biblical truth was instrumental in enabling him to distance himself from the notoriety of his fanatically millenarian brother.

By the mid-1820s in New York, Cole was seeking to paint in an ambitious manner that went beyond the naturalistic depiction of native scenery. In 1826 he expressed a desire, conventional in art academies, to make elevated compositions, as opposed to working exclusively from nature: "If the imagination is shackled, and nothing is described but what we see, seldom will anything truly great be produced in either Painting or Poetry."[12] In May 1828 he exhibited eight paintings at the National Academy of Design in New York, and in a letter he singles out two paintings, *The*

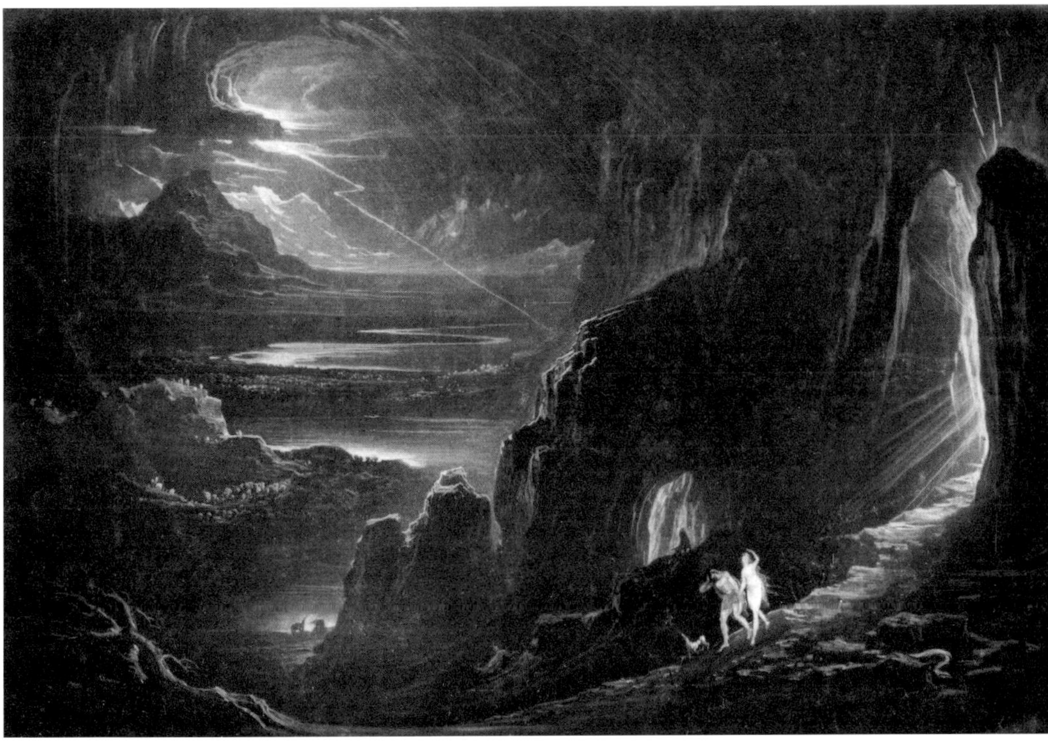

Figure 8.1. John Martin, *The Expulsion of Adam and Eve,* 1824–1827. Mezzotint, 5.74 x 8.3 in. (14.6 x 21.1 cm). The British Museum.

*Garden of Eden* and *The Expulsion from the Garden of Eden,* which he described as "two attempts at a higher style of landscape than I have hitherto tried."[13] These were the ones that caused him to be accused of plagiarizing prints by John Martin, *The Paphian Bower* and *The Expulsion of Adam and Eve* (fig. 8.1), by a writer in the *New York Morning Courier* of June 21, 1828.[14]

Cole denied the accusation indignantly. Though the charge was unfair, it is clear that he borrowed from Martin's mezzotints then available in New York, and he used Martin's manner to elevate his own approach to landscape. Yet what I want to focus on is not the similarities but the differences. Martin's mezzotints were available in New York within a very short time of their publication in London.[15] Cole claimed he could not put his hands on an impression of Martin's *Expulsion* to show next to his own, and to have painted his version "before I knew that such a print was in the country," a claim that is hard to believe, but he did show an impression of Martin's *Paphian Bower* next to his *Garden of Eden.*[16] While it is possible that impressions of Turner's *Liber Studiorum,* published in 1807–1819, had reached New York, it is fair to say that Martin would have been for Cole the most prominent model for the modern historical landscape, along with prints after Gaspard Poussin and Salvator Rosa.

If the scale of the figures in relation to the landscape is comparable in both artists' pictures of the Expulsion, the landscape itself is very different, and not only in the glimpse of paradise lost on the right of Cole's version. The landscape in the Cole painting is both more allegorical of the fallen world in its rugged precipitate landscape, and more studied from real nature of the kind the artist encountered in America. There is a strong suggestion that the American landscape was, unlike that of Europe, unchanged from the beginning of human time. One is reminded of John Locke's famous remark "In the beginning all the world was America."[17]

Martin's landscape, by contrast, though rugged at first, opens out into a wonderful sense of distance and light, as if the travails of life are of brief duration before mankind's redemption. Cole's world is described by him, in a note of 1827–28, in geological terms as made up of volcanic mountains: "The world in its deformity [is made up of] rugged dark stormy Broken Rocks," by definition formed by geological shifts.[18] Cole's primeval animal kingdom is, however, made up of still-existing animals: "Vulture, Hyena, Tiger, Birds of Prey of several kinds."[19]

The animals in Martin's mezzotint *The Expulsion* are more intriguing, and suggest that Martin was more up to date than Cole in his knowledge of extinct animals. The serpent in the foreground has an obvious theological meaning, and the stag chasing the deer is also a reference to the struggle for existence in the fallen world. But what of the creatures silhouetted against the water in the distance? They have been identified by Michael Campbell as dinosaurs,[20] though that is unlikely, because such extinct animals were pictured only in specialized books in skeletal form before 1830. One creature looks more like an elephant with an upraised trunk, but given its enormous size in relation to the other animals pictured, I would suggest that it is a mastodon or mammoth.[21] Cuvier had already published the skeleton of a mastodon in 1822, and we know that Martin was an admirer of his, as Cuvier was later to be of Martin.[22] The mastodon was particularly associated with the United States because of Charles Willson Peale's sensational excavation in Ohio of a complete skeleton in 1801 and his display of it in Baltimore. His sons Rembrandt and Rubens Peale traveled to London with a second skeleton as early as 1802. The showman William Bullock exhibited a huge model of one in the Egyptian Hall in Regent Street from at least 1810, and it was very likely still on view when Martin exhibited his *Destruction of Pompeii and Herculaneum* there in 1822.[23]

The discovery of the mastodon was a matter of national importance in the early United States, for it enabled Jefferson to respond to the condescension of French commentators such as Buffon, who dismissed America as a continent without ancient history or early inhabitants like Europe. Martin's placement of a mastodon in the world inhabited by Adam and Eve would also fix their place in a biological time when extinct creatures roamed the earth, but this was before the identity of other prehistoric creatures that later became known as dinosaurs had been fixed and visualized. It thus provides an early and perhaps not fully thought-out answer to the later question of whether or not early mankind cohabited with extinct creatures. Martin's only comment, probably made in the 1830s, on the early history of man, as recorded by his friend Serjeant Thomas, is that the earth was "peopled first with inferior animals, then a grade superior, and finally with man."[24]

Given that Martin's painting *The Deluge* of 1826 is now lost, the mezzotint of 1828 (fig. 8.2) is the *locus classicus* of the painter's encounter with contemporary geology. Nonetheless, as most writers on it have observed, it follows the biblical account quite literally, even including a figure of Methuselah. Martin quotes extensively in the accompanying pamphlet from the Bible, and also from Byron's play *Heaven and Earth: A Mystery.* According to the preface to Byron's *Cain: A Mystery* of 1821, "the author has partly adopted in this poem the notion

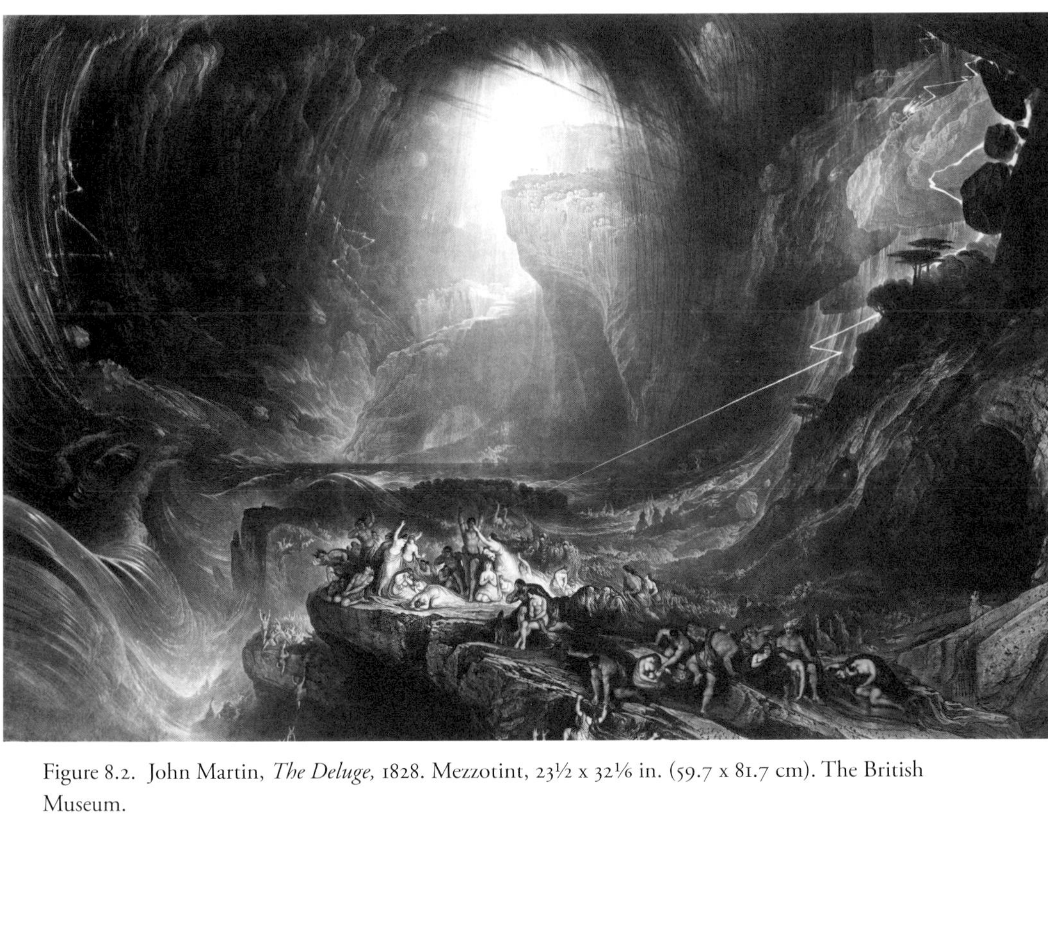

Figure 8.2. John Martin, *The Deluge,* 1828. Mezzotint, 23½ x 32⅙ in. (59.7 x 81.7 cm). The British Museum.

of Cuvier, that the world had been destroyed several times before the creation of man."[25] Martin's print is in sympathy with this interpretation of Cuvier (who talked of "Révolutions" rather than cataclysms) in representing the Deluge as a physical and geological cataclysm in which mighty waters rush and displace mountains, especially on the right, where boulders are falling down the mountainside. Another concession to modern physical theory is the conjunction, noted with approval by Cuvier when he saw the painting, of the sun, moon, and a comet,[26] as if God's wrath is expressed through natural and scientifically observable means. This was seen by the contemporary novelist Edward Bulwer Lytton as a notable instance of Martin's joining of art and science: "Martin gives . . . a possible solution to the phenomena he records, and in the gloomy and perturbed heaven, you see the conjunction of the sun, the moon and a comet! I consider this the most magnificent alliance of philosophy and art of which the history of painting can boast."[27] Martin is very precise about the moment represented by the scene, and he distinguishes between the geological layers of the earth, the valleys, the low hills, and the mountains, which are all inundated except for Ararat. Strata break away, leaving people stranded; erratic boulders tumble down the mountains on the right, and some are carried away on the left by the torrent. As he claims in the accompanying pamphlet, "This representation of the universal inundation of the earth comprehends that portion of time when the valleys are supposed to be completely overflowed, and the intermediate hills nearly overwhelmed, and the people who have escaped from drowning there are flying to the rocks and mountains for safety."[28]

There is also a great deal of animal life in the background of Martin's *Deluge.* Large elephants, or more probably mastodons on account of their enormous relative size, abound in the middle distance, and there is a group of curious creatures with very long necks like giraffes but with humped backs like camels. There is a possibility that these are antediluvian animals now extinct, though Martin in his pamphlet accompanying the print describes them as "Lions and tygers."[29] The print was published a couple of years before prehistoric animals like iguanodons were actually pictured in publications.

We know the *Deluge* mezzotint reached New York and was on display by the end of 1828, though it had only been published in London in September of the same year.[30] Cole made a drawing of it before he went to England, and his larger response to the painting was his famous picture *The Subsiding of the Waters of the Deluge* of 1829 (plate 14). Given that it represents the period after the Deluge, there are no human figures except a skull in the foreground representing the destruction of humanity outside the ark, which floats in the sunlit distance as a sign of a more glorious future for mankind. Unlike Martin's picture, it has a classic calm probably derived from an engraving after Nicolas Poussin's version of the subject, dismissed by Bulwer Lytton as representing "the dreary waste of inundation but not the inundation of a world."[31] Like his *Expulsion,* Cole's painting shows nature disrupted by cataclysm but in a way that once again suggests close observation of actual nature, as it can be observed in the Catskills and the mountains of New Hampshire. Signs of cataclysmic disruption which involved widespread dispersal of matter can be seen in the loosened boulders on the left, with an immense split rock balancing precariously on a smaller one, and the sense that the broken wood in the foreground will merge eventually with the damp earth beneath it. Perched on the right is an erratic boulder, moved into a precarious position from a distance by the force of the waters. What we see in the foreground is a landscape moved, broken up, and reconstituted by immense natural forces; yet the ark floating in the sunlight makes it clear that the cataclysm was an act of a wrathful but ultimately benign God working through natural forces.

What it lacks, strangely, is any sense of the marine life that would have survived in the form of fossils and was much discussed by geologists at the time. It may be compared with Martin's painting of ten years later, *The Assuaging of the Waters,* of virtually the same event, but more precisely contextualized in the biblical story. The sea is more dynamic than Cole's Claudeian calm expanse, and it shows the raven and the dove that Noah had released to test whether the waters were subsiding. There are also in the foreground shells and fossils of sea creatures, some fully embedded within the strata revealed by the cataclysm, locating their origins in deep time before mankind and the period of the Deluge.

The presence of fossils in that painting and the presumed mastodon in Martin's *Expulsion of Adam and Eve* suggest a major difference between Martin's and Cole's geology, and perhaps between the subject as practiced in Britain and in the United States in the 1820s and 1830s. Despite the discovery of the mastodon in the United States, and the interest of Benjamin Silliman of Yale in fossils (he corresponded with Buckland and his followers), there was a more active engagement with cave paleontology in England and in France with Cuvier and his followers.[32] There are also signs that Martin's interest in geology was reciprocated by geologists, not only by Cuvier but also by Gideon Mantell, a follower of Buckland and the discoverer of the iguanodon. Mantell commissioned from Martin a drawing, *The Country of the Iguanodon,* which Martin himself developed as a mezzotint (fig. 8.3) used as a frontispiece to Mantell's textbook *Wonders of Geology,* first published in 1838.[33] This vision of dinosaurs in their original habitat is one of the first by a serious artist to show them as living creatures, and it led to two other commissions by

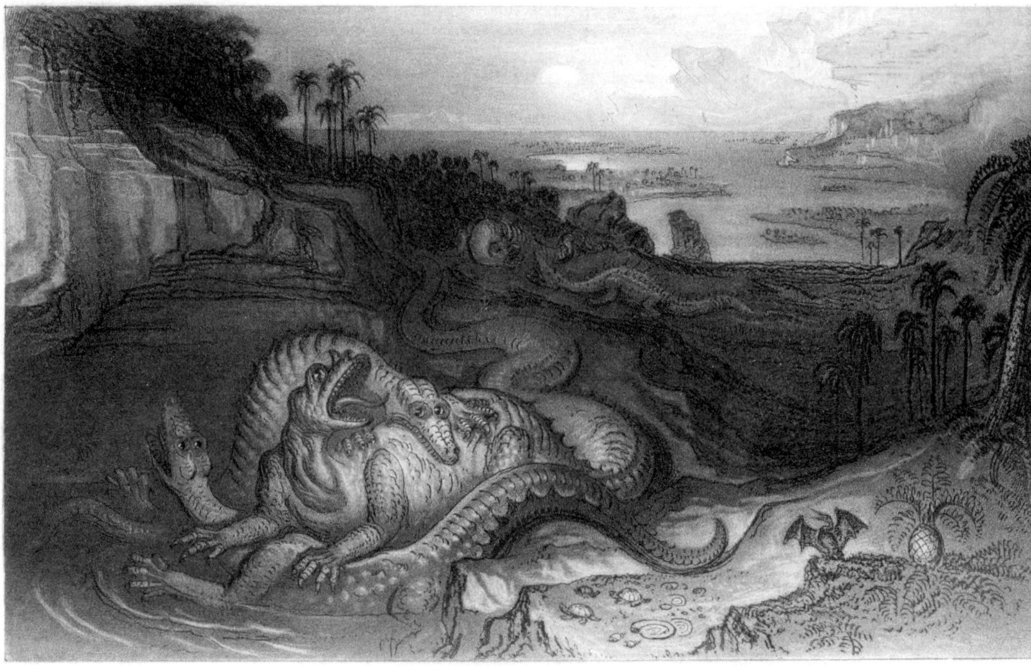

Figure 8.3. John Martin, frontispiece to Gideon Mantell, *Wonders of Geology*, 1838. Mezzotint, 3½ x 5¾ in. (8.89 x 14.58 cm). Collection of Michael Campbell.

geologists for similar scenes. Mantell described Martin as "the celebrated—most justly celebrated—artist, whose wonderful conceptions are the finest productions of modern art," claiming "no other pencil but his should attempt such a subject."[34]

Though Cole is known to have collected fossils, and he was a friend of Silliman's, there is no sign in his paintings of an attempt to integrate them into his geological vision, which is, unlike Martin's, broadly mineralogical; it is the movement of rocks and the way in which the American landscape bears evidence of earlier cataclysms that interests him.[35] In June 1829 he went back to England for a period of twenty-two months. There he mingled with the London art world, meeting Martin himself as well as Constable and Turner. The result was not to move away from Martin, though his subsequent work shows the influence also of the other two painters.

For both Cole and Martin, geology was among other things a way of associating their art with social and intellectual respectability. It is clear that Martin's contemporaries in both Britain and the United States generally saw in his images not—as is now commonplace—crude sensationalism and playing to popular taste, but an up-to-date and consoling exposition of the way in which the new and disturbing ideas of deep time could be reconciled with the Christian account of the Creation. Though Cole was perhaps less aware of recent scientific developments than Martin, geology, under the latter's influence, played a comparable part in his work and contributed to his own reputation.[36]

## NOTES

1. For a full catalogue of his prints, see Michael J. Campbell, *John Martin: Visionary Printmaker* (England: Campbell Fine Art, 1992). All references to Martin's prints are to this catalogue.

2. Thomas Cole to Robert Gilmor, May 21, 1828, reprinted in Ellwood C. Parry III, *The Art of Thomas Cole: Ambition and Imagination* (Newark: University of Delaware, 1988), 78.

3. For a full account of the affair, see Christopher Kent Wilson, "Rediscovered Thomas Cole Letter: New Light on *The Expulsion from the Garden of Eden*," *American Art Journal* 18, no. 1 (Winter 1986): 73–74.

4. See Rebecca Bedell, *The Anatomy of Nature: Geology and American Landscape Painting, 1825–1875* (Princeton: Princeton University Press, 2002), esp. 27–30.

5. See Martin J. S. Rudwick, "Geologists' Time: A Brief History," in *The New Science of Geology: Studies in the Earth Sciences in the Age of Revolution* (Aldershot: Ashgate, 2004), 1–5.

6. See ibid., 313.

7. For the imagery of apocalypse, see Frances Carey, ed., *The Apocalypse and the Shape of Things to Come* (London: British Museum, 1999).

8. David Bindman, "John Martin," *Print Quarterly* 4, pt. 4 (1987): 36.

9. Thomas Balston, *Jonathan Martin: Incendiary of York Minster* (London: Macmillan, 1945).

10. See Campbell, *John Martin,* nos. 74, 82, 78, and 88, respectively.

11. William Feaver, *The Art of John Martin* (Oxford: Clarendon Press, 1975), 188–204.

12. Thomas Cole to Robert Gilmor, December 25, 1826, quoted in Franklin Kelly, *Thomas Cole's Paintings of Eden* (Fort Worth, Tex.: Amon Carter Museum, 1994), 19.

13. Thomas Cole to Robert Gilmor, May 21, 1828, quoted in Parry, *Art of Thomas Cole,* 78.

14. Ibid., 87–88; Wilson, "Rediscovered Thomas Cole Letter," 73.

15. Wilson, "Rediscovered Thomas Cole Letter," 73.

16. Ibid.

17. John Locke, *Two Treatises of Government* (London: Printed for Awnsham Churchill, 1690), 343.

18. Sketchbook page with study for *Expulsion,* Manuscripts Division, New York State Library, Albany, reproduced in Kelly, *Thomas Cole's Paintings of Eden,* 30.

19. Ibid.

20. Campbell, *John Martin,* no. 49, though the word "dinosaurs" is in quotation marks.

21. Here I take a different view from Martin Rudwick, who claims that in this painting "there is no suggestion that the species of wild animals caught in the rising deluge were any

other than those on view in the newly opened gardens of the Zoological Society in London and in the menagerie attached to the great Museum of Natural History in Paris." Martin J. S. Rudwick, *Scenes from Deep Time: Early Pictorial Representations of the Prehistoric World* (Chicago: University of Chicago Press, 1992), 23–24.

22. Cuvier evidently called on Martin twice and expressed appreciation of the *Deluge* painting; see Balston, *Jonathan Martin,* 90.

23. Richard D. Altick, *The Shows of London* (Cambridge: Belknap Press, 1978), 289.

24. Mary L. Pendered, *John Martin, Painter, His Life and Times* (London: Hurst & Blackett, 1923), 231–33.

25. *Byron: Poetical Works,* ed. Frederick Page (Oxford: Oxford University Press, 1970), 521.

26. Pendered, *John Martin, Painter,* 133–34.

27. Edward Bulwer Lytton, *England and the English* (London, 1836), 261.

28. *A Descriptive Catalogue of the Engraving of The Deluge, by John Martin* (London, 1828), 3.

29. Ibid.

30. Parry, *Art of Thomas Cole,* 87.

31. Bulwer Lytton, *England and the English,* 261.

32. Rebecca Bedell, "The History of the Earth: Darwin, Geology and Landscape Art," in *Endless Forms: Charles Darwin, Natural Science and the Visual Arts,* ed. Diana Donald and Jane Munro (Cambridge: Fitzwilliam Museum; New Haven: Yale Center for British Art, 2009), 52–54.

33. Campbell, *John Martin,* no. 130.

34. Gideon Algernon Mantell, *The Wonders of Geology* (London: Relfe & Fletcher, 1838), preface.

35. Bedell, *The Anatomy of Nature,* 17.

36. See Christine Stansell and Sean Wilentz, "Cole's America," in *Thomas Cole: Landscape into History,* ed. William H. Truettner and Alan Wallach (New Haven: Yale University Press, 1994), 14.

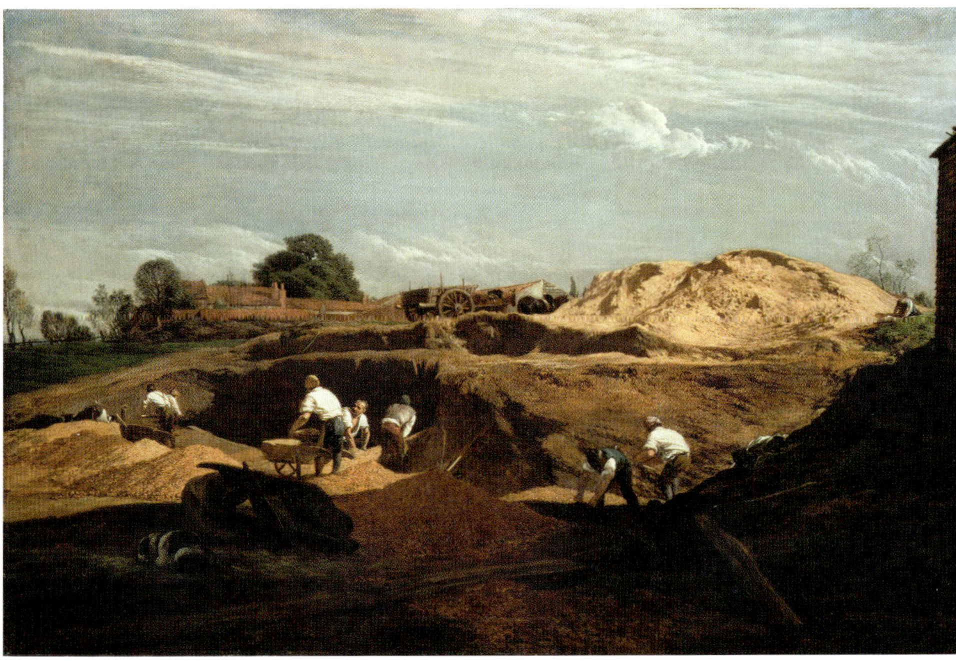

Plate 1. John Linnell, *Gravel Pits at Kensington,* 1811–12. Oil on canvas, 28 x 42 in. (71.1 x 106.7 cm). Tate Britain, © Tate, London, 2013.

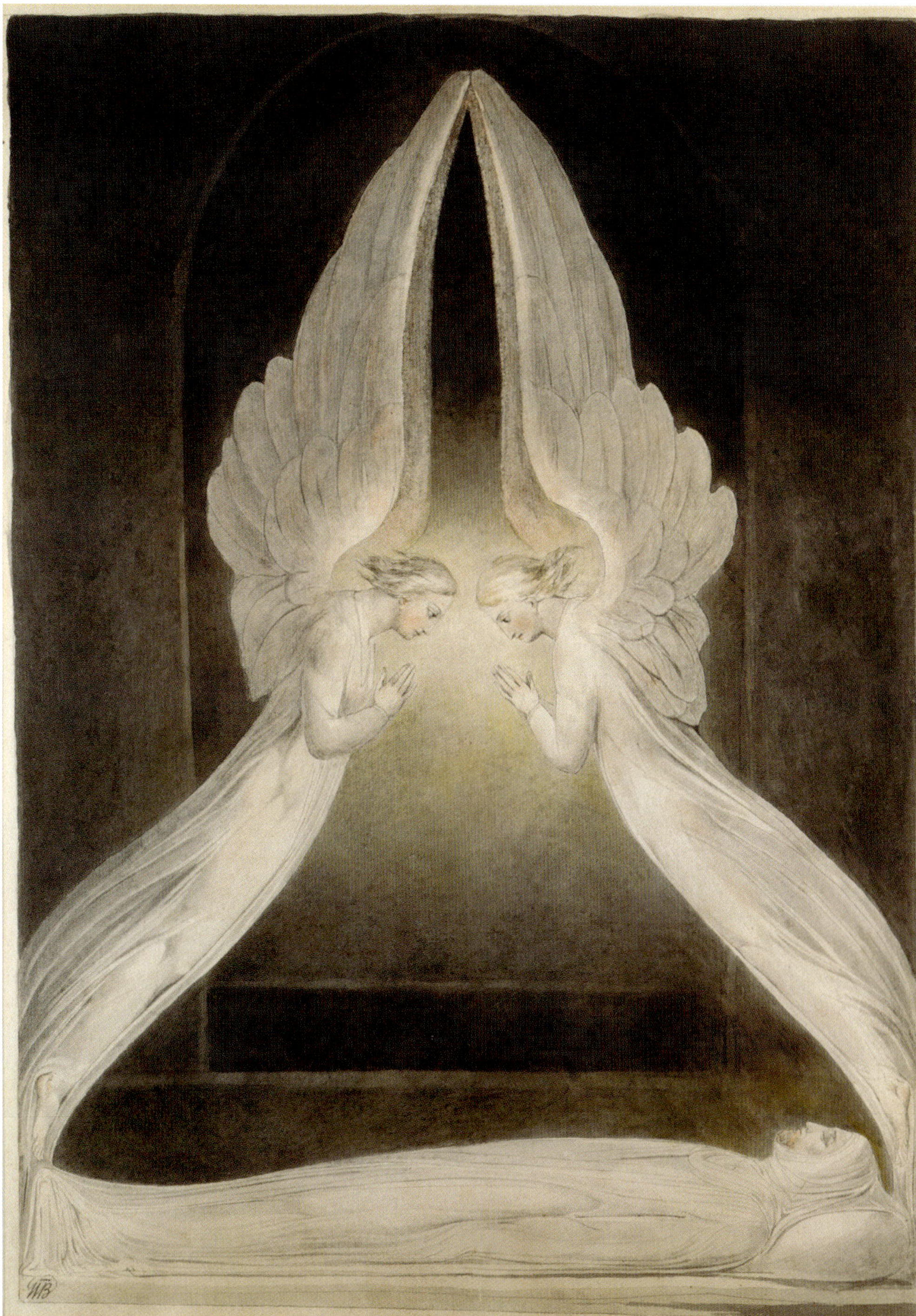

Plate 2. William Blake, *The Angels hovering over the Body of Jesus in the Sepulchre,* ca. 1805. Watercolor, pen and ink, 16½ x 12¼ in. (42.2 x 31.4 cm). Victoria and Albert Museum, London, Given by the heirs of Esmond Morse, © Victoria and Albert Museum.

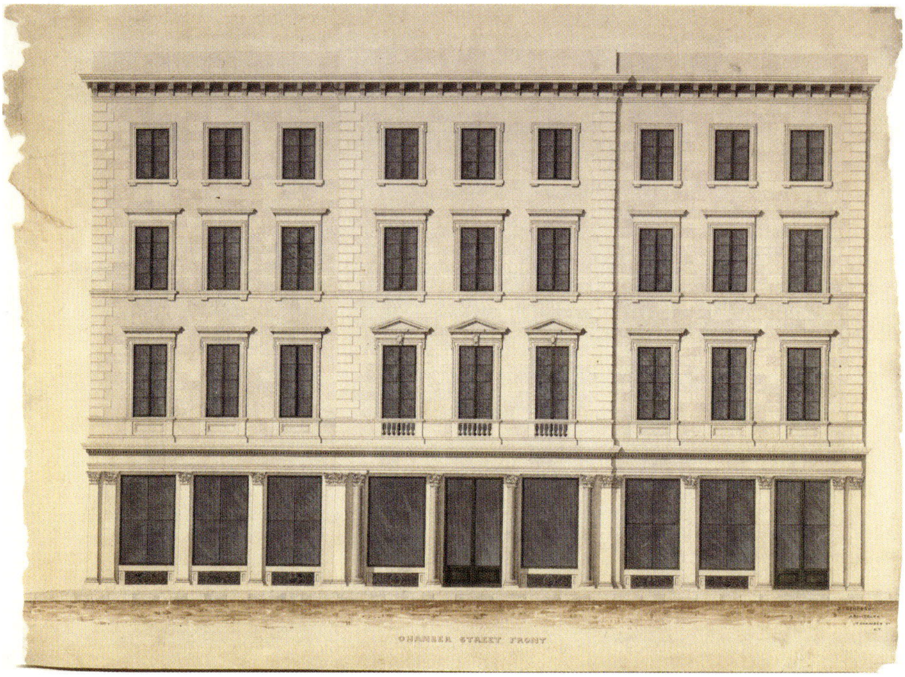


Plate 3. J. Trench & Co., elevation of A. T. Stewart store, Chambers St. front, ca. 1850. Collection of the New-York Historical Society.

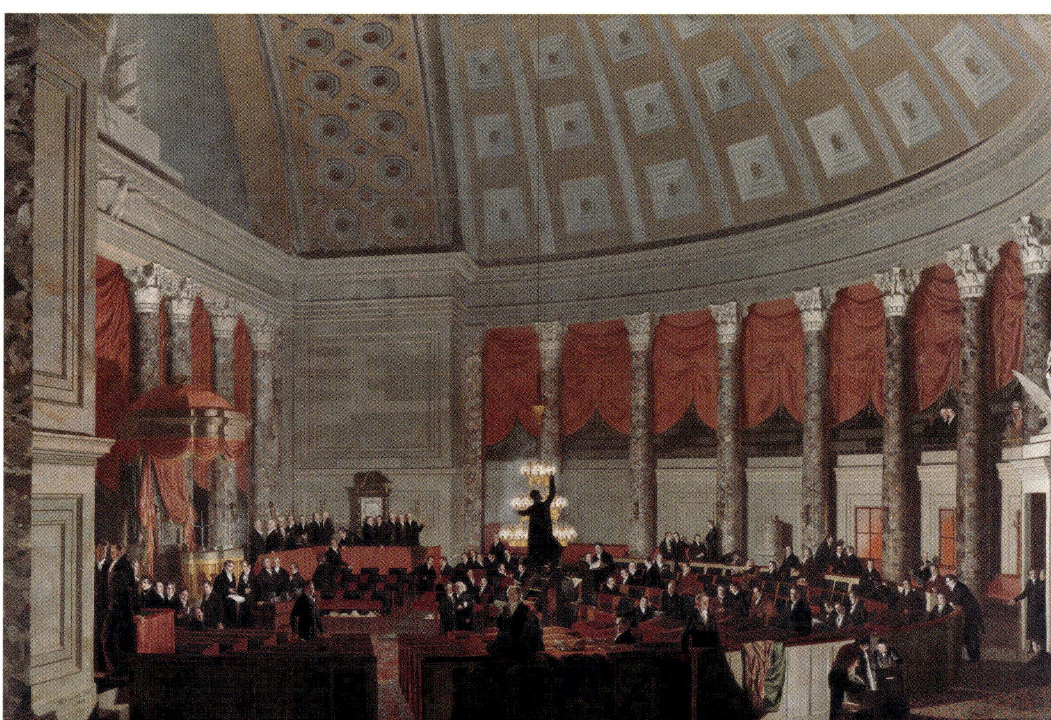

Plate 4. Samuel Finley Breese Morse, *The House of Representatives,* completed 1822, probably reworked 1823. Oil on canvas, 7 ft. 2⅞ in. x 10 ft. 10⅝ in. (2.2 x 3.2 m). Corcoran Gallery of Art, Washington, D.C., Museum purchase, Gallery Fund.

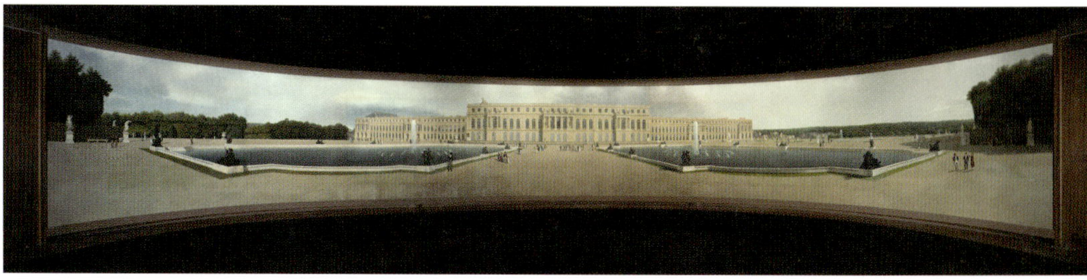

Plate 5. John Vanderlyn, *The Palace and Gardens of Versailles,* 1818–19. Oil on canvas, 12 x 165 ft. (3.6 x 49.5 m). Metropolitan Museum of Art, Gift of the Senate House Association, Kingston, N.Y. Panorama created for display in Vanderlyn's rotunda. Image © The Metropolitan Museum of Art.

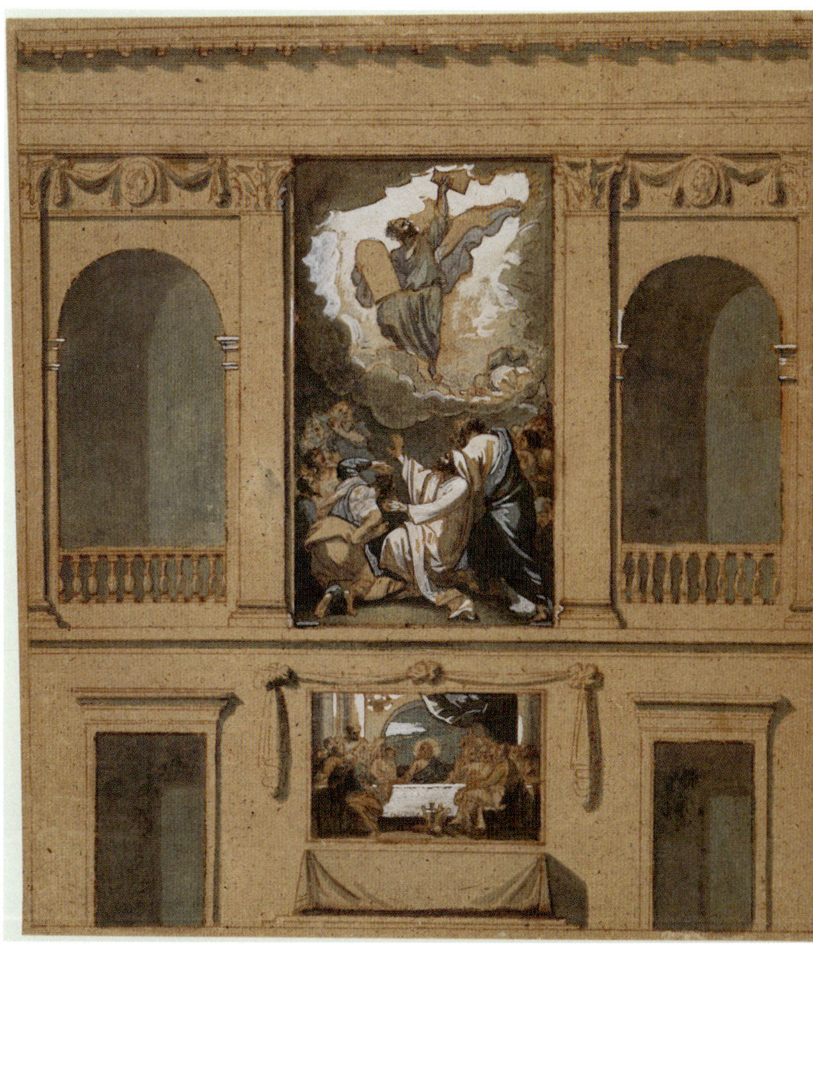

Plate 6. Benjamin West and Sir William Chambers (?), *Design for the Altar Wall of the Royal Chapel at Windsor,* ca. 1779–80. Pen and brown ink on brown paper, wash, watercolor heightened with white, 11 x 9¾ in. (27.9 x 24.8 cm). Royal Collection Trust / © Her Majesty Queen Elizabeth II, 2013.

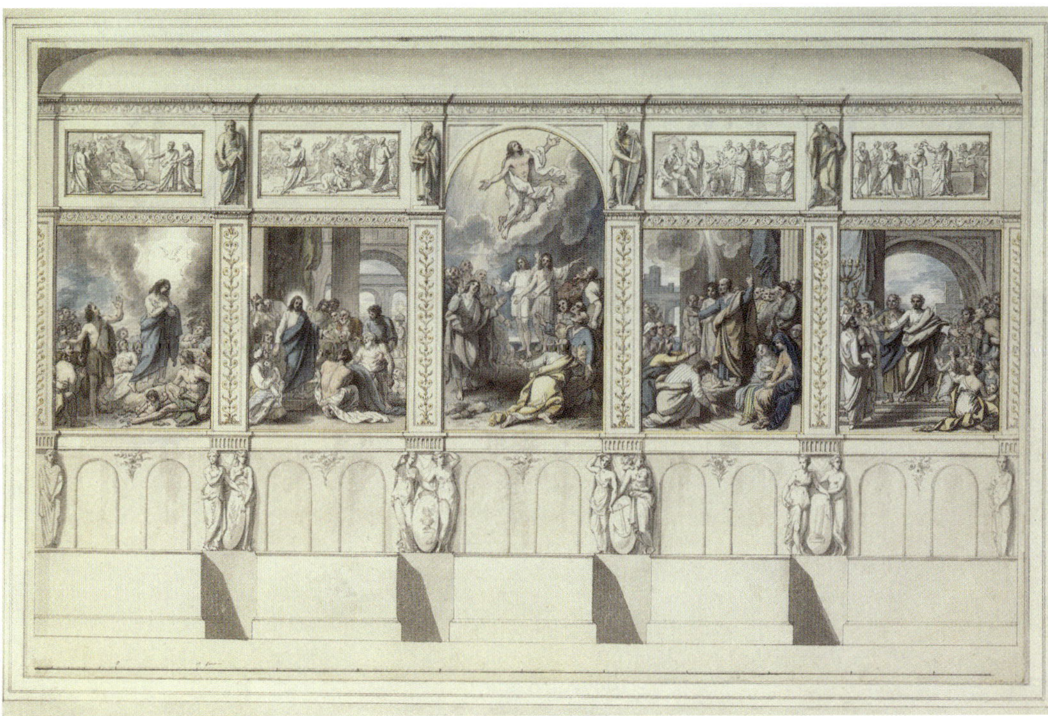

Plate 7. Benjamin West and Sir William Chambers (?), *Design for a Wall of the Royal Chapel at Windsor,* ca. 1779–80. Pen and black ink, gray wash, and watercolor, 11½ x 18⁷⁄₁₆ 7/16 in. (29.1 x 46.7 cm). Yale Center for British Art, Paul Mellon Collection.

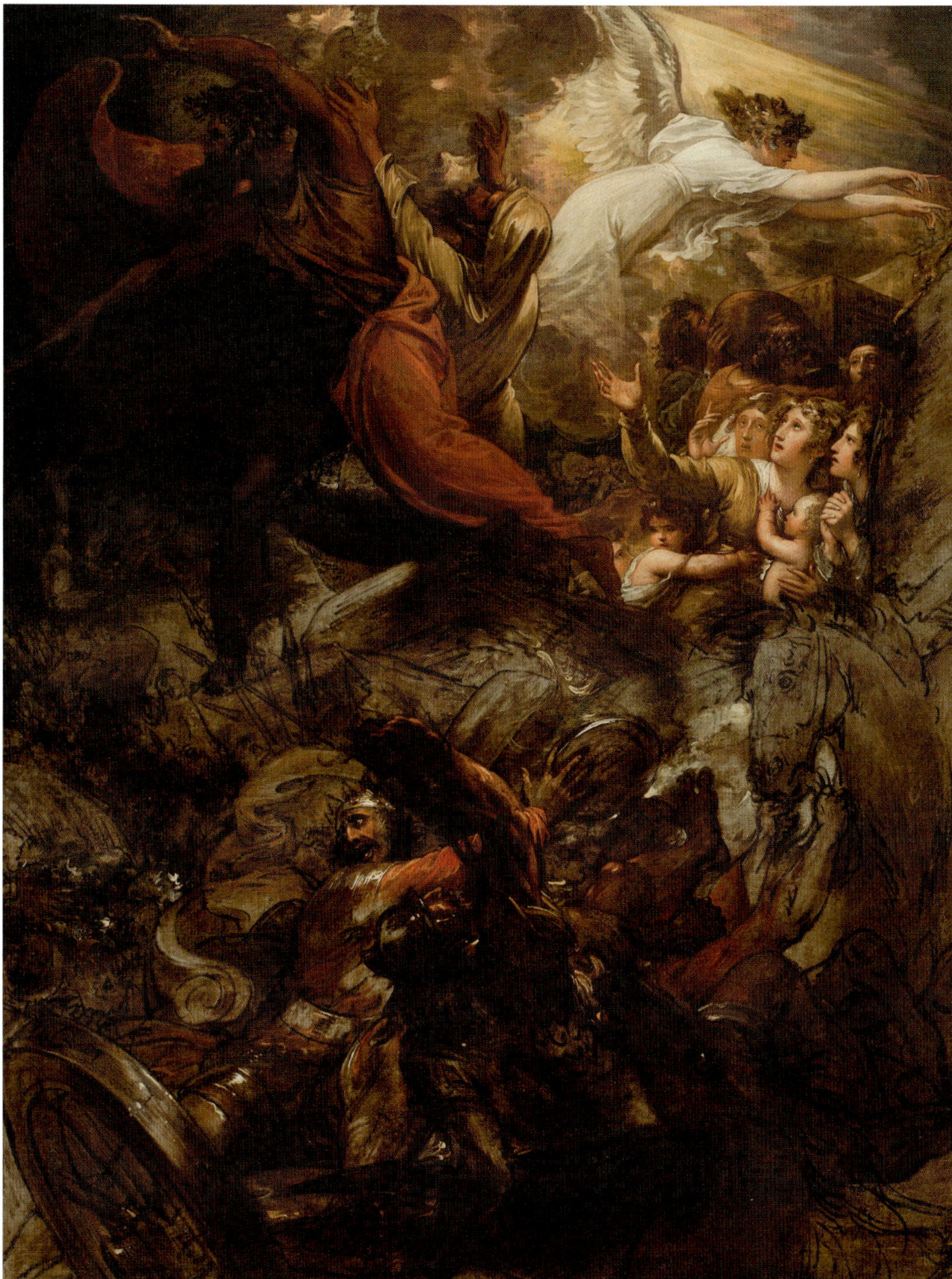

Plate 8. Benjamin West, *The Triumph of Moses over Pharaoh and His Host,* ca. 1792. Oil on canvas, 38⅛ x 30 in. (96.8 x 76.2 cm). Worcester Art Museum, Worcester, Mass., Museum Purchase, 1960.18.

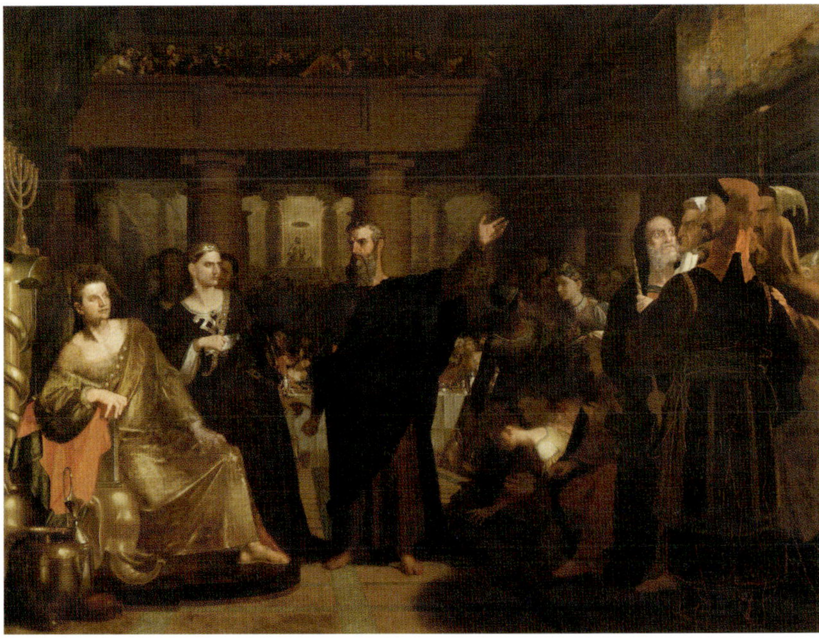

Plate 9. Washington Allston, *Belshazzar's Feast,* 1817/1843. Oil on canvas, 12 ft. ⅛ in. x 16 ft. ⅛ in. (3.66 x 4.88 m). Detroit Institute of Arts, Gift of the Allston Trust, 55.515. Photo: Detroit Institute of Arts.

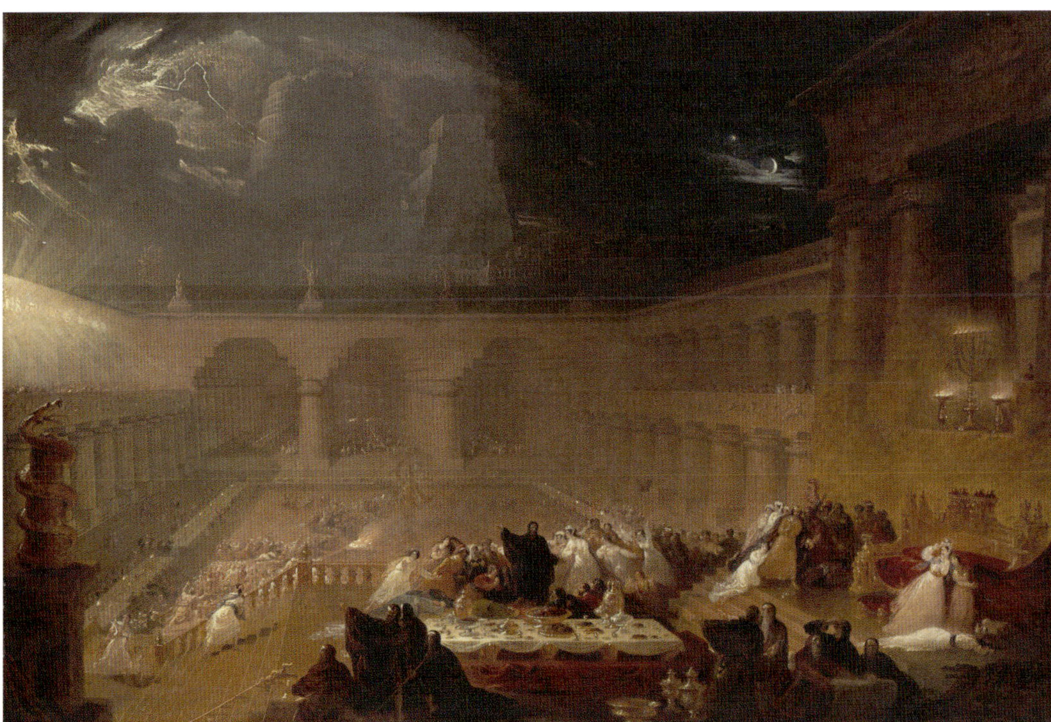

Plate 10. John Martin, *Belshazzar's Feast,* 1820. Oil on canvas, 31½ x 47½ in. (80 x 120.7 cm). Yale Center for British Art, Paul Mellon Collection, B1981.25.440. Photo: Yale Center for British Art. This is a smaller version of the picture exhibited in 1821 (160 x 249 cm), which is in a private collection.

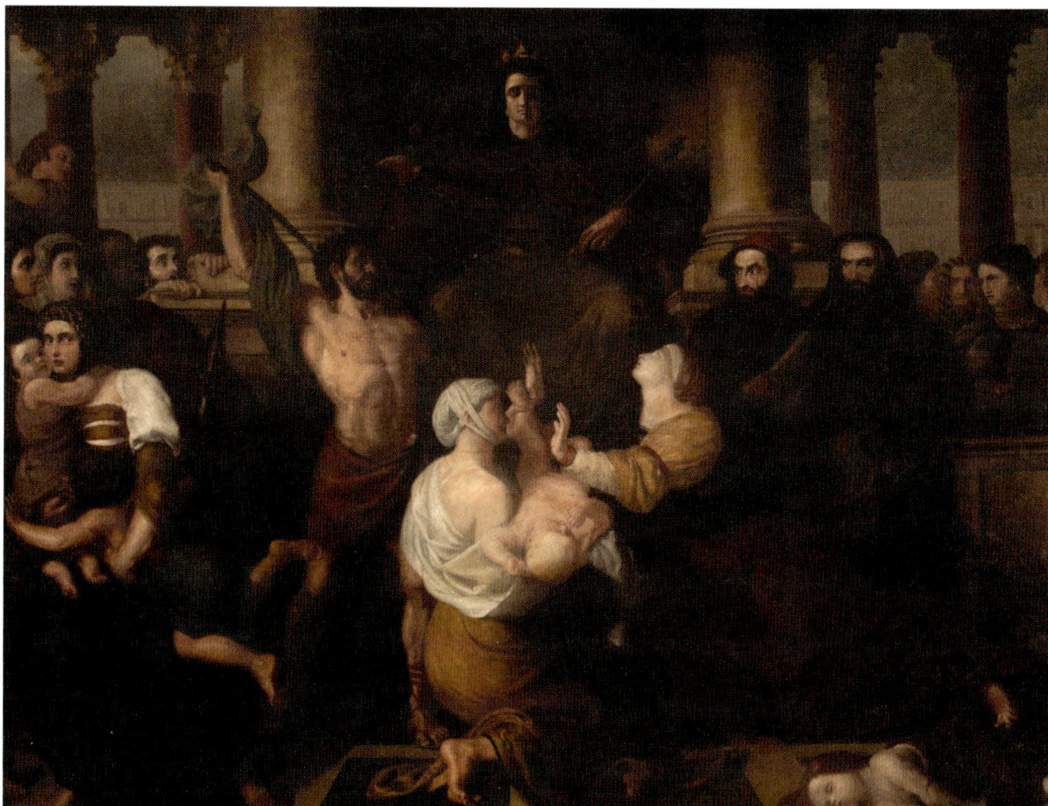

Plate 11. Benjamin Robert Haydon, *Judgment of Solomon,* 1814. Oil on canvas, 9 ft. 5 in. x 12 ft. 9½ in. (2.89 x 3.9 m). Plymouth City Council, Plymouth Museum and Art Gallery.

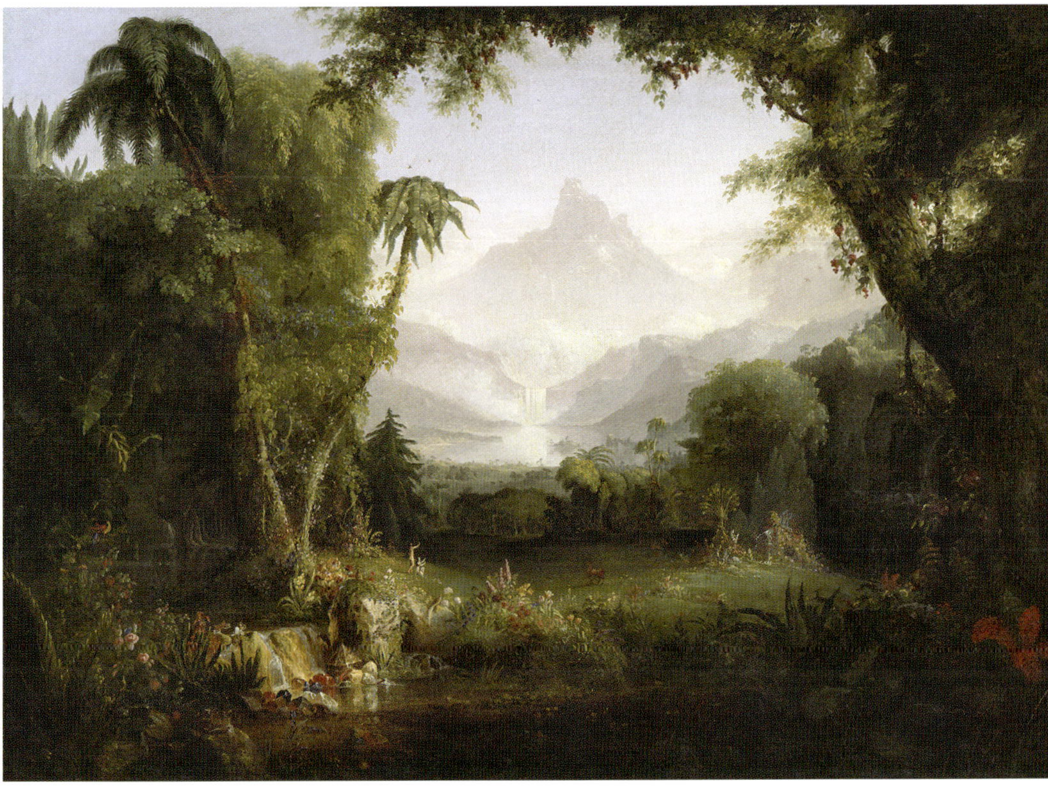

Plate 12. Thomas Cole (1801–1848), *The Garden of Eden,* 1828. Oil on canvas, 38½ x 52¾ in. (97.8 x 134 cm). Amon Carter Museum of American Art, Fort Worth, Tex., 1990.10.

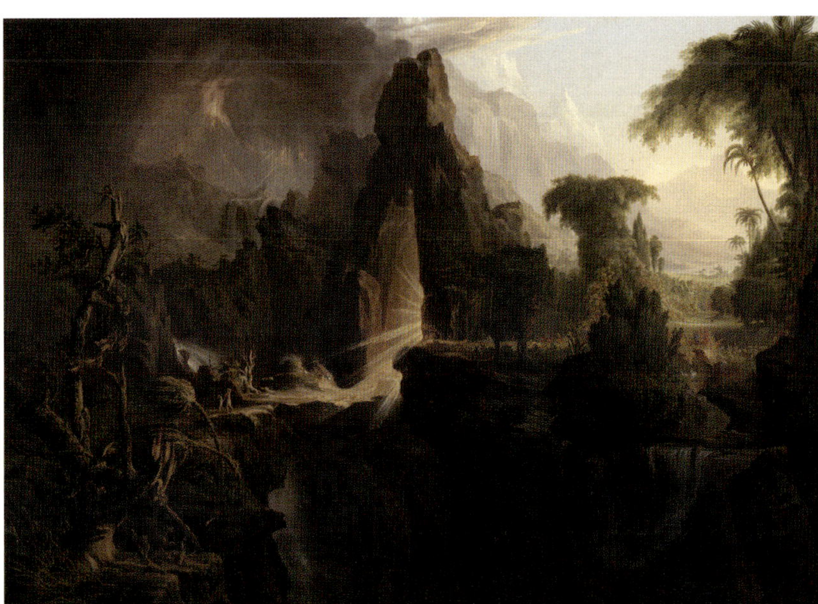

Plate 13. Thomas Cole, *Expulsion from the Garden,* 1828. Oil on canvas, 39¾ x 54½ in. (100.96 x 138.43 cm). Museum of Fine Arts, Boston, Gift of Martha C. Karolik for the M. and M. Karolik Collection of American Paintings, 1815–1865, 47.1188.

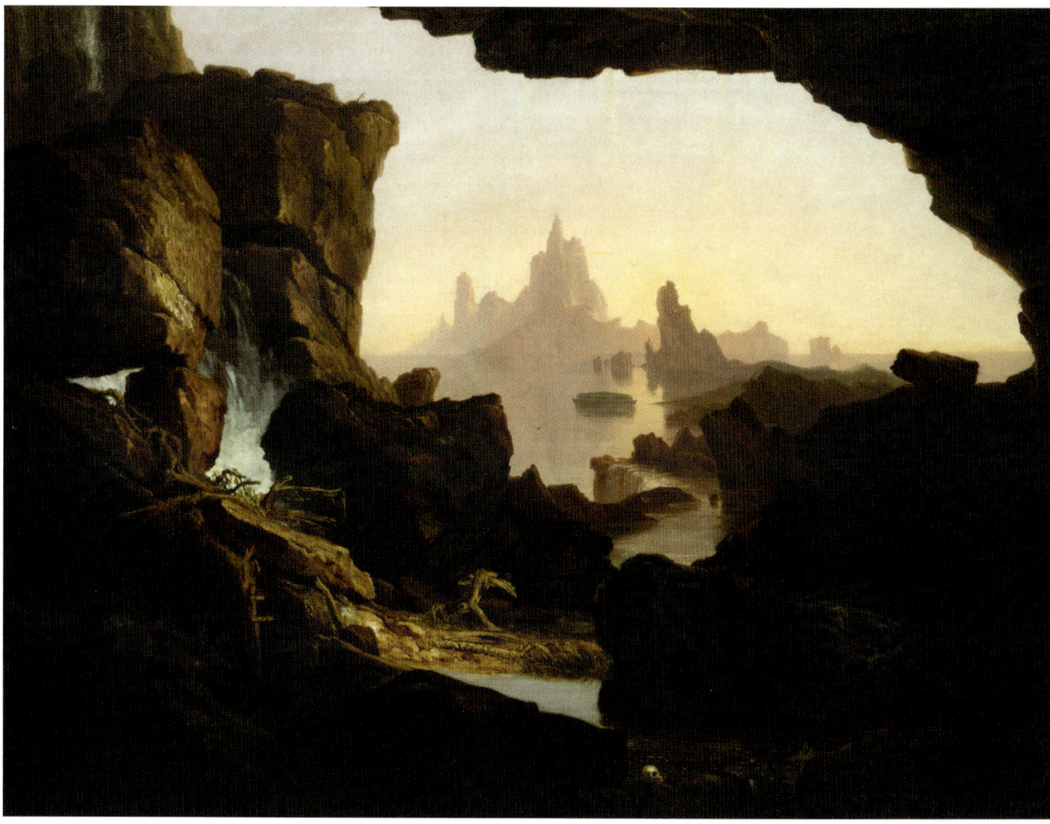

Plate 14. Thomas Cole, *The Subsiding of the Waters of the Deluge,* 1829. Oil on canvas, 35¾ x 47¾ in. (90.8 x 121.4 cm). Smithsonian American Art Museum, Washington, D.C., Gift of Mrs. Katie Dean in memory of Minnebel S. and James Wallace Dean and museum purchase through the Smithsonian Institution Collections Acquisition Program, 1983.40.

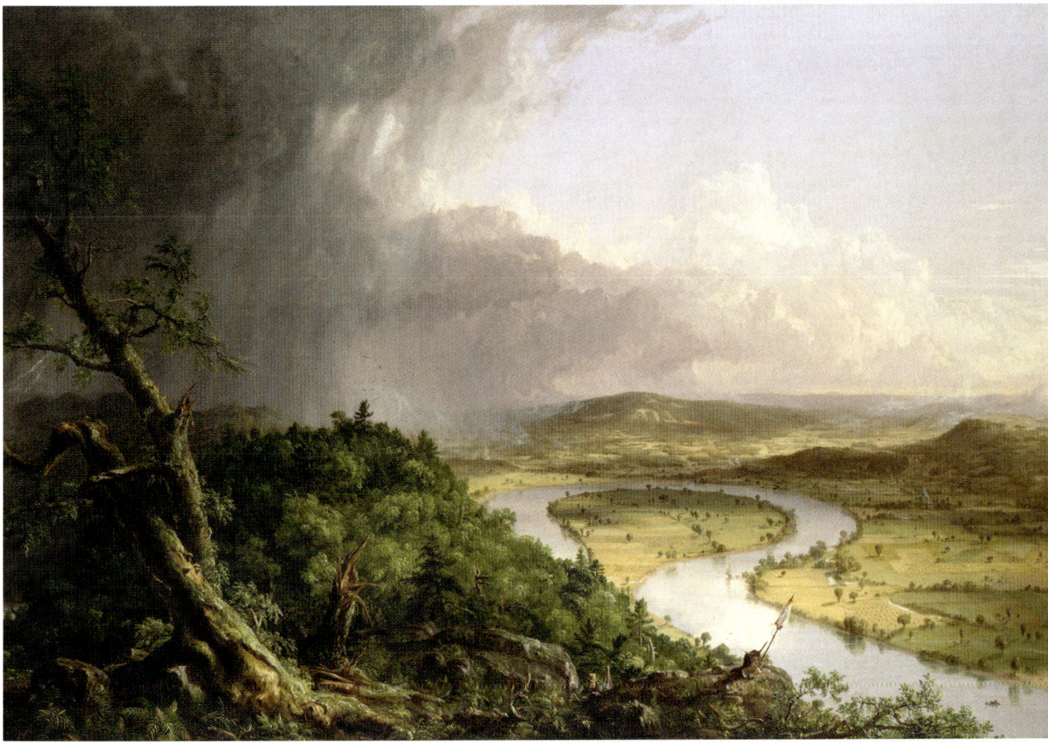

Plate 15. Thomas Cole, *View from Mount Holyoke, Northampton, Massachusetts, after a Thunderstorm—The Oxbow,* 1836. Oil on canvas, 51½ x 76 in. (130.8 x 193 cm). Gift of Mrs. Russell Sage, 1908 (08.228). The Metropolitan Museum of Art, New York. Image copyright © The Metropolitan Museum of Art. Image source: Art Resource, New York.

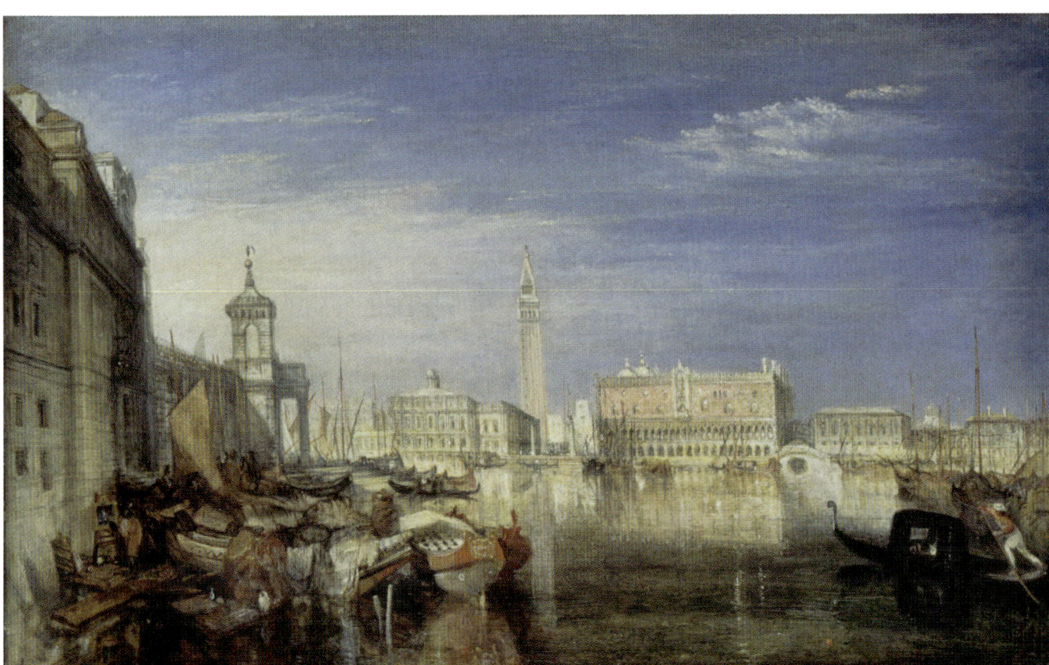

Plate 16. Joseph Mallord William Turner, *The Bridge of Sighs, Ducal Palace and Custom-House, Venice: Canaletti Painting,* 1833. Oil on canvas, 20 x 32 in. (51.1 x 61.6 cm). © Tate, London, 2013.

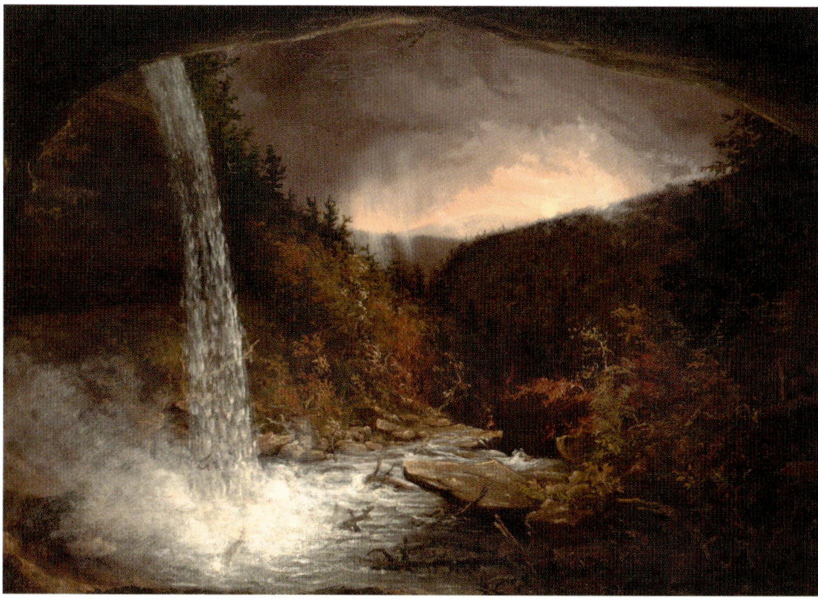

Plate 17. Thomas Cole, *Kaaterskill Falls,* 1826. Oil on canvas, 25¼ x 35⁵⁄₁₆ in. (64.1 x 89.2 cm). The Wadsworth Atheneum, Hartford, Conn., Bequest of Daniel Wadsworth, 1848.15. Photo: Wadsworth Atheneum Museum of Art/Art Resource.

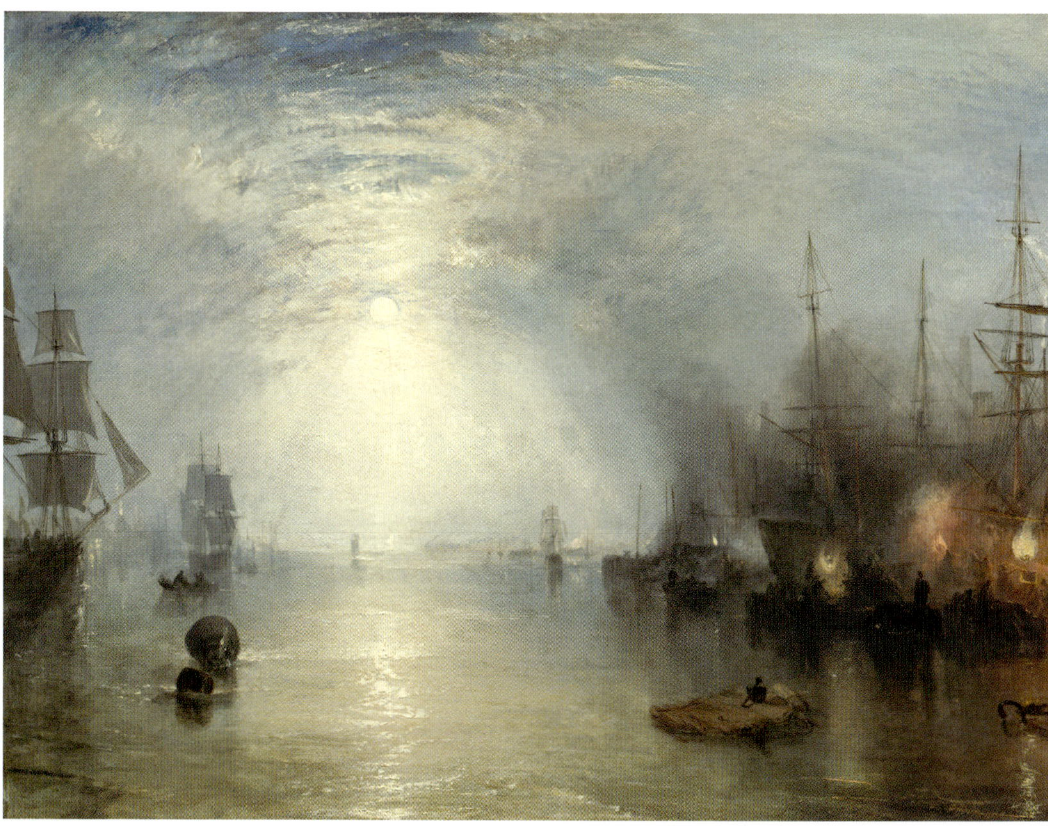

Plate 18. Joseph Mallord William Turner, *Keelmen Heaving in Coals by Moonlight,* 1835. Oil on canvas, 36⅜ x 48⅜ in. (92.3 x 122.8 cm). Widener Collection, Image courtesy National Gallery of Art, Washington, D.C.

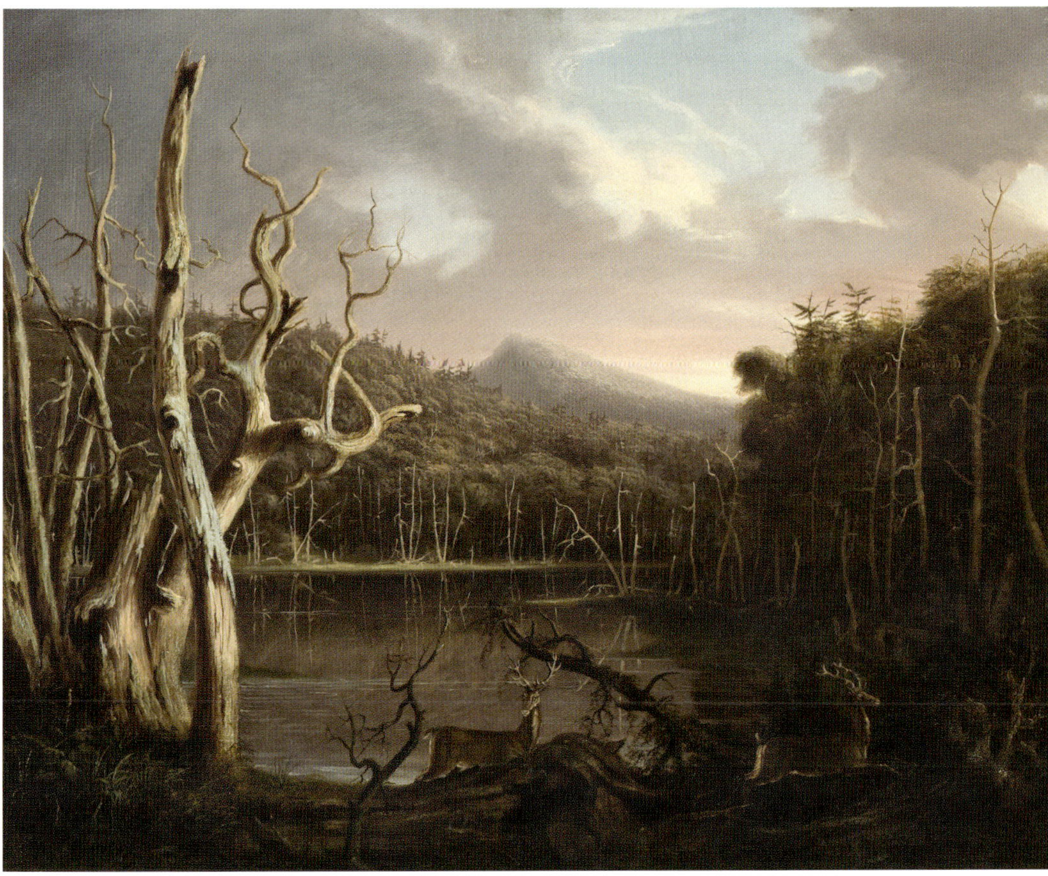

Plate 19. Thomas Cole, *Lake with Dead Trees,* 1825. Oil on canvas, 27 x 34 in. (68.6 x 86.4 cm). Allen Memorial Art Museum, Oberlin College, Gift of Charles F. Olney, 1904.

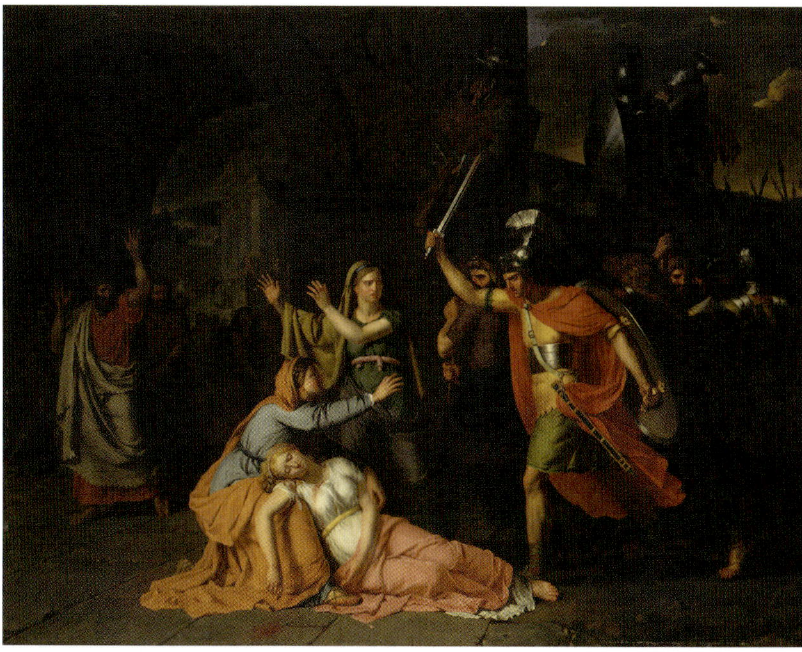

Plate 20. Anne-Louis Girodet, *Death of Camilla,* 1785. Oil on canvas, 43¾ x 58¼ in. (111 x 148 cm). Musée de Montargis, France.

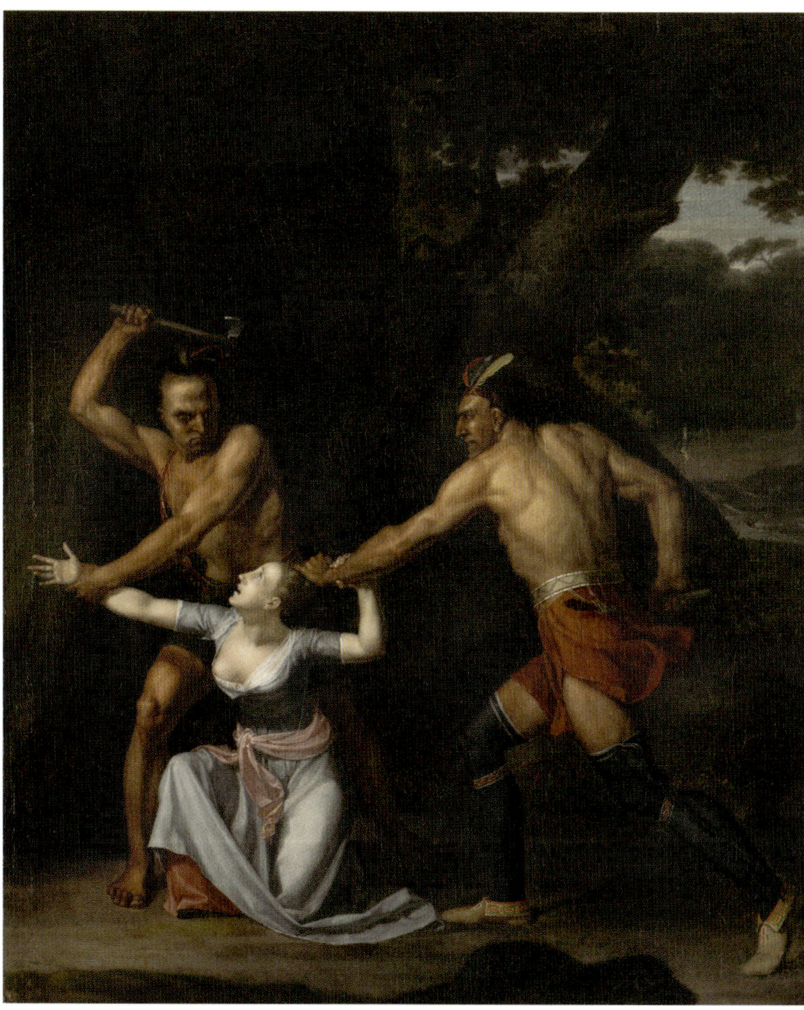

Plate 21. John Vanderlyn, *The Murder of Jane McCrea,* 1804. Oil on canvas, 32½ x 26½ in. (82.4 x 67.3 cm). Wadsworth Atheneum, Hartford, Conn.

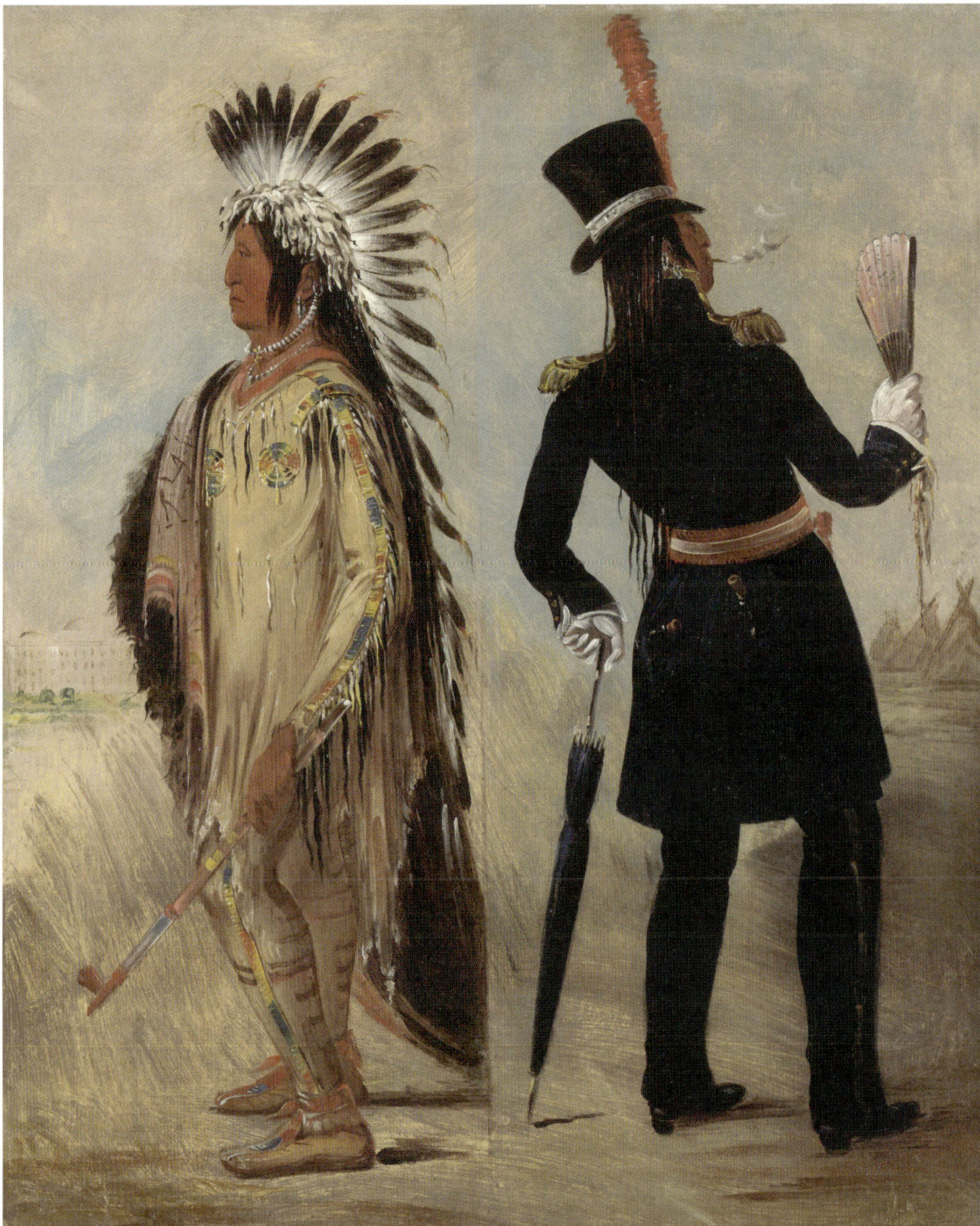

Plate 22. George Catlin, *Wi-jún-jon, Pigeon's Egg Head (The Light) Going to and Returning from Washington*, 1837–1839. Oil on canvas, 29 x 24 in. (74.7 x 61.0 cm). Smithsonian American Art Museum, Washington, D.C.

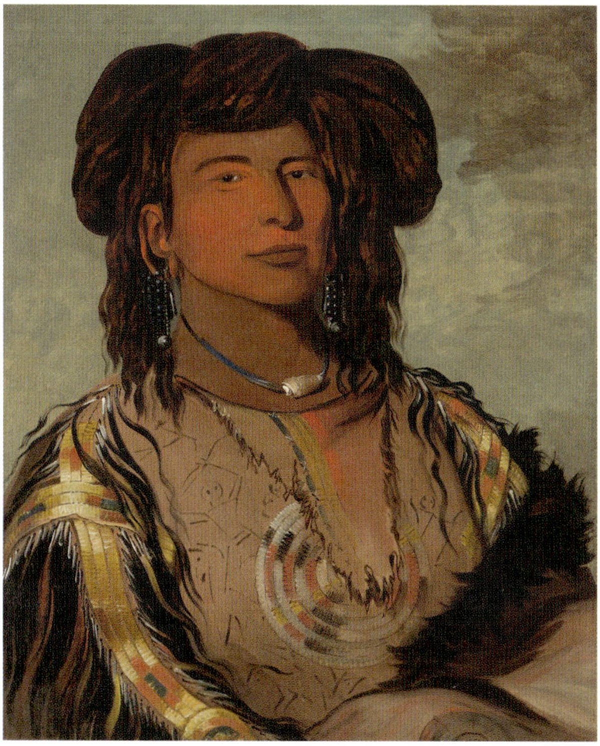

Plate 23. George Catlin, *Ha-wón-je-tah, One Horn, Head Chief of the Miniconjou Tribe.* Oil on canvas, 29 x 24 in. (73.7 x 60.9 cm). Smithsonian American Art Museum, Gift of Mrs. Joseph Harrison Jr., 1985.66.69.

Plate 24. George Catlin, *Kee-o-kuk, The Watchful Fox, Chief of the Tribe, on Horseback.* Oil on canvas 29 x 24 in. (73.7 x 6 0.9 cm), Smithsonian American Art Museum, Gift of Mrs. Joseph Harrison Jr., 1985.66.1A.

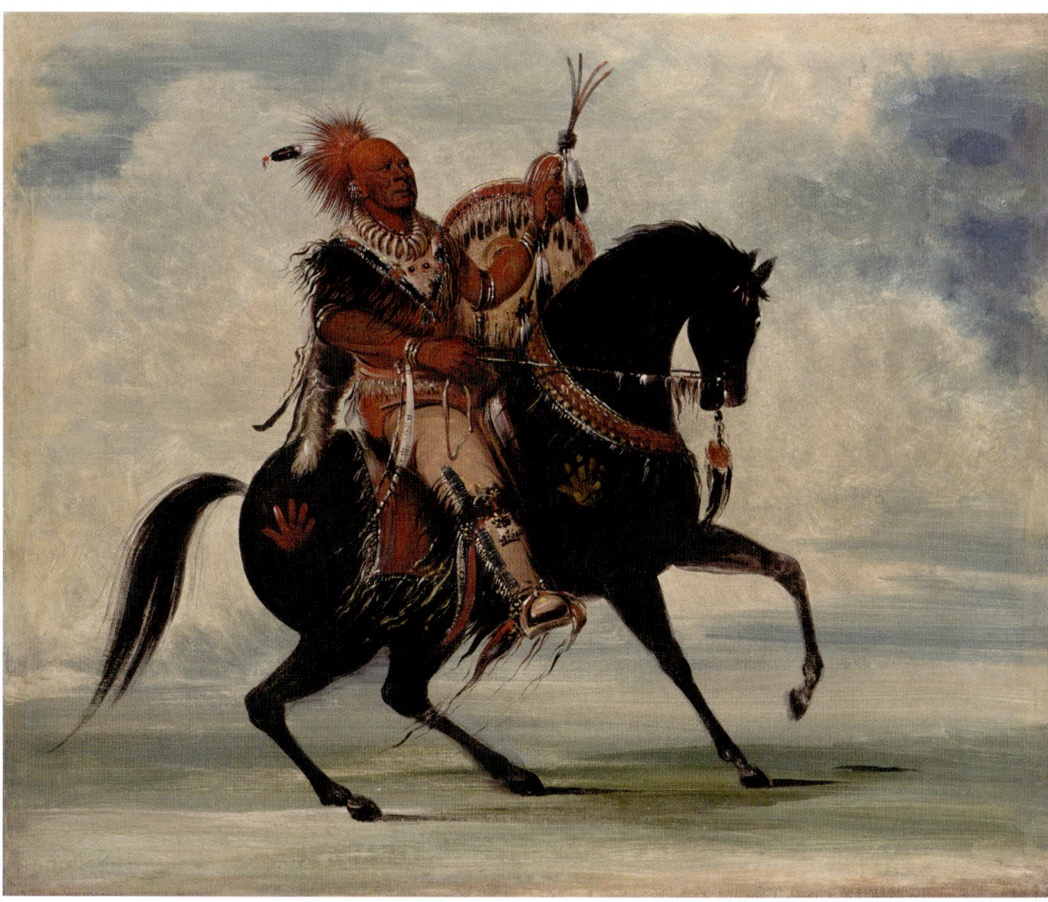

# 9

# "Gorgeous, but altogether false"

## Turner, Cole, and Transatlantic Ideas of Decline

*Leo Costello*

Writing to Charles Eliot Norton, John Ruskin once declared: "I profoundly think it useless for Americans to look at Turner. He is English to the sole of his foot."[1] The remark is unusually harsh for Ruskin in the context of this correspondence, even though elsewhere he had teased Norton about America's unfitness as a source for either art or its appreciation, wondering whether any kind of art might emerge amidst the rattlesnakes and bears of such an "ugly" country.[2] But it is useful to me here because it indicates the degree to which, from a very early point, national identity has been understood as central to the production and reception of Romantic landscape art.

Indeed, an ongoing concern with national identity has often precluded other kinds of more searching analyses into the issues raised by the work of American and British Romantic landscape painters in the first half of the nineteenth century. In this essay, therefore, I attempt to reopen some of these questions by comparing aspects of Turner's work to that of his younger contemporary Thomas Cole. In particular, I revisit Cole's own statements about Turner's work, made during his stay in London in 1829–30. Typically these comments have been understood within a model of the emergence of Cole's own artistic identity and that of American art as a whole as it began to take shape as a distinct school separate from European influences. I show that they also offer a means of investigating how formal issues can be opened onto a discussion of matters of empire, progress, class, and artistic identity. In so doing, I wish to indicate some of the ways in which we may seek insight into a Romantic *Weltanschauung*, as discussed by Andrew Hemingway in the introduction to this volume in a way that augments the nationalist framework within which Cole and Turner have traditionally been compared. As Hemingway says there, New York and London ultimately share a determinant status as "capitalist metropolises."

When Cole arrived in London in June 1829, Turner was already established for Americans as a dominant figure in modern European painting and the first name in the English school. Washington Allston had advised Cole, through an intermediary, to look in particular at Turner, as had Cole's patron Robert Gilmor. Not surprisingly, Cole attended closely to Turner's work at the Royal Academy exhibition that summer. He made pencil sketches (fig. 9.1) of Turner's *Ulysses Deriding Polyphemus* (1829),[3] carefully noting the colors of the blazing sunset, and twice adding the seemingly unnecessary label/signature "Turner" at the bottom of his sheet. Cole can hardly have expected to forget the picture's author, so the repeated signature acts as part reinscription and part appropriation of the authoritative name of the artist-father. This sense of Turner as a kind of paternal authority figure may go some way toward explaining Cole's disillusionment at meeting Turner in his studio in December of that same year. Writing privately, the younger artist expressed disappointment at not finding Turner more worthy of reverence, more paternal: "I had expected to see an older looking man, with a countenance pale with thought; but I was entirely mistaken."[4] Cole also assessed Turner's appearance in tellingly classed terms, comparing him to "a seafaring man, a mate of a coasting vessel, and his manners in accordance with his appearance."[5] Such responses to Turner were not uncommon. Delacroix famously remembered him as having "the look of an English farmer, black coat of a rather coarse type, thick shoes—and a cold, hard face."[6]

Writing in a more official voice to Gilmor, however, Cole was more circumspect and still had much to praise in Turner's work, noticing in particular the *View of the Temple of Jupiter Panellenius* (1816, B&J 134), which he thought "as fine as anything the world has produced," and *Dido building Carthage; or the Rise of the Carthaginian Empire* (1815, fig. 9.2), which he called "a splendid composition, and full of poetry. . . . The figures, vessels, &c., are all very appropriate. The composition resembles very closely some of Claude's. The colour is fine, and the effect of the sunshine excellent. . . ."[7] As a number of critics had done when *Dido building Carthage* was shown the previous decade, Cole praised both the picture's representation of nature and its poetic/narrative qualities. But also in Turner's studio at this point were more recent productions such as *Dido directing the Equipment of the Fleet, or The Morning of the Carthaginian Empire* (1828, B&J 241) and *Boccaccio relating the Tale of the Birdcage* (1828, B&J 244), and Cole reacted very differently to these. Citing "a great falling off," Cole told Gilmor that the pictures were "the strangest things imaginable."[8] He elaborated in his notebook: "When

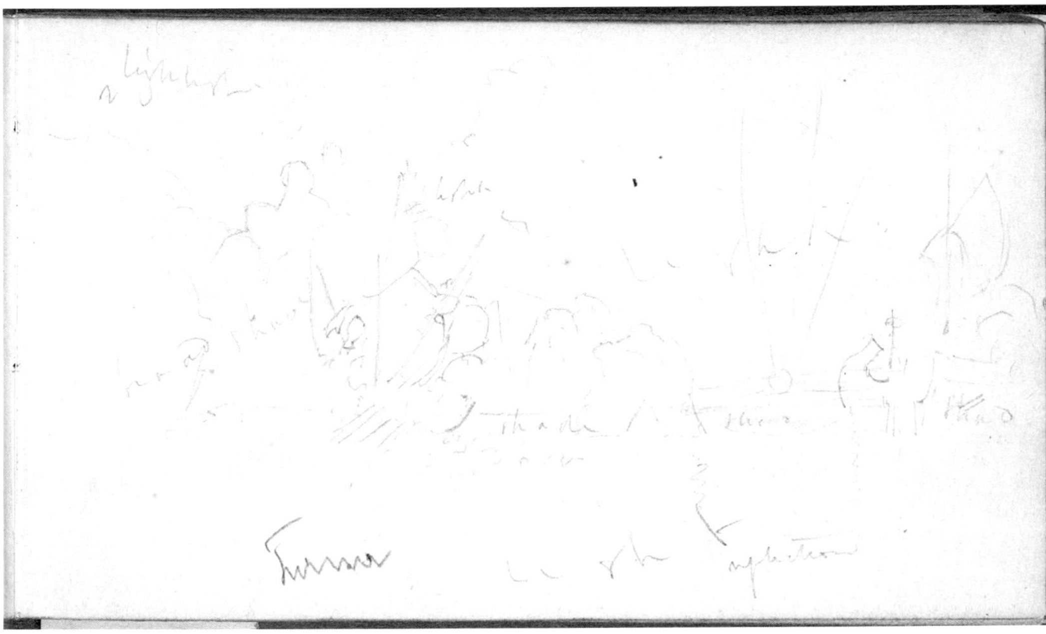

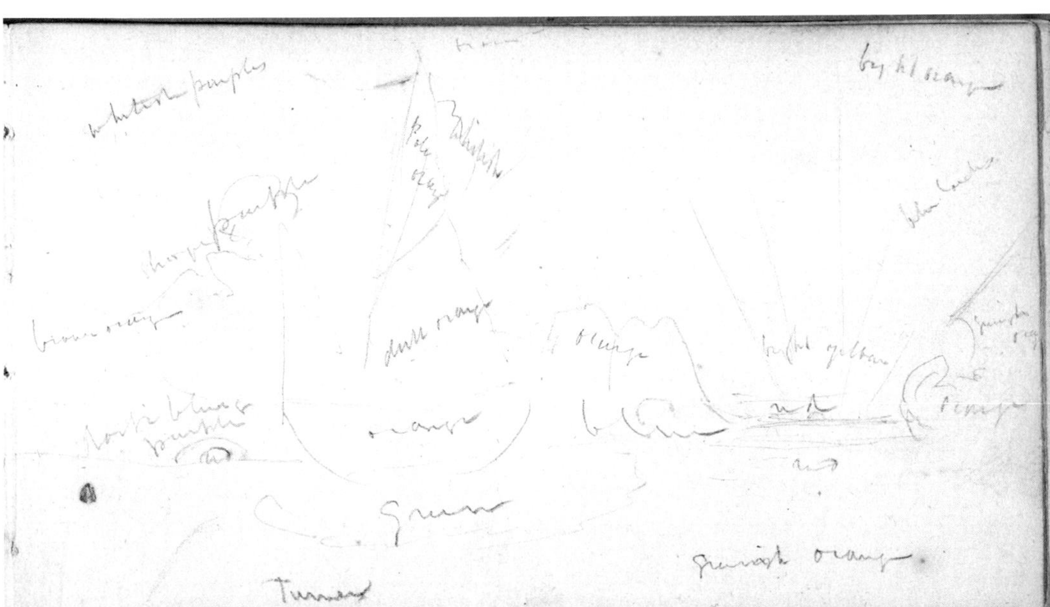

Figure 9.1. Thomas Cole, *Untitled,* 1829. Pencil on paper, each image 3½ x 6½ in (8.9 x 16.5 cm). Detroit Institute of Arts, USA / Founders Society Purchase, William H. Murphy Fund / The Bridgeman Art Library.

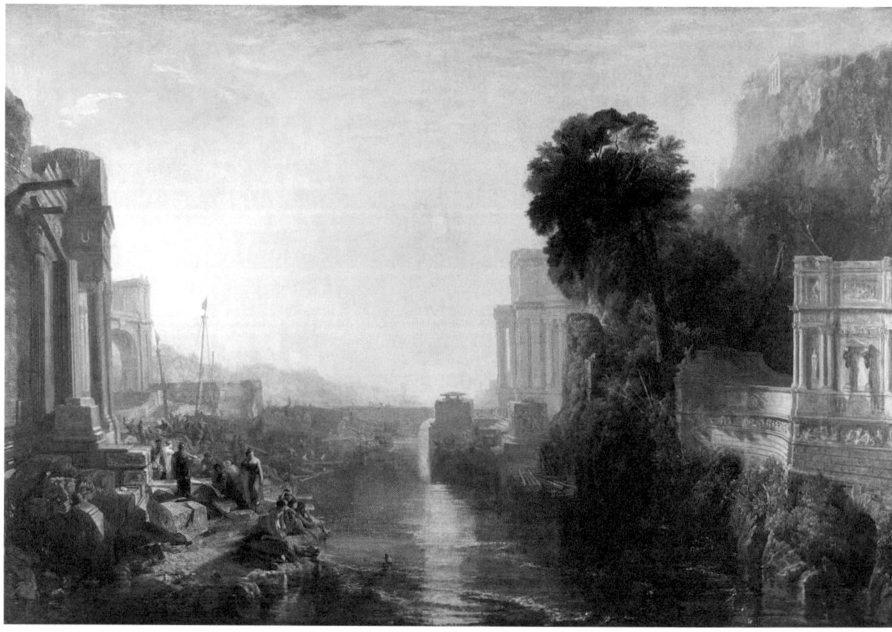

Figure 9.2. Joseph Mallord William Turner, *Dido Building Carthage, or The Rise of the Carthaginian Empire,* 1815. Oil on canvas, 61¼ x 90½ in. (155.6 x 229.9 cm). National Gallery, London, Turner Bequest, 1856. © The National Gallery, London.

considered separately from the subject, they are splendid compositions of colour. But they are destitute of all appearance of solidity: all appears transparent and soft, and reminds one of jellies and confections."[9] Cole, perhaps more confident now, but also self-conscious in crafting his own public identity, went still further in a letter printed by William Dunlap in 1834, calling Turner "the prince of evil spirits." Cole criticized Turner's recent work for sacrificing the balance between nature and art that he had admired in the earlier pictures: "With imagination and a deep knowledge of the machinery of his art, he has produced some surprising specimens of effect. His early pictures are really beautiful and true, though rather misty; but in his late works you see the most splendid combinations of color and chiaroscuro—gorgeous but altogether false—there is a visionary, unsubstantial look about them that, for some subjects, is admirably appropriate; but in pictures, representing scenes in this world, rocks should not look like sugar candy, nor the ground like jelly."[10]

Because of the biographical foundation of so much of the work on Cole, starting with Dunlap, these comments are most often treated in terms of Cole's own progression from a self-tutored artist into the father of American art, and one suspects that this sense of emerging independence is exactly what Cole had in mind in writing thus to Dunlap. The subtly Freudian aspect of Cole's comments here is useful because it suggests an artist coming into his own by defining himself against a rejected senior figure. He claimed a kind of willful individualism in resisting Turner's critical reputation in favor of the direct relationship to nature that would be the basis of his claims to originality: "These opinions of existing English art, I know, may be considered heterodox; but I will venture them, because I believe them correct. The standard by which I form my judgment is—beautiful nature; and if I am astray, it is on a path which I have taken for that of truth."[11] In the first place, Cole's very conventional sense of chiaroscuro and form may have been challenged by Turner's innovative mid-career practice. Even more, despite his strategic claims to heterodoxy, Cole's comments were in fact thoroughly conventional and closely matched a strain in Turner's critical reception in England which stressed the undoubted brilliance of Turner's facility with paint but similarly divided his effects from the natural and the true, as well as from comprehensible subject matter. An anonymous reviewer for *The Times* called the *Dido* and *Boccaccio* "extremely beautiful and powerful" but "like nothing in nature" and said that *Dido* "might as well be called anything else."[12] Even more important, critics also shared Cole's view that Turner's recent work marked a decline from his earlier pictures. Indeed, Cole had arrived in Turner's studio at an awkward moment in the artist's career. The period after his return from an Italian trip in 1819–20 produced a growing critical discomfort with his new commitment to Mediterranean light, which seemed to many critics to produce an excess of yellow tones and dramatic atmospheric effects.

As a result of these changes, critics increasingly lamented the passing of Turner's greatness into a style they called "gaudy," "mannered," and "extravagant." Speaking of *Mortlake Terrace, the Seat of William Moffat, Esq. Summer's Evening* (1827, B&J 239), for instance, *John Bull*'s critic compared Turner to a cook with an obsession for curry and complained, "When we look back at the work of Turner, of some twenty or five and twenty years standing, and see nature in all her healthfulness glowing under his powerful hand, it really makes us as sick as she looks in his pictures now to see so sad, so needless a falling off."[13] The rhetoric of disease and bodily deterioration used here is one that would recur often in Turner's reception. By the mid-1830s, decline had become a common cry among critics, who routinely claimed that the tragedy was not even so much Turner's disregard for subject, natural appearance, and drawing but the loss of those qualities from his earlier, great work. The re-exhibition of earlier works often prompted these laments. On seeing *Apullia in Search of Appullus vide Ovid* (1814, fig. 9.3) and other early works on display in Turner's gallery in 1835, an anonymous reviewer for *The Spectator* in essence repeated Cole's verdict, writing, "These pictures are finished with the utmost care; and the effect is proportionately real and beautiful. We wish Turner would return to the sober beauty and elaborate truth of his earlier works, and cease to 'gild refined gold and paint the lily.' "[14]

While it is not unusual for a rhetoric of decline to be mobilized in regard to the later work of an aging artist, what makes this particularly notable in Turner's case is not just its pervasiveness but the fact that such a discourse had existed for much of Turner's career already. In a review of 1820, for instance, *Annals of the Fine Arts*—a magazine not overly friendly to landscape painting at the best of times—could already describe the progression of Turner's career as a descent into mannerism: "The earlier works of Turner before he visited Rome, and those which he has done since, for this collection, are like works by a different artist. The former, natural, simple and effective; the latter, artificial, glaring and affected." Turner, the reviewer concluded, "should really look back at some of these works, and keep nearer to their truth, than to run riot, as he now does, after a thousand yellow fantasies and crimson conceits."[15] Reviewers of the 1840s, by which time Turner was in his sixties, often connected his advancing age to a decline leading to increased looseness of handling and incomprehensible subject matter. But even this discourse of age and decline had been voiced as early as 1806, when he had been exhibiting

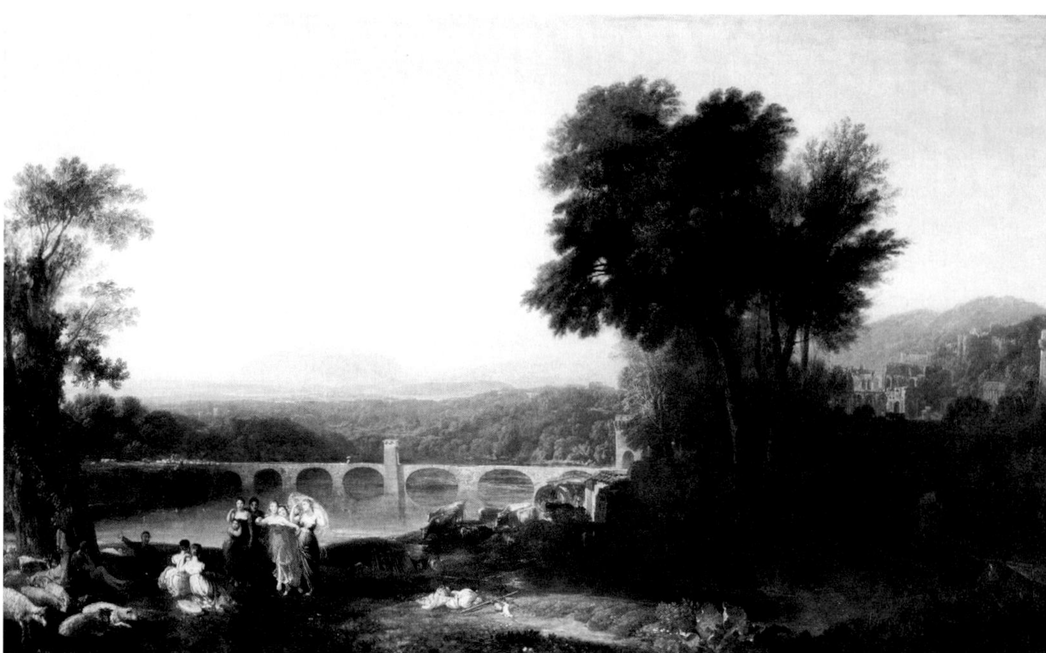

Figure 9.3. Joseph Mallord William Turner, *Apullia in Search of Appullus,* 1814. Oil on canvas, 58½ x 95 in. (48.5 x 241 cm). © Tate, London, 2013.

for less than a decade. Joseph Farington reports that the conservative painter and connoisseur Sir George Beaumont had said that Turner's pictures at the British Institution that year, such as *The Goddess of Discord choosing the Apple of Contention in the Garden of the Hesperides* (B&J 57) and *The Battle of Trafalgar, as seen from the Mizen Starboard Shrouds of the Victory* (B&J 58), "appeared to Him to be like the works of an *old man* who had ideas but had lost his power of execution."[16] Thus, while Ruskin would place Turner's overall career within a model of rise and fall that hinged on the 1829 *Ulysses,* Cole, at the very moment of that picture, placed Turner within an already elaborated, but still emerging, model of an artist who had been in a state of decline for much of his career.[17] What these critics were suggesting was that even when Turner's genius was evident, it was a genius better suited to un-forming than forming, better applied to taking things apart than putting them together, a paradoxical creation of disintegration rather than of unity. Beaumont suggested as much when he connected the innovations of young painters like Turner to a broader destruction of tradition and order, declaring that "that harmony and modesty which distinguishes great masters is not seen, —but crudeness and bravura are substituted." He further called these artists an "influenza" and concluded, "The British school is affected by it."[18] In another letter Beaumont connected this approach to progressive politics, sarcastically observing that these young artists have "the sagacity to discover that in politics, poetry and painting all that has hitherto been done is fit only for the flames."[19]

Such laments about Turner's innovations were connected to broader concerns over the state of the British school as a whole, which were in turn rooted in a larger set of social anxieties. As John Barrell has demonstrated, in 1800, at the very beginning of Turner's career, the Royal Academy was already considered by some to have failed in its task of consolidating a style of painting that would create unity amidst the increasing complexity, division of labor, and prevalent self-interest of a commercial society.[20] Part of this failure had to do with the fundamentally commercial nature of the Academy, which seemed to many to be more concerned with generating income for its artists than promoting painting that would benefit the nation as a whole. Henry Fuseli voiced these concerns in one of his lectures as professor of painting, saying:

> We have now been in possession of an Academy more than half a century; all the intrinsic means of forming a style alternate at our commands. . . . And what is the result? If we apply to our Exhibition, what does it present, in the aggregate, but a gorgeous display of varied powers, condemned, if not to the beasts, at least to the dictates of fashion and vanity? What, therefore, can be urged against the conclusion, that, as far as the public is concerned, the art is sinking, and threatens to sink still deeper, from the want of demand for great and significant works?[21]

The point to emphasize here is Fuseli's invocation of a decline in both art and taste, an idea that was mobilized particularly in respect to the exhibitions. Fuseli notes exactly the combination of technical genius and lack of a higher moral goal that would be applied to Turner by Cole and others. Exhibitions were a source of particular ambivalence, because there was widespread concern that artists were competing with one another for the attention of a commercial audience, rather than with the Old Masters for the glory of the nation and art as a whole. In his Fifth Discourse, Sir Joshua Reynolds had prominently warned artists against being seduced by "an ambition of pleasing indiscriminately the mixed multitude" of the exhibition,[22] and later Martin Archer Shee, who would later be president of the Royal Academy, took up this theme in his 1809 *Elements of Art.* Exhibition, Shee wrote, can be "the spur of Genius," but can mislead the artist toward self-interest "if it quickens to the profitable rather than the praise-worthy: if in short, it prompts to a contention of meretricious allurements rather than of modest merit."[23]

Over the course of his career, the kinds of dramatic effects, high-key colors, and loose painting style Cole and others mentioned with respect to Turner were connected to his desire to appeal to this "mixed multitude" by attracting attention to himself at exhibitions, and to seek his own fortune and reputation at the expense of the British school as a whole. By the 1820s and 1830s, this theme was picked up mainly by conservative critics lamenting the intrusion of the commercial values and classes into the spaces of high culture. Most well known in this regard is the Reverend John Eagles, writing for *Blackwood's Edinburgh Magazine,* whose diatribes against Turner emerged in a larger environment of social change in the wake of the 1832 Reform Bill. Like many of the critics we have already seen, Eagles at times, and rather disingenuously one suspects, acknowledged elements of greatness in Turner's work of the past, but felt that he had renounced the just cause of art in favor of a crude appeal to the crowd. In his review of the 1835 exhibition, he pointedly accused Turner of seeking novelty and effect simply to maintain his popularity. "Why," he asks, "for the sake of this trickery fame, will Turner persist in throwing the gauze of flimsy novelty over his genius, as great as it is?"[24] Cole expressed the same concerns about the English school as a whole, writing to Dunlap in 1834, "My *natural* eye was disgusted with its gaud and ostentation: to color and chiaroscuro all else is sacrificed—design is forgotten; to catch the eye by some dazzling display, seems to be the grand aim."[25]

Despite his claims to heterodoxy, therefore, Cole's opinions were solidly rooted in a set of well-established critical opinions about Turner in Britain. In understanding Cole's reaction to Turner, I think it is therefore more instructive look at a set of shared social concerns between Britain and America rather than issues of national identity. Cole took this critical framework and strategically deployed it to emphasize his own independence, and that of developing American landscape art, from corrupt European models. This account has been influential. James Flexner's *That Wilder Image,* for instance, published in the early 1960s as the international dominance of Abstract Expressionism in the NATO countries was being consolidated, identified Turner and Constable as sources for an American landscape tradition. Flexner grounded the English artists' innovations in the broader movement of European democracy that followed the French Revolution. In Flexner's account, as democracy took root in the United States, Cole joined this newly liberated approach to an investigation of the unique landscape of the New World.[26] I turn now to explore some of the ways that both artists' work seems to support this reading of European decline and American rise. But I also seek to complicate this picture, showing that both artists shared a deeply ambivalent position regarding the rise and fall of empire and the position of the artist in relation to it.

By casting Turner's career in these terms, Cole can be seen as portraying the decline of Turner and the English school as symptomatic of the decay of Old World culture. Indeed, the greed, luxury, and ostentation which for Cole tainted art and artists overseas are precisely the elements that are seen contributing to the downfall of society in Cole's own picture of decline, the *Destruction* scene from the *Course of Empire* series (1836). We can understand Cole's repeatedly stated goals of remaining close to nature and resisting manner as indications of his desire to avoid the kind of decline that he saw in Turner and other artists. At first glance, this appears consistent with the image of the American nation on the rise in Cole's *View from Mount Holyoke, Northampton, Massachusetts, after a Thunderstorm—The Oxbow* (1836, plate 15), with its depiction of fires burning, workers, livestock, and baled hay in the newly cultivated fields, and boats on the river. Cole named futurity as the defining condition of the American landscape in his well-known statement "Where the wolf roams, the plough shall glisten; on the grey crag shall rise temple and tower—mighty deeds shall be done in the now pathless wilderness."[27]

These contrasting positions for the artist, one predicated on an interaction with rise and the other with fall, would further appear to be tidily summarized by comparing the *Oxbow* to Turner's *Bridge of Sighs, Ducal Palace and Custom-House, Venice: Canaletti painting* (1833, plate 16). At core, the paintings are structurally very similar. Both place the viewer before a scene that is divided between a view onto a distant prospect in the background and a diagonal foreground that features an artist at work, at left. While Cole's artist, a self-portrait, is positioned before the American landscape as one of futurity, John Gage has shown that *The Bridge of Sighs* concerns the fall of a commercial empire, though in less overt fashion than Turner's *Decline of the Carthaginian Empire* (1817, B&J 135).[28] By this time it had become commonplace to connect the rise and fall of the Carthaginian and

Venetian empires, and to see in both a warning to Britain's own maritime empire and an imagining of its own inevitable collapse. Ruskin repeated this idea at the beginning of *The Stones of Venice:* "Since first the dominion of men was asserted over the ocean, three thrones, of mark beyond all others, have been set upon its sands: the thrones of Tyre, Venice, and England. Of the First of these great powers only the memory remains; of the Second the ruin; the Third, which inherits their greatness, if it forget their example, may be led through proud eminence to less pitied destruction."[29] Turner's return to painting Venice in the 1830s also followed a difficult period in which the painter was grieving a number of losses, including that of his friend and patron Walter Fawkes, and, most seriously, his father in the same year he met Cole. These events, we may assume, caused him to think seriously about his own mortality.[30] Thus, while decline became a frequent critical refrain in reference to Turner, it was clearly an issue that was of ongoing concern at both historical and personal levels in this period.

This personal component should alert us to the position of the artist in both pictures. While Cole's artist is a self-portrait, Turner names his predecessor in painting the Venetian harbor, Canaletto. Undoubtedly, as with his Claudian scenes, this is an example of Turner placing himself in visible competition with an Old Master, and critics in 1833 certainly took it this way.[31] But the point is that where Cole seems to be alone before nature, Turner was well aware that to some extent previous artists always stood between him and his subject. This fits well with Cole's own statements about his sense of artistic priority. In a diary entry of 1836 Cole proclaimed the "virginal" state of the American landscape, referring to "green woods, whose venerable masses had never figured in annuals, and overlooked by the stern mountain peaks, never beheld by Claude nor Salvator, nor subjected to the canvass by the innumerable dabblers in paint of all past time."[32] A similar sense of unencumbered subjectivity informs Cole's report to his parents after seeing the Royal Academy exhibition in 1829. Cole mentions some "excellent" pictures by Turner and A. W. Callcott, but on the whole claims to find little to make him doubt his own ability: "You may suppose that when I visited the exhibition of the Royal Academy, I went with great expectations. . . . But really I think that most of them are very far from perfection in the art. They do not altogether come up to my expectations; and I cannot but think that I have done more than any of the English painters."[33]

Turner, by contrast, seemed to feel the example of the Old Masters as a burden for much of his career.[34] Indeed, for many artists in Britain, the Renaissance seems to have created a standard of perfection that could not be rivaled but only modified. In discussing the course of Greek art, Fuseli had described a period of ideal public art followed by one of refinement in which the perfection earlier achieved could only be revised.[35] Whereas Shee had worried that exhibition would lead artists to pursue "qualities inconsistent with the perfection of Art," in this view Britain was in a stage in which that perfection was no longer possible. An awareness of this sense of belatedness might add a layer of subtlety to our understanding of the oft-cited story of Turner's reaction to seeing the work of Claude in the collection of J. J. Angerstein. According to George Jones: "Angerstein came into the room while the young painter was looking at the Sea Port by Claude, and spoke to him. Turner was awkward, agitated, and burst into tears. Mr. Angerstein enquired the cause and pressed for an answer, when Turner said passionately, 'because I shall never be able to paint any thing like that picture.'"[36]

Something more than individual ability may have been behind Turner's anxiety. That is, as with Cole, this story is usually taken as a signpost in the artist's developing sense of individual subjectivity, but it is also possible to see it as a recognition that the kind of unified pictorial statements that constituted the "perfection" of the Old Masters was no longer available. In understanding the broader context of Turner's reaction to Claude, we might usefully think of Georg Lukács's discussion of the fragmented cultures of modernity. In Lukács's terms, the vision of wholeness available to Claude was no longer possible for Turner, who faced a range of stylistic possibilities, none of which was specifically demanded or unproblematically privileged by the current culture, or *Weltanschauung*.[37] While academic theory had emphasized the ability of painting to create a unified, harmonious pictorial space, Turner was aware that this unity could no longer be achieved in straightforward terms. In response, Turner seems to have understood that he would need to make his reputation in the first place as a painter of destruction and disintegration and that it would have to be out of this state that compositional unity would emerge. When he saw Poussin's *Winter (The Deluge)* (1660–1664) in the Louvre in 1802, Turner criticized the picture for not giving vivid enough form to a world being pulled apart by flood, but also for failing to bring the parts of his picture together into a cohesive whole.[38] Thus, I have elsewhere argued that in pictures like *The Shipwreck* (1805, fig. 9.4), Turner sought at once to portray disintegration more intensely than any artist had done before, but also to create unity out of that very scene of destruction.[39] In particular, Turner developed the strange motif of the fishing boat whose sail blocks most of the capsized ship from view. Turner had used a similar blocking motif in *Venus and Adonis or Adonis departing for the Chase* (ca. 1803–1805, B&J 150), where he was reprising elements of Titian's *Death of St. Peter Martyr* (1527–1529), which he had also seen at the Louvre in 1802 and which many considered to be a paradigmatic model for the unity of figure and landscape.[40] This odd composition would normally be taken as evidence of Turner's disregard for figures in favor of their setting, but in light of the foregoing discussion, I am inclined to explain it as an awkward attempt at managing originality in the face of an established master.

Thus, again, *The Oxbow* might be taken as a representation of the American artist before nature, unencumbered by the past, painting a scene of the rise of empire and individual creative freedom. Conversely, *The Bridge of Sighs* could be seen as the product of a European artist burdened with the past, painting a scene of both personal and individual decline. But this would misrepresent the complexity of both paintings as representations of history and as indices of the artists' sense of their own position. In the first place, just as Turner's early pictures seem to arise from a refusal of the Fuselian conception of belatedness, Turner could also in these same years imagine himself and the British school as on the rise. Concluding one of his lectures to the Royal Academy as professor of perspective, Turner exhorted the students to build on the successes of past British artists for the glory of the Academy and the nation: "To you therefore this institution consigns [past artists'] efforts looking forward with the hope that by your zealous guardianship

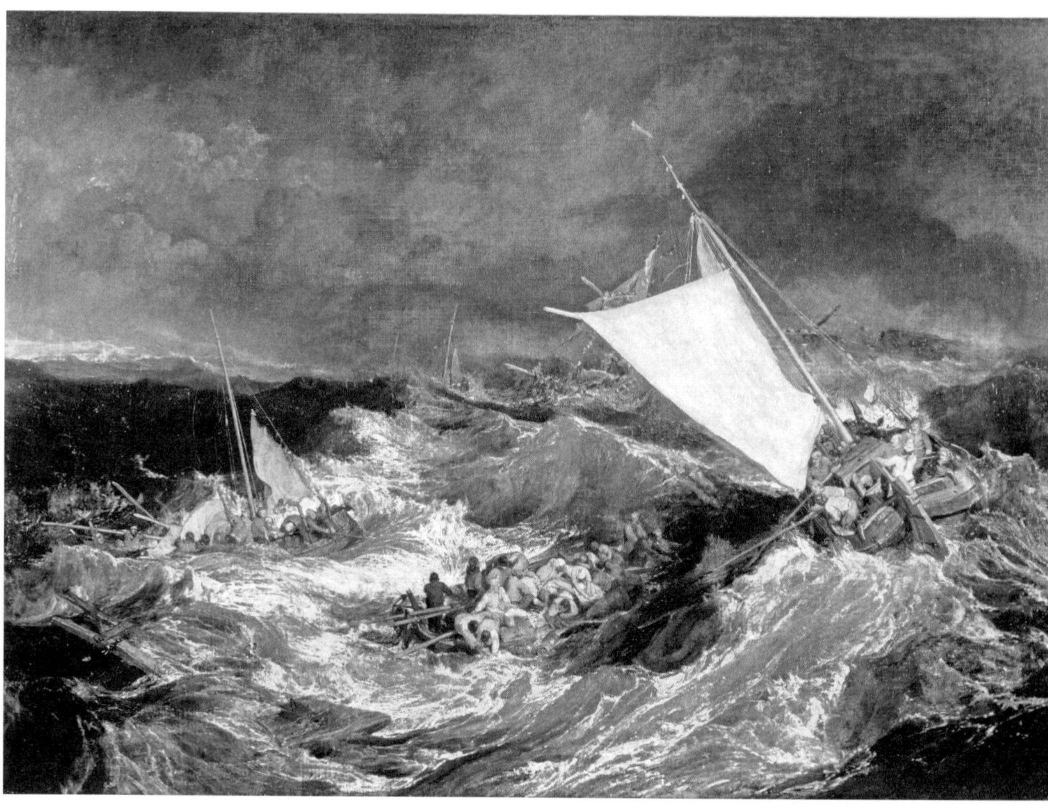

Figure 9.4. Joseph Mallord William Turner, *The Shipwreck,* 1805. Oil on canvas, 67⅛ x 95⅛ in. (170.5 x 241.5 cm). © Tate, London, 2013.

to all who follow that ultimately the joint endeavors of concording activities in the pursuit of all that is meritorious . . . may fix irrevocably the triple standard of the Arts in the British Empire."[41]

For his part, we know that Cole was deeply ambivalent about the progress of civilization in the New World and its effect on the landscape. Even as he was extolling the "virgin waters" of America, Cole lamented the rampant "utilitarianism" that he saw leading to its wanton destruction, as Alan Wallach and Angela Miller have discussed.[42] This ambivalence is present in *The Oxbow,* a picture that, for all its ostensible support for the notion of an Edenic America of infinite possibility, also intimated profound concerns over the effects of industrialization and commercial development.[43] Thus, just as Turner's picture cannot be seen as unconcerned with the past, so too must we see Cole's vision of the future in *The Oxbow* as profoundly ambivalent. Cole's condemnation of the commercialism of the English school, and Turner specifically, was related to these concerns and may have helped form it. We may also, I think, be more specific now about what Cole lamented exactly. Alan Wallach has emphasized Cole's aristocratic patrons and the outlook he shared with them, and we should see that outlook as one common to elements of both British and American society. In this regard it is instructive to remember that Cole had very likely read the *Discourses* of Sir Joshua Reynolds. Because of the emphasis on nationalism and on the relative unimportance of landscape for Reynolds, such a connection is not often made, but it is revealing.

Reynolds cast world history in terms of a progress toward civilization and away from barbarism, and his claims for the importance of art were based in its ability to contribute to this movement by transforming base material desires into ideas. He viewed the world in terms of a broad hierarchy, between savage people and civilized Europeans, and more specifically between a leisured landowning class, capable of this kind of intellectual process, and the mechanical laboring class, who must work to provide for the gentleman's leisure. For Reynolds the material/idea dichotomy meant that parts of the picture were imagined as physical resources to be harnessed to the good of the elevated central idea, which was, in turn, to be distanced from these details.[44] Reynolds describes a process by which creation becomes a kind intellectual manufacture: "It is indisputably evident that a great part of every man's life must be employed in collecting materials for the exercise of genius. Invention, strictly speaking, is little more than a new combination of those images which have been previously gathered and deposited in the memory: nothing can come of nothing: he who has laid up no materials, can produce no combinations."[45] In its emphasis on the collection of raw material, to be transformed by the elite Western male subject into something refined, Reynolds's approach is at root similar to English colonial practice, which, according to Nicholas Canny, emphasized the exploitation of raw material and sacrifice of local distinctions in favor of creating a uniform imperial culture that was justified by its claims to advance civilization as a whole.[46] Reynolds's focus on the importance of the elite male subject is also of a piece with the stewardship theory of virtual representation most powerfully expounded by Edmund Burke. Burke expressed this pithily at the end of the century, saying, "We procure reverence to our civil institutions on the principle upon which nature teaches us to revere individual men."[47] Reynolds's unpublished *Ironic Discourse* makes clear his allegiance with Burkean social hierarchy, and Andrew Hemingway has convincingly argued that Reynolds's academic theory worked to naturalize that hierarchy.[48] Reynolds's aesthetics were therefore useful to both aristocratic and empire-building discourses (these were of course separate, but also overlapped) because of his focus on the elite male subject and on masking material relations behind abstractions and claims of universality.

The aristocratic outlook, which argued against expanded suffrage and for the continued importance of the landowning gentleman as a bulwark against the moral decay of society, was shared with Cole's Federalist patrons in the 1820s and 1830s. It would also have been buttressed by Cole's interest in the associationist aesthetics of Archibald Alison, which, as Andrew Hemingway has shown, was based in the same social assumptions, and legitimated the cultural authority of the landed classes by stressing the necessity of a disinterested relationship to the landscape.[49] Cole's work also responded to ongoing colonialist fantasies. In his "Essay on American Scenery," Cole spends several pages almost ecstatically describing the vast abundance and range of natural wonders in the New World: mountains, lakes, waterfalls, and skies, a catalogue of plenitude that compares quite closely to eighteenth-century British accounts of the New World offered in newspapers and journals during and after the Seven Years' War. Wolfe's victory on the Fields of Abraham brought with it a similar sense of ecstasy at the promise of apparently limitless raw materials to be transformed into British wealth and security. In 1761 the *Royal Magazine* declared that "the . . . variety of soils and climates in America, capable of producing every necessary and convenience of life, joined to the fishery on its coast must infallibly prove to our Mother Country an inexhaustible source of wealth."[50] Reynolds and Cole are a part of a larger colonial trajectory in which aesthetic theory was deployed in part to mask and in part to justify the exploitative nature of white European expansionism in the New World and to argue for the continued importance of an aristocratic, hierarchical society.

Seeing Cole's viewpoint as influenced by issues of class outlook that transcend national distinctions ultimately speaks to Andrew Hemingway's important point in the introduction to this volume about a dialectical form of Romanticism between Britain and America, as well as to Paul Giles's observations, cited by Hemingway, about American and British culture working as "mirror images" over this period. Going even further, then, we may say that Cole's pictures provided precisely the kind of disembodied elite male subject who was central to both Reynolds and Burke by incorporating the raw American wilderness into the accepted formula of European landscape—beautiful, in *View on the Catskill—Early Autumn* (1837), or sublime, in *Kaaterskill Falls* (1826, plate 17)—Claude or Salvator Rosa. Cole signals the viewer's distance from the material, wild state of nature in *Kaaterskill Falls* by the presence of Native Americans, who he and Reynolds would have agreed lived too close to the savage state of nature themselves to have any means of understanding it in anything other than material terms. In contrast, the viewer of the picture maintains a discreet distance from the landscape. Cole's lament in *View on the Catskill—Early Autumn* is not so much with the disappearance of the landscape but the mode of its loss—industrial, commercial, and democratic—which made the process of transforming the landscape too obvious, too direct, and less predicated on superior cultural knowledge. In short, this rendered it unfit for the aristocratic kind of transformation taking place here. I think Alan Wallach is exactly right in finding in Cole's work the celebration of aristocratic values, even as he mourned their loss.[51] Pictures like *View on the Catskill—Early Autumn* create a sense of longing not just for the landscape itself but for a moment in the past when that utopia could at least be pictured by means of a certain kind of artistic interaction with nature, when a particular kind of elite male subject could still be formed by aesthetics. Seen this way, Cole's lament was less for the loss of a landscape itself than for the loss of a set of conditions of production and its replacement by a very different one.

Cole was astute, then, in recognizing that something disturbing was taking place in Turner's work, even as Turner experienced some of the same sense of loss. Both artists reacted, in different ways to be sure, to the sense of pervasive loss that Michael Löwy and Robert Sayre describe as so formative of Romanticism's critique of modernity.[52] Because his painting defined itself and its viewers by their distance from the material landscape, Cole sought to create a purely visual and disembodied subject. In much of Turner's work we see the creation of an opposite mode of subjectivity. Specifically, I mean that many of Turner's pictures are based on a bodily presence within the landscape. To bring this out, we might compare representations of work in Cole and Turner. As Elaine Scarry has discussed, while modern scholarship has been consistently drawn to the issue of desire with respect to investigations of cultural embodiment, work has received much less attention. But work, she says, is fundamentally about the material relation of human beings to the world around them, and was a dominant theme in nineteenth-century novels, especially Thomas Hardy's.[53] With this in mind, we might compare two

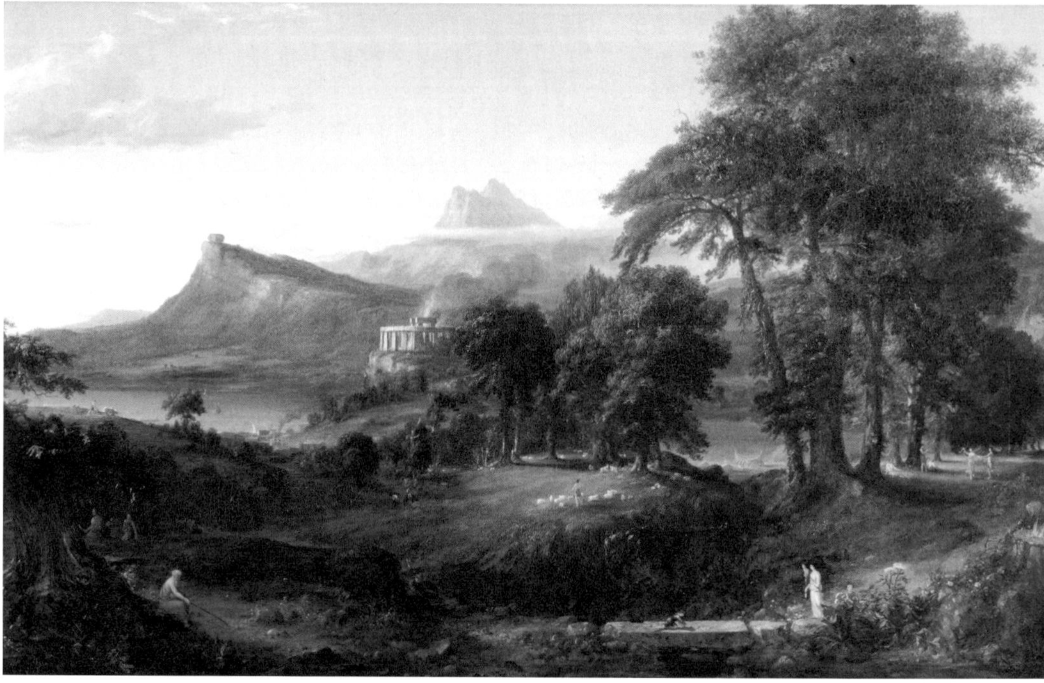

Figure 9.5. Thomas Cole, *The Course of Empire: The Arcadian or Pastoral State,* 1836. Oil on canvas, 39¾ x 63¼ in. (99.7 x 160.7 cm). Collection of the New-York Historical Society.

paintings of the rise of empire, Cole's *Arcadian or Pastoral State* from *The Course of Empire* (1836, fig. 9.5), and the same *Dido building Carthage* (1815, fig. 9.2) that Cole had seen in 1829. Although Cole's picture concentrates on agrarian pursuits, the development of science, and the emergence of religion, no physical labor is shown, except for a distant scene of boat building. Turner's seaport, by contrast, is a hive of activity. Behind Dido are scenes of boats being unloaded and heavy materials being hauled ashore. All along the left-hand shore, stretching into the distance, bodies twist, bend, pull, and lean with the effort of physical exertion. In fact, Turner chose to follow a section of Book One of the *Aeneid* that emphasizes the work of constructing the new city:

> The Prince, with Wonder, sees the stately Tow'rs,
> Which late were Huts and Shepherd's homely Bow'rs.
> The Gates and Streets; and hears, from ev'ry part,
> The Noise and busy Concourse of the Mart.
> The toiling *Tyrians* on each other call,
> To ply their Labour: some extend the Wall,
> Some build the Citadel; the brawny throng,

> Or dig, or push unweildy [*sic*] Stones along.
> Some for their Dwellings chuse a Spot of Ground,
> Which, first design'd, with Ditches they surround.[54]

To be sure, Cole's image is a pastoral, and Turner painted a number of similar landscapes throughout his career, but the point is that Turner stressed the physical process of the rise of empire. This was exactly the kind of development that Cole could not picture, a process that he saw as leading to the destruction rather than the creation of empire. Consider, for instance, the stacked logs on the right-hand shore juxtaposed against the verdant green woods behind them. In a scene of ancient myth, Turner alludes to an industrialized harnessing of natural resources with a directness that we can never imagine having a place in Cole's work. For Cole, sensuality can be pictured only in negative terms, transformed into pleasure and luxury. *The Consummation of Empire* is decidedly not a scene of labor; there is no representation of the means of production, but rather an elite enjoyment of the fruits and pleasures built by the invisible hand of labor.

It is further remarkable, then, to note the prevalence of vivid depictions of bodies at work in pictures in different media from throughout Turner's long career: fisherman straining to fight their way off a lee shore (*Fisherman Upon a Lee-Shore, in Squally Weather,* 1802, B&J 16), a man struggling to pull horses against a strong Scottish wind (*Borthwick Castle,* 1818),[55] the working painter and leaning gondolier in *The Bridge of Sighs* (see plate 16), fishers bending low to collect bait in the shallows (*Calais Sands, Low Water, Poissards collecting Bait,* 1830, B&J 334), and the leaning bodies of workers struggling to tow a barge against the current in *The Bridge of Meulan* (ca. 1833, fig. 9.6), all of which attest to a physical interaction with the natural world that is the opposite of Cole's disembodied visual distance from the landscape. Turner shows precisely the kind of activity that Cole tried to eliminate from representation. Nowhere is this more clear, perhaps, than in another picture of imperial rise, *Keelmen Heaving in Coals by Moonlight* (1835, plate 18). The painting is remarkable in its admission not just of labor but of industrial labor, highlighting the coalmen against the industrial fires burning into the night. *Keelmen* has been understood as a pendant for *Venice,* which had been exhibited the year before and was also a commission from the industrialist Henry McConnell.[56] The pairing would seem to connect British industriousness and industrialism to the continued viability of empire as opposed to the midday languor of Venice in decline.[57] Turner thus seems to suggest that the very forces that Cole saw as leading to the downfall of empire were to be its basis.

Turner also seems to have imagined himself as an artist physically within the spaces he depicted, in possession of a sensual relationship to both nature and art, figured in terms of both desire and labor. Coming back to *The Bridge of Sighs,* we see that his surrogate, Canaletto, is involved in the unlikely task of painting the picture within an elaborate gilded frame. This replicates the actual circumstances of the picture's creation, in its frame on the walls of the Academy, during the Varnishing Days.[58] Turner's performances on those days, creating finished pictures from nearly abstract beginnings, made visible the physical creation of a painting, its labor. This contrasts with so much academic art theory, which had emphasized the importance of hiding the hand of the artist, the material conditions of creativity, as Turner was aware. A thought scribbled at the margins of his notes for a lecture at the Academy reads, "The artist in his picture ought to be completely hid."[59] Turner is voicing the conventional demand that the hand of the artist must be obscured in the final work, but in phrasing it like this he actually implies the exact opposite as well: that the artist's engagement with the work of art

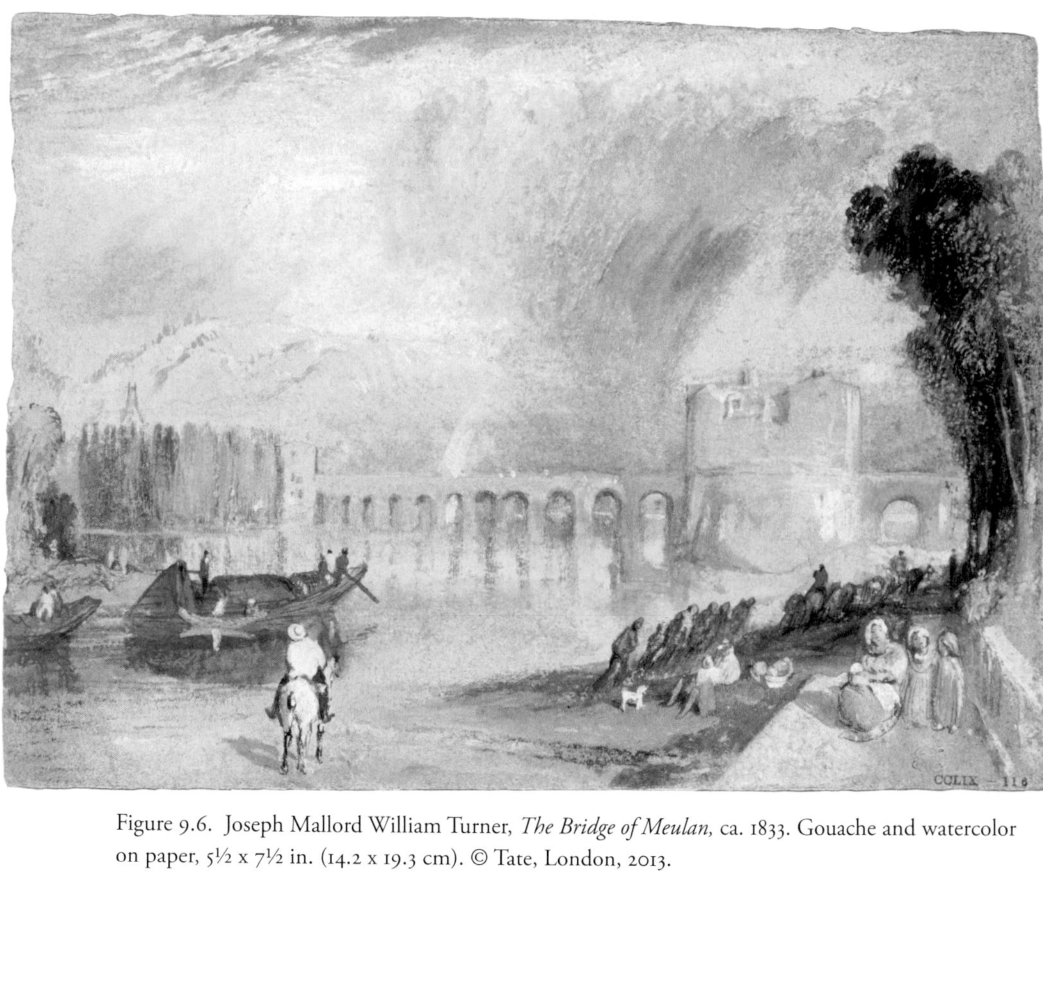


Figure 9.6. Joseph Mallord William Turner, *The Bridge of Meulan,* ca. 1833. Gouache and watercolor on paper, 5½ x 7½ in. (14.2 x 19.3 cm). © Tate, London, 2013.

must be complete, even to the point of a physical immersion in the picture. Such an immersion seems to be precisely what has taken place for the artist in *Bridge of Sighs,* as he has been drawn from the Academy into the space he depicts, and is also what it offers its viewers, with the richness of paint providing an analogue to a sensual penetration of the spaces of the city in decline.

Part of what made Cole and others uncomfortable about Turner's later work was surely the immediacy of this sensual experience. The references by Cole and others to Turner's seductive colors are usually taken, not incorrectly, to allude to the debased sensuality that Reynolds and others rejected. But I hope to have made it clear that work was another part of that sensuality and one that carried an equally dangerous social charge. We should remember now Cole's comments comparing Turner to a "sea-faring mate," which can be placed alongside Richard Doyle's caricature of Turner as a janitor applying yellow paint with a mop (1846, fig. 9.7), and the critical jabs comparing him to a sloppy chef rather than a fine painter. Undoubtedly, many of these traded on Turner's low birth and rough manners, but they also registered the physical impact of Turner as a worker of pictures and a creator of pictures of workers.

In conclusion, Cole's reactions to Turner were complex and paradoxical and represent an opposite, but linked, pole to his proclamations on the New World landscape. On the one hand, Cole found English painting, and Turner's work specifically, too insubstantial: "full of sound and fury signifying nothing," as he put it.[60] Turner was thus characterized by an excess of "nothing"; in short, his work was too far from nature, too much removed from all that was stable and full of meaning. On the other hand, he found Turner to be excessively present in his pictures, overly materialized in his emphasis on bodily experience, sensuality, and labor. But the landscape was equally present and absent for Cole. Even as he sought to ground himself in the solidity of the land and nature, it is a "pathless" wilderness, a virginal landscape, which needs to be cultivated, acted upon by the imagination of the elite male subject to achieve significance and meaning. In his ambivalent reaction to Turner, therefore, Cole sought to balance these concerns, staking his right to a subjective self-determination and exceptionalism defined through his unmediated access to the American landscape, while simultaneously laying claim to possession of a venerable and esteemed tradition that would validate his project.

I hope to have demonstrated what were fundamental differences between Cole and Turner, best seen as emerging not from primarily national distinctions, nor merely in aesthetic choices, but in relation to the material social conditions that precede but do not determine those choices. I have placed Cole within the

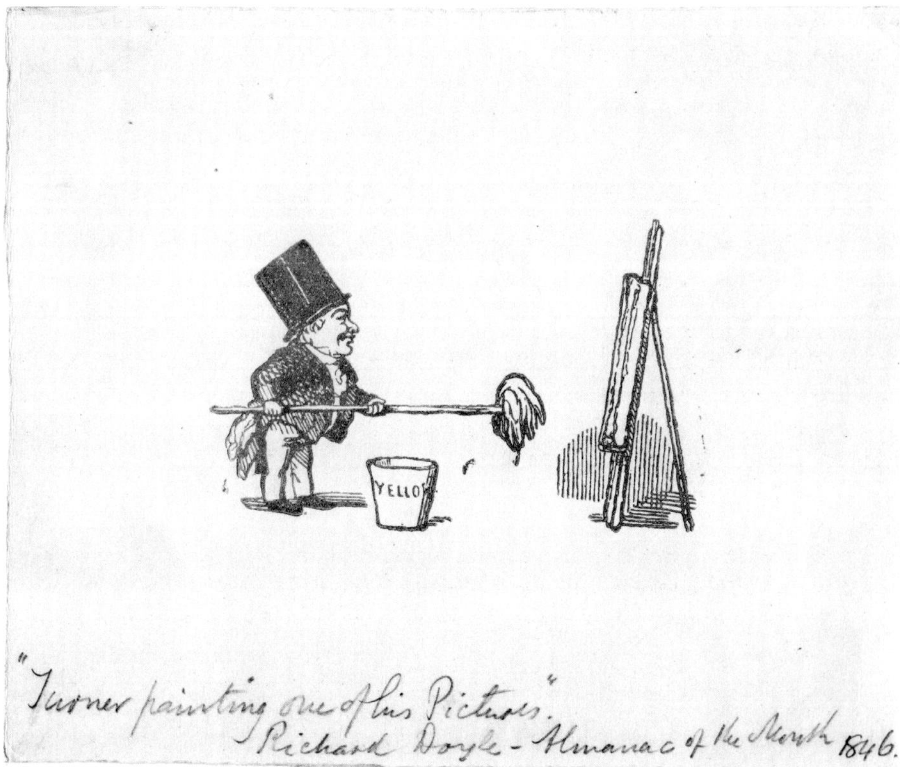


Figure 9.7. Richard Doyle, *Joseph Mallord William Turner,* 1846. Woodcut, 3⅜ in. x 4⅛ in. (8.5 cm x 10.5 cm). © National Portrait Gallery, London.

anti-capitalist critique of modernity that characterized other figures discussed in this volume, such as Allston, Cooper, and Irving. Turner's position is perhaps rather more complex. It seems to me that *Keelmen* and *Dido building Carthage,* in finding a place for depicting and enacting labor, even industrial labor, represent a willingness to see work as central to change and modernity. Whether they celebrate those changes unproblematically, however, is a different question. Works like the watercolor *Loss of an East Indiaman* (ca. 1818, W 500) are willing to register the negative effects of empire on the anonymous figures who suffer them in all too material terms, showing perhaps the ambivalent outcomes of the activity of *Dido building Carthage.* At the same time, however, we must also acknowledge that pictures like *Rain, Steam and Speed—the Great Western Railway* (1844, B&J 409) bring with them their own ambivalence, their own blindness, and their own tendency to aestheticize social injustice and exploitation. I hope it is clear, then, that the work of both artists is richly indicative of the ambivalent position of

Romantic landscape painters on either side of the ocean in the face of a rapidly changing world that seemed at once to be both too present and too absent.

## NOTES

1. *The Correspondence of John Ruskin and Charles Eliot Norton,* ed. John Lewis Bradley and Ian Ousby (Cambridge: Cambridge University Press, 1987), 312.

2. Ibid., 31–32.

3. Martin Butlin and Evelyn Joll, *The Paintings of J. M. W. Turner,* 2 vols. (New Haven: Yale University Press, 1984), 330; hereafter cited parenthetically in the text as B&J.

4. Louis Legrand Noble, *The Life and Works of Thomas Cole* (Cambridge: Belknap Press of Harvard University Press, 1964), 81.

5. Quoted in Ellwood Parry, *The Art of Thomas Cole: Ambition and Imagination* (Newark: University of Delaware Press, 1988), 99.

6. *The Journal of Eugène Delacroix,* trans. Walter Pach (New York: Crown Publishers, 1948), 458.

7. Quoted in Gertrude Rosenthal et al., *Studies on Thomas Cole, an American Romanticist* (Baltimore: Baltimore Museum of Art, 1967), 68.

8. Noble, *Life and Works of Thomas Cole,* 86.

9. Ibid., 81.

10. William Dunlap, *A History of the Rise and Progress of the Arts of Design in the United States* (1834), 3 vols. (New York: Benjamin Blom, 1965), 3:153.

11. Ibid. I am grateful to Alan Wallach for emphasizing the importance of Cole's strategies of self-presentation in writing.

12. *The Times,* May 6, 1828.

13. Martin Butlin and Evelyn Joll, *The Paintings of J. M. W. Turner* (New Haven: Yale University Press, 1984), 148.

14. *The Spectator* 8, no. 356 (April 26, 1835): 404.

15. [James Elmes], *Annals of the Fine Arts* (1820): 421.

16. *The Diary of Joseph Farington,* vol. 7, ed. Kathryn Cave (New Haven: Yale University Press for the Paul Mellon Centre for Studies in British Art, 1978), 2710.

17. John Ruskin, *Notes on the Turner Collection at Marlborough House* (London: Smith, Elder & Co., 1857).

18. *The Diary of Joseph Farington,* vol. 6, ed. Kenneth Garlick and Angus MacIntyre (New Haven: Yale University Press for the Paul Mellon Centre for Studies in British Art, 1978), 2023.

19. Cited in Felicity Owen and David Blayney Brown, *Collector of Genius: A Life of Sir George Beaumont* (New Haven: Yale University Press for the Paul Mellon Centre for Studies in British Art, 1988), 144.

20. John Barrell, *The Political Theory of Painting from Reynolds to Hazlitt: "The body of the public"* (New Haven: Yale University Press, 1986), 64.

21. Henry Fuseli, *Lectures on Painting* (New York: Garland Publishers, 1979), 558, reprint of Ralph Wornum, ed., *Lectures on Painting, by the Royal Academicians* (London: Henry G. Bohn, 1848).

22. Sir Joshua Reynolds, "Discourse V," in *Discourses on Art,* ed. Robert Wark (New Haven: Yale University for the Paul Mellon Centre for Studies in British Art, 1975), 90.

23. Sir Martin Archer Shee, *Elements of Art: A Poem in Six Cantos* (London: William Miller, 1809), 297.

24. Rev. John Eagles, "The Sketcher No. XII," *Blackwood's Edinburgh Magazine* 8, no. 238 (August 1835): 200.

25. Dunlap, *History of the Rise and Progress,* 152.

26. James Flexner, *That Wilder Image: The Painting of America's Native School from Thomas Cole to Winslow Homer* (Boston: Little, Brown, 1962), 12–14.

27. Thomas Cole, "Essay on American Scenery," in *American Art, 1700—1860: Sources and Documents,* ed. John McCoubrey (Englewood Cliffs, N.J.: Prentice Hall, 1965), 109.

28. John Gage, "Turner in Venice," in *Projecting the Landscape,* ed. J. C. Eade (Canberra: Humanities Research Centre, Australian National University, 1987), 72–77.

29. John Ruskin, *The Stones of Venice,* vol. 1 (New York: John B. Alden, 1885), 15.

30. On Turner and mortality in this period, see Anthony Bailey, *Standing in the Sun: A Life of J. M. W. Turner* (London: Pimlico, 1998), 260. On pictorial formations of mortality in Venice, see Lindsay Stainton, *Turner in Venice* (London: British Museum Publications, 1985), 34; and Eric Shanes, *Turner's Human Landscape* (London: Heinemann, 1990), 92–94.

31. On issues of competition and the Varnishing Days, see Leo Costello, "'This cross-fire of colours': Turner and the Varnishing Days Reconsidered," *British Art Journal* 10, no. 3 (Spring 2010): 56–68; and Michael Rosenthal, "Turner Fires a Gun," in *Art on the Line: The Royal Academy Exhibitions at Somerset House, 1780–1836,* ed. David Solkin (New Haven: Yale University Press, 2001), 144–55.

32. Noble, *Life and Works of Thomas Cole,* 148.

33. Ibid., 79.

34. For an excellent discussion of the dilemma of tradition and originality in this period, see David Solkin, "Turner and the Masters: Gleaning to Excel," in *Turner and the Masters,* ed. David Solkin (London: Tate Publishing, 2009), 18–26.

35. Barrell, *Political Theory of Painting,* 270–72.

36. George Jones, "A Short Memoir of Turner," in *The Collected Correspondence of J. M. W. Turner,* ed. John Gage (Oxford: Oxford University Press, 1980), 4.

37. Georg Lukács, *The Theory of the Novel: A Historico-Philosophical Essay on the Forms of Epic Literature,* trans. Anna Bostock (Cambridge: MIT Press, 1989), 29–39.

38. Notebook, "Studies in the Louvre," Tate Britain, Turner Bequest LXXII, 41a–2.

39. Leo Costello, *J. M. W. Turner and the Subject of History* (Farnham, Surrey: Ashgate, 2012).

40. Solkin, *Turner and the Masters,* 138.

41. British Library, Add. MS. 46151, 41.

42. Angela Miller, "Thomas Cole and Jacksonian America: *The Course of Empire* as a Political Allegory," *Prospects* 14 (1989): 65–92, and *The Empire of the Eye: Landscape Representation and American Cultural Politics, 1825–1875* (Ithaca: Cornell University Press, 1993); Alan Wallach, "Thomas Cole and the Aristocracy," *Arts Magazine* 56 (November 1981): 94–106, and "Thomas Cole: Landscape and the Course of American Empire," in *Thomas Cole: Landscape into History,* ed. William Truettner and Alan Wallach (New Haven: Yale University Press; Washington, D.C.: National Museum of American Art, Smithsonian Institution, 1994), 90–98.

43. See Wallach, "Thomas Cole: Landscape and the Course of American Empire," 76–77; Miller, "Cole and Jacksonian America," 82–83 (in *Empire of the Eye,* 39–49, Miller argues that *The Oxbow* "is neither apocalypse nor millennium" but instead seeks to prompt viewers to an active response in positing the two alternative possibilities); and Rochelle Johnson, *Passions for Nature: Nineteenth-Century American Aesthetics of Alienation* (Athens: University of Georgia Press, 2009), 86–89.

44. For an important discussion of Reynolds's approach to details, which opens directly onto these issues, see Elizabeth Bohls, "Disinterestedness and Denial of the Particular: Locke, Adam Smith, and the Subject of Aesthetics," in *Eighteenth-Century Aesthetics and the Reconstruction of Art,* ed. Paul Mattick (Cambridge: Cambridge University Press, 1993), 17.

45. Sir Joshua Reynolds, "Discourse II," in Wark, *Discourses,* 27.

46. Nicholas P. Canny, "The Ideology of English Colonization: From Ireland to America," in *Theories of Empire, 1450–1800,* ed. David Armitage (Aldershot: Ashgate, 1998), 179–202.

47. Edmund Burke, *Reflections on the Revolution in France* (Mineola, N.Y.: Dover Publications, 2006), 32, republication of 7th ed. (1790).

48. Andrew Hemingway, *Landscape Imagery and Urban Culture in Early Nineteenth-Century Britain* (Cambridge: Cambridge University Press, 1992), 91–92.

49. Andrew Hemingway, "Academic Theory versus Association Aesthetics: The Ideological Forms of a Conflict of Interests in the Early Nineteenth Century," *Ideas and Production* 5 (1986): 18–42.

50. *Royal Magazine* 4 (January 1761): 14.

51. Alan Wallach, "Thomas Cole: Landscape and the Course of American Empire," in Truettner and Wallach, *Thomas Cole: Landscape into History,* 98.

52. Michael Löwy and Robert Sayre, *Romanticism against the Tide of Modernity,* trans. Catherine Porter (Durham: Duke University Press, 2001), 22–25.

53. Elaine Scarry, *Resisting Representation* (Oxford: Oxford University Press, 1994), 49–90.

54. John Dryden, trans., *Virgil's Aeneid* (New York: Penguin Classics, 1997), 17–18. Turner probably knew the text through Dryden's translation; see Jan Piggot, "Virgil," in *The Oxford Companion to J. M. W. Turner,* ed. Evelyn Joll, Martin Butlin, and Luke Herrmann (Oxford: Oxford University Press, 2001), 365–66. On Turner's Carthage pictures, see Kathleen Nicholson, *Turner's Classical Landscape* (Princeton: Princeton University Press, 1990), 105.

55. Andrew Wilton, *The Life and Work of J. M. W. Turner* (Fribourg: Academy Editions, 1979), 1060; hereafter cited parenthetically in the text as W.

56. Julian Treuherz, "The Turner Collector: Henry McConnell, Cotton Spinner," *Turner Studies* 6, no. 2 (Winter 1986): 37–42.

57. Ian Warrell, "Contemporary Approaches to British Art," in *Turner and Venice,* ed. Ian Warrell (London: Tate Publishing, 2003), 107. See also Gerald Finley, *Angel in the Sun: Turner's Vision of History* (Montreal: McGill–Queens University Press, 1997), 33–36, 146–47.

58. Rosenthal, "Turner Fires a Gun," 148.

59. British Library, Add. MS. 46151 A, 19.

60. Dunlap, *History of the Rise and Progress,* 152.

# 10

# Thomas Cole and Transatlantic Romanticism

*Alan Wallach*

The terms that define this anthology, *Transatlantic* and *Romanticism,* are not too often juxtaposed. Of course, it is frequently acknowledged that romanticism was an international movement, and much important work has been done on international contacts and influences, such as, for example, the exhibition *Crossing the Channel: British and French Painting in the Age of Romanticism,* which was seen at Tate Britain, the Metropolitan Museum of Art, and the Minneapolis Institute of Arts in 2003–4.[1] And yet while scholars have long been aware of the romantic movement's international dimension, the art-historical study of romanticism tends to focus more on its national than its international manifestations.

The problem here is twofold. To begin with, we confront the fact of historical contexts and artistic careers. To take a familiar example, Benjamin West was born an English subject in Pennsylvania in 1738, traveled to Italy in 1760, and in 1763 set up a studio in London. In 1772 George III appointed him historical painter to the court, and from 1791 until his death in 1820 he served as president of the Royal Academy, succeeding Joshua Reynolds.[2] West belongs to the history of English art, but in light of his role as mentor to several generations of American artists beginning with Charles Willson Peale in the 1760s and ending with Samuel F. B. Morse in the 1810s, he also belongs to the history of American art. To describe West as exclusively English or exclusively American is, obviously, to distort the facts of his career and his impact on the history of painting on both sides of the Atlantic. Such terms as *Transatlantic* and *Anglo-American* suggest a different approach to understanding West's career, since they signal the many points of connection and influence between two evolving national cultures. Or perhaps it would be better to say that the two terms (*Transatlantic, Anglo-American*) allow us to comprehend West's career in relation to a hybrid culture, one that cannot be subsumed under the rubric English or American.

And yet a shift in terminology only begins to resolve the problem of the transatlantic relation, since the conventional organization of the history of art along national lines tends to work against scholarly awareness of international cultures and cultural connections. To be sure, the practice of dividing the history of art in this fashion itself has a history going back to the eighteenth century, when collectors and writers on art divided the history of European art into national schools. This division along national lines coincided with the political revolutions of the early modern period and the rise of the modern nation-state. The nationalist ideologies that are their ongoing legacy resulted not only in claims of national superiority but also in a belief in inherent national and racial characteristics. These ideologies have left an indelible mark upon the historiography of the art-historical discipline. Moreover, these beliefs are not simply relics of the romantic nationalisms and unabashedly chauvinist discourses of the nineteenth century; in the latter half of the twentieth century, students of the history of English and American art expended much energy attempting to define, mainly in formalist terms, "the Englishness of English art" and "the Americanness of American art." Such attempts may now seem futile, benighted, opportunistic, or, for that matter, ominous. Yet until quite recently they were a feature of the study of the history of English and especially American art, for example, the concerted effort during the 1970s and 1980s to promote so-called luminist painting—the work of such artists as Fitz Henry Lane and Martin Johnson Heade—as an epitome of "Americanness."[3]

Still, ideologies are as much a part of history as the historical facts they represent. Consequently, doing justice to the theme of this anthology—Transatlantic Romanticism—requires, among other things, a dual critique. First, we need a critical-historical approach to the ways in which nationalist ideologies influenced the production and reception of the work of the artists under consideration. And second, given a predominantly one-sided relation, we will want to examine closely how American artists of the period drew upon or rejected English cultural and institutional precedents. The issue here might be construed in terms of influence, but "influence" is too weak and passive a term to describe the participation of such artists as Benjamin West, Washington Allston, and Thomas Cole in the cultural exchanges that played a crucial role in the rise of romanticism in the United States.

Of the three artists just named, perhaps none more fully exemplifies the dialectic between nationalist ideology and transatlantic cultural reality than Thomas Cole. Born in Bolton-le-Moors, Lancashire, in 1801, the son of a small-time woolens manufacturer, Cole was at fourteen apprenticed as an engraver at a calico print works in Chorley and later worked as an engraver's assistant in Liverpool.[4] Cole's father's business failed in the depression following the end of the Napoleonic Wars, and in 1818 the Cole family—mother, father, three sisters, and an aunt—emigrated to the United States, where Cole's father tried and repeatedly failed to repair the family's fortunes. The experience of displacement, downward mobility, and poverty—an experience Cole shared with thousands of his contemporaries whose lives were similarly upended by the industrial revolution—resulted in an almost unbearable tension between the aspiring artist's actual situation and the pretensions to gentility he had acquired growing up in the Lancashire "middling class." Cole resolved this tension—although never completely, certainly never to his own satisfaction—via his artistic ambition. He may not have consciously linked success as an artist to a rise in social status. Indeed, he was inclined to dismiss as unworthy any equation between the spiritual and the material. Still, there was something relentless about the way he worked to realize his ambition, attempting to paint portraits as an itinerant in the backwoods of Ohio in the early 1820s, and then, as his vocation as a landscapist came into clearer focus, moving to Philadelphia in 1823, where he survived by working as an artistic jack-of-all-trades, and spent what free time he had drawing from casts and studying the paintings on view at the Pennsylvania Academy of the Fine Arts. By 1824 he was showing a landscape of his own at the Academy's annual exhibition.[5]

Critics have described Cole's move to New York City in April of the following year as fortuitous, a result of a shift in his family's circumstances, but it was also probably inevitable. By 1825, as Dell Upton has observed, "New York's economic dominance [had been] secured," and the opening that year of the Erie Canal, the "artificial river" connecting the city to the Great Lakes, "assured [its] future preeminence at the geographical and financial center of a web of national and international commerce."[6] A burgeoning local economy went hand in hand with a rapidly expanding art scene. At its center stood John Trumbull, scion of an old, politically powerful Connecticut family, president from 1817 to 1835 of New York's American Academy of Fine Arts, and considered by many the United States' foremost history painter.[7] A student of Benjamin West during the 1780s and author of the four mammoth Revolutionary War scenes that Congress had commissioned for the Capitol rotunda, Trumbull commanded a large patronage network consisting primarily of members of the old Federalist aristocracy. He was also deeply involved both privately and in his capacity as president of the Academy in the exhibition and sale of American and European painting.[8]

Cole first met Trumbull in November 1825, an encounter that soon became the stuff of New York art world legend. Shortly after arriving in the city, Cole exhibited a number of works at the carving and gilding shop of George Dixey, where they were seen by the merchant George Washington Bruen, a patron of the Academy. Bruen bought one or more of Cole's paintings and later provided the artist with money to visit the Hudson Highlands and the Catskills, where the recently opened Catskill Mountain House, perched atop a palisade and giving onto a panoramic view of the Hudson Valley, had become a fashionable resort. In late August or early September, Cole traveled up the Hudson accumulating a portfolio of sketches. When he returned to New York, he executed perhaps as many as five landscape paintings. In October, Bruen helped the artist place at least three of these paintings at the shop of the bookseller and art dealer William A. Colman, where Trumbull, who had business dealings with Colman, first saw them. Trumbull paid twenty-five dollars for Cole's *Kaaterskill Falls,* a tourist attraction near the Mountain House (plate 17).[9] Later he expressed his excitement over Cole's work to the engraver Asher B. Durand and the playwright, historian, and history painter William Dunlap (who, like Trumbull, had studied with West in the 1780s). Durand acquired a second painting, *View of Fort Putnam,* which has recently resurfaced. Dunlap purchased Cole's *Lake with Dead Trees* (plate 19), and almost immediately resold it at a substantial profit to the auctioneer, politician, and diarist Philip Hone. The three artists soon met Cole, although whether they first encountered him together or individually remains unclear.[10]

According to an anecdote repeated and embroidered upon by Cole's biographers, on first seeing the artist's landscapes at William Colman's bookstore and gallery, Trumbull had exclaimed to Colman: "I am delighted, and at the same time mortified. This youth has done at once, and without instruction, what I cannot do after fifty years' practice."[11] Whatever his actual words, Trumbull's enthusiasm proved genuine. After his initial meeting with Cole, Trumbull put the young landscapist in contact with his network of aristocratic collectors and patrons, including Robert Gilmor of Baltimore and Daniel Wadsworth of Hartford. Gilmor, the owner of an extensive collection of European painting, purchased altogether five works from Cole; Wadsworth, an amateur landscapist and the founder of the Wadsworth Atheneum, bought six or seven. Patronizing American artists was for them not only an opportunity to acquire works of art but also an occasion for assuming the patriotic responsibility of encouraging the arts in the young republic.[12]

Why did Cole's early canvases so impress Trumbull, Dunlap, and other knowledgeable artists and collectors? What did they find in Cole's paintings that was absent or missing from the work of other American landscapists of the period? As his statement to Colman implied, Trumbull himself had seriously pursued the study of landscape. Indeed, he had in 1808 tried to sell the inventor-entrepreneur Robert Barker on the idea of commissioning a panorama of Niagara Falls for

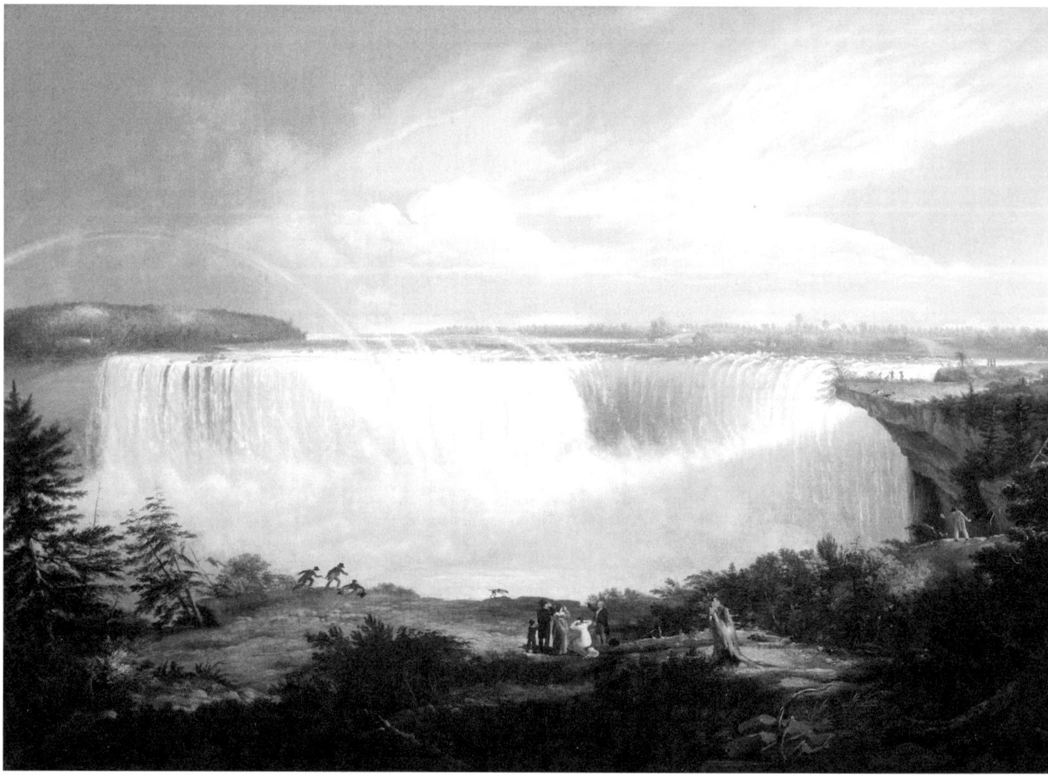

Figure 10.1. Alvan Fisher, *The Great Horseshoe Falls, Niagara,* 1820. Oil on canvas, 34⅜ x 48 in. (87.2 x 122.0 cm). Smithsonian American Art Museum, Washington, D.C., Museum Purchase, 1966.82.1.

Barker's Leicester Square rotunda.[13] Still, Trumbull's attempts at painting American scenery seem leaden by comparison with such works as Cole's *Lake with Dead Trees.* Similarly, paintings by the leading American landscapists of the 1820s, Alvan Fisher and Thomas Doughty, look formulaic and uninspired—too literal in the case of Fisher (fig. 10.1), too vague in the case of Doughty—by comparison with Cole's early efforts. Those efforts might also be characterized as in some respects formulaic. Nonetheless, both *Kaaterskill Falls* and *Lake with Dead Trees,* though deliberately cast in the past or historical tense, possess an immediacy, a specificity of detail, and above all a dramatic—one might say melodramatic—dimension (for example, Cole's signature writhing trees) that appealed to an intensely patriotic American elite, an audience already familiar with landscape tourism and landscape literature, and primed to see realistic representations of American landscape as symbolic of the United States.

Cole may have become acquainted with the novelist James Fenimore Cooper in New York in the fall of 1825.[14] Two years earlier, Cooper had scored an unprecedented success with *The Pioneers,* which introduced the reading public to Natty Bumppo, Cooper's ideal frontiersman. As Donald Ringe and James Franklin Beard have observed, Cooper's descriptions of American nature in *The Pioneers* and later novels in the Leatherstocking series paralleled Cole's painting technique, in which closely observed natural details—trees, rocks, mountains, clouds—are set within an idealized framework.[15] Indeed, Cole to some degree developed the wilderness iconography of his early paintings of the American wilderness from *The Pioneers* and *The Last of the Mohicans* (1826), which he took as a subject for at least five of the works he painted between 1826 and 1829.[16]

Early on, Cole also formed a friendship with the poet William Cullen Bryant, who had moved from Massachusetts to New York in 1825 to embark on a career as a journalist and editor. Cole, who was widely read in English literature and was a capable poet in his own right, became closely familiar with Bryant's poetry. For his part, Bryant became a great admirer of Cole's art.[17]

Dunlap, Bryant, and Cooper presided over what might be called the Americanization of Cole, naturalizing the artist in both senses of the word by passing over his English birth and upbringing when they could, and celebrating his paintings as unmediated records of American nature. In late November 1825, Dunlap, writing under the patriotic pseudonym "American," penned the first published account of the artist, praising Cole as "an American boy" who "has equalled those works which have been the boast of Europe and the admiration of the ages."[18] (Dunlap's praise may seem hyperbolic, but given what then passed for a European Old Master painting on the New York art market, it may well have been justified.) In 1829 Bryant apostrophized the artist as *the* painter of American landscape in "To an American Painter Departing for Europe." Bryant began his sonnet:

> Thine eyes shall see the light of distant skies:
>   Yet, Cole! thy heart shall bear to Europe's strand
>   A living image of thy native land,
> Such as on thy own glorious canvass lies.[19]

Thirty-six years later, Bryant still recalled the nationalist enthusiasms Cole's early landscapes awakened: "Here, we said, is a young man who does not paint nature at second hand, or with any apparent remembrance of the copies made by others. Here is the physiognomy of our own woods and fields; here are the tinges of our own atmosphere; here is American nature and the feeling it awakens. You have only to look at his pictures to see that they represent the features of no region but that in which we dwell."[20] Cooper wrote in a similar vein in *Notions of the Americans,* a book intended as a defense of American society against foreign critics and published simultaneously in London and Philadelphia in 1828: "There are some highly respectable professional landscape painters. One of them, a Mr. Cole, possesses the rare faculty of giving to his pictures the impression of nature to a degree so extraordinary that he promises to become eminent. . . . To me his scenery is like the scenery from which he drew, and as he has taste and skill enough to reject what is disagreeable and to arrange the attractive parts of his pictures. I only hope he will continue to study the great master from whom he has drawn his first inspirations."[21] When the fact of Cole's English birth proved inescapable, his early biographers alluded to the artist's American relatives, including a grandfather who had been a Maryland farmer, "a yeoman cultivating his own soil," in Dunlap's picturesque phrase.[22] Indeed, to clinch the case for Cole's Americanness, Dunlap felt it necessary to include an elaborate piece of admitted hearsay in his two-volume *History of the Rise and Progress of the Arts of Design in the United States,* which he published in 1834 (and which in fact contains a great deal of hearsay). As Dunlap wrote, "So strong is [Cole's] desire to have the right to call [the United States] his, which he feels *to be his,* that I have heard it said he has exclaimed, 'I would give my left hand to identify myself with this country, by being able to say I was born here.' "[23]

As THE historian Robert Gross has argued, American cultural nationalism was rooted in the concerns of the founding fathers. Republican theory held that "only a small republic close to the people could safeguard 'the public good.' "[24] As James Madison maintained in *The Federalist,* political thinkers on both sides of the Atlantic believed an extensive republic was incapable of surviving the competition of "a great variety of interests, parties and sects" since "no single faction could readily gain sway."[25] In addition to creating a republican government based on countervailing checks and balances, the framers of the Constitution and those who followed their lead concerned themselves with building a national culture that would, in the realm of ideology and myth as well as in the domain of everyday life, bind the American people together—or at least the American upper classes. The four decades preceding Cole's arrival in New York witnessed the rise of academies of arts and sciences; the founding of libraries, athenaeums, and historical societies; the publication of journals, such as the *American Monthly Review* and the *American Monitor,* which proclaimed nationalist ambitions in their titles; and the appearance of textbooks and reference works such as Jedidiah Morse's *American Geography* (1789) and *Universal Geography of the United States* (1797), Noah Webster's widely used *American Spelling Book,* and his authoritative *American Dictionary of the English Language* (1828)—all conceived to advance the dream of a nation, in Webster's words, as "independent in literature as she is in politics, as famous for arts as for arms."[26]

After his spectacular New York debut, Cole's name was indissolubly linked to the cultural-nationalist project. As Bryant asserted in his funeral oration for the artist, from the time he was discovered by Trumbull, Dunlap, and Durand, Cole "had a fixed reputation, and was numbered among the men of whom our country had reason to be proud."[27] But what of Cole's view of the role that in effect had been created for him? To what extent did he share the cultural nationalists' enthusiasms? Was he concerned with the fate of a specifically American culture? The evidence suggests an ambivalence that only grew with time.

He was, of course, fully aware that his career rested on his reputation as the United States' foremost painter of native scenery, and for the first decade of that career he embraced the role of standard-bearer for American landscape painting. Yet if he was celebrated at home, he was mainly ignored abroad. In a lengthy and extraordinarily candid letter to Dunlap, which, to his mortification, Dunlap published unedited in his *History,* Cole described his experience during the twenty-two months he spent in London between 1829 and 1831 in terms that would gratify the most outspoken cultural nationalist. English artists were "cold and selfish"; English art was "with few exceptions . . . meretricious"; and even Turner, "prince of the evil spirits," as Cole put it, having earlier produced pictures that were "beautiful and true, though rather misty," was now creating works that were "gorgeous but altogether false." He complained that the London art world had for the most part ignored his work; that even two nominally American artists living in London, C. R. Leslie and Gilbert Stuart Newton, had shown scant interest in his art; and that the paintings he sent for exhibition at the Royal Academy and British Gallery ended up "in the most *exalted* positions" (that is, hung near the ceiling or, in the language of the day, "skied"). He went on: "My own works, and myself most likely, had nothing to interest them sufficiently to excite attention: the subjects of my pictures were generally American—the very worst that could be chosen in London. I passed weeks in my room without a single artist entering, except Americans."[28] Cole allowed that at the Gallery of the Society of British Artists he had enjoyed a moderate success with his *Tornado in the American Wilderness,* and that via introductions from Gilmor and Cooper he had profited from contact with the president of the Royal Academy, Sir Thomas Lawrence, the poet Samuel Rogers, and Samuel's brother Henry. Yet Cole's letter to Dunlap is striking for what it omits—a point I will return to in a moment—and for the way Cole portrays himself as an American painter of American landscape who, inevitably, suffers neglect in the sophisticated and corrupt London art world, and whose "heterodox" opinions of Turner and other contemporary English artists were based on nothing other than the standard of "beautiful nature" itself.

Cole's "Essay on American Scenery," which he read before the American Lyceum in New York in 1835 and subsequently published in the *American Monthly Magazine,* marks the high point of the artist's career as cultural nationalist. In defense of what he described in the essay as "the less fashionable and unfamed American scenery," he made a series of predictable rhetorical moves, equating the national landscape with national identity, and defending its beauty and sublimity against the opinions of "those who through ignorance or prejudice strive to maintain that American scenery possesses little that is interesting or truly beautiful."[29]

Cole's letter to Dunlap and the passages just quoted from his "Essay on American Scenery" recall the prickliness and xenophobia that so often characterized American responses to foreign criticism—responses that, when it came to the former "mother country," compensated for unacknowledged or barely acknowledged feelings of dependency and inferiority. Consequently, if we ask what accounts for the aggrieved tone that permeates Cole's letter to Dunlap, or for his sarcasm in his "Essay on American Scenery," the answer seems obvious. The scorn Cole heaped on the London art world represented a backhanded acknowledgment of its cultural authority, his bitterness a displacement of the chagrin he felt at its failure to recognize his accomplishments.

Cole may never have felt more American than he did during his first London sojourn. And yet he had to have been aware, as were so many of his American contemporaries, of how deeply American art was rooted in English artistic practice and tradition. As might be expected, Anglophobia went hand in hand with Anglophilia. Filiopiety pervaded the American art world, especially when it came to West and Allston, who had achieved stunning successes in London, and who symbolized the transatlantic dimension of American art. Thus in 1816 the Pennsylvania Academy mortgaged its building in order to acquire Allston's then famous *Dead Man Restored to Life by Touching the Bones of the Prophet Elisha.* Twenty years later the academy again took out a mortgage on its building to purchase West's *Death on a Pale Horse.*[30] In a similar vein, in 1818 the American Academy of Fine Arts raised the large sum of $2,000 to commission a full-length portrait of Benjamin West from Thomas Lawrence—a work that, as Carrie Rebora has noted, would allow John Trumbull "to assert a connection between his academy and West's academy in London."[31]

Moreover, as Cole must also have recognized, landscape painting as it was practiced in the United States—and as he himself practiced it—was deeply rooted in English tradition and convention. In the spring of 1825 Cole closely studied William Oram's *Precepts and Observations on the Art of Colouring in Landscape Painting,* which had been published in London in 1810 but had been written many years earlier by a royal official and amateur landscapist who had died in 1777.[32]

Oram's *Precepts* epitomized conventional English landscape taste, though more that of the eighteenth than the early nineteenth century. Still, Oram furnished Cole with a method for sketching landscape, which he adhered to throughout his career, and for producing a uniform if relatively dark, or one might say Claudeian, effect. Oram's *Precepts* also introduced him to the work of such major European landscapists as Poussin, Domenichino, Gaspard Dughet, Jan Both, and Aert van der Neer.

Oram's *Precepts* represents one of many instances of Cole's reliance on English landscape precedent. English publications informed his practice, shaped his taste, gave form to his artistic ambition. An omnivorous reader, he was very likely familiar with the writings of Reynolds, Gilpin, and Alison. From books and conversations with critics, artists, and knowledgeable patrons, he developed an almost entirely conventional set of artistic aspirations, although unlike his more fastidious American admirers, he tended to ignore distinctions between high and popular art forms. His early success had derived in some measure from his skill in applying traditional landscape techniques and formats—the prospect, the pastoral, the sublime prospect—to American subjects. His taste in landscape, though perhaps somewhat *retardataire* by London standards, pretty much paralleled that of his English counterparts. When he left for England in 1829, the American art public tended to think of him as the American Salvator Rosa on account of his penchant for the sublime. (In the 1830s he produced a small painting titled *Salvator Rosa Sketching Banditti,* a playful homage to a preferred artist and perhaps a fantasy self-portrait.)[33] By the time he returned to the United States in 1832, Claude, so central to the English romantic landscape tradition, had become his favorite, and during the 1830s, as a new tranquility began to manifest itself in his art (fig. 10.2), he acquired a reputation as the "American Claude"—or as one writer put it, "our American Claude."[34]

The friends and patrons who supported and in part helped to finance his trip shared with him the idea that an American landscapist, especially an autodidact, needed to advance his artistic education by familiarizing himself with contemporary English art as well as the work of the Old Masters. As Cole wrote Gilmor from London in March 1830, the Old Masters were his "greatest study and admiration," especially Claude and Gaspard Dughet.[35] Still, his encounters with the work of English artists were to prove as consequential for his subsequent career as the study of the Old Masters, if not more so.

When Cole arrived in London, he was already an admirer of the work of John Martin, whose mezzotints of scenes from Milton's *Paradise Lost* had inspired his own *Garden of Eden* and *Expulsion from the Garden of Eden* of 1827–28, a pair of paintings he had hoped to sell in order to finance his European trip. During the

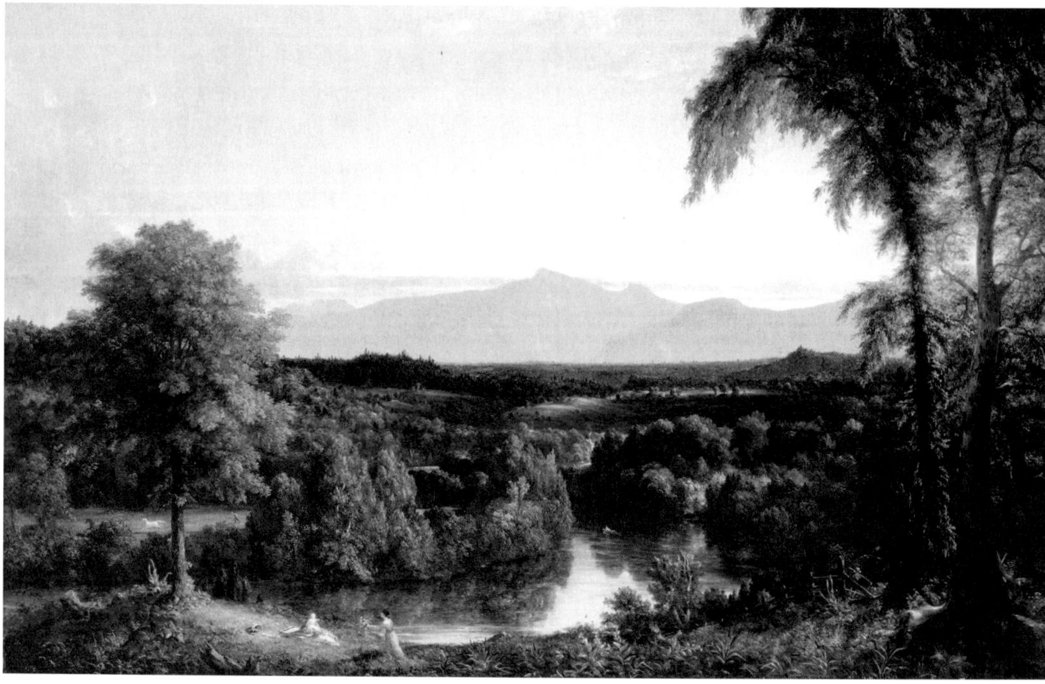

Figure 10.2. Thomas Cole, *View on the Catskill, Early Autumn,* 1836–37. Oil on canvas, 39 x 63 in. (99.1 x 160 cm). Metropolitan Museum of Art, New York. Gift in memory of Jonathan Sturges by his children, 1895 (95.13.3). Image copyright © The Metropolitan Museum of Art. Image: Art Resource, New York.

1820s, Martin's work was becoming popular in the United States, although not among the American cognoscenti. As Christopher Kent Wilson discovered, in 1828 a newspaper reviewer writing under the pseudonym "Middle Tint the Second" castigated Cole for plagiarizing Martin—a charge Cole vehemently denied since, following Reynolds, he distinguished between slavish copying and imitation.[36] Still, a critic for the staid *American Monthly Magazine* disparaged Martin's influence on Cole: were the young artist to continue working in this vein, the critic warned, he would suffer "the degradation" of being known as "an imitator of *Pandemonium Martin.*"[37] Nonetheless, in London Cole sought an introduction to Martin, who, writing to C. R. Leslie on June 7, 1830, invited Leslie and Cole to an evening "conversazione."[38]

In 1827 Cole solicited Washington Allston's recommendations regarding a European tour. In his letter the Anglophile Allston wrote that he found "no modern school of landscape equally capable with the English," and that Turner, " 'take him all in all,' has no superior of any age."[39] Gilmor struck a similar chord, advising Cole that "by studying the works of English artists, particularly Turner, you will be able to improve your style."[40] When Cole arrived in London, he was no doubt eager to see Turner's work. As Ellwood C. Parry III noted, "of the four paintings by . . . Turner in the Royal Academy exhibition in [July] 1829, Cole must have been profoundly impressed by . . . *Ulysses Deriding Polyphemus,*" since he made two drawings of the painting in one of his London sketchbooks.[41] Five months later, after visiting the artist in his gallery, he was full of praise for *The Building of Carthage,* "a splendid composition, and full of poetry. . . . The composition resembles very closely some of Claude's."[42] He also admired Turner's *Snow Storm: Hannibal and his Army Crossing the Alps,* and *The Temple of Jupiter,* which he rated, à la Allston, "as fine as anything the world has produced."[43] Yet he was not overawed by Turner, as his sharp criticisms of the English artist's more recent paintings make clear. Still, Turner exerted a powerful influence, sparking Cole's growing attachment to Claude (it is probably no coincidence that two days after his visit to Turner's gallery, Cole went to study the collection of Claude drawings at the British Museum),[44] inspiring an interest in color effects and extended perspectives, and reinforcing his fascination with the rise and fall of empire. Suffice it for now to say that Cole's *Course of Empire* of 1836 is unimaginable without his experience of Turner's art.

I touch on only two other instances of Cole's encounters with English landscape painting. In 1830, if not earlier, Cole made the acquaintance of John Constable. In June of that year the two artists visited the Grosvenor Gallery on Park Lane. Constable memorialized the visit and the two artists' shared interest in Dutch landscape painting with a tiny sketch of Paulus Potter's *The Hague with Cattle and Figures,* which he inscribed on the verso with the words "for his friend Cole." No other direct evidence remains of Cole's contact with Constable, but it is probable, as Parry and others have speculated, that Cole admired Constable's *Hadleigh Castle,* which he no doubt saw, along with Turner's *Polyphemus,* at the 1829 Royal Academy exhibition—a work that very likely has everything to do with his *Ruined Tower* (fig. 10.3), which he painted after his return to the United States.[45]

The second encounter was with the work of the eighteenth-century landscape painter Richard Wilson. Gilmor had advised Cole to copy a painting by Claude, Poussin, Ruysdael, or Cuyp, but, as Cole somewhat shamefacedly admitted to his patron, in London he had "only copied a Wilson."[46] The painting in question, which I have so far been unable to identify, belonged to Henry Rogers. Parry believed that Wilson's *Destruction of Niobe's Children* influenced Cole's large *Tornado in the American Wilderness,* the work the artist exhibited at the Gallery of British Artists in 1831.[47] Be that as it may, Cole's decision to copy a Wilson attests to his interest in an artist who was himself very much involved with Claudeian landscape and who was often considered the founder of the (then modern) English landscape tradition.

Cole left London in May 1831 for France and Italy, where he traveled as far south as Naples and spent several months in Rome working in a studio once occupied by Claude. He returned to New York in November 1832. The next nine years, in which he painted *The Course of Empire* and *The Voyage of Life* and a series of major landscapes including *The Oxbow,* were the most fruitful and successful of his career. Nonetheless, he grew increasingly restive. American patronage, he believed, was failing him. Moreover, whatever hopes he may have harbored for the future of the United States succumbed to a deepening historical pessimism evident in *The Course of Empire* and in the dystopian fantasies he set down in his journals.

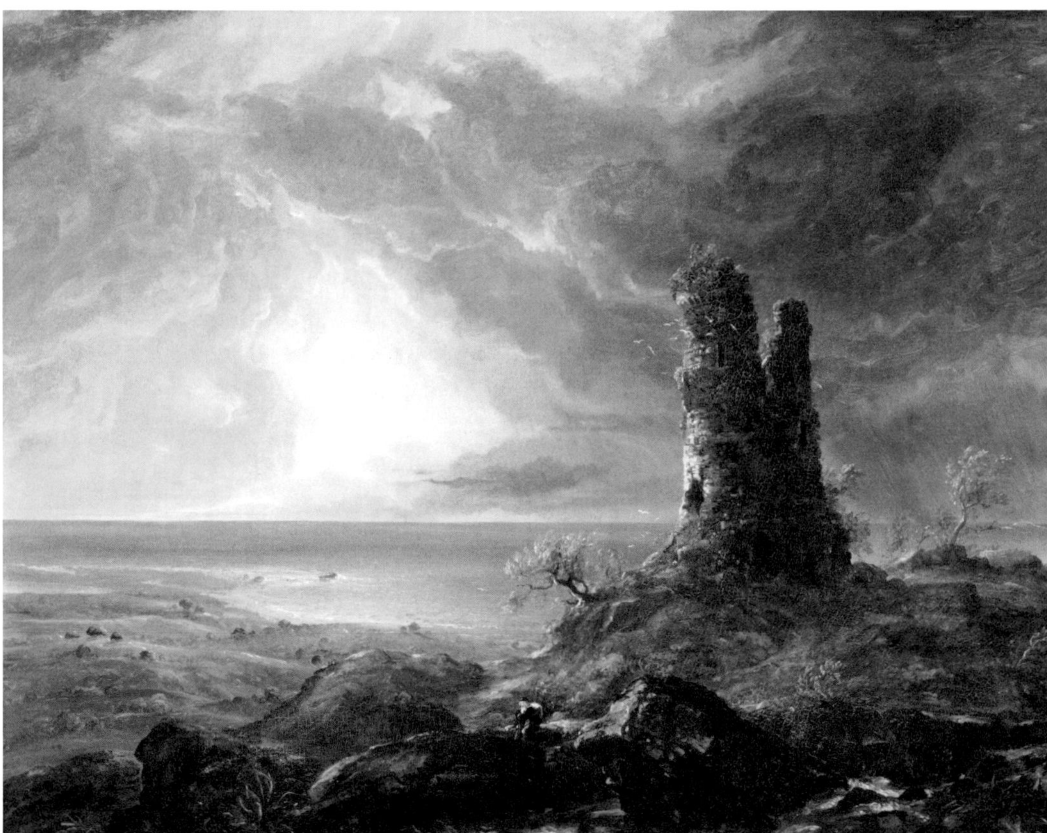

Figure 10.3. Thomas Cole, *Ruined Tower (Mediterranean Coast Scene with Tower),* 1832–1836. Oil on canvas, 26¾ x 34 in. (68 x 86.4 cm). Albany Institute of History and Art, Albany, N.Y., 1965.1.

He struggled to focus his ambition. He argued for the significance of American landscape as a subject for art, but he had, almost from the beginning of his career, believed he was destined to be more than a painter of landscape. "I do not feel I am a mere leaf painter," he wrote in 1838, forgetting his penchant for nature worship. "I have higher conceptions than a mere combination of inanimate, uninformed nature."[48] Before his first European trip he had aspired to what he called "a higher style of landscape," and produced works, such as *The Garden of Eden* and *The Expulsion from the Garden of Eden,* that may have satisfied his ambition but were less appreciated than his American landscapes.[49]

Fascinated by Rembrandt's etching *The Angel Appearing to the Shepherds,* which he had studied in London, he had, shortly after his return to the United States in 1833, painted his own version of the subject on a canvas measuring eight and a half by fifteen and a half feet. The failure of this undertaking did nothing to deter his pursuit of "higher conceptions."[50] Although he championed "historical landscape," he believed with the intensity of an autodidact in the traditional academic hierarchy of genres, and thus could not escape the notion that historical landscape was inferior to history painting, and that only as a painter of history could he win lasting renown. He lamented his lack of training in drawing and painting the figure, and while in Florence in 1831–32 attended a life class at the Academy of St. Luke, where he painted a *Dead Abel* in preparation for an elaborate history painting which he never executed.[51] In 1843, shortly after his return from his second European tour, he painted *After the Temptation,* an eight-foot-wide canvas that was subsequently cut into two sections. The painting, which probably reflected an increasingly conservative turn in his religious thinking (his pastor and later biographer, the Reverend Louis Legrand Noble, was a High Church Episcopalian and an enthusiastic follower of Cardinal Newman), failed to find a buyer—a failure that Cole, who was by the 1840s very much focused on religious subject matter, probably anticipated.[52] As he observed in a letter written to his wife eight months before *After the Temptation* went on display, he had on a visit to New York City "found out . . . that a Subject from Scripture particularly if a figure of Christ is introduced or even supposed is disgustful to the popular taste," which, as he well knew, tended to identify traditional Christian imagery with Catholicism.[53]

Cole's motives for his 1841–42 trip to Europe have never been closely examined. But given his dissatisfaction with his situation in the United States and his interest in developing an international reputation, it is evident that in addition to refurbishing his stock of European landscape subjects, he hoped to connect with an international audience. Although he did not spend much time in England on this trip, he had over the years kept an eye on the London art world. (Thus in a letter to his wife written in December 1840, he noted with some envy that Leslie had realized £26,000 or £27,000 from his painting of the coronation of Queen Victoria.)[54] By the time Cole reached London in August 1841, it is likely he had already in conversation with his wife entertained the possibility of an English or, perhaps, a European career. After traveling from London to Paris in October 1841 in the company of the writer Anna Jameson, he visited the Louvre, later writing his wife, "I am not overwhelmed I yet feel that I am a painter & that I have in my particular way achieved what has not been attempted before & I know that were I inclined to take a stand in the old world I should not remain unnoticed long."[55] (This from the United States' foremost painter of native scenery!) Cole spent the winter of 1841–42 in Rome producing a second version of *The Voyage of Life.* He showed the series to the sculptor Bertel Thorwaldsen and then exhibited it publicly, gaining in the eyes of the Italians "great honor," or so he told his wife. In the same letter he wrote that the series "evidently created a sensation in the outside world of Rome" (that is to say, among foreign visitors), and formulated plans to ship the paintings to London, where he was convinced they would find a buyer.[56]

The plan fell through, but Cole's transatlantic ambitions remained very much alive. He had long been interested in mural painting and had closely followed the competitions for the decoration of the Houses of Parliament. In 1844, when a third competition was announced, he decided to enter, knowing that his work might win a premium of £200, £300, or £500, and it might be purchased for display in the building.[57] Moreover, as Patricia Junker has remarked, entrants were aware that "this venue afforded other, more far-reaching opportunities [since] the competition would be seen by tens of thousands of visitors [at Westminster Hall] as well as scrutinized by critics[,] [that] the most popular works would be reproduced in the widely read *Illustrated London News* and possibly elsewhere," and that a prestigious mural commission might also result.[58] Aware of what was at stake, Cole did everything in his power to maximize his chances. He recruited the English watercolorist Peter Ainsley to serve as his agent and oversee the framing and submission of his painting. (Ainsley was the brother of the painter Samuel Ainsley, with whom Cole had traveled in Italy in 1841.) He wrote Ainsley a letter notable for the vehemence with which he insisted on his eligibility to enter the competition: "In the first place I was born in England of English parents. In the second I have lived in England the full term required of foreigners who are according to the announcement considered eligible."[59] Believing that success, in his words, depended "so greatly on the influence of friends," he contacted C. R. Leslie, who was persuaded to pass on a letter to Charles Eastlake, secretary of the Royal Commission. Leslie reported back to Cole that he had sent "[the] letter to Mr. Eastlake . . . as the best means of securing attention to your picture."[60]

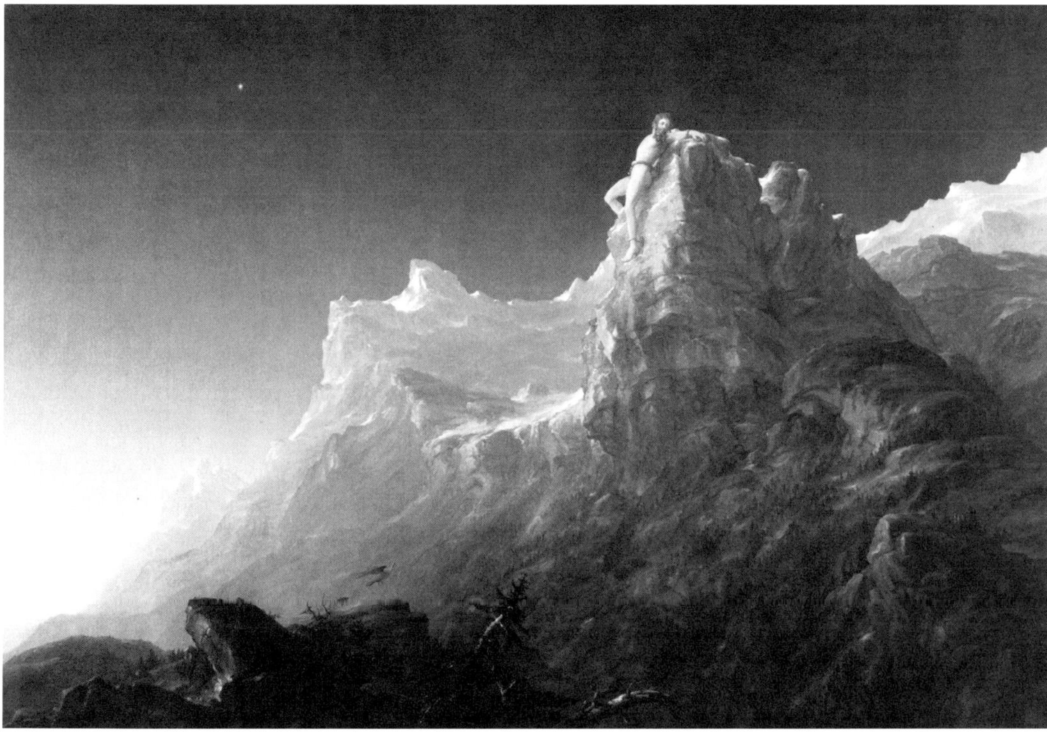

Figure 10.4. Thomas Cole, *Prometheus Bound*, 1847. Oil on canvas, 64 x 96 in. (92.1 x 210.8 cm). Fine Arts Museums of San Francisco, Museum Purchase, Gift of Mr. and Mrs. Steven McGregor Read and Joyce I. Swader Bequest Fund, 1997.28.

Cole may have thought that his *Prometheus Bound* (fig. 10.4), an eight-foot canvas set within a large frame, would attract the judges' and the public's attention, but the painting was badly hung and went unremarked by all but one London newspaper. In May 1847, a month before the opening of the Westminster Hall exhibition, a writer for the *Literary World* (New York) applauded Cole's *Prometheus* when it was displayed at the New-York Gallery of the Fine Arts for the way it gave "a dignity to art which the mass of modern artists do not seem to appreciate."[61] But Cole's New York celebrity did not translate to London. The *Art-Union* (London) carried a brief notice of the picture, concluding rather noncommittally that "the work is distinguished by valuable points."[62] While Cole's mythological subject fell within the guidelines set forth by the Royal Commission, landscape painting at the competition was, as one London commentator observed, "out of court."[63] Unsurprisingly, the biggest prizes went to figure paintings with subjects drawn from English history.

If, by 1847, improvements in transportation and communication had in a material sense brought New York and London closer together, culturally they were growing farther apart. The Hudson River School, which Cole had done so much to engender, was on the verge of gaining international recognition as the first truly independent American school of art. Cole was not much older than the new generation of Hudson River School painters, but he belonged to a different world. A conservative anti-modernist, he shared none of the new generation's optimism, its faith in American democracy, American expansion, and American progress. Instead, a decade earlier, in *The Course of Empire,* his most ambitious work, he had attempted to alert Americans to the dangers of imperial hubris. As a motto for his series, he chose a passage from Byron's *Childe Harold:* "first freedom and then glory; when that fails, wealth, vice, corruption."[64] An American work inspired by Martin, Turner, and Byron, Cole's series epitomizes the tensions I've been attempting to describe: the tensions between nationalist ideology and the reality of a transatlantic romantic culture.[65]

## NOTES

1. See Patrick Noon, ed., *Crossing the Channel: British and French Painting in the Age of Romanticism* (London: Tate Publications, 2003). At Tate Britain the exhibition was called *Constable to Delacroix: British Art and the French Romantics.*

2. For biographical information, see Helmut von Erffa and Allen Staley, *The Paintings of Benjamin West* (New Haven: Yale University Press, 1986).

3. See Nicholas Pevsner, *The Englishness of English Art* (1956; repr., Harmondsworth: Penguin, 1976); Barbara Novak, *American Painting of the Nineteenth Century,* 3rd ed. (New York: Oxford University Press, 2007); John Wilmerding, ed., *American Light: The Luminist Movement, 1850–1875* (Washington, D.C.: National Gallery of Art, 1980).

4. For biographical information, see Ellwood C. Parry III, "Thomas Cole's Early Career, 1818–1829," in *Views and Visions, American Landscape before 1830,* ed. Edward J. Nygren and Bruce Robertson (Washington, D.C.: Corcoran Gallery of Art, 1986), 161–87; Ellwood C. Parry III, *The Art of Thomas Cole: Ambition and Imagination* (Newark: University of Delaware Press, 1988); Alan Wallach, "Thomas Cole and the Course of American Empire," in *Thomas Cole: Landscape into History,* ed. William Truettner and Alan Wallach (New Haven: Yale University Press; Washington, D.C.: National Museum of American Art, Smithsonian Institution, 1993), 23–111; and Margy P. Sharpe, "Timeline," in Truettner and Wallach, *Thomas Cole: Landscape into History,* 161–68.

5. For the painting Cole showed at the Pennsylvania Academy's annual exhibition in 1824, see Parry, "Thomas Cole's Early Career," 166.

6. Dell Upton, "Inventing the Metropolis: Civilization and Urbanity in Antebellum New York," in *Art and the Empire City: New York, 1835–1861,* ed. Catherine Hoover Voorsanger and John K. Howat (New York: Metropolitan Museum of Art; New Haven: Yale University Press, 2000), 3.

7. For Trumbull's career, see Irma B. Jaffe, *John Trumbull: Patriot Artist of the American Revolution* (Boston: New York Graphic Society, 1975).

8. See Carrie Rebora [Barratt], "Mapping the Venues: New York City Art Exhibitions," in Voorsanger and Howat, *Art and the Empire City,* 50–55.

9. Cole's original painting was thought lost, but a work that may well be the 1825 painting was recently in the hands of an art dealer in New York. So far, however, the painting has been neither published nor sold. Plate 17 is the copy Cole painted for Daniel Wadsworth in 1826.

10. See Rebora, "Mapping the Venues," 47–50; Wallach, "Thomas Cole and the Course of American Empire," 23–24; Parry, *Art of Thomas Cole,* 21–27.

11. Trumbull quoted in American [William Dunlap], *New-York Evening Post,* November 22, 1825. Parry, *Art of Thomas Cole,* 25–26, reproduces in its entirety Dunlap's article. Variants of the story appear in subsequent biographical accounts of the artist. See Wallach, "Thomas Cole and the Course of American Empire," 23.

12. See Rebora, "Mapping the Venues," 47–50; Wallach, "Thomas Cole and the Course of American Empire," 33–38; and Parry, *Art of Thomas Cole,* 24–28.

13. For Trumbull's career as a landscapist, see Bryan Wolf, "Revolution in the Landscape: John Trumbull and Picturesque Painting," in *John Trumbull: The Hand and the Spirit of a Painter,* ed. Helen Cooper (New Haven: Yale University Art Gallery, 1982), 206–15; see also the catalogue entries, ibid., 216–30.

14. There is no record, however, of their meeting before Cooper left on June 1, 1826, for an extended European stay. In any case, as Parry notes, Cole was in Duanesburg, New York, "from as early as the third week in December [1825] until perhaps as late as the end of March 1826" (*Art of Thomas Cole,* 29), and left New York again in late May for Lake George, so chances for a meeting were slim. For Cooper's departure from New York, see Wayne Franklin, *James Fenimore Cooper: The Early Years* (New Haven: Yale University Press, 2007), 517–21.

15. See Donald A. Ringe, "James Fenimore Cooper and Thomas Cole: An Analogous Technique," *American Literature* 30, no. 1 (March 1958), 26–36; Donald A. Ringe, "Chiaroscuro as an Artistic Device in Cooper's Fiction," *PMLA* 78, no. 4 (September 1963): 349–57; James F. Beard, "Cooper and His Artistic Contemporaries," in *James Fenimore Cooper: A Re-Appraisal,* ed. Mary E. Cunningham (Cooperstown: New York State Historical Association, 1954), 480–95.

16. See Ellwood C. Parry III, "Cooper, Cole, and *The Last of the Mohicans,*" in *Art and the Native American: Perceptions, Reality, and Influences,* ed. Mary Louise Krumrine and Susan Clare Scott, special issue, *Papers in Art History from the Pennsylvania State University* 10 (2001): 155.

17. See William Cullen Bryant, *On the life of Thomas Cole: A funeral Oration delivered before the National Academy of Design, New York, May 4, 1848,* www.catskillarchive.com.

18. American [Dunlap], in Parry, *Art of Thomas Cole,* 25–26.

19. Today Bryant's sonnet is better known as "To Cole the Painter Departing for Europe," but its original title is symptomatic for my argument. See William Cullen Bryant, "To an American Painter Departing for Europe," in *Poems* (Boston: Russell, Odiorne, & Metcalf, 1834), 182; compare John W. McCoubrey, ed., *American Art, 1700–1960: Sources and Documents* (Englewood Cliffs, N.J.: Prentice Hall, 1965), 95; see also the Web page for

Bryant in Paul Lauter, ed., *Heath Anthology of American Literature,* 5th ed., http://college.cengage.com, where the poem is titled "To Cole, the Painter, Departing for Europe."

20. William Cullen Bryant, "The Academy of Design," April 28, 1865, in *Prose Writings,* ed. Parke Godwin, vol. 2 (New York: D. Appleton, 1884), 232.

21. James Fenimore Cooper, *Notions of the Americans: Picked up by a Travelling Bachelor,* ed. Gary Williams (1828; repr., Albany: State University of New York Press, 1991), 357.

22. William Dunlap, *A History of the Rise and Progress of the Arts of Design in the United States,* ed. Rita Weiss, 2 vols. (1834; repr., New York: Dover Publications, 1969), 2:351. For obvious reasons, Cole or Dunlap may have concocted the story of the artist's American relatives, including the "yeoman" grandfather. As of this writing, no corroborating evidence has come to light.

23. Ibid.

24. Robert Gross, "Introduction: An Extensive Republic" (unpublished manuscript, 2009), 2.

25. Madison cited ibid., 3.

26. Webster cited ibid., 19.

27. Bryant, *On Cole: A funeral Oration.*

28. Dunlap, *History,* 2:361.

29. Thomas Cole, "Essay on American Scenery," *American Monthly Magazine,* n.s. 1 (January 1836): 1–12. See also Thomas Cole, "Essay on American Scenery," in *The Collected Essays and Prose Sketches,* ed. Marshall Tymn (St. Paul: John Colet Press, 1982), 3–19.

30. See Frank H. Goodyear Jr., "A History of the Pennsylvania Academy of the Fine Arts, 1805–1976," in *In This Academy: The Pennsylvania Academy of the Fine Arts, 1805–1976* (1976; repr., n.p.: Resource Library, Traditional Fine Arts Organization, 2008).

31. Carrie Rebora [Barratt], "Sir Thomas Lawrence's 'Benjamin West' for the American Academy of the Fine Arts," *American Art Journal* 21, no. 3 (1989): 22.

32. See William Oram, *Precepts and Observations on the Art of Colouring in Landscape Painting* (London: Charles Clarke, 1810). See also Wallach, "Thomas Cole and the Course of American Empire," 27–28.

33. See "Salvator Rosa Sketching Banditti," www.mfa.org. See also Richard Wallace, *Salvator Rosa in America* (Wellesley, Mass.: Jewett Arts Center, 1979). Gilmor emphasized Cole's affinity for Rosa in his correspondence with the artist. See "Correspondence between Thomas Cole and Robert Gilmor, Jr.," in "Studies on Thomas Cole, an American Romanticist," ed. Howard S. Merritt, special issue, *Baltimore Museum of Art Annual* 2 (1967): 41–81.

34. The phrase appears in a letter from Samuel B. Ruggles to William H. Seward, July 24, 1841, quoted in Parry, *Art of Thomas Cole,* 222.

35. See Cole to Gilmor, March 1, 1830, in "Correspondence between Thomas Cole and Robert Gilmor, Jr.," 69.

36. See Christopher Kent Wilson, "Rediscovered Thomas Cole Letter: New Light on the Expulsion from the Garden of Eden," *American Art Journal* 18, no. 1 (Winter 1986): 73–74.

37. *American Monthly Magazine* 1 (August 1833): 402.

38. Parry, *Art of Thomas Cole,* 103.

39. Ibid., 95.

40. Gilmor to Cole, December 5, 1827, in "Correspondence between Thomas Cole and Robert Gilmor, Jr.," 96.

41. Parry, *Art of Thomas Cole,* 96–97.

42. Thomas Cole, "Notes on Art," December 12, 1829, in Louis Legrand Noble, *The Life and Works of Thomas Cole,* ed. Elliot S. Vesell (Hensonville, N.Y.: Black Dome Press, 1997), 81.

43. Parry, *Art of Thomas Cole,* 96. See also Franklin Kelly, "Turner and America," in *J. M. W. Turner,* ed. Ian Warrell (London: Tate Publishing, 2007), 232–34.

44. Cole's 1829 Notebook, Thomas Cole Papers, New York State Library, Albany, 16, 17; noted by Parry, *Art of Thomas Cole,* 101.

45. See Parry, *Art of Thomas Cole,* 100, 103–4.

46. See Cole to Gilmor, May 1, 1831, in "Correspondence between Thomas Cole and Robert Gilmor, Jr.," 71–72. See also Cole's letter in Dunlap, *History,* 2:366, where he asserts, "I made but one copy during my sojourn in Europe, and that was from a small Wilson of H Rogers."

47. Parry, *Art of Cole,* 113.

48. Thomas Cole, "Thoughts & Occurences," May 19, 1838, in *Collected Essays and Prose Sketches,* 156.

49. See Frank Kelly, *Thomas Cole's Paintings of Eden* (Fort Worth, Tex.: Amon Carter Museum, 1994).

50. For *The Angel Appearing to the Shepherds,* see Parry, *Art of Cole,* 101, 120, 149–51.

51. Dunlap, *History,* 2:363; Parry, *Art of Cole,* 119.

52. The larger section, which is approximately six by four and three-quarters feet, is now *Angels Ministering to Christ in the Wilderness* and is in the collection of the Worcester Art Museum; the smaller section, *The Tempter,* is at the Baltimore Museum of Art. See William H. Gerdts Jr., "Cole's Painting 'After the Temptation,'" in Merritt, "Studies on Thomas Cole, an American Romanticist," 282–85.

53. Thomas Cole to Maria Cole, January 28, 1843, Cole Papers.

54. Thomas Cole to Maria Cole, December 15, 1840, ibid.

55. Thomas Cole to Maria Cole, October 7, 1841, ibid.

56. See letter from Thomas Cole to Maria Cole, May 21, 1842, private collection, reproduced in Parry, *Art of Cole,* 271–72. For Cole's work on the second version of *The Voyage of Life* and Thorwaldsen's visit, see Noble, *Life and Works of Cole,* 232–41; Parry, *Art of Cole,* 265–68, 271–72.

57. See Patricia Junker, "Thomas Cole's *Prometheus Bound:* An Allegory for the 1840s," *American Art Journal* 21, nos. 1 and 2 (2000): 40–41. As will be evident, I have relied on Junker's research for my discussion of Cole's painting.

58. Ibid.

59. Cited ibid., 45.

60. Ibid. Cole's letter to Eastlake is lost, but very likely it reproduced the arguments the artist set forth in his letter to Leslie.

61. Cited ibid., 43.

62. Cited ibid., 45.

63. Cited ibid.

64. See Alan Wallach, "Cole, Byron, and the *Course of Empire,*" *Art Bulletin* 50, no. 4 (December 1968): 375–79.

65. Timothy Barringer, "The Englishness of Thomas Cole," in *The Cultured Canvas: New Perspectives on American Landscape Painting,* ed. Nancy Siegel (Hanover: University Press of New England, 2011), 3, argues that "the experience of [Cole's] early years [in England] shaped, even determined Cole's later cultural and aesthetic positions. While Cole distanced himself—through a careful campaign of self-fashioning—from the modern, the industrial and, after 1818, the English circumstances of his formation, I suggest that his creative project was defined—albeit negatively—by the geographical, economic, and cultural milieu of his early life. Cole's paintings . . . can be seen to make frequent, if tacit, references to British art and culture." In his essay, Barringer gives an account of Cole's childhood and adolescence in Bolton, Chorley, and Liverpool, and offers a number of valuable insights into how Cole's art reflected or was shaped by his English experience. Still, in my view Barringer exaggerates the extent to which Cole's career was determined by the circumstances of his early life in the north of England, and overestimates the English dimension of the artist's *Course of Empire* series.

# IV RACE

# 11

# Picturing the Murder of Jane McCrea

## A Critical Moment in Transatlantic Romanticism

*William H. Truettner*

Since it was first published in 1967, Robert Rosenblum's *Transformations in Late Eighteenth Century Art* has offered art historians a closely observed visual route through a bewildering array of late eighteenth-century Salon-inspired history paintings.[1] It was Rosenblum's genius to see neoclassicism and romanticism not as separate and distinct but as artistic movements that had much in common, the former merging slowly into the latter, with late eighteenth-century neoclassicism previewing almost every romantic tendency that would appear in more distinct form in the first several decades of the nineteenth century. Indeed, so thoroughly did Rosenblum dispose of old clichés about neoclassicism that he almost single-handedly recalled from the margins of art history works that had previously been dismissed as grim and moralizing accounts of ancient history. The content of these works, he argued, should be viewed against the unsettling background of contemporary events—several decades of violent social and political change in Europe and North America. And it was the emotionally charged byproduct of these chaotic times that often surfaced in the representation of otherwise obscure classical subjects, painted by artists who had, while composing their large canvases, intentionally or unintentionally introduced a similar aura of revolutionary activity into a no less perilous ancient world. Vividly representing this era of Salon painting is Anne-Louis Girodet's *Death of Camilla* (plate 20), a work that bears a haunting resemblance to the painting that is the subject of this essay, John Vanderlyn's *Murder of Jane McCrea* (plate 21).

If French and other European artists led the way in representing this troubled modern era with works that indirectly referenced the tension and conflict of everyday life, American artists participated also, but with fewer willing or able to take on such epochal events. Benjamin West and John Singleton Copley, for example, did few history paintings before going abroad, and later, when they were presiding over large London studios, their work more often dealt with the global reach of British imperialism than with events in North America. (West's *Death of Wolfe* is a notable exception.) That left Charles Willson Peale, John Trumbull, Washington Allston, and John Vanderlyn to fill the void at home. Several of Peale's major paintings featured the history of science and the arts in the new republic, and Allston, the most prolific history painter of the four, spent more time on biblical and literary subjects than on picturing events in America, past or present. Trumbull and Vanderlyn, however, did take on major political issues of the day: Trumbull with a series of Revolutionary War battles and momentous national events that preceded and followed (four of these subjects became mural-size oil paintings in the U.S. Capitol); and Vanderlyn, deeply indebted to French neoclassicism, with three memorable Salon paintings—the previously mentioned *Jane McCrea* (1804), *Marius amid the Ruins of Carthage* (1807), and *Ariadne Asleep on the Island of Naxos* (1809–1812). Whatever the relationship of the second painting to events in America, the first directly and unequivocally depicts a gruesome event that took place during the Revolutionary War.[2] Moreover, it stands out as the most brutal and provocative history painting done by an American-born artist in the decades preceding or following the war, although popular illustrations, published during the same years, sometimes recorded similar tragedies.

Like many of the examples that Rosenblum illustrates and describes, *Jane McCrea* diligently follows a then-current formula for Salon painting. The horrific effects of the *Death of Camilla* have been transported from ancient Rome to the wilds of North America, where a similar tragedy unfolds. But this time violent purposeful action has been confined to a format even more rigidly drawn than in Girodet's painting, perhaps causing Vanderlyn to lose sight of the pictorial initiatives with which he began. The murderous impulse of the savages, for example, is offset by figures that are stiff and wooden, and by a composition that severely restricts whatever vision of mayhem the artist intended. The result is a painting that looks uncomfortably stillborn, a studio exercise struggling to gain more convincing form and expression. Not for a moment, however, did Vanderlyn take his eye off the formula he hoped would gain him admission to the Salon of 1804.[3] Nor, as we shall see, did he seem to have reservations about showing two Indians as brutal savages prepared to murder an innocent white woman, despite telling differences between the subject and more moderate images of North American

Indians that preceded and followed his work. That makes *Jane McCrea* an uncomfortable departure in the history of British and American art: among a succession of images that reach back to 1710 and extend forward to about the mid-nineteenth century, few white American artists chose to show Indian hostility toward white subjects in such an uncompromising manner, despite a long and bitter history of provocation on both sides, sometimes ending in events no less horrifying than the one Vanderlyn has depicted.

If indeed *Jane McCrea* is an uncomfortable departure from major historical paintings that featured North American Indians, why did Vanderlyn undertake such a subject? The short answer is that it was a commission, negotiated by the artist-inventor Robert Fulton, to illustrate an epic poem by Joel Barlow (1754–1812), a Connecticut Wit who later became a Jeffersonian Democrat and achieved major financial and political success as a diplomat in Holland and France. Barlow had begun the poem, subsequently called *The Columbiad,* in 1787 as a tribute to a brave new post–Revolutionary War America, with selected scenes from the war previewing the subsequent outcome. One of those describes the murder by two "savages" of a loyalist heroine who had all the attributes of a Jane McCrea figure. Barlow had originally engaged Fulton to illustrate the poem, but Fulton, after completing only a few drawings, one of which was the Jane McCrea scene, withdrew in favor of Vanderlyn. Vanderlyn took over the commission, apparently with Barlow's consent, and was supposed to finish it, but instead turned Fulton's drawing (now lost) into a full-fledged Salon painting that subsequently became known as *The Murder of Jane McCrea.*[4] This turn of events, which seems to have taken Barlow by surprise, left him to find yet another artist to finish the illustrations for *The Columbiad.* Vanderlyn, however, never looked back. He was by then beginning his second stay in Paris (1803–1815), and was determined to enhance his reputation in the United States by succeeding at the annual Paris Salon. When Barlow's commission dropped into his lap, developing the Jane McCrea scene must have seemed to him a golden opportunity. Terrified, helpless women facing the unchecked passion of brutal warriors was by then standard Salon fare.[5] Vanderlyn had only to play up the moment when the Indians attacked Jane—a moment from which she could neither escape alive nor keep her honor intact—in order to advance toward his goal. Call it art or exploitation or both; Vanderlyn was determined to match the horror stories told in similar Salon history paintings. But his technique, he also realized, had to meet the high standards of French academic painting. During his first trip to Paris (1796–1800), he trained under François-André Vincent, a follower of David, in order to master Salon-style brushwork and composition. By 1804, a year into his second stay in Paris, the effort had paid off. *Jane McCrea* seems to have closed the gap between Vanderlyn and his Salon competitors, at least enough to get his painting hung in the most prestigious art showcase in Europe at that time.

## The Jane McCrea Story

If Vanderlyn's commitment to Salon success comes as no surprise, it still does not fully explain why *Jane McCrea* looks the way it does. For the rest we are indebted to Samuel Edgerton's pioneering research that brought to light the political alignment of Barlow, Jefferson's ambassador to France; Fulton; and Vice President Aaron Burr, Vanderlyn's principal supporter during his early years in Paris.[6] In addition to their Republican (as opposed to Federalist) political leanings, all three shared an interest in French art and culture, and Vanderlyn, as a young student in Paris, must have seen himself following in their footsteps. With the more immediate goal of advancing his career, Vanderlyn mastered the techniques of French Salon painting and subsequently came up with a subject (courtesy of Barlow) that would gain him entry to the Salon of 1804. Moreover, that subject, which was sure to revive lingering Revolutionary War animosities against the British, was also bound to have political appeal for French audiences. When the painting hung in the Salon of 1804, it was accompanied by a label that read "A Young Woman Slaughtered by Two Savages in the Service of the English During the American War." That left little doubt as to how the painting should be interpreted.[7]

To explain the label further, we must go back to a notorious and unfortunate series of events early in the war that culminated in Jane McCrea's death. The daughter of a Tory family living in New Jersey, Jane was betrothed to a young officer in General Burgoyne's army, which in 1777 was encamped near Fort Edward in northern New York State. While traveling across the frontier to meet him, she was attacked by Indians, who murdered and scalped her. The blame was placed on Mohawk warriors, who frequented the area, although the actual identity of the Indians who accosted her was never known for certain. In any case, as the story spread through the northern colonies, guilt was assigned to the Mohawks, enabling Barlow to blame Jane's death on the British, for whom the Mohawks had fought during the Revolution.[8]

Vanderlyn recounts the story in no uncertain terms, driving home the point that by 1804, it was difficult for many (but certainly not all) Americans to see the Mohawks in a favorable light and, by extension, the British, who had encouraged Mohawk scalp-taking during the war. Most recent scholars have followed the same argument to account for the zeal with which Vanderlyn made his case against the Indians.[9] What seems missing, however, is the recognition that perhaps Vanderlyn had complementary objectives in mind: he could launch his career with a Salon-style history painting that indirectly favored expanding French influence in Europe, *and* he could simultaneously fulfill his patron's wish to vilify the Indians who had pursued and murdered Jane McCrea. The result can be seen as a rather conventional example of French neoclassical composition, conceived in a way that makes it look like a nightmare today but that early nineteenth-century Salon audiences surely considered more acceptable.

Does such an explanation complicate our understanding of the picture without overturning the scholarly attention it has already received? Vanderlyn knew his competition: *Jane McCrea* was not a picture intended for exhibition at the American Academy of the Fine Arts in New York (although it eventually ended up there); it was meant to compete with neoclassical history paintings that featured violence, chaos, and tragedy. All such melodramatic effects, Rosenblum argues, found their way into Salon subjects of that period. After several years' residence and study in Paris, Vanderlyn had evidently mastered such effects.[10] Dark savage Indians, whose angry, distorted features and powerful bodies cast them as implacable foes, are poised to attack (and undoubtedly violate) a cowering, pathetic, terrified white woman. Surely more than anti-British feelings are at work here; what we also see is ambition—that of a young American painter eager to test his skill against a daunting array of European masters.

What else suggests that Vanderlyn's determination to produce a Salon painting might have led us to overestimate the anti-British feelings we perceive in *Jane McCrea* today? Surely Barlow's response to the picture needs further consideration. When it was offered to him (admittedly at almost twice the price of the original contract, but after the painting had been shown at the Salon), Barlow, in a cool and restrained letter to Vanderlyn, refused to pay the additional amount and directed the artist to send the picture back to the United States. Fulton, undoubtedly embarrassed by the turn of events, purchased the picture for the collection of the American Academy of the Fine Arts in New York, where it remained (and was hung from time to time) until in 1842 a group of subscribers, acting on behalf of the Wadsworth Atheneum in Hartford, purchased the collection from the Academy, which by then had ceased operation.[11]

One could argue, of course, that Barlow refused the painting (which he had probably seen either in Vanderlyn's studio or at the Salon of 1804) solely on the basis of its higher price. But Barlow was a wealthy man and could easily have paid the additional amount. So was Barlow perhaps uneasy about the way Vanderlyn had staged the painting? Had *Jane McCrea* as a Salon entry become too violent (and perhaps too harshly critical of Indian behavior) for the taste of a progressive American statesman and literary figure, even though he had earlier spared no detail in describing a similar event in his epic poem? And what of Fulton's role?

Did he act out of concern for Vanderlyn and carry through with the purchase of the painting because he had originally brought artist and patron together? Or did he simply know that there was no market for such a painting among American collectors, no matter how strong their anti-British feelings? Finally, one wonders, had Vanderlyn's Salon formula betrayed him? Had it turned protest into a polemic that sent too strong a message of Indian-hating, even to those in his own country who had no particular affection for the native population? In a public collection the painting might have been tolerated, or seen as a historical curiosity. But who among the few American private collectors of that period would have wanted to hang such a painting on his walls?

If the motives of those trying to deal with *Jane McCrea* after it had been exhibited at the Salon seem to raise questions, one also wonders, along with Edgerton, why Vanderlyn's success at the Salon elicited so little comment back home?[12] No other American artist had done so well when competing at the Salon. The best evidence may again be the shocking nature of the subject, and how it applied to the larger issues of Indian-white relationships during the Jefferson administration. During the years when Vanderlyn was in France, painting and exhibiting *Jane McCrea,* Barlow's good friend Jefferson was busily courting Indians at the White House. The president's two main objectives were finding new homelands in the Ohio Country for eastern Indians driven west by the Revolution, and securing the friendship of Upper Missouri Indians who resided within the unsecured boundaries of the newly acquired Louisiana Purchase. As minister to France during the Jefferson administration, Barlow must have had second thoughts when asked to pay double for a painting that might have caused a negative reaction among government officials in Washington as well as private collectors in New York. Through the first half of the nineteenth century, Vanderlyn's painting also seems to have lost appeal as the model for popular illustrations of the Jane McCrea story.[13] More benign and sentimental compositions took over, presumably because public taste for Indian images during those years favored less hostile encounters. That would again change, but not until the Army of the West had permanently overturned a short-lived pre–Civil War era of relative toleration and peace.

## *Jane McCrea* as Misfit

Another way to address the question of *Jane McCrea's* impact on a patron like Barlow is to consider its unique position among images of North American Indians. What we find is that *Jane McCrea* is an exception that falls between two more positive trends in the painting of Native Americans. The first, dating to before 1800, consisted mainly of works by British artists and American expatriates, such as Benjamin West and Gilbert Stuart, operating out of London; the second, based in the United States, included American artists trained abroad, as well as in New York and Philadelphia.[14] The variety of artists and styles considerably complicates the range of Transatlantic Romanticism, adding to the overwrought temper of French neoclassicism the more measured, "scientific," and deeply nostalgic Indian images coming from Britain and North America before and after 1800. Consider, for example, Gilbert Stuart's impressive portrait of the Mohawk leader Joseph Brant (fig. 11.1), painted in London in 1786, some twenty years before *Jane McCrea;* or Charles Willson Peale's benign and uplifting portrait of Brant, painted in Philadelphia in 1797, a year after Vanderlyn first went to study in Paris. Despite Brant's—or perhaps more accurately Mohawk warriors'—well-publicized raids through the Wyoming Valley of Pennsylvania during the Revolutionary War, British and American artists most often portrayed Brant as an enlightened Indian, usually wearing a hybrid ensemble of Indian and European dress.[15] Accordingly, both the Stuart and Peale portraits play down racial characteristics. In Stuart's portrait, Brant assumes a thoughtful, somewhat melancholy air, perhaps in recognition of his postwar circumstances, which left him and the Mohawk warriors who had followed him during the Revolution bereft of their extensive homelands in upper New York State. And yet Peale later shows him, according to Charles Coleman Sellers, "full of . . . hope . . . for the betterment of his people."[16]

On the other side of *Jane McCrea,* or in some cases concurrent with Vanderlyn's painting, are tightly drawn neoclassical heads by artists working in Washington, including Europeans such as C. B. J. Févret de Saint-Mémin (fig. 11.2) and native artists such as Charles Bird King (fig. 11.3). These artists share with Vanderlyn's *Jane McCrea* a preoccupation with linear style and with consistent ethnographic detail. Vanderlyn's Mohawks no longer wear the hybrid clothing of Stuart's Brant; they are instead carefully dressed in Mohawk leggings, perhaps copied from a pair that Vanderlyn had in his studio. And the Saint-Mémin and King figures are correctly turned out in Plains Indian dress. But that's as far as one can take the comparison. Unlike *Jane McCrea,* the Saint-Mémin and King images are static and restrained, and neither depicts overt hostility toward whites. *Jane McCrea,* as we have noted, belongs to a different tradition, one more closely associated with Vanderlyn's understanding of French Salon aesthetics. Why then was Vanderlyn so out of step with what was going on in his own country? Perhaps because by the early nineteenth century, romanticism had taken a scientific turn in the United States, at least as far as painting Indians was concerned.[17] Indians were more often represented as natural history specimens, part of the new order of flora and fauna encountered by artists roaming through a North America that, beyond the Atlantic coast settlements, remained almost untouched. As such, Indians were no

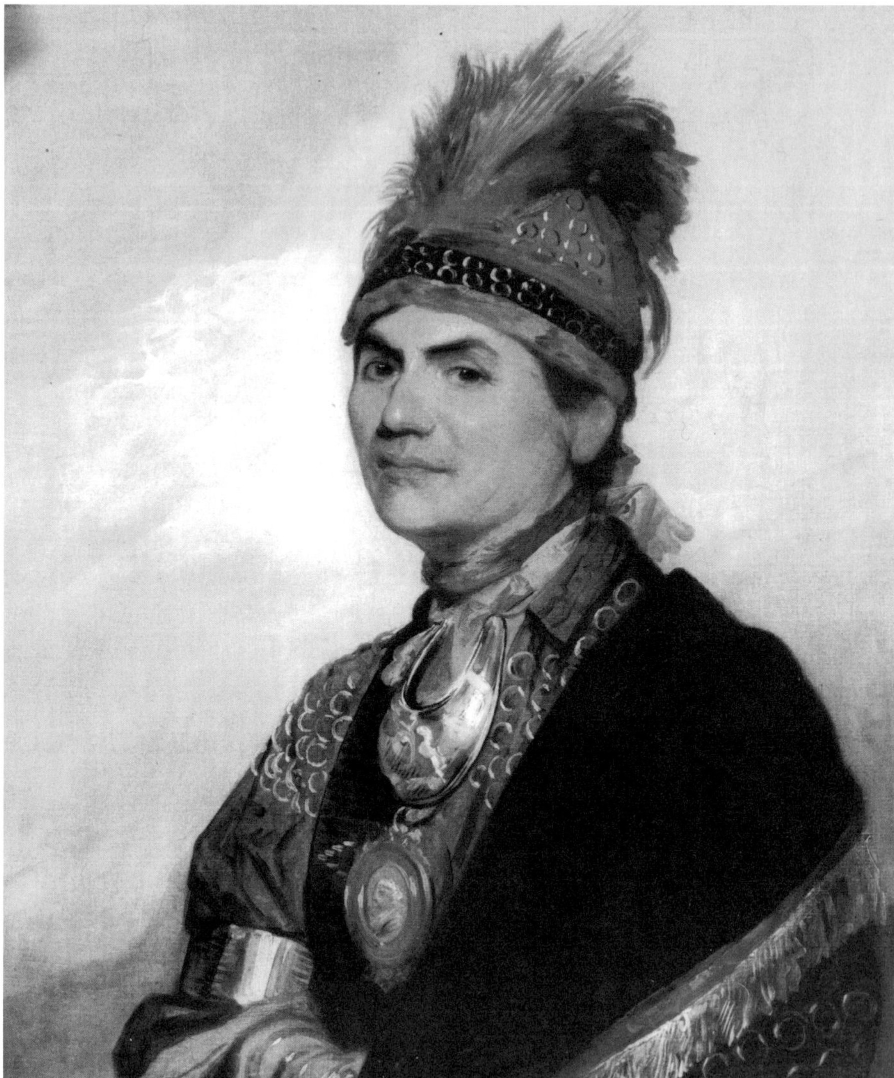

Figure 11.1. Gilbert Stuart, *Joseph Brant,* 1786. Oil on canvas, 23½ x 24 in. (59.7 x 61.0 cm). Collection of the Duke of Northumberland, Syon House, London.

more savage than their surroundings, although their behavior would soon become a matter of how fast their surroundings began to disappear and what measures they subsequently took to defend themselves. Whatever those measures may have been, they appear to be less sensational than those that attracted attention at the Paris Salons of the early nineteenth century.

## Jane McCrea in and out of Context

Not only does Vanderlyn's *Jane McCrea* stand out as unique among North American Indian subjects that immediately preceded and followed it, but also, within the larger sequence of Indian images painted between 1710 and about 1840, it is one of a kind, at least among those by white artists well known for painting Indian subjects during that period. One can't assume, of course, that none of those images

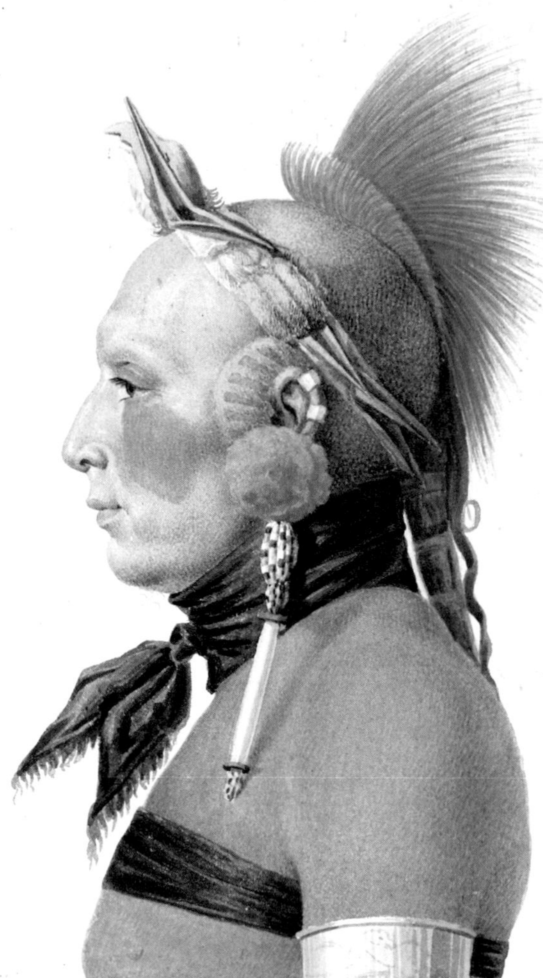

Figure 11.2. Charles Balthazar Julien Févret de Saint-Mémin, *Osage Warrior,* 1804. Watercolor on paper, 7½ x 6¾ in. (19.1 x 17.2 cm). Courtesy Winterthur Museum, Winterthur, Del.

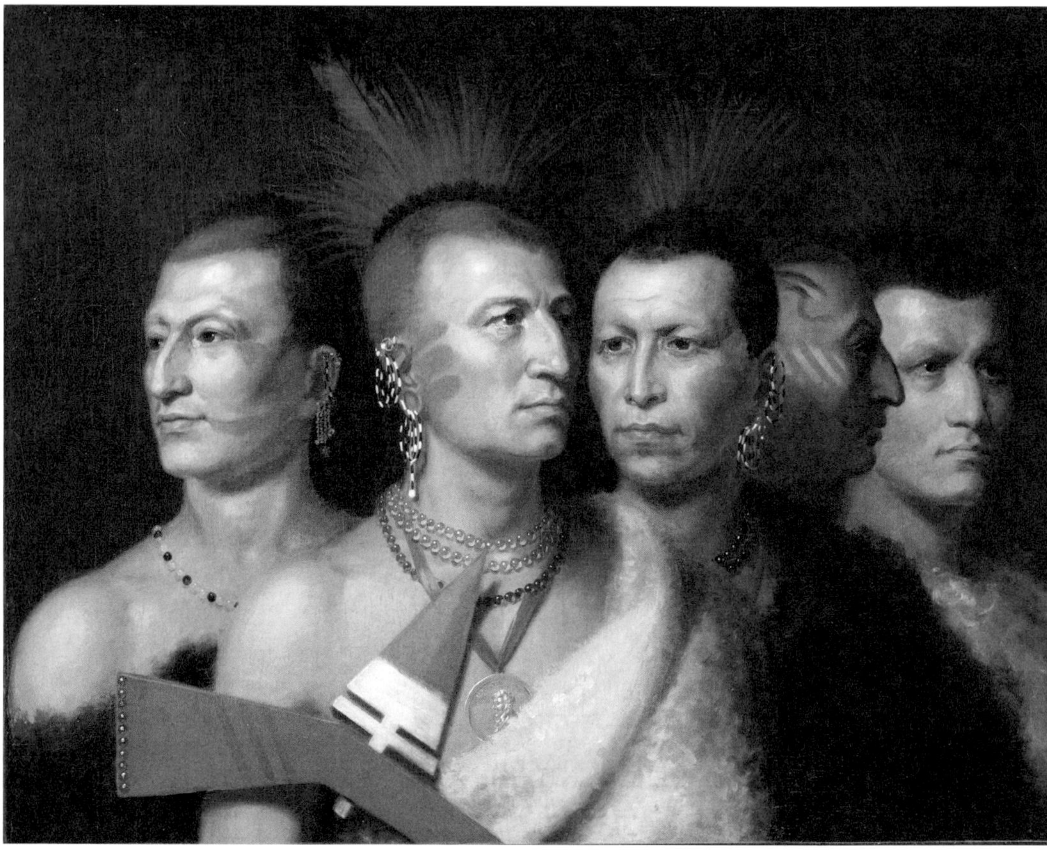

Figure 11.3. Charles Bird King, *Young Omahaw, War Eagle, Little Missouri, and Pawnees,* 1821. Oil on canvas, 36⅛ x 28 in. (91.8 x 71.1 cm). Smithsonian American Art Museum, Washington, D.C., Gift of Miss Helen Barlow.

demeaned Indians; but their biases were usually more subtle, aimed at dismantling traditional Indian life or showing Indians unable to survive in a technologically advanced white world. Images of Indians and whites locked in vicious combat were few, except for those that appeared as popular prints, published individually or as illustrations in American and English periodicals of the period.

A review of additional Indian images will help reinforce these points. Conveniently enough, the images can be divided into two groups, each carrying an imperialist message but, unlike the brutal act featured in *Jane McCrea,* whispered rather than shouted. The first of these groups can be called by the familiar term Noble Savages; the second has been given the more arbitrary name Republican Indians.[18] Those who assigned the mythical status of Noble Savage to North

American tribes such as the Mohawks were mostly Europeans—British colonials, French missionaries, and romantic writers living in England and France. Although they originally cast these tribes as innocent primitives living peacefully in the dense woodlands that ranged from the eastern seaboard to the Alleghenies, by the early eighteenth century, rival colonial powers had already claimed much of the surrounding land. As a result, many of these Indians, from the Mohawks in the north to the Cherokees and the Creeks in the south, were at best part-time Noble Savages, regularly conscripted by competing European powers (and sometimes by other Indian tribes) to deal with the real-world problems of trying to protect their land and fur trade routes from further encroachment. If this somewhat modified their status as innocents, no one seemed to mind; indeed, the North American wilderness was thought to provide Noble Savages with a certain nature-learned cunning when it came to defending themselves against their enemies, white or red. And yet Noble Savages were rarely referred to or pictured as "wild." Instead they were usually shown in hybrid dress—an often deliberate mix of Indian and white costumes—or submitting to white leadership, both signifying the degree to which they acknowledged the presence of Europeans in the New World.

After numerous bloody battles between American colonials and so-called Noble Savages during the Revolutionary War, their reputation as ideal Indians began to wane, and for a time such Indians seem to have vanished from North America. But by the beginning of the nineteenth century, another group, designated here as Republican Indians, came along to take their place. Republican Indians, so called because they flourished on the Great Plains during the early years of the American republic (and were also admired by a New York Republican elite), were no less a mythical construction than Noble Savages. The former are more familiar to us today; collectively they constitute the stereotype we think of as American Indians.[19] They are generally associated with the first decades of the nineteenth century, a period of active territorial expansion, and with a West in which Anglo-Americans were gaining a first tentative foothold. These Indians lived near overland trails to the Southwest or along the Upper Missouri River, main corridors for the fur trade and eventually for settlers headed for rich agricultural lands in Texas and the Far West. To some extent Republican Indians could monitor, if not control, these two activities, vital to the development of the young nation. When we see them in pictures today, they wear clothing that appears to be ethnographically correct, made of hides and fur, and decorated with feathers, beads, and animal parts. They are also shown riding horses, hunting buffalo, taking part in religious ceremonies, and fighting other Plains tribes.

## Painting Noble Savages

Even a brief survey of Noble Savage imagery must start with four monumental portraits of Indian "Kings," three of whom were Mohawks (fig. 11.4). The "Four Kings," summoned to London in 1710 by Queen Anne, who also commissioned the portraits, were nominally present to serve the queen as potential allies in North America. But the portraits were a new twist—a subtle mixture of flattery and intimidation that made the Mohawks party to British imperial designs on the New World.[20]

During the visit, at a time when Queen Anne's War preoccupied Britain and France, plans were made for a combined British-Mohawk attack on Montreal and Quebec. The attack never happened. What remains of the visit are portraits of the Kings by John Verelst, billed in his day as "a noted Face-Painter." More interesting than the facial features, however, are the settings of the portraits—forest interiors that represent the New World—and the costumes of the Four Kings. Hendrick, the grand or head chief, wears court dress; the others, like the King named Brant (see fig. 11.4), the grandfather of Joseph Brant (fig. 11.5), wear tunics of a sort, over which long red robes have been draped, reminding one of shepherds found in classical landscapes of the previous century. Hendrick also holds a wampum belt, symbolizing the agreement arrived at between the Mohawks and the British. The others wear beaded belts, moccasins, and earrings. In the lower register of each painting is an animal (a wolf for Hendrick, a bear for Brant). In addition, Brant proudly displays across his face, chest, and arms a spectacular tattoo. Otherwise, except for mildly aboriginal face types and darker skin, the figures don't necessarily stand out as Indians.

Not long after West arrived in Rome, he painted his first Indian picture, *Savage Warrior Taking Leave of His Family* (1760), whose central figure, a warrior departing from his home, reminds us how often artists drew on classical figures, such as the Apollo Belvedere, to assert the dignity of their Indian subjects. Over the next decade West followed with three more paintings that include Indians; in each, one or more figures are Mohawks. The first, *General Johnson Saving a Wounded French Officer from the Tomahawk of a North American Indian* (1764–1768), shows an incident that occurred during the French and Indian War. Sir William Johnson, an Irish baronet, fur trader, and unofficial steward of Mohawk affairs, was leading a force of local militia and Mohawk warriors along the shores of Lake Champlain when he was attacked by French soldiers under the command of Baron von Dieskau. The English engaged and defeated the French, leaving Dieskau exposed to the scalping knives of the Mohawks, when Johnson intervened, saving Dieskau's life. West's Indian looks and acts a bit like those in Vanderlyn's *Jane McCrea,* but with a major difference. What changes the outcome in West's picture is the Indian's response to Johnson, who formally deters the Indian's advance through a series of reciprocal movements and gestures. These, in effect, tell a moral tale: Johnson steps forward to arrest the Indian's attack, causing the Indian to restrain himself, even in the heat of battle. Thus, under Johnson's influence, he arrives at a standard of civilized behavior.

The next Indian, seated in the left foreground of West's famous painting *The Death of General Wolfe* (fig. 11.6), also appears willing to sample civilized behavior, but in this case the viewer is hard-pressed to know what West had in mind. Although they had fought on the side of the British earlier in the war, no Mohawks or other Indians were present at Quebec when Wolfe defeated Montcalm, thus ending French claims to Canadian North America.[21] When he placed the Indian (marked with a tattoo that identifies him as a member of a Mohawk clan) in such a prominent position in the picture, was West alluding to that alliance with the British, or did he have something more in mind? Apparently he did. The Indian and Wolfe face each other along a diagonal, each highlighted to contrast their physical appearance: the Indian in the prime of life, his strong young body a model of classical perfection; Wolfe, hovering on the edge of death, limp and recumbent, supported by two aides. Still, the Mohawk doesn't appear to act on his advantage. More likely the viewer sees his attitude as one of contemplation, even caution; he is perhaps the one figure in the painting unsure of the future. How would the British deal with the Mohawks in a postwar North America, when, with the French gone, British regulars and a subservient colonial militia would hold a distinct military advantage over the tribe?

That question more than any other seems to determine the Indian's prominent role in the painting. And yet the Mohawk appears to be swept along by a compositional thrust that directs the attention of those who surround him toward the dying Wolfe. The immediate concern of these figures, expressed through their focus on Wolfe, is the loss of their victorious commanding general. But perhaps West was also reaching for a higher, more universal meaning: great military victories are often accompanied by tragic human loss. Is it this that so deeply affects the Indian? If we assume, as with the previous picture, that the Mohawk is guided by the beliefs of a white officer corps, then he will be led by those surrounding him to reflect on the tragic consequences of Wolfe's death. But here West seems to suggest that the Mohawk's thoughts might not always align with those of the men he had fought beside in the previous war. For the British, death on a foreign battlefield was a more or less familiar event, the price paid for building and maintaining an empire. For the Indian, and for his future in North America, the moment clearly has a darker significance.

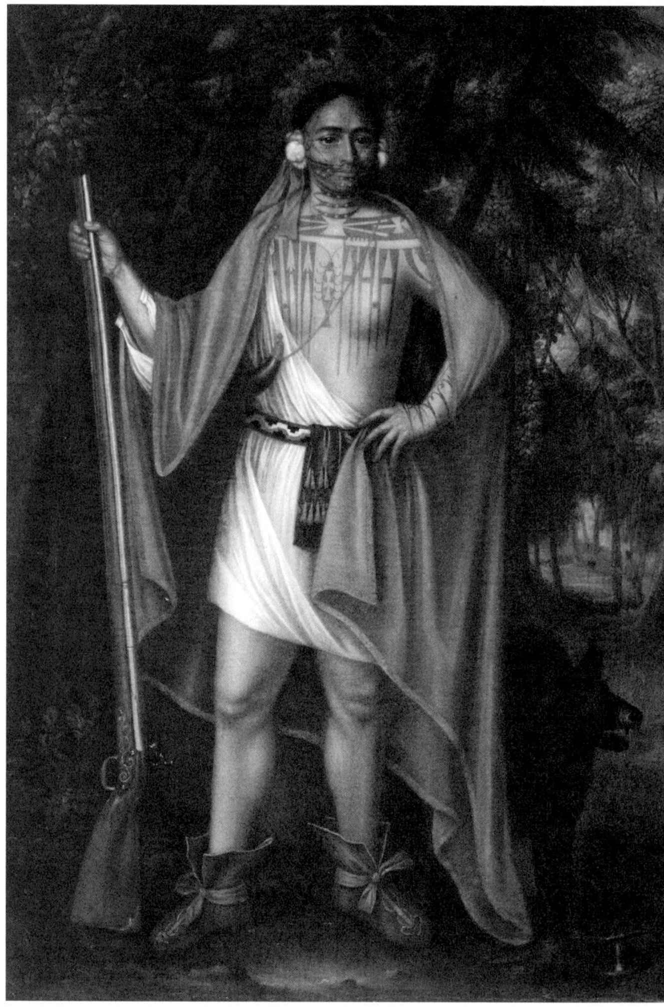

Figure 11.4. John Verelst, *Sa Ga Yeath Qua Pieth Tow (Christianized Brant),* 1710. Oil on canvas, 36 x 25⅞16 in. (91.4 x 64.5 cm). Library and Archives Canada, Ottawa, acquired with a special grant from the Canadian Government in 1977.

Six years after *The Death of General Wolfe,* West painted Sir Guy Johnson, his last picture in which an Indian appears (fig. 11.7). Johnson, who commissioned the portrait, was a nephew and son-in-law of Sir William, and succeeded his father-in-law as superintendent of Indian affairs for the Iroquois Confederacy.[22] Standing behind and to the right of Johnson is Captain David Hill (Karonghyontye), a Mohawk chief who accompanied Johnson to London in 1776, presumably at the request of British officials anxious about keeping the Mohawks on their side during the Revolutionary War. Hill has dressed up for the portrait (or West has done it for him), with richly detailed native accessories and a fringed robe worn classical-style to achieve a level of exoticism suitable for a London portrait studio. Johnson, by contrast, has dressed down to look less military, more like an elegant

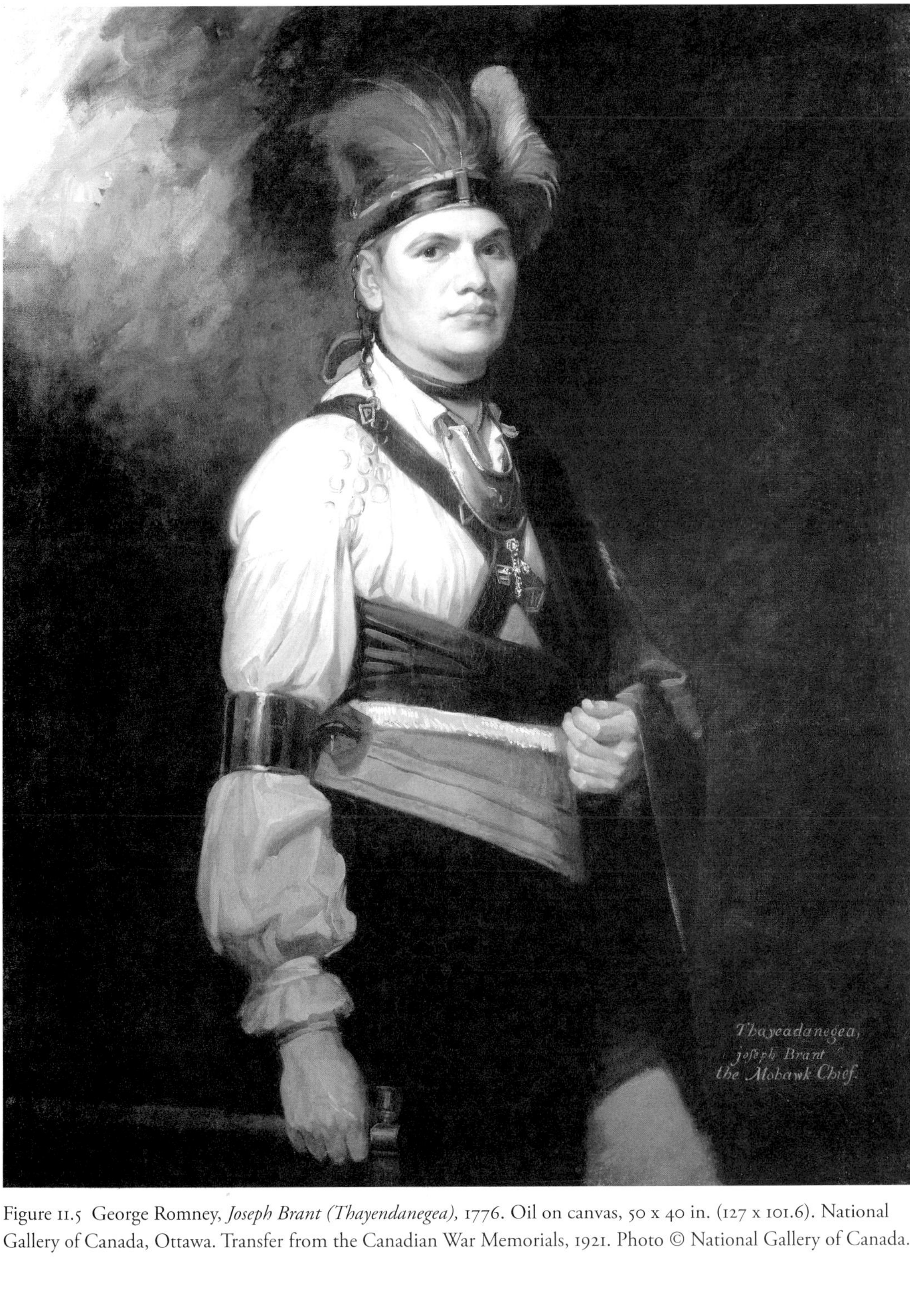


Figure 11.5 George Romney, *Joseph Brant (Thayendanegea)*, 1776. Oil on canvas, 50 x 40 in. (127 x 101.6). National Gallery of Canada, Ottawa. Transfer from the Canadian War Memorials, 1921. Photo © National Gallery of Canada.

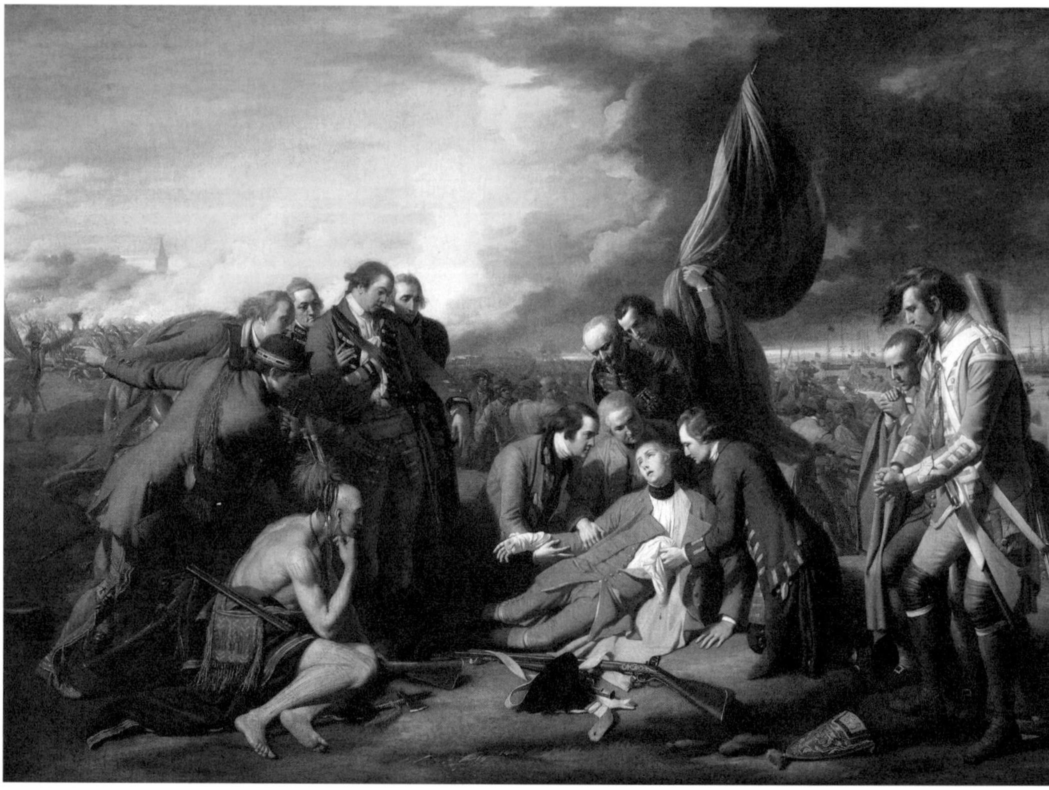

Figure 11.6 Benjamin West, *The Death of General Wolfe,* 1770. Oil on canvas, 60 x 84½ in. (152.4 x 214.6 cm). National Gallery of Canada, Ottawa. Transfer from the Canadian War Memorials, 1921. Gift of the second Duke of Westminster, 1918.

frontiersman. Beaded sashes, deerskin leggings, moccasins, and a beautifully decorated fur blanket moderately downgrade the authority of his red military jacket. Johnson's clothing, more than Hill's, implies a willingness to cross boundaries. But Hill responds in his own way; he seems ready to understand his authority as an Indian leader through the good offices of Johnson—to allow Johnson's judgment to supplement his own. This again is the mark of a Noble Savage: the capacity to recognize and receive the wisdom of civilized mentors. Johnson assumes his role with perfect equanimity; Hill stays by his side, both in the portrait and in the real world, ensuring Mohawk cooperation with the British during the war.

With Gilbert Stuart's portrait of Joseph Brant (see fig. 11.1), Noble Savage imagery reaches new heights.[23] Brant, as noted, was a prominent Mohawk chief, a leader of the Iroquois warriors allied with the British during the Revolution, and subsequently an accomplished diplomat, who twice went to London to seek restitution of Mohawk land lost during the Revolution. On the first trip (1776),

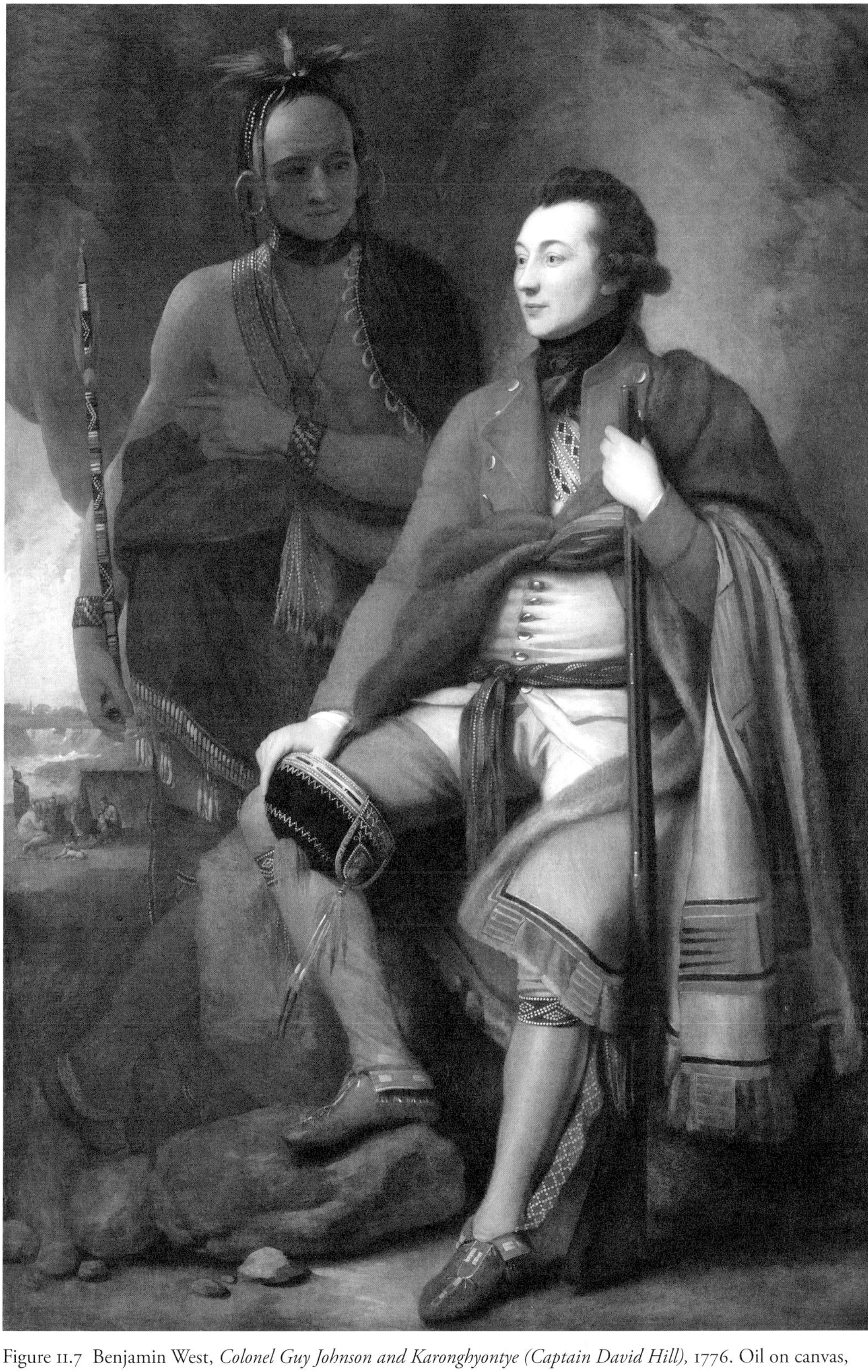

Figure 11.7 Benjamin West, *Colonel Guy Johnson and Karonghyontye (Captain David Hill),* 1776. Oil on canvas, 79½ x 54⅜ in. (201.9 x 138.1 cm). National Gallery of Art, Washington, D.C., Andrew W. Mellon Collection. Image courtesy of the Board of Trustees, National Gallery of Art, Washington, D.C.

he sat for George Romney (see fig. 11.5).[24] On the second (1786), at the request of the Duke of Northumberland, like Brant a veteran of the French and Indian and Revolutionary wars, he sat for Stuart. On both trips, Brant's "polished" manners, personal appearance, and fluent command of English made a deep impression at Court. Clearly this was not lost on him. In the Romney and Stuart portraits, he dresses the part so splendidly that one suspects he was no less adept at manipulating his image than were the two artists. Indeed, both Romney and Stuart stressed Noble and played down Savage, to the point where the latter barely exists. Except for the tomahawk Brant holds in his left hand in the Romney portrait, and the slightly swarthy color of his skin in Stuart's image, he could easily be taken for an exotically dressed white man.

What makes Stuart's *Brant* such an exceptional portrait is that his conversion to an alternate white man never quite takes hold, despite the standard pose and the sitter's impressive demeanor. Hanging from a blue ribbon around Brant's neck is the gorget, received from George III in 1776, which appears in the earlier portrait. But in the Stuart portrait, a medallion of George, contained in a brass locket, is attached to the bottom of the gorget. The decorative ensemble looms much larger than it did in the Romney portrait, no doubt because the gorget and medallion are strikingly set off against the fringed black shawl Brant wears around his shoulders. Equally striking is Brant's red headdress, adorned with feathers, in effect the only item in the portrait that looks even partially Indian. Brant's face, positioned between vividly contrasting background colors, encourages us to see him between two different worlds. So does his expression. No longer does it contain the hint of self-satisfaction we saw in the previous portrait; age, resignation, even world-weariness have altered his features. Either Brant performed for Stuart, or Stuart, perhaps aware of the post–Revolutionary War plight of the Mohawks, has introduced a note of tragedy into Noble Savage portraiture. For unlike Romney's *Brant,* Stuart's cannot forsake his tribe. His manner, perhaps also his somber dress, conveys his obligation to return to North America. There he would escort his tribe to a new and greatly diminished home in Canada.

## Painting Republican Indians

The iconography of Noble Savage portraiture continues through the end of the century with works by C. W. Peale, Ezra Ames, and others. At this point, however, it's more helpful to highlight *Jane McCrea*'s unique position by moving on to pictures of Republican Indians. The transition was in part brought about by the failure of the Iroquois Confederacy during and after the Revolutionary War. Not long after, Republican Indians rose to assume the new mantle of "chosen savages." Along the Upper Missouri River, on the buffalo-filled northern Great Plains, lived the Mandan, Sioux, Blackfoot, Crow, and numerous other tribes. By the 1820s, these tribes had gained another kind of romantic allure among western travelers—not for perceived assimilationist tendencies but for the opposite, their commitment to freedom, independence, even wildness. Whether these values actually guided the behavior of Upper Missouri Indians or were imposed by a republican society back east is probably a moot point. Let's assume that both parties benefited in separate ways: the Indians received praise for a courageous and enduring lifestyle; elite white republicans, usually Federalists, saw Indian life as a model for preserving their own values against political change already under way by the early 1800s. Whatever sympathy Indians as model aristocrats generated, however, did not prevent the real distance between Indians and whites from increasing. Republican Indians, as distinct from Noble Savages, were seen as more remote geographically, more confined to an ethnographic ranking, and more likely to remain in a "primitive" state. Hence they were destined not to assimilate but to become a vanishing race.

As the new century began, Republican Indian portraiture was still a studio process, underwritten by officials in the War Department, who brought hundreds of Upper Missouri Indians to Washington during the Jefferson, Madison, Monroe, and John Quincy Adams administrations. Softening up these Indians, making them more amenable to the passage of white men through their territories, was at first a matter of diplomacy. Included in the package were peace medal ceremonies at the White House, a sobering glimpse of gunboat drills at the Washington Navy Yard, and a visit to one or more portrait studios. Many of the Indians who came east sat for notable portrait painters—Saint-Mémin, Charles Bird King, John Neagle, and John Wesley Jarvis, to name a few, each of whom made a considerable effort to copy closely characteristic features and dress. In King's landmark portrait of five members of an 1821 delegation (see fig. 11.3), for example, each subject is identified by name or tribe, and each wears distinct individual accessories.[25] War Eagle, the lead figure of the group, holds a menacing war club, but the peace medal hanging around his neck, presumably a recent gift from President Monroe, modifies its impact. Those behind him look remarkably alike, a community of stern, silent warriors from several different tribes. But what makes them a community—their common and forcefully repeated image as Plains Indians—seems all important to King. As if by design, he abandons Noble Savagery to create an alternate stereotype, focusing less on shifting cultural circumstances than on the common ethnography that he believed identified them as Plains Indians.

By the 1830s, as one gets further into Republican Indian portraiture, a romantic naturalism begins to soften the severe classical forms in the work of King and his contemporaries. But if more individual-looking Indians emerge, they can also be seen as more human and fragile, their power as much on the line as the Indian delegations systematically recruited to visit official Washington. In some cases that process was fed by old warriors, like Black Hawk, whose tribes or bands had lost their last battles with white men, and who then posed for white painters eager to capitalize on their notoriety. George Catlin, for example, painted separate portraits of Black Hawk (fig. 11.8) and his son Whirling Thunder in 1832 at Jefferson Barracks, near St. Louis, at the conclusion of the Black Hawk War. The father's face, an oval, is composed of angles and planes that form deeply undercut aboriginal features. They reveal age but little about the Indian's state of mind. What strikes the viewer more forcefully is the poignant contrast between those hard features and the soft, inert form of the dead hawk that lies in the crook of his left elbow. In the son's portrait, the facial features are less rigid, more open; his future, unlike Black Hawk's, is not yet firmly settled. When Black Hawk and his son came to New York the next year, John Wesley Jarvis placed both figures in a moving double portrait, this time with Black Hawk in European dress, perhaps a sign of resignation echoed in his aging features. But those features and the beaded ear decorations tell us that Black Hawk remains an Indian, regardless of his European dress. No such compromise is entertained by his son, who, in a portrait also painted at Jefferson Barracks, standing close behind his father, supports him as a younger double, as if he were the young Black Hawk, the leader of a strong, independent Sauk tribe before white settlers overran their midwestern homeland. Time is of the essence in this portrait and in the two preceding. They represent, in their different ways, past, present, and future, the unfolding of a white narrative that takes Plains Indians from their original state, savage and free, to their present condition.

King was the last of these early nineteenth-century painters of Indians who confined himself to an eastern studio, or who worked, either directly or indirectly, for the federal government. But one can argue that those who followed him—Catlin, Karl Bodmer, and Alfred Jacob Miller, among others—were equally effective in serving the government's cause. They were ethnographers of a sort, dedicated to observing (Catlin on his own, Bodmer and Miller with encouragement from their respective patrons, Prince Maximilian zu Wied-Neuvied and the Scotsman William Drummond Stewart) Upper Missouri Indians on their home grounds, and to transcribing not just characteristic features and dress—the "true" look of a precontact Indian—but customs and rituals as well. A more accurate record of Indian life, however, did not necessarily bring about a greater understanding of Indians. Through most of the eighteenth century, Enlightenment science had opened up a dialogue for improving man, on the assumption that so-called primitive societies were passing through an early stage of human development. They were, in effect, still ascending the ladder, at the top of which stood post-Renaissance Europeans, especially the Anglo-Europeans who had recently settled North America. But by the early nineteenth century, a shift in attitude toward native people had begun, dampening the belief that their upward progress was inevitable.

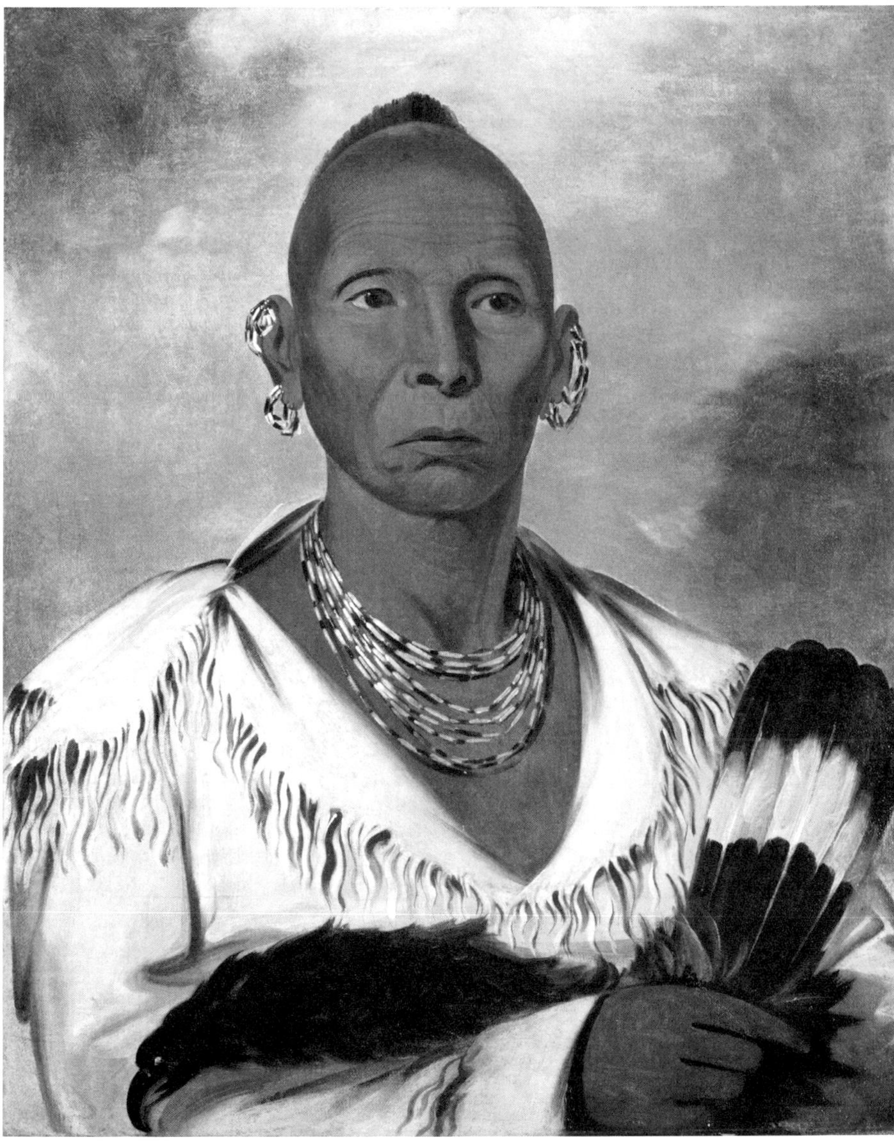

Figure 11.8 George Catlin, *Múk-a-tah-mish-o-káh-kaik, Black Hawk, Prominent Sac Chief,* 1832. Oil on canvas, 29 x 24 in. (73.7 x 61.0 cm). Smithsonian American Art Museum, Washington, D.C., Gift of Mrs. Joseph Harrison Jr.

The historian Robert Berkhofer explains the shift as a growing reluctance to believe in the virtues that had formerly been attributed to Noble Savages. By the end of the eighteenth century, he observes, the literary primitive was being transformed "from a man of reason and good sense into a man of emotion and sensibility." While "the true Noble Savage of rationalism comprehended nature's laws through reason as well as instinct, the romantic savage depended upon passion and impulse alone" to understand the world around him.[26] Berkhofer's analysis of changing white perceptions of Indian life has been generally accepted by scholars, but the distinction he makes between the two stereotypes doesn't necessarily leave room for a painting like *Jane McCrea.* Instead, the trend toward identifying Indians as "romantic savages" seems to have led naturalists in the United States to classify Indians according to an ethnography fixed within a divinely ordered universe whose visual counterpart had less to do with passion or impulse than a specimen-like cataloguing of Indian features and dress. So-called savage and civilized races were assigned fixed and separate niches; native peoples did not necessarily pass from a lower to a higher stage (nor did they become more capable of assimilation). Educated, highly motivated individual Indians might still climb the ladder, but Indians as a race had fewer choices; their customs and rituals, according to many of these naturalists, were too deeply ingrained to allow them to change. And Indians who couldn't change, who didn't have a Brant-like capacity to cross racial and cultural boundaries, became increasingly vulnerable.

Catlin and Bodmer, and to a lesser extent Miller, set out to demonstrate that Indians were locked in an immutable past, although the three artists would surely have been reluctant to admit that their mission was more an ideological quest than a deliberate search for evidence. Only Catlin went so far as to call Indians a vanishing race, and he qualified his belief so often that the edge it might have had was considerably blunted. Still, the pattern of travels by the three artists exhibits an unmistakable ethnographic design. Catlin led and the others followed him across the Great Plains, searching for Indians they believed were still in their "primal" state, more or less untouched by commerce with whites. The most convincing proof of a common mindset among the three artists was their focus on "authentic" Indian subjects—those that were repeated time and again. The major examples are the chiefs and tribal leaders painted by Catlin and Bodmer (and some by Miller, too); tribal scenes, such as buffalo hunting, horse racing, archery contests, and mock war exercises; and villages, including lodge interiors and exteriors. In addition, all three artists recorded major fur trade centers and activities. Chief among these were scenes in and around fur trade forts, steamers that carried trade goods up the Missouri and furs downriver, and fur trade gatherings on the Upper Missouri and in the Wind River Mountains.

Following this trend takes us even farther away from the picture of Indian life Vanderlyn paints in *Jane McCrea,* especially when we view the work produced by Catlin and his contemporaries on the Upper Missouri in the 1830s. By then the river had been a highway to Indian country for almost a hundred years. Prominent chiefs like Four Bears, who lived beside the river, became a magnet for painters like Catlin and Bodmer, each of whom spent months at his village. So closely matched were the two artists' ideas of how to present Four Bears that each did half- and full-length portraits.[27] But Four Bears may have had his own agenda, too: Prince Maximilian, Bodmer's patron, noted that the chief wore a different outfit every time he came to visit the Prince. The half-lengths by each artist might be called the warrior images of Four Bears (figs. 11.9 and 11.10). Catlin's half-length is broadly painted, with head, shoulders, and chest of monumental proportions. Prominent aboriginal features, a high forehead, and a steady gaze match that monumentality, while across Four Bears' arms and upper body are battle scars and self-inflicted wounds that attest to a lifetime of courageous exploits. Bodmer chooses to emphasize these same traits with a more detailed narrative. Four Bears' lean body is taut with energy, striking patterns of paint cover his face and torso, his war club is held ready for action, and feathers stand erect above his head. He is as much a savage as a Republican Indian ever becomes. Catlin's full-length portrait of Four Bears is even more monumental than the half-length. The chief has become a statue—solid, imposing, dignified (fig. 11.11). This was accomplished, Catlin admits, by stripping from Four Bears' dress "such trappings and ornaments as interfered with the grace and simplicity of his figure."[28] But to a white audience, Four Bears looked no less authentic. Indeed, he must have fulfilled to perfection the image of a Republican Indian—proud and colorful but not half so savage as the Indians in *Jane McCrea.* And much more vulnerable. Five years after Catlin painted him, Four Bears died of smallpox, brought upriver by American Fur Company employees.

In *The Light Going to and Returning from Washington* (plate 22), a two-part narrative that indirectly replays the fate of Four Bears, Catlin reveals how other Indians would suffer from contact with white men.[29] The first part shows The Light, a young Upper Missouri Indian newly arrived in Washington. In the sequential image, The Light, after sampling the amusements of the capital, has fallen from grace. The formal narrative is a bit more subtle. On the left, The Light stands erect and in profile, so that his aboriginal features, proud bearing, and feathered headdress are prominently displayed. On the right, he is a swaggering dandy, his figure a caricature of what it once was. The bottles in his back pockets tell only part of the story. His uniform and hat, both form-fitting, show how confining civilized dress and customs are, how they place restrictions on Indian life. The Light's pipe is exchanged for an umbrella and the fan he holds, which tell the same story in a different way: both diminish his former "manliness," and both are as useless as a tight-fitting uniform.

The irony is that the darker meaning of the image, though delivered with a certain grim humor rather than by two murderous savages, is not so different

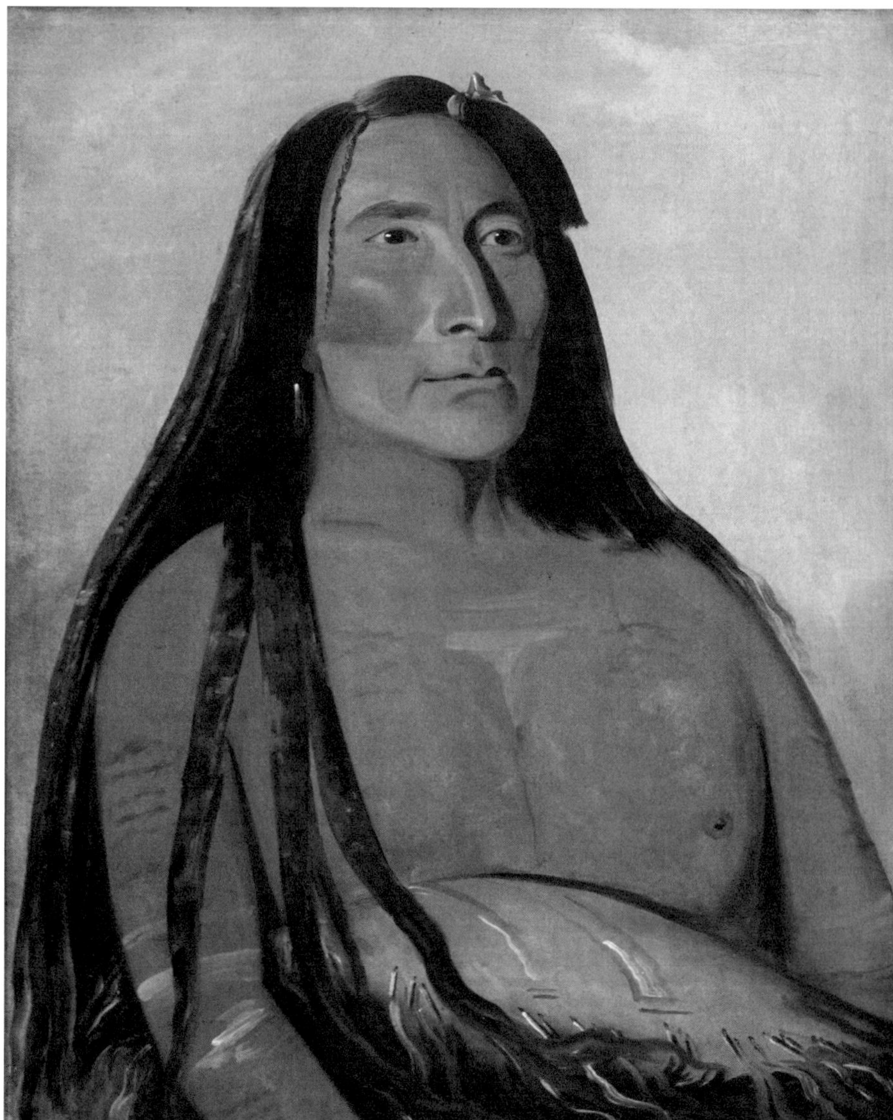

Figure 11.9 George Catlin, *Máh-to-tóh-pa, Four Bears, Second Chief in Mourning,* 1832. Oil on canvas, 29 x 24 in. (73.7 x 61.0 cm). Smithsonian American Art Museum, Washington, D.C., Gift of Mrs. Joseph Harrison Jr.

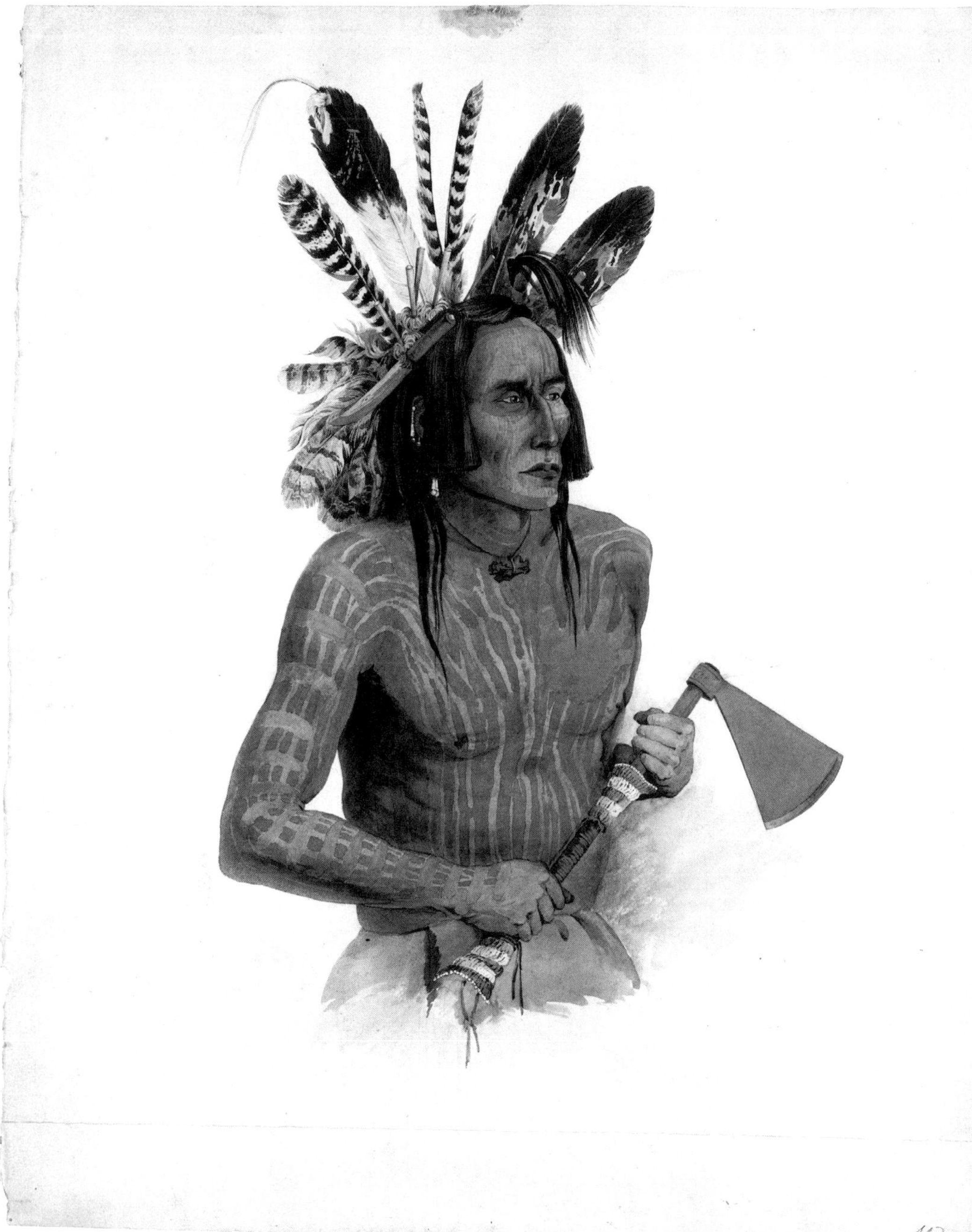

Figure 11.10 Karl Bodmer, *Mató-Tõpe, Mandan Chief,* 1833–34. Watercolor on paper, 13¾ x 11¼ in. (34.9 x 28.6 cm). Joslyn Art Museum, Omaha, Gift of the Enron Art Foundation, 1986.

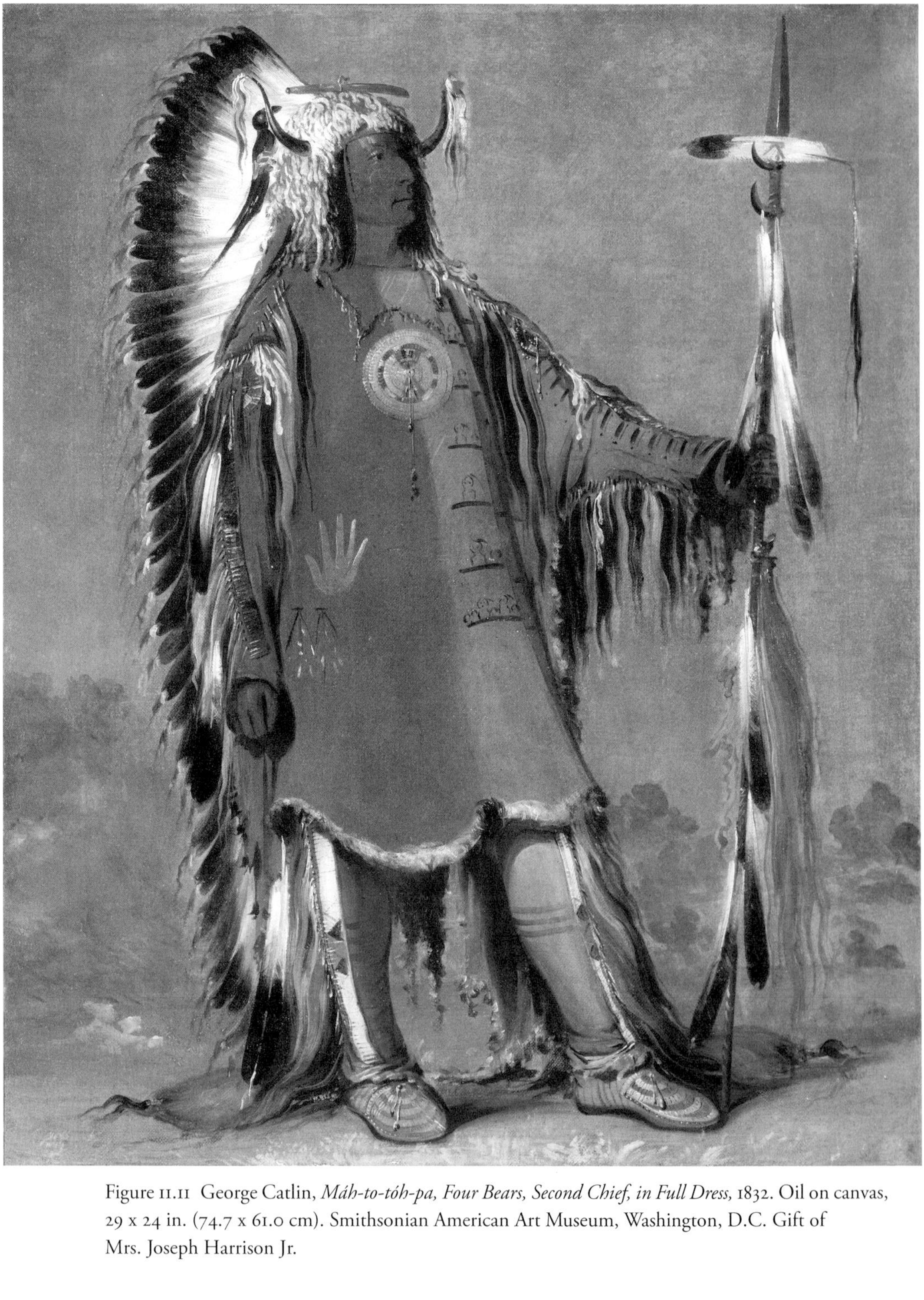

Figure 11.11 George Catlin, *Máh-to-tóh-pa, Four Bears, Second Chief, in Full Dress,* 1832. Oil on canvas, 29 x 24 in. (74.7 x 61.0 cm). Smithsonian American Art Museum, Washington, D.C. Gift of Mrs. Joseph Harrison Jr.

from what Vanderlyn says in *Jane McCrea.* Regardless of how much the behavior of the two Indians was a reflection of American animosity toward Britain, both were under the control of a white painter who could compose them as he wished. And Catlin, to be sure, could use The Light's encounter with official Washington as a way to remind his viewers that a deep gulf still remained between Indian and white societies, a condition from which Indians would inevitably emerge as the losers. This once again brings us back to Transatlantic Romanticism. Deeply embedded in both paintings is a message that conveys the links between romanticism and imperialism, a veil that the former draws across the latter in order to soften and defuse the aggressive campaigns—military, political, and cultural—that Europeans and Americans launched against Indians to gain control of North America. Vanderlyn's *Jane McCrea* and Catlin's *The Light* show it at two different stages; they were only a warm-up for what was still to come.

## NOTES

1. Robert Rosenblum, *Transformations in Late Eighteenth Century Art* (Princeton: Princeton University Press, 1967), see esp. 3–29.

2. Kenneth C. Lindsay, *The Works of John Vanderlyn* (Binghamton: University Art Gallery, State University of New York, 1970), 72, suggests that *Marius* was Vanderlyn's response to Aaron Burr's severely damaged national reputation following his duel with Alexander Hamilton. Vanderlyn's major history painting was *The Landing of Columbus,* completed in 1847 for the Capitol rotunda. The subjects of Allston's history paintings seem more closely tied to his academic training in London and Rome than to his brief stay in Paris with Vanderlyn. But in view of Rosenblum's theories about early nineteenth-century Salon subjects, might scholars have overlooked more immediate connections between Allston's work and then-contemporary events in the United States and Europe? E. P. Richardson suggested, in 1948, that Allston's work could be seen in a broader context, which he described as "a generation of war and revolution, beginning in America, spreading to France, and then sweeping over the civilized world." See E. P. Richardson, *Washington Allston: A Study of the Romantic Artist in America* (Chicago: University of Chicago Press, 1948), 100. More recent scholars have taken different approaches to Allston's work, none of which follow Richardson's lead; see Elizabeth Johns, "Washington Allston's Dead Man Revived," *Art Bulletin* 61 (March 1979): 78–99; William H. Gerdts and Theodore E. Stebbins, Jr., "*A Man of Genius*": *The Art of Washington Allston 1779–1843* (Boston: Museum of Fine Arts, 1980); and David Bjelajac, *Millennial Desire and the Apocalyptic Vision of Washington Allston* (Washington, D.C.: Smithsonian Institution Press, 1988).

3. For more about why young American painters, especially Vanderlyn, sought success at the annual Paris Salons, see Lois Fink, *American Art at Nineteenth-Century Paris Salons* (Cambridge and New York: Cambridge University Press for the National Museum of American Art, 1990), xiv, 12–13, 18–20, 23–26, 29.

4. For further information about the commission and the subsequent history of the painting, see Elizabeth Mankin Kornhauser, *American Paintings before 1945 in the Wadsworth*

*Atheneum,* vol. 2 (New Haven: Yale University Press, 1996), 765–74; and Samuel Y. Edgerton Jr., "The Murder of Jane McCrea: The Tragedy of an American *Tableau d'Histoire,*" *Art Bulletin* 47 (December 1965): 481–92.

5. Rosenblum, *Transformations,* 1–22; Thomas Crow, "Classicism and Romanticism," in *Nineteenth Century Art: A Critical History,* ed. Stephen F. Eisenman, 2nd ed. (New York: Thames & Hudson, 2002), 38–40, 46–47, 49–50. See also Thomas Crow, *Emulation: Making Artists for Revolutionary France* (New Haven: Yale University Press, 1995), which provides a thematic overview of Salon subjects from the 1780s to about 1820, relating them to events that were taking place during various phases of the Revolution. Crow remarks that major artists such as David and Girodet saw "their most passionate efforts slide from tragic grandeur to melodrama" (*Emulation,* 2), especially after the new century began.

6. See Kornhauser, *American Paintings,* 765–64; and Edgerton, "The Murder of Jane McCrea," 481–92.

7. The Salon label is cited (and translated) in Fink, *American Art at the Nineteenth-Century Paris Salons,* 18. See also Kornhauser, *American Paintings,* 2:773. A helpful description of the issues that divided Federalists and Republicans at the turn of the century can be found in Gordon S. Wood, *Empire of Liberty: A History of the Early Republic* (New York: Oxford University Press, 2009), 250–67. Federalists generally supported Great Britain, while Republicans, like Jefferson, more often favored France. As the War of 1812 approached, newspapers sharpened this division, calling Federalists "Tory Monarchists" and Republicans "Filthy Jacobins." In some cities the arguments carried over into taverns, where newspapers advocating one side or the other were read aloud.

8. Edgerton, "The Murder of Jane McCrea," 483–84.

9. John Wilmerding, *American Art* (New York: Penguin, 1976), 62; David Lubin, *Picturing a Nation: Art and Social Change in Nineteenth-Century America* (New Haven: Yale University Press, 1994), 1–2; and Frances K. Pohl, *Framing America: A Social History of American Art* (2002; New York: Thames & Hudson, 2008), 116–17, among others, follow Edgerton's argument.

10. William Townsend Oedel, who first noted Vanderlyn's embrace of the neoclassical themes on view at then-current Paris Salons, called those themes "a popular strain of exotic, horrific genre in modern French art." Oedel also observed that the "figural composition" of *Jane McCrea* "refers to the moralizing tradition of ancient Greek art . . . while [Vanderlyn's] narrative presentation is charged with emotion. By these means, the thematic strains of ancient Greek virtue and Romantic horror merge in his painting, as they do in much of the art of this unsettled, contradictory time when lofty ideals clashed with harsh realities." See William Townsend Oedel, "John Vanderlyn: French Neoclassicism and the Search for an American Art" (Ph.D. diss., University of Delaware, 1981), 234–38.

11. Kornhauser, *American Paintings,* 2:474.

12. Edgerton, "The Murder of Jane McCrea," 482.

13. Ibid.

14. William H. Truettner, *Painting Indians and Building Empires in North America, 1710–1840* (Berkeley: University of California Press, 2010), 28–60, 70–119.

15. For more on the Mohawks' wartime campaign through the Wyoming Valley, see Alan Taylor, *The Divided Ground: Indians, Settlers, and the Northern Borderland of the American Revolution* (New York: Knopf, 2006), 86–96; and Isabel Thomson Kelsay, *Joseph Brant,*

*1743–1807: Man of Two Worlds* (Syracuse: Syracuse University Press, 1984), 216–22. More recent evidence suggests that Brant may have helped plan the raids in Pennsylvania but did not accompany those who carried them out.

16. Charles Coleman Sellers, "Portraits and Miniatures by Charles Willson Peale," *Transactions of the American Philosophical Society* 42, pt. 1 (1952): 40–41.

17. See note 27 for more on early nineteenth-century trends in Philadelphia science.

18. For more on the presumed differences between Noble Savages and Republican Indians, see Truettner, *Painting Indians,* 11–17.

19. John C. Ewers, "The Emergence of the Plains Indian as the Symbol of the North American Indian," in *Indian Life on the Upper Missouri* (Norman: University of Oklahoma Press, 1968), 187–203.

20. For a discussion of the portraits of the "Four Kings," see Kevin Muller, "From Palace to Longhouse: Portraits of the Four Indian Kings in a Transatlantic Context," *American Art* 22 (Fall 2008): 26–49.

21. See Helmut von Erffa and Allen Staley, *The Paintings of Benjamin West* (New Haven: Yale University Press, 1986), 212.

22. For more on the portrait of Guy Johnson, see Leslie Kaye Reinhardt, "Colonel Guy Johnson and Karonghyontye (Captain David Hill)," in *American Paintings of the Eighteenth Century,* ed. Ellen G. Miles (Washington, D.C.: National Gallery of Art, 1995), 321–28.

23. For more on the Brant portrait by Stuart, see Carrie Rebora Barratt and Ellen G. Miles, eds., *Gilbert Stuart* (New Haven: Yale University Press for the Metropolitan Museum of Art, 2004), 68–71.

24. A brief entry on the Brant portrait appears in Humphrey Ward and W. Roberts, *Romney: A Biographical and Critical Essay with a Catalogue Raisonné of His Works,* vol. 2 (New York: Charles Scribner's Sons, 1904), 135, which notes that the portrait was commissioned by the second Earl of Warwick and that Brant is shown "meditating a war against the United States."

25. For more on Charles Bird King's role in these Washington visits, see Herman J. Viola, *The Indian Legacy of Charles Bird King* (Washington, D.C.: Smithsonian Institution Press; New York: Doubleday, 1976). Rowena Houghton Dasch has discovered that the first three names in the title of the Smithsonian American Art Museum's King portrait don't match those of any of the Indians in the delegation from which King is supposed to have taken the five subjects; see her dissertation, "'Now Exhibiting': Charles Bird King's Picture Gallery, Fashioning American Taste and Nation, 1824–1861" (University of Texas, 2012).

26. Robert F. Berkhofer Jr., *The White Man's Indian: Images of the American Indian from Columbus to the Present* (New York: Vintage Books, 1979), 78–79. Classifying New World flora and fauna according to Enlightenment standards continued into the first decades of the nineteenth century, but Romantic Savages never regained the status of Noble Savages. Instead, they were subjected to a more pronounced effort to categorize Indians as a primitive race whose level of development could be determined by applying data that had rarely been used for such purposes in the past.

What drove this new program, according to George H. Daniels in *American Science in the Age of Jackson* (New York: Columbia University Press, 1968), 63–117, was not so much a new methodology as a new belief system. Philadelphia scientists, the best trained in the young nation, turned from broad-based secular studies to the narrower task of finding order in God's universe, and to discovering why Indians had remained in a primitive state (still under the sway of passion and impulse) while other races had progressed. The end result of this search, claimed Maryland natural philosopher Samuel Tyler, was to reaffirm the existence of the Creator, and to discover the laws and the relationships that he had set in motion (Daniels, *American Science,* 74–85). Thus facts, observations, and experiments became part of a system more tightly built than ever, an "edifice" that was based on faith as much as reason, and therefore less permissive of change than before.

Ordering God's universe also put a higher priority on data gathering than had Enlightenment science. When, in 1838, George Catlin completed his Indian Gallery, which consisted of a survey of Indian life on the Great Plains, he claimed that he had "visited forty-eight tribes, the greater part of which [he] found speaking different languages, and containing in all 400,000 souls." More facts and figures followed. See George Catlin, *Letters and Notes on the Manners, Customs, and Conditions of the North American Indians,* 2 vols. (1844; New York: Dover Publications, 1977), 4. But if Catlin proceeded as a conscientious ethnographer, with high praise for many of the Plains tribes he visited, he also believed that they and other Indians in remote areas of the West had changed little over the past centuries. That was their virtue; they still remained in their original state. At the same time, he thought them so wedded to their traditional ways that increased contact with white civilization would, in time, cause wholesale destruction of their culture (Catlin, *Letters and Notes,* 1:61). A few decades later, that opinion was more forcefully reiterated by the historian Francis Parkman, who wrote: "The Indian is hewn out of a rock . . . You cannot change the form without destruction of the substance. . . . [H]e and his forest must perish together." Quoted in Steven Conn, *History's Shadow: Native Americans and Historical Consciousness in the Nineteenth Century* (Chicago: University of Chicago Press, 2004), 207. Also helpful in developing this discussion were George W. Stocking Jr., *Victorian Anthropology* (New York: Free Press, 1987), 9–19; Berkhofer, *The White Man's Indian,* 40–55; and Reginald Horsman, *Race and Manifest Destiny: The Origins of American Racial Anglo-Saxonism* (Cambridge: Harvard University Press, 1981), 116–32.

27. For more on the half-length portraits of Four Bears, see William H. Truettner, *The Natural Man Observed: A Study of Catlin's Indian Gallery* (Washington, D.C.: Smithsonian Institution Press, 1979), 180; and William H. Goetzmann, "The Man Who Stopped to Paint America" in *Karl Bodmer's America* (Omaha: Joselyn Art Museum and University of Nebraska Press, 1984), 14–17, 309.

28. For more on Catlin's full-length portrait of Four Bears, see Truettner, *The Natural Man Observed,* 23, 26, 92, 103, 178–79.

29. For more on The Light's visit to Washington and his subsequent fate, see Catlin, *Letters and Notes,* 1:55–57; 2:194–200; Viola, *The Indian Legacy of Charles Bird King,* 88–91; and Ewers, *Indian Life on the Upper Missouri,* 75–90. For more on the dual image of The Light, see Truettner, *The Natural Man Observed,* 18–20, 280.

# 12

# The Romantic Indian Commodified

## Text and Image in George Catlin's *Letters and Notes* (1841)

*Robert Woods Sayre*

Although his principal subject matter is thoroughly American, the painter and writer George Catlin (1796–1872) is a transatlantic figure in the fullest sense of the term. For he spent more than half of his adult life in Europe—England, France, and Belgium—presenting the Indians of the American West whom he had visited, painted, and written about earlier, as well as continuing to produce pictorial and textual representations of them there. After a brief period as a society portrait painter in Philadelphia and New York in the 1820s, Catlin decided to devote himself single-mindedly to the preservation—visual and verbal—of what he, like many of his American contemporaries, saw as a "vanishing race." A period of travels in the trans-Mississippi West followed in the 1830s, during which Catlin painted western Indians and their environment, made voluminous notes, and collected artifacts. These activities culminated in a series of lectures and exhibitions of his "Indian Gallery" in major cities on the East Coast at the end of the decade. After initial public interest in his work waned, though, and after failing to persuade the U.S. Congress to buy his Gallery, Catlin left for Europe in 1839, hoping to better his fortunes there. From late 1839 to 1845 he was based in London, lecturing, showing his paintings, and producing "spectacles" of Indian life. When the popularity of his productions subsided there as well, he moved them to Paris, then Brussels. In the following twenty-five years, hounded by chronic insolvency, he transferred the stage of his various activities—all involving the American Indian—back and forth between London, Paris, and Brussels, though according to his own accounts, he interrupted his European sojourn with a series of travels in South America (and more briefly on the West Coast of North America) in the

1850s.[1] Catlin did not return to the United States to settle until 1871, the year before his death.[2]

Catlin's work has generated a growing interest—both scholarly and popular—since World War II. During the 1950s, the books that appeared on Catlin focused mainly on the paintings and were largely celebratory in tone, presenting the artist as a superb visual chronicler of the American West and its native inhabitants.[3] The early 1960s saw a series of publications that provided samples of Catlin's artistry alongside those of other, approximately contemporaneous painters of similar scenes and subjects.[4] In the 1970s several collections of Catlin's paintings alone were printed, but there also appeared—as a first sign of a shift of interest—two editions, one a reprint of the original and the other an edited text for a wider public, of what is arguably Catlin's best and most significant piece of writing: the travel account of his years with the western Indians in the 1830s, which is the main focus of this essay.[5] Several publications at the end of the decade signaled a willingness to study not just the paintings, and isolated ones at that, as had often been the case before, but also on the one hand the writings and on the other the Indian Gallery and Catlin's career as a whole.[6]

A new trend had been initiated, one that was expanded and diversified considerably beginning in the 1990s, as publications of all sorts on Catlin multiplied. This period of accelerated production has seen the appearance of further collections and exhibition catalogues of his paintings, most notably *George Catlin and His Indian Gallery,* based on a 2002–3 Smithsonian exhibition in Washington, D.C., subsequently on tour in a number of American cities in 2004,[7] and a new edition of Catlin's *Letters and Notes* published by Penguin.[8] Catlin's art has also been included in several large-format collections of imagery of the West for a broad public,[9] and excerpts of his writing have appeared in anthologies of environmentalist writing.[10]

But most important, a significant number of scholarly articles, chapters of books, and in one case a full-length monograph have begun to take a more strongly critical view of Catlin, bringing into their analyses all the multifarious aspects of his career: paintings and writings, talks and promotional activities, the Gallery, and the variety of Indian "shows" he put on at different times. Inspired by recent developments in cultural and postcolonial studies, ethnohistory, radical environmentalism, and art-historical ideology critique, their authors have explored, from different vantage points, the ways in which Catlin participated in the very evils—the wanton destruction of "wild" nature and its "wild" Indian inhabitants—he wished to denounce and combat. Among these critics one finds different emphases and approaches, and disagreements on specific points. But there is broad consensus that Catlin's work is to the highest degree paradoxical, contradictory, and ambivalent.[11]

There has, then, been much important critical and historical work done on Catlin. But one aspect of his production has received little attention. Although recent studies have often drawn on them extensively, Catlin's published travel accounts have generally not been treated as travel literature per se, as part of a well-established genre of writing: accounts of travel in "Indian territory." During his own lifetime, Catlin was in fact no less well known as a writer in this genre than as a painter of Indians and producer of Indian shows. In what follows I discuss from this perspective his 1841 publication *Letters and Notes*—the first of his travelogues and by consensus the one of greatest value and interest.[12] I first deal with the trip on which the work was based in its historical context, and sketch in some background on the genre of writing about travel in Indian territory. Then I discuss the text itself, both from a formal point of view and in terms of content, stressing the close linkage between text and image. Finally, I highlight some connections that seem particularly relevant between *Letters and Notes* and larger sociocultural developments in the nineteenth century: ethnological shows, ethnology and the museum, and tourism.

As the title of my essay suggests, an aspect of Romanticism features—in highly problematic form—in the material under consideration, and in the course of my discussion I attempt to bring out some of the paradoxes of Catlin's position as regards Romanticism, such as I and Michael Löwy conceive it, and as it is developed in the introduction to this volume. I return to the question of Catlin's relation to Romanticism in the conclusion to my essay.

THE LONG subtitle to the first edition of *Letters and Notes* reads as follows: "written during eight years' travel amongst the wildest tribes of Indians in North America, in 1832, 33, 34, 35, 36, 37, 38, and 39." This seemingly precise delineation of the scope of the travels that form the experiential basis for the textual account does not, however, entirely correspond to the actual itineraries and chronologies of Catlin's trips in Indian territories in the 1830s. Although the subtitle enumerates the years from 1832 to 1839 one by one, as if to emphasize that he was traveling among "wild Indians" during each of them, this was not the case: in 1833, and from 1837 to 1839, the year in which he left for England, Catlin did not in fact travel in the West but was engaged in various activities in the East (completing his paintings, organizing and carrying out lectures and exhibitions). The author, then—this is characteristic of him, but many other travelers have done the same—inflated and scrambled his dating, speaking of eight years among the "wildest tribes," when what was involved was a number of trips of several months each during a six-year period, only some of which were among "wild" tribes.

Of these, three were particularly important: in 1832, a trip from Saint Louis far up the Missouri River by steamboat, as far as Fort Union in Assiniboin, Crow, and Cree country (near the present-day North Dakota–Montana border), and the return trip—by canoe—including a prolonged stay at Fort Clark (North Dakota), near the Mandan settlements; in 1834, a trip from New Orleans up the Mississippi and Arkansas rivers, then, starting from Fort Gibson (Oklahoma), on foot and horseback accompanying an expedition of dragoons into Comanche territory (Texas); and finally, in 1836, a trip through the Great Lakes, up the Mississippi to Fort Snelling (near the present Wisconsin-Minnesota border), then west to a sacred pipestone quarry in Sioux territory (Minnesota).[13]

These trips, as well as the general period of Catlin's travels and dealings with Indians before publication of *Letters and Notes*—starting in 1830, when he met General William Clark, then superintendent of Indian Affairs in the West, in Saint Louis—have significant historical contexts in terms of evolving relations between indigenous tribes, whites, and the U.S. government. The 1830s was a decade in which crucial developments occurred in this respect. Trappers, traders, and settlers moved into and through the trans-Mississippi West in greatly increasing numbers (the Santa Fe and Oregon trails were both open and active by 1830), and there were repeated conflicts between these encroachers and Indian tribes resisting them, from the Dakotas and Montana in the north to Texas in the south. In Illinois, in 1831–32, Black Hawk waged a fierce though short-lived war that was a prelude to many others west of the Mississippi later in the century. The 1830s was a period in which the U.S. Army invested unprecedented resources in securing continental, imperial expansion through building roads and forts, and engaging in various kinds of military action. At the same time, Jackson's removal policy for the Indians east of the Mississippi was being applied, from the time of its passage into law in 1830 through to the arrival in Oklahoma of the last remnants of the Trail of Tears in 1838. The Seminoles of Florida continued to resist removal violently throughout the decade and beyond, though the capture of their leader Osceola in 1838 was a major blow to their struggle.[14]

One commentator sees *Letters and Notes* as a whole as "parallel[ling] the removal campaign of Indian peoples in the 1830s,"[15] and indeed each volume of the work is preceded by a map of the trans-Mississippi West, the first before and the second after the removal of the eastern Indians, with the southwestern territories created for them drawn in on the second map. But there are also specific links between the historical background I have alluded to and the principal trips that Catlin recounts in the book. The 1832 trip up the Missouri was made on the maiden voyage of a steamboat of the American Fur Company, which was the spearhead of U.S. commercial exploitation of the upper Missouri. The 1834 overland trek from Fort Gibson on the Arkansas River was undertaken with dragoons who were attempting to make a show of force in the area through which the Santa Fe Trail passed.[16] Moreover, when in Fort Gibson, Catlin painted a number of Indians from tribes "removed" from the East.[17] The 1836 trip to the pipestone quarry relates more generally to the continuing history of white intrusion on Indian sacred grounds.

Catlin's *Letters and Notes,* in addition to being framed by these historical contexts, falls into a rich tradition of accounts of travel in Indian territory since the beginnings of exploration and colonization in North America, accounts that were—in greatest numbers and significance—Spanish, French, and Anglo-American. In the last case, it was mainly in the eighteenth century that they developed, the two best-known works being those of Jonathan Carver and William Bartram.[18] Catlin's *Letters and Notes* has a good deal in common with these earlier ones, and he certainly drew on the tradition, at least unconsciously, in writing his account. But it is in important ways different, and even unique in certain respects. One of the major differences is the presence, in Catlin's work, of abundant pictorial illustration, with the illustrations being an entirely integral part of the work. Before the early nineteenth century, there was little illustration in texts involving encounters with North American Indians. Even Bartram, who was an artist, did very few drawings of Indian subjects. (Most of his illustrations were botanical and zoological.) This has meant that modern-day publishers of such accounts, in search of enticing visuals, have sometimes resorted to using John White's quite exceptional set of drawings of sixteenth-century Virginia natives to illustrate texts involving other times and places.

The situation changed quite radically in the first half of the nineteenth century, however, and in that period modern publishers have found a particularly rich vein to exploit. Although Lewis and Clark had no artist on their expedition, soon thereafter travelers who wrote about sojourns in Indian territories—now west of the Mississippi—often either were artists themselves or were accompanied by one. In addition, with the multiplication of visits to Washington by Indian delegations, many portraits of Indians were carried out there, without travel. The best known of the sedentary portraitists is Charles Bird King. Of the traveling artists, and travelers with artists accompanying them, some were Americans and some foreign visitors, usually noblemen with scientific interests. Many of the foreigners were of Germanic origin—Prussian or Swiss German. The most famous traveling pair of this kind—traveling within the same time period as Catlin and covering many of the same locales—was Prince Maximilian zu Wied-Neuvied and the Swiss artist Karl Bodmer, whom he engaged in his service.[19]

Catlin's illustrated travel book, then, falls within this new trend, one that was to be largely supplanted in the second half of the nineteenth century by that of photographers traveling in Indian country (the most illustrious being Edward Curtis). But Catlin's work is unique among the artist-travelers in its extremely close-knit relation between text and visual representation. Not only are the artist and the writer one and the same, but also the two elements of the work are conceived of as equal parts of an indissoluble whole with a systematic cross-referencing of the two.

Though Catlin's work differs from most earlier accounts of travel in Indian territory in this important pictorial aspect, it does otherwise resemble earlier examples of the genre in certain general ways. Like them, it provides information and analysis, value judgments and representations of interaction, coming out of encounters with the Indian "Other." Earlier accounts do these things in two ways: at the very least through a diachronic account of the travel, since this is what defines a travel narrative, but also often in a synchronic, synthetic presentation of the lifeways of the Indians encountered. These presentations are either entirely separated from the travel narrative, in a section apart, or inserted as blocks of text within it. Catlin in fact does both, stopping to make lengthy comments on the ways of life of tribes encountered over the course of the travelogue, and then attempting to generalize in his last letter.

Indeed, as indicated in the title, the author adopts the epistolary convention, as do a number of important earlier accounts of the same type (French rather than Anglo-American, though).[20] The novelty in the case of Catlin is that his letters are addressed not to specific, imaginary persons but to the reader. Letter 1 begins, "The following pages have been hastily compiled, at the urgent request of a number of my friends, from a series of Letters and Notes written by myself during several years' residence and travel [among wild Indians]," and the author/narrator goes on to beg his readers to understand that he must dispense with a preface and begin directly with his opening remarks.[21] In this way letter 1 suggests the artificiality of the epistolary mode, since the authorial persona refers to letters written during the trip. At the end of letter 2 and the beginning of letter 3, the pretense of an actual letter is introduced, and it is maintained in many subsequent ones. Letter 3 opens, "Since the date of my former Letter, I have been so much engaged in the amusements of the country, and the use of my brush, that I have scarcely been able to drop you a line until the present moment" (1:17). The correspondent is never given a name or the slightest indication of identity. In fact, Catlin had originally published some of the material as a series of open letters to several New York newspapers.[22] Yet strangely this origin is entirely erased, never mentioned in the book. In the context of the book, since in the letters that subdivide it the author continually addresses himself to his readers, imagining what they may think or feel, the readers can only conclude that the letters are metaphorical and are addressed to them.

"Notes" are also referred to, both in the title of the book and in the opening sentence of letter 1. Occasionally later on the author speaks of a notebook that he carried with him, making entries in it as he went along (for example, 1:66, 2:97). At certain points within the so-called letters Catlin even transcribes passages from the notebook verbatim, or claims to do so. He also from time to time transcribes long dialogues and stories that he has been told. A final element of composition is the footnote, which comments on the text from the perspective of a later date, shortly before publication. All of these elements can be found in some form or other in earlier travel accounts, but nowhere else are they so fully subordinated to what is the main structural feature of Catlin's book: a direct address by the author to the reader (or to his collective readers; sometimes the singular, sometimes the plural is used). All the other compositional elements seem to be manipulated in a way that is calculated to create effects in the reader.

This applies, in addition, to Catlin's method of chronological organization of his material. When the travel narrative per se begins in letter 2, after the introductory material of letter 1, it starts not with the departure from Saint Louis on the 1832 excursion but with the arrival three months later of the steamer at its ultimate destination, Fort Union, the farthest it would penetrate into "wild" Indian country. The intent to catch the reader's interest from the outset seems clear. But this organizational decision obliges Catlin to introduce material relating to what occurred on the way upriver at points in the account of the trip downriver where (or near where) the earlier events took place. The procedure—which is repeated elsewhere later on—is convoluted and clumsily executed, leading to a good bit of confusion and repetition. This explains the decision of the Penguin editors to reorganize and condense. Paradoxically, in the interest of gaining the attention of the twenty-first-century reader, they undo a construction that was aimed at seducing the nineteenth-century reader.

An overriding concern with, and direct address to, the reader is reflected also in the style and tone of the work. There is tremendous variety in these, running from the intensely serious, lyrical, or even quasi-mystical to the broadly comic, the burlesque, and the coy. But in all its modulations, Catlin's style seems motivated mainly by the desire to establish a rapport with his reading public—to involve them, to instruct and entertain them. Here also the huge gap between his immediate, intended public and that of our own time is evident. Many of Catlin's literary effects strike the modern reader as overblown, unconvincing, even ridiculous. There are numerous patches of purple prose, much tiresome repetition to hammer home a point, hyperbole (everything is the *most,* the *best,* and so on of its kind), and heavy-handed humor. In one passage Catlin plays on the words "sticks" and "Styx," (1:18); in another he winks at the reader, noting that in the place where he is next visiting he'd better watch out for his scalp (1:59). The Penguin edition eliminates much of this material. Whatever its failings may appear to be to the modern reader, though, Catlin's prose is clearly meant to be a kind of virtuoso performance before the audience of his contemporaries.

As for the illustrations, there were over three hundred of them in the original edition. They took the form of line cuts from the paintings that Catlin had made while on his journeys, since the more sophisticated forms of reproduction available at the time—lithograph and aquatint—would have taken much time and expense to prepare. In the Dover edition most of the line cuts have been replaced by photographic reproductions of the corresponding oil painting, presumably as Catlin would have wished if the technology had been available. The illustrations fall into several broad categories: posed portraits of Indians (some full-length, some from the waist up); scenes of Indian life (dances, ceremonies, buffalo hunting); drawings of objects used by Indians in their daily life (Catlin collected many of these, and they are often presented as part of his collection); landscapes, with little or no human presence; and, finally, scenes in which Catlin himself appears, sometimes also with the two *voyageurs* who did the canoe paddling on his first trip (Baptiste and Bogard).

As mentioned earlier, there is a continual cross-referencing between the text and these illustrations. They are intended as a visual complement to or extension of the text, the latter continually referring to different numbered plates, and in some cases commenting on them at length. The most extended and significant of these cross-references involves the Mandan chief Four Bears, to whom an entire letter is devoted (1:145–54), and who is illustrated by a portrait, a drawing of the author being honored by him at a feast, and another of his buffalo robe, with a detailed analysis of the meaning of the figures on it. Thus the pictorial and the written are closely intertwined, forming a "multimedia" whole, as we might say today.

I TURN NOW to the meanings conveyed by these representations. It should first be emphasized that there is a main thread running throughout the long written text, supported by the tenor of many of the images. Repeated again and again, in different tonalities but always passionate ones, is the conviction that North American Indians—highly admirable in their native or "classic" state,[23] such as Catlin encountered them on the Upper Missouri and elsewhere—are being or will soon be corrupted and exploited by whites, particularly traders, and are almost surely doomed to extinction. One of Catlin's major purposes is to correct misconceptions and prejudices concerning Indians commonly held by "civilized" whites—his potential readers—whose only contact with Indians, if any, has been with those in the frontier areas, where they have already been severely debased by white influence. The contrast between Indians in their own culture and those degraded by white contact is the subject of one of his best-known paintings. An Assiniboine Indian named Wi-Jun-Jon is pictured "before and after" (plate 22): in the left-hand panel, resplendent in his full tribal regalia before a trip to Washington as a delegate, and in the right-hand panel, after his return home, in an awkward, mismatched outfit of assorted Anglo-American clothing, with a bottle of liquor protruding from a back pocket.[24]

Catlin is often at pains to explain (and in most cases to justify, up to a point) Indian customs and practices that he knows will appear bizarre, absurd, revolting, or objectionable to his readership. Thus his work presents itself first and foremost as a celebration of the "wild" Indian and a criticism of the cupidity of white society, which is destroying the "savage" (undoubtedly a noble one, for Catlin). Sometimes Catlin's awareness of what is happening and his condemnation of white America become intensely bitter, as in the very last lines of the book, where he prophesies that "for the Nation, there is an unrequited account of sin and injustice that sooner or later will call for *national retribution*" (2:256).

This message would seem extremely clear and straightforward, and would appear to associate Catlin with the "primitivism" that is characteristic of some forms of Romanticism. But a closer look at Catlin's text reveals greater complexities and some surprising ambiguities and contradictions. First, although Catlin's main theme regarding Indians is situated on the moral plane, this dimension of his discourse alternates with others—the aesthetic and the "scientific"—which, if not necessarily contradictory, are at least in a situation of ambiguous admixture or uneasy coexistence with it. In many passages, Indians are treated not as beings with a morally interesting culture, in a morally distressing predicament, but as purely aesthetic objects. Beautiful bodies, perfect subjects for the painter, they are "picturesque" (a word he uses often, in reference to Indians as well as to landscapes; for example, 1:23, 192).[25] Numerous other passages put the Indian under a quasi-scientific scrutiny, speaking of Indian individuals, as well as their clothes and other accoutrements, as "specimens"—another word that recurs regularly (for example, 1:22, 193). This ambiguity in the textual material is reflected in the illustrations as well: beside portraits that are strongly individualized and seem to project inner qualities, we find those that place emphasis on plastic beauty and stunning costume, and also many catalogued arrangements of ethnological phenomena (plates 23–24).

Another area in which an ambiguity exists, if not an outright contradiction, involves the place of the author in the work. In principle the Indian is the hero and the focus in *Letters and Notes,* yet at times it seems as if Catlin himself has taken over that role. Many passages foreground the author in his thoughts, feelings, and actions, making the Indians recede into his shadow. We see the author both dramatized and glorified in various roles in the text, and some of these also are represented visually in the category of illustration mentioned earlier, in which the artist puts himself in view: Catlin as artist (painting Indians),[26] as adventurer (hunting buffalo, alone on a plain with wolves in the distance), as friend of the Indian (being fêted by a chief). In both text and image, Catlin's courage on the one hand and good faith toward the Indians on the other are the characteristics most often insinuated or asserted. This focus on the (admirable) self of the author-traveler can be found to a certain extent in some earlier accounts, but Catlin takes the tendency considerably further.[27]

These aspects of the work complicate the seeming simplicity of the primary message but are not necessarily problematic in themselves, nor need they be incompatible with a romantic perspective. As the work progresses, however, it becomes clear that Catlin is inhabited by some very stark, glaring contradictions, many of which he shared with other Americans of his period. These raise more serious questions, and finally negate any romantic critique of modernity that some passages might seem to point to. Although parts of the text treat—or show the author-protagonist as treating—Indians and Indian customs with respect and sensitivity, other parts reveal a tendency toward condescension and ethnocentrism. On the one hand, for instance, concerning the strange (for his culture) burial customs of the Mandans, Catlin comments that the traveler who comes to "study and learn" can "draw many a deduction that will last him through life" (1:89). In another instance, when treated to a feast of dog meat by the Sioux, he willingly accepts it in the spirit in which it is offered (though, as he says, other visitors often react with disgust and ridicule), and explains to the reader the sacrificial nature of the custom, related to the role of dogs in Indian societies (1:230).

On the other hand, elsewhere the author himself ridicules Indian practices, particularly shamanistic ones, which are dismissed as "hocus pocus" or "laughable farce," often with a wink to the reader (for example, 1:35, 111, 134). The text creates a bond of cultural superiority between author and reader at the expense of the "benighted" savage. Several tribes that Catlin visits believe that his painting, of a realistic kind they have never seen before, is "medicine," that is, a manifestation of sacred power. Catlin quickly discovers that this can give him strong leverage with his hosts, and he uses the awe that he inspires in ways that are sometimes manipulative. He informs the reader in one passage that he purposely made some gestures to suggest magical operations, in effect playing at being a shaman, and enjoying it (1:109).

More than this, though, in pursuing his own purposes Catlin is often prepared to engage in actions that are anathema to the Indians in terms of their belief systems, and use his own culture as a standard. He continually tries to *buy* for his collection sacred objects, or irreplaceable, highly valued ones (such as a warrior's robe with his deeds painted on them), and he often wheedles, in an attempt to have his way in the end, after a first refusal. (One chief finally *copies* for Catlin the figures from his robe onto another, thereby making a *replica;* 1:148). Perhaps the most striking case of this cultural insensitivity took place on the third of Catlin's major excursions to the West, when he set out to discover the location of a fabled pipestone quarry (stone for the making of the calumet), common to many tribes of the region, which he had been told of by Indians on earlier trips. When he reached it, he was stopped by a party of Sioux, who at the time controlled access to it and who told him that he should not continue onto the site because it was sacred ground. He continued on anyway. Once there he painted the site, took samples of the rock, and later wrote an article on it for a scientific journal.[28] In the text of *Letters and Notes,* Catlin builds reader curiosity about this visit early on, and then when he recounts the incident proudly extols his achievement and attempts to discredit the Sioux who opposed him (1:31, 234; 2:166–68, 172–76, 201–2).

Most crucially of all, though, Catlin contradicts the very celebration of wildness that appears to be at the heart of his message, recognizing, implicitly or explicitly, the need for wild Indians to acquire the blessings of civilization, to become sedentary agriculturalists, adopt Christianity, and give up some of their "ignorant" superstitions and "disgusting" customs. (One such passage comes after his lengthy description of the Mandan *o-kee-pa,* a self-torture ceremony; 1:183.) In the same way, Catlin sometimes bewilderingly takes the very opposite tack from his common theme of criticism of white encroachment on Indian land and condemnation of the cupidity that often motivates it. The passages that make this shift appear mainly in volume two, which concerns the later period of travels, generally among "semi-civilized" Indians farther east, therefore coming, perhaps, after the intensity of his first response to the wild tribes has worn off. The contradiction is nonetheless breathtaking. In one passage the author urges "the enterprising capitalists of the North" to come and prosper in Pensacola, a highly promising location now that a railroad is projected to reach it (2:34). In another he enthuses about the then-new town of Dubuque, on the Mississippi, promising, "A visit of a few days to Dubuque will be worth the while of every traveller; and for the speculator and man of enterprise, it affords the finest field now open in our country"; with its nearby mines, Catlin claims, "it is to be the mint of our country" (2:149). Another passage describes the author's "sublime contemplations" of civilized man advancing joyfully farther west, and sings the praises of the pioneer as the true American, though all the while expressing deep regret at the coming demise of the Indian (2:157–59). Given such passages in *Letters and Notes,* it is perhaps not surprising that in the late 1840s, when living abroad, Catlin wrote a pamphlet encouraging immigration to the frontier and even touted the Gold Rush.[29]

Catlin's apparent blindness to these discrepancies is remarkable, as is his seeming unawareness that those whites he willingly associates with on his travels, and he himself to a certain extent, are participants in the process of destruction of one culture by another. On his first excursion Catlin travels up the Missouri on a steamboat of the American Fur Company that is penetrating deeper than ever before into Indian territory, thus enabling further extension of the trade in buffalo hides. Catlin reports that when it arrives at Indian encampments, it fires its cannon as a means of impressing fear and awe in the minds of the natives. Yet he reports their reactions only with amusement (1:20).[30] On the second excursion Catlin joins dragoons whose purpose is to lay the bases for the extension of U.S. government control in Comanche territory. He opens his account of that journey in volume two by commenting that "the *natives* are again 'to be astonished,' and I shall probably again be a witness to the scene," but assures the reader, "I care not how badly we frighten them, provided we hurt them not, nor frighten them out of *sketching distance*" (2:37). Later Catlin uneasily notices the brutality of the officers' treatment of the Pawnees (encountered before his expedition reaches the Comanches; 2:47), but the issue is quickly dropped and in the end the author has only praise for the commanders (2:84). On the third major trip, as already mentioned, Catlin was imperturbably prepared to desecrate what, from an Indian point of view, was a sacred site. Looking to the future, he approvingly sees the day when the quarry will be the domain of the geologist rather than the Indian (2:202).

A final instance might be mentioned. Although he elsewhere harshly criticizes whites for creating the conditions for the extinction of the buffalo on which the Plains Indians rely, and discusses the reverent attitude of the latter toward the animals they hunt, Catlin tells the reader that he merely wanted a trophy when he went hunting, and describes how he delayed delivering the coup de grâce to a wounded buffalo so that he could make a dramatic sketch, close-up, of its agony (1:26–27; fig. 12.1).

Such, then, are some of the ambiguities and contradictions that emerge from a reading of *Letters and Notes,* though in them Catlin often reflected attitudes that were current among Anglo-Americans of the period. Their presence, in an extreme form, in this travel account produced during the 1830s would tend to support John Hausdoerffer's contention in *Catlin's Lament* that—contrary to a common interpretation of his European period as a betrayal of an earlier purity of mission—there is an essential continuity of conflicted vision throughout Catlin's

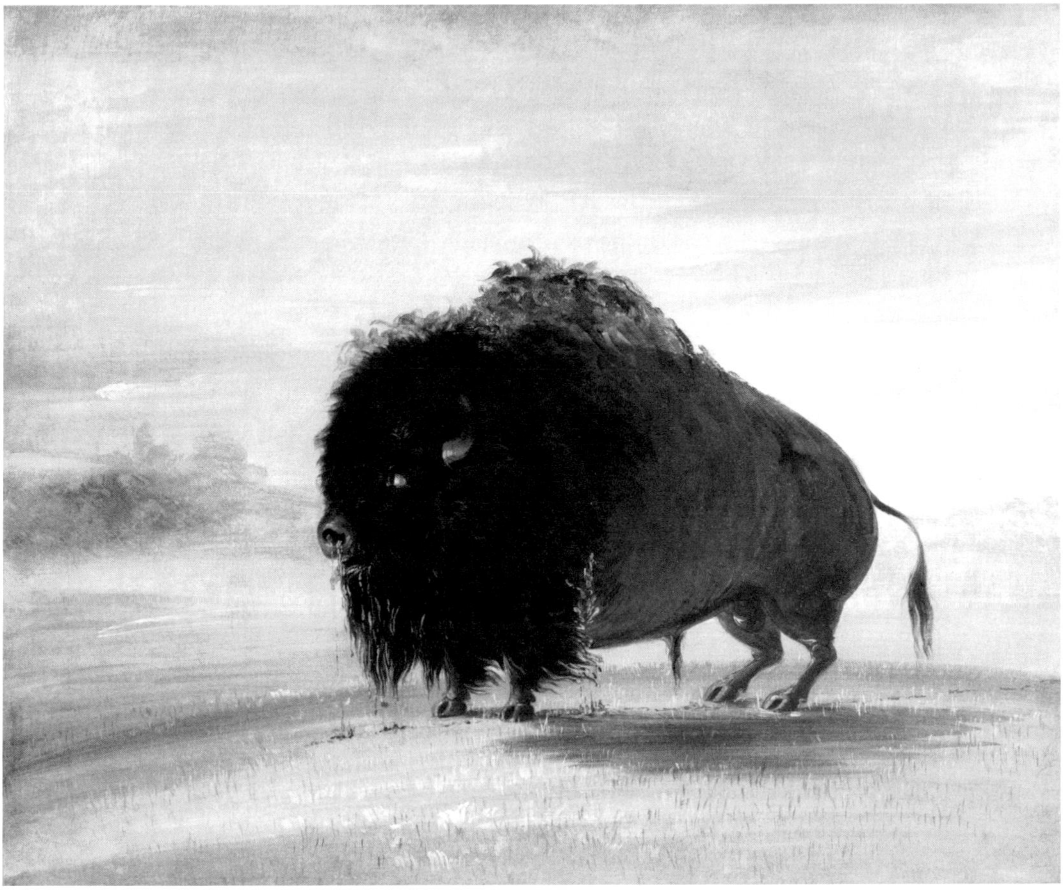

Figure 12.1 George Catlin, *Wounded Buffalo, Strewing His Blood over the Prairies.* Oil on canvas, 24 x 29 in. (60.9 x 73.7 cm), Smithsonian American Art Museum, Gift of Mrs. Joseph Harrison Jr., 1985.66.406.

life.[31] In this context, some important aspects of his travel account, and of his larger life work seen as a unified whole, can be linked to cultural trends already developing in early nineteenth-century America but destined to take on added importance later in the century and beyond. Three of these connections seem most significant: ethnological show business, ethnology and its collections and museums, and finally the development of tourism.

The history of exhibition of "savage" or "primitive" peoples to audiences in "civilized" countries goes far back in time, as does that of displays of "abnormal" creatures or "freaks," with which the former kind of exhibition has significant similarities. In the case of American natives, such spectacles date back as far as the discovery of the "New World." But in the nineteenth century they proliferate and are transformed by a growing commercialism and consumerism in Europe and North America. Ethnological displays become a part of the early development of "show business"; their impresarios are submitted to the pressures of competition and make extensive use of advertising to attract profitable publics. In Europe in the early nineteenth century—particularly in London, but also in some continental capitals—a series of shows involving primitive peoples were put on: from the "Hottentot Venus" of the 1810s and "Eskimos" of the twenties, to "Bushmen" in the forties and "Zulu Kaffirs" in the fifties (fig. 12.2). Catlin's Indian shows in Europe fall within this series. His productions at first used whites, including himself, dressed in Indian garb and playing Indian roles, but later added live performances by actual imported Indians (Ojibway and Iowa), who danced, enacted ceremonies, and mimed the gestures of their daily life.[32]

In the second half of the nineteenth century and into the early twentieth, this kind of ethnological show was carried to a further level of development, becoming a "major form of public entertainment" as a crucial component of wild west shows, circuses, world's fairs, colonial expositions, and the like.[33] In relation to this later period, Catlin's Indian shows bear the strongest resemblance to "Buffalo Bill's Wild West" show of the last two decades of the nineteenth century and first decade of the twentieth. Like Catlin, "Buffalo Bill" Cody produced his shows first in the United States and then in Europe, and both men focused on dramatizing western Indians in their western habitat. In spite of differences—Cody's shows achieved greater popularity than Catlin's by concentrating on creating grand spectacle and enacting conflict—there was much continuity between the two. That this continuity extends beyond Buffalo Bill to the movie western is suggested by Paul Reddin in his comprehensive study of wild west shows, which devotes the first two chapters to Catlin, the middle three to Cody, and the concluding ones to later shows and their relation to the western film.[34]

Catlin the showman was thus an important early exponent of a nineteenth-century trend. And this aspect of his career is directly linked in several ways to the travel account I have been analyzing. In addition to including materials also used in it, *Letters and Notes* is a kind of *advertisement* for Catlin's show.[35] Throughout the text we find references to a production, called the "Indian Gallery," which the author is preparing, though when the travel account was published in 1841 the Gallery had in fact already been running for some years (fig. 12.3). The book announces the show as a coming attraction, giving a preview to the reader through text and sketches, creating interest and curiosity, often suggesting that it is impossible to convey fully in words what the spectator at the Gallery will be able to see with his or her own eyes. This form of enticement includes some rather

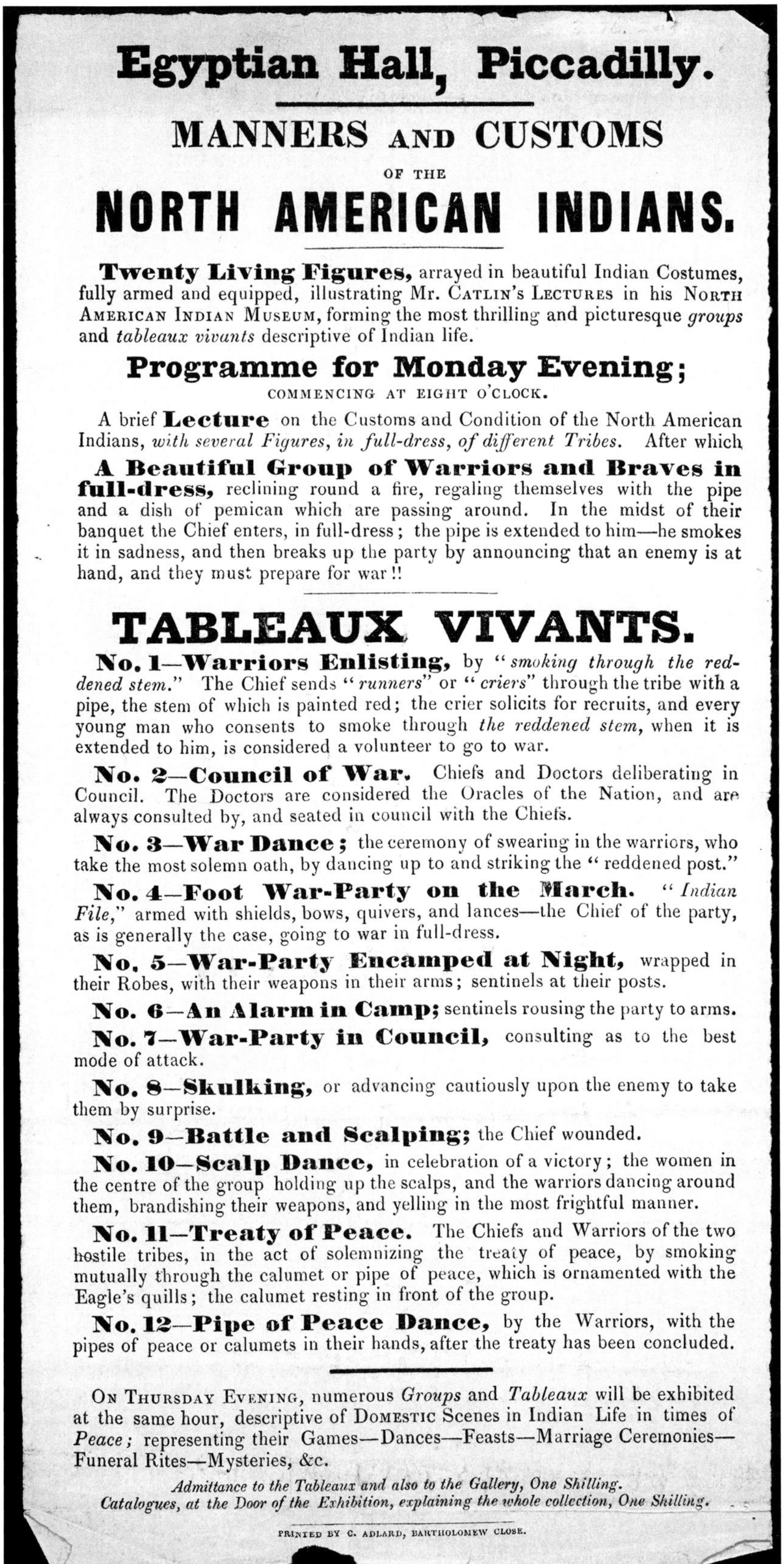

# Egyptian Hall, Piccadilly.

## MANNERS AND CUSTOMS OF THE NORTH AMERICAN INDIANS.

**Twenty Living Figures,** arrayed in beautiful Indian Costumes, fully armed and equipped, illustrating Mr. CATLIN'S LECTURES in his NORTH AMERICAN INDIAN MUSEUM, forming the most thrilling and picturesque *groups* and *tableaux vivants* descriptive of Indian life.

## Programme for Monday Evening;

COMMENCING AT EIGHT O'CLOCK.

A brief **Lecture** on the Customs and Condition of the North American Indians, *with several Figures, in full-dress, of different Tribes.* After which

**A Beautiful Group of Warriors and Braves in full-dress,** reclining round a fire, regaling themselves with the pipe and a dish of pemican which are passing around. In the midst of their banquet the Chief enters, in full-dress; the pipe is extended to him—he smokes it in sadness, and then breaks up the party by announcing that an enemy is at hand, and they must prepare for war!!

## TABLEAUX VIVANTS.

**No. 1—Warriors Enlisting,** by "*smoking through the reddened stem.*" The Chief sends "*runners*" or "*criers*" through the tribe with a pipe, the stem of which is painted red; the crier solicits for recruits, and every young man who consents to smoke through *the reddened stem,* when it is extended to him, is considered a volunteer to go to war.

**No. 2—Council of War.** Chiefs and Doctors deliberating in Council. The Doctors are considered the Oracles of the Nation, and are always consulted by, and seated in council with the Chiefs.

**No. 3—War Dance;** the ceremony of swearing in the warriors, who take the most solemn oath, by dancing up to and striking the "reddened post."

**No. 4—Foot War-Party on the March.** "*Indian File,*" armed with shields, bows, quivers, and lances—the Chief of the party, as is generally the case, going to war in full-dress.

**No. 5—War-Party Encamped at Night,** wrapped in their Robes, with their weapons in their arms; sentinels at their posts.

**No. 6—An Alarm in Camp;** sentinels rousing the party to arms.

**No. 7—War-Party in Council,** consulting as to the best mode of attack.

**No. 8—Skulking,** or advancing cautiously upon the enemy to take them by surprise.

**No. 9—Battle and Scalping;** the Chief wounded.

**No. 10—Scalp Dance,** in celebration of a victory; the women in the centre of the group holding up the scalps, and the warriors dancing around them, brandishing their weapons, and yelling in the most frightful manner.

**No. 11—Treaty of Peace.** The Chiefs and Warriors of the two hostile tribes, in the act of solemnizing the treaty of peace, by smoking mutually through the calumet or pipe of peace, which is ornamented with the Eagle's quills; the calumet resting in front of the group.

**No. 12—Pipe of Peace Dance,** by the Warriors, with the pipes of peace or calumets in their hands, after the treaty has been concluded.

ON THURSDAY EVENING, numerous *Groups* and *Tableaux* will be exhibited at the same hour, descriptive of DOMESTIC Scenes in Indian Life in times of *Peace;* representing their Games—Dances—Feasts—Marriage Ceremonies—Funeral Rites—Mysteries, &c.

*Admittance to the Tableaux and also to the Gallery, One Shilling.*
*Catalogues, at the Door of the Exhibition, explaining the whole collection, One Shilling.*

PRINTED BY C. ADLARD, BARTHOLOMEW CLOSE.

Figure 12.2
Catlin Collection.
Egyptian Hall
Broadside—3576.203.
Gilcrease Museum
Archives, Tulsa.

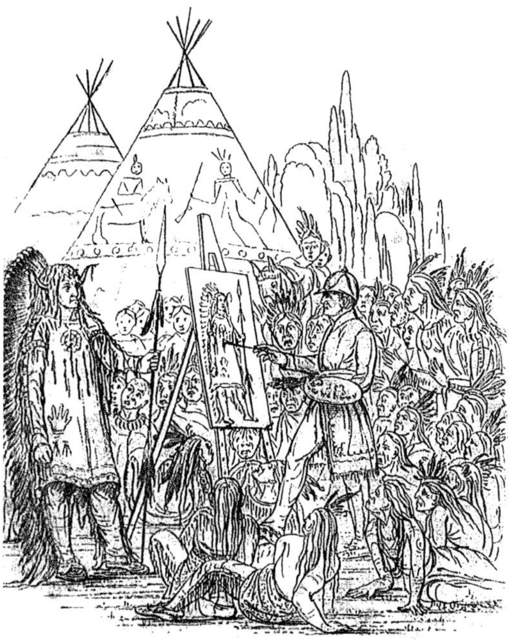

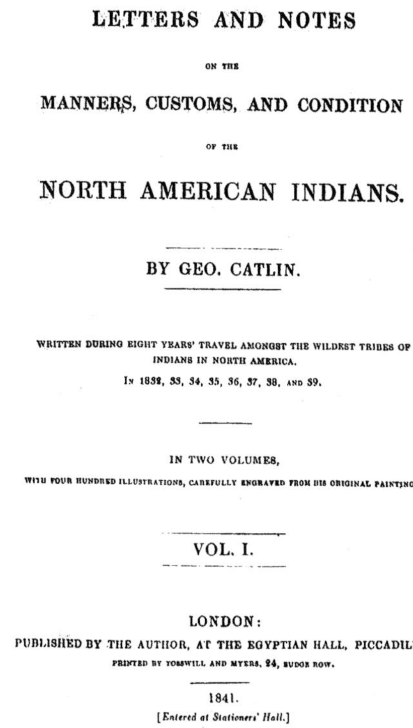

LETTERS AND NOTES
ON THE
MANNERS, CUSTOMS, AND CONDITION
OF THE
NORTH AMERICAN INDIANS.

BY GEO. CATLIN.

WRITTEN DURING EIGHT YEARS' TRAVEL AMONGST THE WILDEST TRIBES OF INDIANS IN NORTH AMERICA.
IN 1832, 33, 34, 35, 36, 37, 38, AND 39.

IN TWO VOLUMES,
WITH FOUR HUNDRED ILLUSTRATIONS, CAREFULLY ENGRAVED FROM HIS ORIGINAL PAINTINGS.

VOL. I.

LONDON:
PUBLISHED BY THE AUTHOR, AT THE EGYPTIAN HALL, PICCADILLY.
PRINTED BY TOSSWILL AND MYERS, 24, BUDGE ROW.
1841.
[*Entered at Stationers' Hall.*]

Figure 12.3 Frontispiece and title page of the first edition of George Catlin's *Letters and Notes,* 1841.

sensationalist appeals, such as announcing that the author has obtained a knife wrested from one chief by another in mortal combat; this knife still has blood on it, blood that will not be removed so that spectators may be able to see for themselves (1:153–54).

But if the publication was an ad for the show, the converse was true as well, since copies of *Letters and Notes* were available for purchase at the entrance to Catlin's London productions.[36] Finally, and most profoundly, it would not be too much to say that the travel account itself, through its rhetorical flourishes, takes on the character of a show, with the author as an impresario opening the curtain to reveal the curiosities, the wonders, and sometimes the horrors or grotesqueries of what he has witnessed in Indian territory—a "grand spectacle," as he calls it in several places, one in which the Indians themselves are the main actors and "supernumeraries" (1:165). In addition to presenting the native denizens of the West as metaphorical players in this way, in several passages Catlin describes Indians living close to white settlements as actually performing for visitors, sometimes for money (for example, 2:237), and it seems plausible that Catlin first had the idea of employing Indian actors through observing these entertainments.[37]

Like ethnological shows, ethnographic discourse and collections of artifacts of "primitive" human groups had a long history—especially in the form of travel accounts and the souvenirs brought back in the baggage of travelers—before they became institutionalized into a discipline and a kind of museum. This institutionalization occurred for the most part only in the second half of the nineteenth century. The American Ethnological Society and the Ethnological Society of London date from 1842 and 1843, respectively, the Smithsonian Institution from 1846, and Harvard's Peabody Museum from 1856; Henry Schoolcraft and Lewis Henry Morgan published works in the area of North American Indian ethnology in the middle of the century. The era of anthropological theorization, as well as of intense collecting of primitive artifacts and "art objects"—in particular those of North American Indians—began somewhat later, in the last quarter of the nineteenth century.[38]

The "scientific" approach to the study of primitive societies, and the constitution of museums documenting their material existence, were thus in their earliest stages in the period when Catlin wrote *Letters and Notes* and developed his Gallery. Yet both of these works had strongly scientific pretensions, aiming to instruct as much as to divert. When Catlin set out on his travels in the early 1830s, he had in mind from the outset to collect data and artifacts of Indian life as much as to represent it pictorially. He amassed huge quantities of both in the following years and integrated them into the book and the exhibition. The text of *Letters and Notes* contains many long descriptions of customs, practices, and beliefs, with interpretations of their meanings in quasi-ethnological terms, while a considerable number of the book's illustrations offer systematically organized visual representations of artifacts (fig. 12.4). As for the Gallery, at least in part it had the aspect of a museum. On display one often found as a centerpiece a full-size tepee that took up much of a room, as well as arranged specimens of Indian weapons, domestic and ritual objects, costumes, buffalo robes painted with scenes of battle, and so on. Since *Letters and Notes* presents many drawings of these same materials, presented in the manner of scientific illustration, it also sometimes takes on a museum-like quality.

Both *Letters and Notes* and the Gallery, then, are hybrid mixes of the museum and the show. In this respect Catlin's work prefigures crosses between the two that

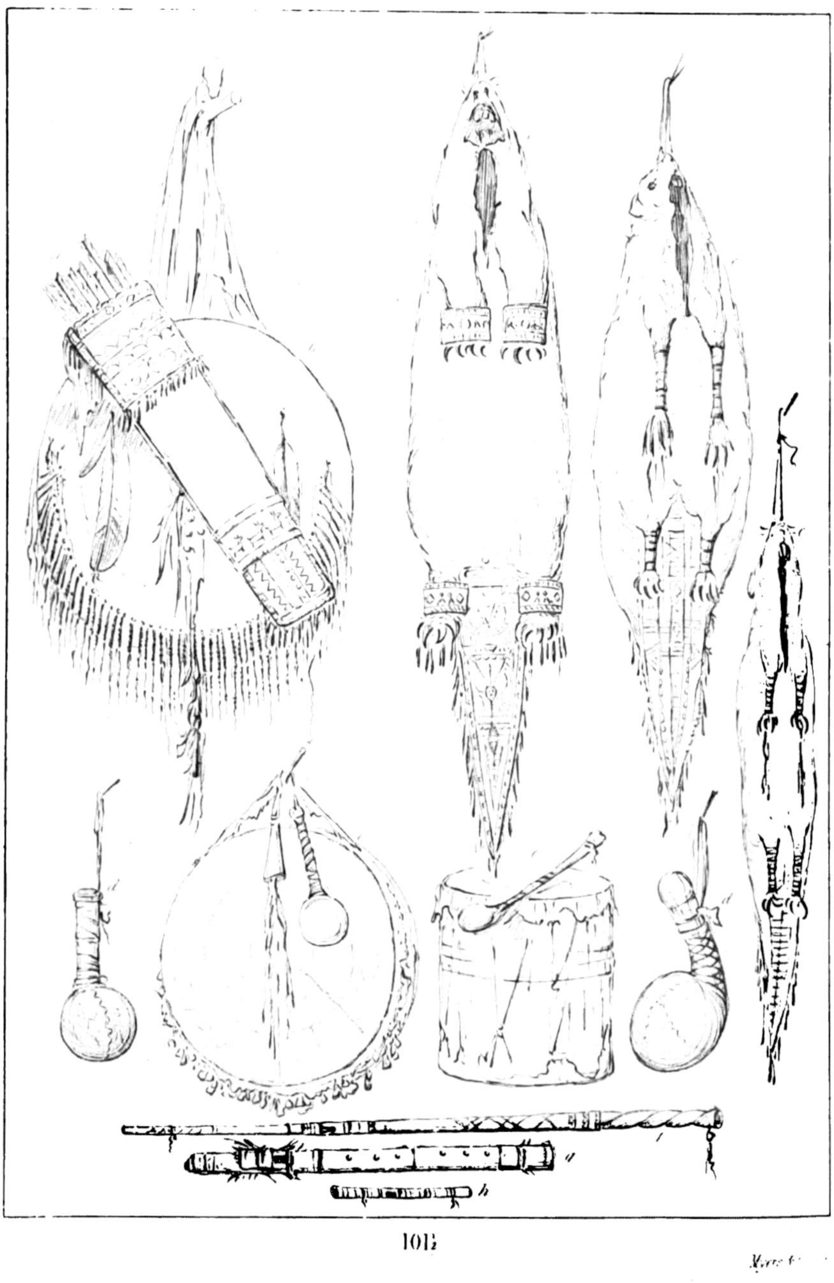

Figure 12.4 Line drawing from the first edition of George Catlin's *Letters and Notes,* 1841: *artefacts,* plate 101½.

came later in the century, most famously—or notoriously—in the ethnological exhibits at world's fairs and universal exhibitions.

A final connection—but one that has been less often noted than the previous two—is with the early development of tourism. Tourism—which might be defined as an organized form of travel, following a prescribed path and facilitated by relatively speedy and comfortable transportation, comfortable lodging at one's destination, and cultural framing in the form of a specialized travel literature, including guidebooks—had already developed to some extent in Europe in the eighteenth century. In the United States, however, it came somewhat later, and took a specific form. The first manifestations of American tourism appeared in the 1820s, in the Hudson River Valley and west to Niagara Falls, following on the introduction of the steamboat and the construction of the Erie Canal. Later, tourism extended to other northeastern destinations and moved progressively farther west, as settlement, industrialization, and modernization proceeded westward. Paradoxically, though, while tourism in the United States was always linked to these phenomena, it often focused on "natural" sites. As several studies have emphasized, tourism played a special and crucial role in the young republic as part of the creation of a national identity, and the predominant image defining its singularity was that of "nature's nation."[39]

By the end of the 1820s, the rudiments of tourism had already burgeoned on the Mississippi River, but it was only in the second half of the nineteenth century that the trans-Mississippi West became an object of the developing tourist industry, in parallel with pacification, settlement, and economic growth in the region.[40] Catlin's *Letters and Notes* represents a significant cultural intervention in both of these moments of western tourism.

In volume two, when the author is reporting on an excursion with his wife up the Mississippi River, he notes, concerning a group of "semi-civilized" Indians encamped near the Falls of Saint Anthony: "[They] are assembled here at this time, affording us, who are visitors here, a fine and wild scene of dances, amusements, etc. They seem to take great pleasure in 'showing off' in these scenes, to the amusement of the many fashionable visitors, both ladies and gentlemen, who are in the habit of reaching this post, as steamers are arriving at this place every week in the summer from St. Louis" (2:132). The area, then, is already a relatively busy tourist stop in the mid-1830s, but Catlin attempts to promote it further, wishing to upgrade its reputation as a tourist experience and increase its frequentation by making it the ultimate destination of a well-defined western tour that will compete with eastern ones. He expresses the hope that a circuit starting in St. Louis, by steamboat up the river to the Falls of Saint Anthony, then returning east via Mackinaw, which he elsewhere calls a "summer's paradise" (2:161), might become "the next 'Fashionable Tour,'" adding, "This Tour would comprehend but a small part of the great 'Far West'; but it will furnish to the traveller a fair sample, and . . . [is] so easily accessible to the world, . . . the only part of it to which *ladies* can have access." (2:130).[41]

Catlin's text reveals that the Indians of the area around the Falls of Saint Anthony—Sioux—are already adjusting to the tourist mode, performing for whites on tour rather than living their normal lives. Catlin seems to be entirely comfortable with this form of relationship between native and visitor. During an earlier sojourn in Sioux territory, while making portraits of a band, he had paid them to dance for him, persuading the head chiefs to join the dance, a departure from their usual practice (1:237). During the later visit to the Falls of Saint Anthony, in an unconsciously ironic gesture he initiated and organized an Indian ball game on the Fourth of July (2:135).

In these passages from volume two, Catlin is simply reinforcing a trend already under way—the opening of the Mississippi (and Great Lakes) to tourism—but he also treats the trans-Mississippi West prospectively in a similar way. Catlin calls his first excursion up the Missouri a "Tour" (1:20), and after describing a particularly "picturesque" landscape[42] near one of the Mandan villages—a vista of bluffs called the "Grand Dome" (1:77)—he speaks of the green turf that protects them from erosion, so that they may "be gazed upon with admiration, by the hardy voyageur and the tourist, for ages and centuries to come" (1:78) (fig. 12.5). Here he seems to envisage a later period when not just the select "hardy voyageurs" but the more numerous group of "tourists" will be attracted to come to an area rarely visited by whites in the past.[43]

In recounting his travels in far western lands inhabited by "wild" Indians, Catlin often uses words such as "fun," "amusement," and "diversion" to characterize the experience, and his animated, enthusiastic descriptions of itineraries and landscapes often take on the accents of a guidebook or promotional brochure. All in all, in spite of Catlin's awareness that the encroachment of "civilization" will destroy the lands and peoples that were still largely "wild" when he visited them, *Letters and Notes* seems to call its readers to become future tourists in the Far West. As for the Indians in this imagined future, Catlin proposes—in a passage that has been much quoted and glossed—the creation, by the U.S. government, of "a magnificent park, where the world could see for ages to come, the native Indian in his classic attire, galloping his wild horse, with sinewy bow" (1:261).

In this essay I have tried to explore some of the fault lines of *Letters and Notes,* some of the ways in which Catlin's travelogue, in both text and image—and in consonance with his work as a whole—is rife with contradictions, appearing to

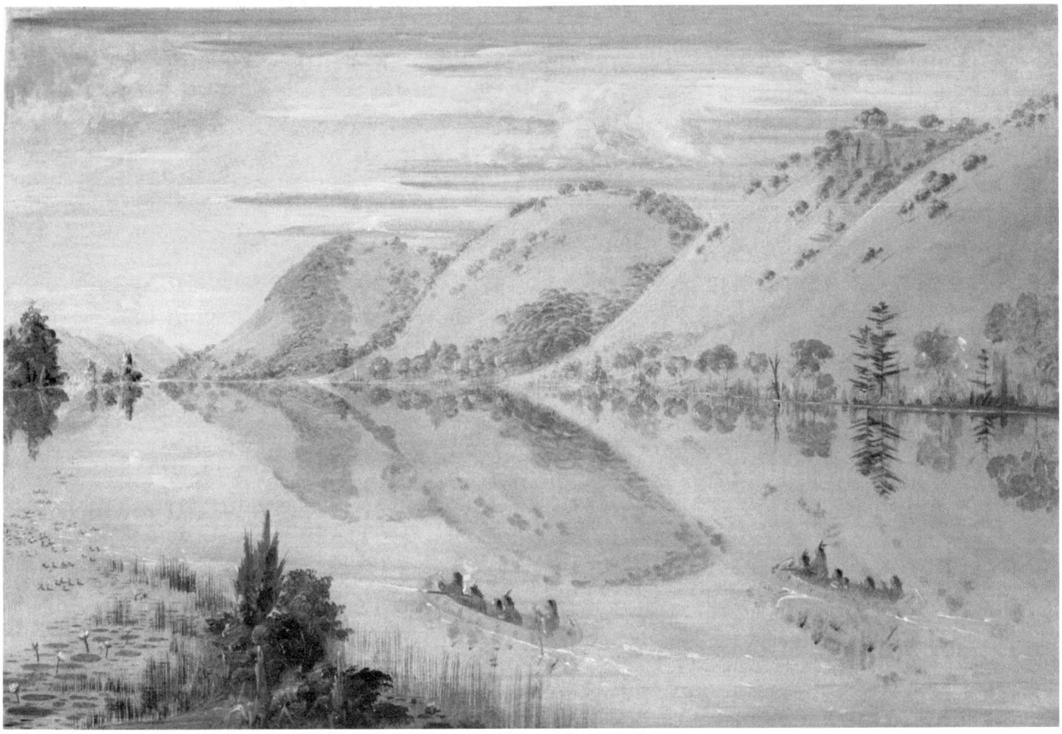

Figure 12.5 George Catlin, *Picturesque Bluffs above Prairie du Chien.* Oil on canvas, 19⅝ x 27½ in. (49.7 x 70.0 cm). Smithsonian American Art Museum, Gift of Mrs. Joseph Harrison Jr., 1985.66.317.

manifest a radically split sensibility. On the one hand, we find the articulation of a passionate affinity for "primitive" indigenous peoples and the natural wilds in which they live, mourning for the imminent destruction of both, and fierce criticism directed against those forces of "civilization" that are carrying it out. The authorial persona that expresses these perspectives in the work seems to be a romantic one. Yet a decidedly anti-romantic persona emerges as well: one that praises, encourages, and takes part in entrepreneurship and the pursuit of profit, science as a desacralizing force, and the imperial spread westward of "American progress."

These two outlooks do not, however, have an equal status in Catlin's intellectual and artistic makeup. Ultimately it is the second of the two that dominates, as my examination of Catlin's work has in fact revealed a personality thoroughly permeated by the modern ethos, especially by the entrepreneurial impulse. As his recent biographer emphasizes, from the beginning Catlin resembled his father in his fixation on wealth and vulnerability to "get-rich-quick schemes,"[44] and he never seems to have felt as alienation the modern artist's dilemma of being torn between the noncommercial values of art and the imperatives of the market. Nowhere in Catlin's praise of "primitive" Indian life, moreover, do we find a searching critique of the mercantile civilization that was destroying it. Consequently, although Catlin's ardent identification with the American Indian does perhaps crystallize an incipient romantic tendency in his temperament, that tendency remains marginal and is entirely co-opted. Entrepreneurship finally provides the organizing framework within which Catlin's "romantic" vision of the Indian expresses itself, and the net effect is the transformation of the latter into a commodity—paradoxical in the extreme, since one of the roots of the authentic romantic sensibility is outrage against commodification in the modern world.

## NOTES

1. According to a 2013 biography of Catlin, there is no independent documentation, outside of Catlin's own writings and iconography, to confirm that he in fact made any of these trips. While their authenticity cannot be entirely ruled out, there are substantial reasons to think that Catlin's presentation of them is partially or wholly fictional. See Benita Eisler, *The Red Man's Bones: George Catlin, Artist and Showman* (New York: Norton, 2013), 371–87.

2. On the European period of Catlin's career, see Christopher Mulvey, "George Catlin in Europe," in *George Catlin and His Indian Gallery*, ed. George Gurney and Therese Thau Heyman (New York: Norton; Washington, D.C.: Smithsonian American Art Museum, 2002). For Catlin's life in the context of the artistic, intellectual, and sociopolitical milieu of the period, see Brian W. Dippie, *Catlin and His Contemporaries: The Politics of Patronage* (Lincoln: University of Nebraska Press, 1990).

3. See especially Harold McCracken, *George Catlin and the Old Frontier* (New York: Dial Press, 1959).

4. *Artist Explorers of the 1830s: George Catlin, Karl Bodmer, Alfred Jacob Miller* (Omaha: Joslyn Art Museum, 1963); Horst Hartmann, *George Catlin und Balduin Möllhausen: Zwei Interpreten der Indianer und des Alten Westens* (Berlin: D. Reimer, 1963); Clide Hollmann, *Five Artists of the Old West: George Catlin, Karl Bodmer, Alfred Jacob Miller, Charles M. Russell, and Frederic Remington* (New York: Hastings House, 1965).

5. The two editions are, respectively, George Catlin, *Letters and Notes on the Manners, Customs, and Conditions of the North American Indians, Written during Eight Years' Travel (1832–1839) amongst the Wildest Tribes of Indians in North America,* 2 vols. (New York: Dover, 1973); and George Catlin, *Letters and Notes on the North American Indians,* ed. Michael Macdonald Mooney (New York: Charles N. Potter Publishers, 1975).

6. Joseph R. Millichap, *George Catlin,* Boise State University Western Writers series, no. 27 (Boise: Boise State University, 1977); William H. Truettner, *The Natural Man Observed: A Study of Catlin's Indian Gallery* (Washington, D.C.: Smithsonian Institution Press, 1979). Truettner's excellent, comprehensive treatment of Catlin's life and work laid the groundwork for later developments. It includes a chapter on the European part of Catlin's career: "Abroad: For European Audiences."

7. Gurney and Heyman, *George Catlin and His Indian Gallery.*

8. This shortened, rearranged version, retitled *North American Indians,* was edited by Peter Matthiessen; originally published in 1989, it was reissued in 1996 and 2004. In the same period a German-language edition also appeared: George Catlin, *Die Indianer Nordamerikas: Abenteuer und Schicksale* (Stuttgart: Edition Erdmann, 1994).

9. William H. Goetzmann, *The West of the Imagination,* 2nd ed. (Norman: University of Oklahoma Press, 2009); Dan L. Flores, *Visions of the Big Sky: Painting and Photographing the Northern Rocky Mountain West* (Norman: University of Oklahoma Press, 2010).

10. Michael P. Branch, ed., *Reading the Roots: American Nature Writing before Walden* (Athens: University of Georgia Press, 2004); Bill McKibben, ed., *American Earth: Environmental Writing since Thoreau* (New York: Literary Classics of the United States / Penguin Putnam, 2008).

11. Articles: Gareth E. John, "Cultural Nationalism, Westward Expansion, and the Production of Imperial Landscape: George Catlin's Native American West," *Ecumene* 8.2 (2001): 175–203; Gareth E. John, "Benevolent Imperialism: George Catlin and the Practice of Jeffersonian Geography," *Journal of Historical Geography* 30 (2004): 597–617. Chapters of books: Miguel A. Cabanas, "With a Colt, a Brush, and a Pen: George Catlin's Preservation of the Indian," in *The Cultural "Other" in Nineteenth-Century Travel Narratives* (Lewiston, N.Y.: Edwin Mellen Press, 2008), 169–207; Joshua David Bellin, "George Catlin, Te-ho-pe-nee Wash-ee," in *Medicine Bundle: Indian Sacred Performance and American Literature, 1824–1932* (Philadelphia: University of Pennsylvania Press, 2008), 21–77. Monographs: John Hausdoerffer, *Catlin's Lament: Indians, Manifest Destiny, and the Ethics of Nature* (Lawrence: University Press of Kansas, 2009). For discussion of the kind of criticism of Catlin that has been leveled by Native Americans themselves, see the introduction to Gurney and Heyman, *George Catlin and His Indian Gallery,* by the director of the National Museum of the American Indian, W. Richard West, himself a Cheyenne-Arapaho Indian.

12. Catlin's later travel accounts are *Notes of eight years' travel and residence in Europe with his North American Indian collection,* 2 vols. (London, 1848; 2nd ed., 1852); *Life amongst the Indians: A book for youth* (New York, 1857; London, 1861); and *Last rambles amongst the Indians of the Rocky Mountains and the Andes* (New York, 1867; London, 1868). None of these has been republished in its entirety in a modern edition. Short excerpts of the last two, rearranged thematically, have, however, been published as *George Catlin: Episodes from Life Among the Indians and Last Rambles,* ed. Marvin C. Ross, Civilization of the American Indian series (Norman: University of Oklahoma Press, 1959).

13. For a map that traces Catlin's western itineraries between 1832 and 1836, see Dippie, *Catlin and His Contemporaries,* 23.

14. For this background of conflict with Indians in the 1830s, see William M. Osborn, *The Wild Frontier: Atrocities during the American-Indian War from Jamestown Colony to Wounded Knee* (New York: Random House, 2000), 180–83; Bill Yenne, *Indian War: The Campaign for the American West* (Yardley, Pa.: Westholme Publishing, 2006), 27–38; Michael L. Nunnally, *American Indian Wars: A Chronology of Confrontations between Native Peoples and Settlers and the United States Military, 1500s—1901* (Jefferson, N.C.: McFarland & Co., 2007), 72–82; Robert Wooster, *The American Military Frontiers: The United States Army in the West, 1783–1900* (Albuquerque: University of New Mexico Press, 2009), 78–95.

15. Cabanas, *The Cultural "Other" in Nineteenth-Century Travel Narratives,* 172.

16. See Wooster, *American Military Frontiers,* 81. In *Catlin's Lament* (15–16), John Hausdoerffer indicates that it was because Catlin had, in lectures and newspaper accounts after 1832, "alienated" the American Fur Company by his criticisms of traders' activities that he was obliged to attach himself to a military expedition in 1834.

17. See the introduction to the Dover edition of *Letters and Notes* by Marjorie Halpin, xi.

18. *Travels Through the Interior Parts of North America In the Years 1766, 1767, and 1768,* by Jonathan Carver, was published in 1778 in London. *Travels through North and South Carolina, Georgia, East and West Florida, the Cherokee Country, the Extensive Territories of the Muscogulges or Creek Confederacy, and the Country of the Chactaws,* by William Bartram, appeared in Philadelphia in 1791. For a study of these accounts, along with an earlier one from the beginning of the century, see Robert Sayre, "Encounters with the 'Other': Three Eighteenth-Century, Anglo-American Travellers in Indian Territory," *Studies in Travel Writing* 4 (2000): 29–53.

19. For publications on some of the major nineteenth-century artist-travelers in the American West, see the sources cited in note 4. For mention of and references for still others, see John, "Cultural Nationalism," 176.

20. Probably the two greatest French accounts of travel in the Indian territories of "New France"—those of Baron de Lahontan (1702) and of the Jesuit father Charlevoix (1744)—both adopt a fictitious epistolary mode.

21. Catlin, *Letters and Notes* (Dover edition), 1:1. All subsequent references are to this edition and are given parenthetically in the text.

22. See Bellin, *Medicine Bundle,* 22; Hausdoerffer, *Catlin's Lament,* 15; John, "Cultural Nationalism," 186.

23. As used by Catlin, this term (see, for example, 1:60, 2:163) may denote excellence or typicality, or may possibly suggest identification with classical antiquity.

24. Catlin had earlier (1831) painted an oil portrait of the same Assiniboine Indian as "a distinguished warrior" (see Gurney and Heyman, *George Catlin and His Indian Gallery,* 201), also included in Catlin, *Letters and Notes.* The text of the travel account discusses him at 1:56–57, 67.

25. Miguel Cabanas comments that, more generally, Catlin "makes the Indian into an aesthetic object to be consumed by Anglo-American and European audiences" (*The Cultural "Other,"* 175).

26. As in the frontispiece of *Letters and Notes;* see fig. 12.3.

27. Cabanes also emphasizes this aspect of *Letters and Notes,* claiming that the author's "narcissistic character controls the narrative" (*The Cultural "Other,"* 173, 186).

28. Catlin was also fascinated by the artistry of calumets, made an extensive collection of them during his excursions of the 1830s, and later in life prepared a monograph on Indian pipes, which is held by the British Museum. It has been published, along with, as an appendix, the text of a letter in which Catlin describes his trip to the quarry and confrontation with the Sioux. See *Indian Art in Pipestone: George Catlin's Portfolio in the British Museum,* ed. John C. Ewers (Washington, D.C.: Smithsonian Institution Press, 1979). In *Medicine Bundle* (57), Joshua Bellin asserts that this is one of the rare instances in which Catlin portrays himself as an interloper in Indian territory. He does, however, acknowledge in other passages the distrust and hostility that Indians sometimes exhibited toward him.

29. See the "handbill advertisement for Catlin's London lecture titled 'Valley of the Mississippi,' April, 1850, Archives of American Art, Washington DC," in Gurney and Heyman, *George Catlin and His Indian Gallery,* 77.

30. John Hausdoerffer comments that Catlin "is on the front lines of Manifest Destiny" in this situation but assumes himself to be innocent (*Catlin's Lament,* 66; see also 82).

31. See ibid., chap. 4, esp. 131 and n. 1. Hausdoerffer's understanding of the roots of Catlin's contradictions is, however, somewhat different from my own.

32. See Bernth Lindfors, "Ethnological Show Business: Footlighting the Dark Continent," in *Freakery: Cultural Spectacles of the Extraordinary Body,* ed. Rosemarie Garland Thomson (New York: New York University Press, 1996), 207–17; Richard D. Altick, *The Shows of London* (Cambridge: Harvard University Press, 1978), 275–81. For a detailed discussion of Catlin's dealings with the Indians in his shows, with a focus on the Iowas, see Joseph B. Herring, "Selling the 'Noble Savage' Myth: George Catlin and the Iowa Indians in Europe, 1843–45," *Kansas History* (Winter 2006–7): 226–45.

33. Lindfors, "Ethnological Show Business," 207.

34. Paul Reddin, *Wild West Shows* (Urbana: University of Illinois Press, 1999); see also L. G. Moses, *Wild West Shows and the Images of American Indians, 1883–1933* (Albuquerque: University of New Mexico Press, 1996), esp. introduction and chap. 1.

35. Joshua Bellin comments that "*Letters and Notes* seems to have been worked up by Catlin as both marquee and script for his traveling show" (*Medicine Bundle,* 22).

36. Altick, *Shows of London,* 276.

37. See Reddin, *Wild West Shows,* 8.

38. See Janet Catherine Berlo, "Introduction: The Formative Years of Native American Art History," in *The Early Years of Native American Art History,* ed. J. C. Berlo (Seattle: University of Washington Press, 1992), 1–9.

39. On these aspects of American tourism, see Richard H. Gassan, introduction to *The Birth of American Tourism: New York, the Hudson Valley, and American Culture, 1790–1830* (Amherst: University of Massachusetts Press, 2008), 1–8; Dona Brown, chap. 1, "Tours, Grand and Fashionable: The Origins of Tourist Industries in the United States, 1815–1830," in *Inventing New England: Regional Tourism in the Nineteenth Century* (Washington, D.C.: Smithsonian Institution Press, 1995), 15–74; John F. Sears, introduction to *Sacred Places: American Tourist Attractions in the Nineteenth Century* (New York: Oxford University Press, 1989), 3–11.

40. See Thomas Ruys Smith, chap. 3, "Travel and Tourism," in *River of Dreams: Imagining the Mississippi before Mark Twain* (Baton Rouge: Louisiana State University Press, 2007), 79–110; J. Valerie Fifer, introduction to *American Progress: The Growth of the Transport, Tourist, and Information Industries in the Nineteenth-Century West* (Chester, Conn.: Globe Pequot Press, 1988), 1–13; Marguerite S. Shaffer, introduction to *See America First: Tourism and National Identity, 1880–1940* (Washington, D.C.: Smithsonian Institution Press, 2001), 1–6.

41. The first American "Fashionable Tour," sometimes also referred to as the "American Grand Tour," was the Hudson Valley–Saratoga Springs–Niagara Falls circuit.

42. It should be noted that this is a different "picturesque" landscape from the one in figure 12.5.

43. One commentator points up Catlin's leading role, especially as a painter of landscape, in "[offering] a vision of the West that was exotic and inviting," to replace the prevailing earlier one of the "Great American Desert"; see Anne Farrar Hyde, *An American Vision: Far Western Landscape and National Culture, 1820–1920* (New York: New York University Press, 1990), 29.

44. See Eisler, *The Red Man's Bones,* 371.

# 13

# Romantic Racialism and the Antislavery Novels of Stowe, Hildreth, and Melville

*Janet Koenig*

In 1861—the year before President Lincoln supposedly greeted Harriet Beecher Stowe at the White House by saying, "So you're the little woman who wrote the book that started this great war!"—Karl Marx commended her for her well-publicized letter to Lord Shaftesbury: "Whatever its intrinsic merit may be, [her letter] has done a great deal of good, by forcing the anti-Northern organs of the London press to speak out and lay before the general public the ostensible reasons for their hostile tone against the North, and their ill-concealed sympathies with the South, which looks rather strange on the part of people affecting an utter horror of Slavery."[1] To Lord Shaftesbury and to the British public, Stowe had proclaimed that the primary reason for the Civil War was to end slavery and not, as many thought, solely to preserve the union. Regarding the union issue, she wrote, "The slave party, finding they could no longer use the Union for their purposes, resolved to destroy it."[2] Hers was a political intervention of some importance, because the British government was using the excuse, broadcast in the conservative press, that slavery was not the issue in order to delay taking sides in the war. In actuality, it was loath to cut off the flow of slave plantation cotton supplying its textile mills and equally reluctant to antagonize the North. The proslavery South believed that the economic power of King Cotton would guarantee the British government's support—or at least its neutrality—and thereby ensure its victory as an independent confederacy and a future slave empire.

After slavery was abolished in Britain and most of its colonies in 1833, British abolitionists worked with American abolitionists to end slavery in the United States—which the South dominated politically and economically until shortly before the Civil War. In the 1840s and 1850s, abolitionist movements in both countries were increasingly anxious over the growth of the slave power as a result of the spread of slavery to Texas and its threatened expansion into the much larger western territory acquired after the Mexican War of 1845–46, a territory that realized the goal of Manifest Destiny to extend the nation to the Pacific. Within a year after the proslavery victories of the Compromise of 1850 and the new, harsher Fugitive Slave Law of the same year, *Uncle Tom's Cabin* first appeared in serial form and in 1852 in book form. Against the political and economic force of the slave power, abolitionists on both sides of the Atlantic saw as their task to change the hearts and minds of Americans and hailed Stowe's work as powerful antislavery propaganda.[3]

Stowe made the acquaintance of Lord Shaftesbury and other members of the British aristocracy when she first traveled through England in 1853 to greet the crowds of admirers of her runaway best-seller.[4] On her next tour in 1856, she met Queen Victoria. It would be hard to exaggerate the success *Uncle Tom's Cabin* enjoyed on both sides of the Atlantic. In less than a year after its publication, the book sold over half a million copies in the United States and over a million and a half copies in England and was soon translated into thirty-seven languages; only the Bible had a greater readership. The British *Eclectic Review* reported in 1856 that Stowe's audience cut across all classes and walks of life, observing that "duchesses and factory-girls, states-men and plough-boys, were reading with an interest equally intense the same fascinating pages."[5] *Uncle Tom*–inspired commercial products in the form of calendars, prints, plates, snuffboxes, and other assorted "Tomitudes" flooded the markets at home and abroad. Those who managed not to read the book could see versions of *Uncle Tom's Cabin* performed in theaters and minstrelsy shows all over the United States and Europe. English critics touted it as the great American novel, finally a national literature from America worthy of their notice. It was, the English historian and novelist Charles Kingsley wrote, "a healthy indigenous growth, autochthonous, & free from all that hapless second- and third-hand Germanism, & Italianism, & all other unreal-isms which make me sigh over almost every American book I open."[6]

Yet other equally if not more "autochthonous" antislavery works had already been published. Several autobiographies of former slaves had appeared in the 1840s, notably those of Frederick Douglass (1845), William Wells Brown (1847), Henry Bibb (1849), and Josiah Henson (1849); and in 1845 Douglass also made a celebrated author's tour to Liverpool, London, and Dublin. Earlier still, more than a dozen slave narratives were published, including that of Olaudah Equiano (aka Gustavus Vassa) in 1789, which British antislavery activists used to promote the anti–slave trade legislation of 1807. In 1836 the first American antislavery novel appeared: *The Slave; or, the Memoirs of Archy Moore* by the New England journalist and historian Richard Hildreth.[7]

What made Stowe's work so extraordinarily popular and so effective in many eyes as antislavery propaganda over and above the other antislavery writings of the period? Her publisher John P. Jewett spent much time and money (in lieu of paying more in royalties) marketing the book, going well beyond abolitionist distribution;[8] and the novel was a gripping melodrama. But these factors alone hardly explain the book's immense success. To try to answer these two questions, I compare Stowe's novel with the relatively unsuccessful novels of two of her New England contemporaries: the aforementioned *The Slave* (1836) by Richard Hildreth—retitled *The White Slave* for the 1852 edition—and Herman Melville's *Benito Cereno* (1855). I suggest that the three authors' different positions on slavery and their different relationships to the romantic critique of capitalist modernity help to explain the success or failure of their works.[9] I also indicate ways in which the three novels can be read as influencing and responding to one another.

## Harriet Beecher Stowe and Romantic Racialism

Stowe said it was the harsh Fugitive Slave Law of 1850 that impelled her to write her abolitionist novel. But it was her experiences in Cincinnati, where she lived from 1832 to 1850, that shaped the ideas presented in it.

In Cincinnati, across the river from the slave state of Kentucky, free African Americans and German immigrants made up the majority of residents. Runaway slaves could find support from the city's large African American community and from its Underground Railroad, which Stowe joined.[10] But prosperous Cincinnati, the Queen City of the West, was divided over the issue of slavery. White workers feared job competition from the influx of African Americans and immigrants, and business interests were anxious to keep their economic ties with the South. There had been white mob violence against the African American community in 1829, and another wave of racial violence (which Stowe witnessed) followed in 1836.[11]

Very likely Stowe saw the nation's first public debates over the contested issue of immediate abolition versus colonization, that is, the return of freed slaves to Africa. Colonization societies (composed of both slaveholders and abolitionists) formed early in the nineteenth century to advocate and sponsor transporting freed slaves back to Africa as the answer to fears of slave insurrections. Slavery would quietly fade away, they claimed, with gradual emancipation through voluntary manumission. To this end, in 1822 the American Colonization Society (which had a strong chapter in Cincinnati) helped found Liberia. In 1834, students at Cincinnati's Lane Theological Seminary, led by the antislavery activist Theodore Dwight Weld, organized a series of public debates on the issue against the advice of the administration. Stowe's father, Lyman Beecher, was at this time the institution's acting president. At the close of the Lane Debates, the majority of students decided in favor of immediate abolition and opposed "colonization" on moral grounds. In a wave of enthusiasm, the student majority formed an antislavery organization reaching out to the African American community. Fearing to alienate the town's businessmen, the seminary's conservative board soon reined in the students' abolitionist activities and shut down their antislavery society. Lyman Beecher (and probably Stowe's husband Calvin, then a professor at the seminary) did not oppose the board's decision.[12]

In 1837 Alexander Kinmont, a Swedenborgian theologian, came to Cincinnati to deliver a series of lectures preaching what the historian George Fredrickson has defined as "romantic racialism." Romantic racialism did not challenge the widespread belief in racial stereotypes but viewed the supposed African American racial attributes—childishness, docility, patience, affection—as positive qualities in the face of the ungentle world of capitalist materialism and ruthless national expansionism. Kinmont proclaimed that Africans were more receptive and closer to true Christianity, hence morally superior to the cold Anglo-Saxon race, and he condemned their forced migration to America. In the distant future, a greater and nobler civilization would emerge from Africa, he predicted. What was new in Kinmont's romantic racialism was the way he linked it to Christianity.[13]

Whether or not Stowe heard Kinmont's lectures, it is clear that she shared his views and applied them in *Uncle Tom's Cabin.* In one of her asides to the reader, she wrote:

> If ever Africa shall show an elevated and cultivated race,—and come it must, some time, her turn to figure in the great drama of human improvement,—life will awake there with a gorgeousness and splendor of which our cold western tribes faintly have conceived. In that far-off mystic land . . . will awake new forms of art, new styles of splendor; and the negro race, no longer despised and trodden down, will, perhaps, show forth some of the latest and most magnificent revelations of human life. . . . In all these they will exhibit the highest form of the peculiarly Christian life, and, perhaps, God [will] make her [Africa] the highest and noblest in that kingdom which he will set up, when every other kingdom has been tried, and failed; for the first shall be last, and the last first.[14]

Through the character of George Harris, Stowe voiced her awareness of the colonization controversy among white and black abolitionists but nevertheless advocated colonization as the future for emancipated slaves. George and his family flee to Canada, then to France, and finally to Liberia, where they will build a new nation for their "race."

Explaining his plans, George says: "I have noted the struggle between abolitionist and colonizationist. . . . I grant that this Liberia may have subserved all sorts of purposes, by being played off, in the hands of our oppressors, against us. . . . But the question to me is, Is there not a God above all man's schemes? May He not have overruled their designs, and founded for us a nation by them?"[15] Stowe further proposed that the northern churches first take in the freed slaves and educate them before sending them to Africa: "Let the church of the north receive these poor sufferers in the spirit of Christ; receive them to the educating advantages of Christian republican society and schools until they have attained to somewhat of a moral and intellectual maturity, and then assist them in their passage to those shores, where they may put in practice the lessons they have learned in America."[16]

It is no wonder that these arguments stirred some abolitionists to object. The black abolitionist Henry C. Wright penned an angry letter to William Lloyd Garrison's antislavery newspaper *The Liberator,* dated July 9, 1852:

> I have just read the above book [*Uncle Tom's Cabin*]. It has affected me and repulsed me at the same time, as a reptile that enchants you, while it excites your loathing and abhorrence. . . . [Stowe is] but a counterpart of Henry Clay and Daniel Webster . . . unscrupulous tyrants. . . . I wonder not at the unprecedented popularity of *Uncle Tom's Cabin.* The conscience of this nation is lashed to madness by uncompromising antislavery. *Uncle Tom's Cabin* comes as a quietus to some extent. Thousands will be satisfied by reading and praising it. The deadliest enemies of immediate, unconditional abolition do read and admire it and still hold, whip, breed, and hunt slaves.[17]

A correspondent for *The Provincial Freeman,* an African American abolitionist paper in Canada, wrote: "Uncle Tom must be killed, George Harris exiled! Heaven for dead Negroes! Liberia for living mulattoes. Neither can live on the American continent. Death or banishment is our doom, say the Slaveocrats, the Colonizationists, and, save the mark,—Mrs. Stowe!"[18]

## Richard Hildreth versus Stowe

In 1836 Richard Hildreth wrote *The Slave; or, Memoirs of Archy Moore,* based on his firsthand observations of slavery in Florida. It is considered to be the first fictional slave narrative and, as Martha Pingel observed, "a forerunner [and possibly the prototype] of all antislavery novels in this country."[19] Unable to find a publisher, Hildreth had to pay for the printing himself. Relying solely on abolitionist distribution, *The Slave* sold only seven to eight thousand copies to a mostly abolitionist market. Even so, some abolitionists refused to distribute it because they were scandalized by the incestuous relationship featured in the story: Hildreth's protagonist Archy marries his half sister, whom their father also desires.[20] As a follower of the utilitarian philosopher Jeremy Bentham, Hildreth believed that sexual relations should be free of interference if consensual (Archy and his half sister love each other) and covered by laws dealing with assault if nonconsensual. Despite the later editions that appeared over the next few years (including one in Britain), Hildreth's novel remained little known outside abolitionist groups.

By contrast, *The Life and Adventures of Jonathan Jefferson Whitlaw* by the British writer Frances Trollope was immediately successful in England and helped lead to the 1838 legislation fully ending slavery in the colonies. Published in London in 1836, her novel preceded Hildreth's by six months and is thus considered to be the first antislavery novel. Like Hildreth, who attacked Thomas Jefferson in his novel, Trollope alluded to Jefferson in the name of her novel's title character, a ruthless slaveholder.[21]

To take advantage of the runaway success of *Uncle Tom's Cabin* and to broadcast his criticisms of Stowe's work, in 1852 Hildreth published an expanded, revised edition of his novel under the title *The White Slave; or, Memoirs of a Fugitive,* giving the story an updated ending. Probably riding on Stowe's success, the 1852 edition sold far better on both sides of the Atlantic, with several European editions, some "highly illustrated." Nevertheless, Hildreth's novel remained far less popular than Stowe's.[22]

In 1854 Richard Hildreth responded in the *Boston Evening Telegraph* to a *New York Post* critic who compared *The White Slave* unfavorably with *Uncle Tom's Cabin.* Hildreth asserted that his novel—first published in 1836—was not, as the critic implied, an unsuccessful imitation of Stowe's novel but rather its "forerunner" and that Stowe had "derived from it, the idea of her story." *Uncle Tom's Cabin* owed its "singular popularity," Hildreth argued, "to its character as a religious novel . . . and to Uncle Tom not as a slave, but as a Christian hero." This and not its antislavery message was the cause of its appeal. He speculated that the success of Stowe's novel would have been more spectacular yet had it not carried an antislavery message, that "its anti-slavery, so far from helping it, rather hurt it." Without that "appeal to the religious sensibilities of Christendom, its admirable realization of the Christian hero, saint and martyr," he wrote, "it would scarcely have been known out of the small circle of antislavery readers."[23] In other words, it would have suffered the same fate as his own work.

As Hildreth observed, there are enough points of similarity between the two works to suggest that Stowe must have drawn many ideas for her plot and characters from his.[24] In both narratives, the reader journeys south with the protagonists—from Kentucky in *Uncle Tom's Cabin,* from Virginia in *The Slave*—to encounter ever harsher conditions of slavery. Along the way, the reader of both works meets a variety of characters, from plantation owners, impoverished shopkeepers and small farmers, overseers, drivers, and preachers to opportunistic northern merchants, all of whom slyly or apologetically justify slavery. Both authors described plantation owners going from profligate wealth to bankruptcy and having to sell off their slaves to pay debts. Both authors railed against the flourishing domestic slave trade that replaced the banned international trade and which further destroyed slave families. But while Hildreth and Stowe both excoriated the use of religion to justify slavery, they did so from different standpoints. Richard Hildreth's father, like Stowe's, was a Congregational minister. But unlike Stowe, who remained devoutly religious, Hildreth became an avowed agnostic and a utilitarian.

Shortly before his death, Stowe's slaveholder character Augustine St. Clare has a religious awakening and voices Stowe's argument that any true Christian would have to oppose slavery: "My view of Christianity is such that I think no man can consistently profess it without throwing the whole weight of his being against this monstrous system of injustice that lies at the foundation of all our society."[25] This is where Stowe's and Hildreth's novels part company on religion. Stowe's title character and Hildreth's Thomas, his most important character after Archy, at first share a number of similarities besides their name. Both Thomases are of unmixed African descent, both are physically strong, and above all, both are devout Christians who cannot be provoked to violence. Like Stowe's protagonist, Hildreth's Thomas first appears as an obedient disciple of religious instruction. But Hildreth's Thomas, unlike Stowe's Uncle Tom, is unable to realize his heroic potential *because* of his religious devotion: "Nature had intended him for one of those lofty spirits who are the terror of tyrants, and the bold asserters of liberty. But under the influence of his religion, he had become a passive, humble and obedient slave."[26]

Unlike Stowe, Hildreth did not believe that African American slaves were more disposed to be religious or docile, and he strongly criticized the use of religion to inculcate submission, "that creed of passive obedience . . . often found more potent than whips or fetters, in upholding tyranny."[27]

In Hildreth's novel, Thomas's passivity, like his piety, is a temporary condition; Hildreth, the utilitarian, offered his Thomas no Christian redemption. Nor did Hildreth excuse Christianity for its use in support of slavery. Whereas Stowe's Thomas dies a Christ-like martyr who forgives his slayers, Hildreth's Thomas rebels. Witnessing the overseer's brutal murder of his wife, Thomas casts off his religious passivity, escapes the plantation, and later kills the overseer without remorse. As Alexander Saxton has observed, it is likely that Stowe's unwaveringly devout Uncle Tom was to some degree her answer to Hildreth's Thomas.[28]

Responding to critics and fans who wanted her to provide sources proving the authenticity of her antislavery novel, Stowe published *The Key to Uncle Tom's Cabin* (1853), which also became popular in Britain. In this work Stowe said that she modeled her Uncle Tom largely after Josiah Henson's 1849 autobiography *The Life of Josiah Henson, Formerly a Slave, Now an Inhabitant of Canada, as Narrated by Himself.*[29] Like Uncle Tom, Henson was a devout Christian who did not succumb to temptations to run away. Though a slave, Henson had become a sort of overseer for his master, and by his account, he even resisted freeing the slaves entrusted to his care: "I had promised that man to take his property [slaves] to Kentucky, and deposit it with his brother; and this, and this only, I resolved to do." His sense of injustice at long last outweighed his fidelity when, on top of proof of his master's unrelenting ingratitude in cheating him out of his promised manumission, he discovered that he was being sold south: "But his attempt to kidnap me again, after having pocketed three-fourths of my market value, absolved me from all obligation, in my opinion, to pay him any more, or to continue in a position which exposed me to his machinations."[30] Henson escaped to Canada and eventually founded a settlement and an industrial school for runaway slaves. He was happy to be known as the model for Uncle Tom and capitalized on the success of *Uncle Tom's Cabin* by republishing his autobiography. He also became a spokesman for abolitionism in the United States and Canada, and made speaking tours in England.

It seems that the real "Tom" was imbued with the capitalist spirit of enterprise and commerce—his respect for "property" and contracts—which Stowe found so admirably lacking in his "race." Stowe believed that African Americans could not easily assimilate into the Anglo-Saxon world of commerce because, she wrote, "they are not naturally daring and enterprising, but home-loving and affectionate." For her, Uncle Tom exemplified the distinctive qualities of the African. He had "the soft, impressible nature of his kindly race, ever yearning toward the simple and childlike." These qualities contrasted with the racial attributes of whites: "The negro, it must be remembered, is an exotic of the most gorgeous and superb countries of the world, and he has, deep in his heart, a passion for all that is splendid, rich, and fanciful; a passion which, rudely indulged by an untrained taste, draws on them the ridicule of the colder and more correct white race."[31]

As George Fredrickson and Alexander Saxton (among others) have pointed out, in *Uncle Tom's Cabin,* Stowe stereotyped "whites" and "blacks" along gender lines. She endowed Africans with more "feminine" traits: more feeling and heart, more sensitivity to the visual world, more childlike dispositions. The colder, more analytical temperament of the masculine stereotype was that of the "white race" or "Anglo-Saxons." From Stowe's romantic outlook, in its striving for material wealth, American society had become too masculine, too unfeeling. She appealed to her female audience to change the outlook of their men and to recognize the immorality of slavery for its destruction of home and family. This appeal to sentiment accorded with the broader *Weltanschauung* of romanticism, which rejected the hard, rational world of commerce.[32] Nevertheless, the logic of Stowe's construction of femininity meant she did not advocate that free women actively join with African Americans to change and improve the cold "Anglo-Saxon" commercial world, nor did she advocate that women leave the sphere of the home.[33]

Stowe's George Harris is similar to Hildreth's protagonist Archy Moore. Like Archy, George Harris is the light-skinned son of his master and a concubine slave. Both George and Archy are well educated; they marry light-skinned house slaves, they get separated from their wives and sons, and eventually they and their families seek freedom abroad. Stowe's description of George Harris is very like Hildreth's of Archy. George is "from one of the proudest families in Kentucky" and "has inherited a set of fine European features, and a high, indomitable spirit."[34] Archy says of himself, "I inherited all my father's proud spirit, sensitive feelings and ardent temperament."[35]

But Hildreth was being ironic in this passage, while Stowe was not. Hildreth presented Archy's father as not just any southern aristocrat: he modeled the father after Thomas Jefferson. In the 1830s, the reader would probably have noticed the strong resemblance to Jefferson in the passage where Archy describes his father, Colonel Moore, head of a wealthy Virginia planter family:

> When the war of the American Revolution broke out, Colonel Moore was a very young man. By birth and education, he belonged, as I have said, to the aristocratic party, which being aristocratic, was of course, conservative. . . . He espoused with zeal, the cause of liberty, and by his political activity and influence, contributed not a little to promote it. Of liberty indeed, he was always a warm and energetic admirer. . . . *The rights of man,* and the *rights of human nature* were phrases . . . I heard so often repeated, that they made an indelible impression upon my memory.

But then Hildreth continues with unmistakable irony: "Had I been allowed to choose my own paternity, could I possibly have selected a more desirable father?—But by the laws and customs of Virginia, it is not the father but the mother, whose rank and condition determine that of the child;—and alas! my mother was a concubine, and a slave!"[36] Some recent scholars have criticized Hildreth for presenting his hero Archy as more of a European American than an African American.[37] But I would argue that Hildreth's purpose was precisely to present

Archy as a man who could have been one of Jefferson's sons. Thomas Jefferson, the champion of democracy, who drafted the Declaration of Independence, collaborated on the Constitution of the United States, and served two terms as president, remained a Virginia slaveholder throughout his life. As was well known at the time, he did have sons and daughters with his concubine slave Sally Hemings, none of whom he acknowledged or freed in his lifetime.[38] Jefferson also espoused colonization.

In Hildreth's view, Jefferson betrayed the meaning of the Virginia Bill of Rights, which was the model for the Declaration of Independence. Hildreth placed Article 1 of the Virginia Bill of Rights on the title page of all of his several editions of both *The Slave* and *The White Slave.*[39] A few veiled and not so veiled criticisms of Jefferson appear in both versions of the novel and in his nonfiction work *Despotism in America,* which was intended to explain slavery more fully. There he sums up Jefferson's racialized conception of democracy as follows: "The democracy which he [Jefferson] preached at home, was democracy among the aristocrats;—and the perfect equality of all the members of the privileged order, has ever been a popular doctrine in all aristocracies. . . . [L]aboring to forget that the unprivileged class—some of whom, to believe the voice of common report, were his own children,—had any greater capacities or rights than beasts of burden, he curtailed the expansive and universal clauses of his political creed."[40]

In his 1852 novel, Hildreth gave his responses to the martyrdom of Uncle Tom and Harris's immigration to Liberia in *Uncle Tom's Cabin.* Thomas returns as even more the opposite of Stowe's Uncle Tom. In the 1836 edition, Thomas chose to remain in the marshes near the plantations to fight against the planters. In that of 1852, the older Thomas is captured by a slave-hunting party and is tried before a vigilante court. As he is about to be burned at the stake—like a Christian martyr—he remains unrepentant and defiantly informs the vigilantes that he has killed several of them in his guerrilla war against slavery. Whereas Stowe presented a pacifist hero to allay fears of slave uprisings, Hildreth offered an insurrectionist one. In *Despotism in America,* Hildreth defined slavery as "a continuation of the state of war," and since slaves were at first "prisoners of war forced to labor for captors," slave insurrection would be justified (fig. 13.1).[41]

In contrast to Stowe's advocacy of colonization through the character of George Harris, Hildreth—having touched briefly on colonization in the first version of his novel—laid out his opposition to it more fully in the second. Most abolitionists who started out in colonization societies, he suggested, came to realize that colonization could not work, that abolition must be immediate and not gradual. Colonization made no economic sense, since it would entail transporting at great cost "some two or three millions of people from their homes, where their labor is

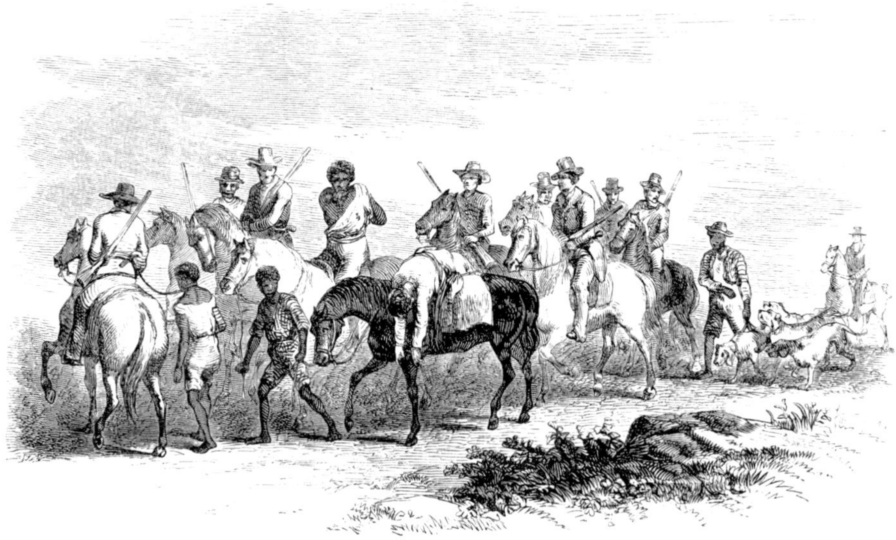

Figure 13.1 Thomas's capture. "The Successful Man Hunt," engraving. Illus. in Richard Hilredth, *The White Slave,* 1852. Online digital image.

greatly needed, and is capable of being productively applied, across the ocean to an uncultivated wilderness, where the native supply of labor already far exceeds the demand." Then further depopulated and deprived of productive labor, the South would sink into poverty and misery.[42]

The appeal of colonization schemes rested upon the preconception that the two "races" could never live side by side as equals—a prejudice that, as we have seen, Stowe shared. But for Hildreth, this belief went against actual fact and contradicted and undermined "the famous national declaration of ours that all men are created free, with certain unalienable rights." Hildreth argued that there was no fundamental difference between the "races" and that skin color was no protection from slavery. Archy, who could pass for a "white" person, is sold at a slave market. A southern gambler remarks to Archy: "You know, here at the south, we reckon all slaves as 'niggers,' whatever their color. Just catch a stray Irish or German girl, and sell her,—a thing sometimes done,—and she turns a nigger at once, and makes just as good a slave as if there were African blood in her veins."[43] Hildreth, like Stowe, dealt frankly with the sexual exploitation of slaves, but he also criticized hypocritical talk of "antipathy of the races" and "the horrors of amalgamation!" Since European Americans and African Americans were in fact already living together, he believed the solution was immediate emancipation and assimilation. For Hildreth, there was in reality no white "Anglo-Saxon" race, and he refused the racial fictions of Stowe's romantic racialism.[44]

Similarly, in addressing the old argument between proslavery and antislavery adherents about the relative advantages of slavery and wage labor, Stowe and Hildreth came to opposite conclusions. Hildreth expressed confidence in a better future for all under a system of free labor. When Archy travels north through the free states, he notices their greater prosperity and well-being in comparison to the slave states. Slavery also kept poor whites in poverty, since, he observes, "manual labor is held to be disgraceful" in the South. Where there is slavery, northern wage laborers and industry will not venture. Slavery, Hildreth argued, by holding back the potential of productive labor, held back progress.[45]

He conceded that in the near future the conditions of newly emancipated slaves in the South would probably resemble those of poor southern whites. But emancipated slaves would eventually become part of the free labor system, rising through their abilities, which were not inferior to those of whites. This optimism about industrial capitalism—Hildreth believed that reforms could solve its unfair distribution of wealth—also reveals Hildreth to be out of step with romanticism.[46]

Through her aristocratic character Augustine St. Clare, Stowe conjectured that there was little to choose between slave labor and free labor. "The American planter is 'only doing, in another form, what the English aristocracy and capitalists are doing by the lower classes;' that is, I take it, *appropriating* them, body and bone, soul and spirit, to their use and convenience. . . . The slave-owner can whip his refractory slave to death,—the capitalist can starve him to death. . . . [Some] slaves are better off than a large class of the population of England."[47] In also saying that "there can be no high civilization without enslavement of the masses, either nominal or real," the cynical St. Clare paraphrases a speech by the intellectual voice of the southern planters, John C. Calhoun, who told the U.S. Senate, "It would be well for those interested to reflect whether there now exists, or ever has existed, a wealthy and civilized community in which one portion did not live on the labor of another; and whether the form in which slavery exists in the South is not but one modification of this universal condition."[48] But Stowe on her second tour in Britain in 1856 was apparently not interested in connecting the abolitionist movement to the British working-class social reform movement. To the call to consider the harsh exploitation of the British working class, she gave a tart Christian temperance response: "It is my belief, from observations and travel in England and Scotland, that almost all the poverty and misery of the lower-classes now arises from the traffic in intoxicating drink."[49]

The British workers wanted to connect their struggles for better pay and working conditions to the abolitionist movement. The American working class was a different story. In the Jacksonian period it had allied with the southern planters against northern capitalists, and so was not interested in—and was even antipathetic to—abolitionism: freed slaves would compete for jobs and free soil. The southern slaveholding planters, a group that included many of the founding fathers, had advocated democratic rights for the northern working class and southern yeoman, but excluded the slaves.[50]

## Stowe, Hildreth, and Blackface Minstrelsy

The contradiction of democratic rights coexisting with slavery and wage slavery fed into the crazy, angry, humorous energy of blackface minstrelsy. Minstrelsy, in effect, performed cultural work important for assimilating immigrants into the new "Anglo-Saxon" republic.[51] It was the "white" working class that constituted the early audiences for blackface minstrelsy.

Blackface minstrelsy got its start in New York City in the 1830s with Thomas Rice's popular blackface performance of his "Jump Jim Crow" song and dance act, supposedly derived from an actual song and dance created by a black man he met in Kentucky. An amalgamation and lampooning of cultures, notably Irish, Scottish, and especially African American, blackface minstrelsy soon became the nation's dominant entertainment form, playing to all audiences across class (if not race) in lowly neighborhood taverns, work camps, circuses, middle- and upper-class theaters, even the White House. Minstrelsy was equally popular in England. While early minstrelsy burlesques addressed a variety of working-class and immigrant concerns avoided in Victorian theater, blackface minstrelsy performers nevertheless always displayed an unquestioned racialism, whether or not they happened to express antislavery sentiment. By the 1850s, minstrelsy had narrowed its focus to delivering mostly proslavery ideology.[52]

The sentimental melodrama of *Uncle Tom's Cabin* and its underlying romantic racialism allowed it to be easily translated into blackface minstrelsy performances. Uncle Tom minstrel shows sometimes carried an antislavery message, but more often than not, they were proslavery counterattacks. To Stowe's representation of slavery destroying slave families, minstrel shows retaliated with depictions of carefree plantation life and happy Uncle Toms. If Stowe aimed to attack proslavery minstrelsy in her novel, she nevertheless intended to tap into its drawing power; she wanted to reach the same vast audience and made unmistakable references to minstrelsy in some of her scenes and characters. In an early scene in the novel, for example, she had Eliza's son dance "Jim Crow": "The boy commenced one of those wild, grotesque songs common among the negroes, in a rich, clear voice, accompanying his singing with many comic evolutions of the hands, feet, and whole body, all in perfect time to the music."[53] In St. Clare's house slave Adolph, Stowe recalled a popular minstrel character, the urban black dandy. Her Uncle Tom suggested another stock minstrel slave character, the asexual "Old Uncle." Topsy and the saintly Eva easily became minstrel characters.[54]

Another feature *Uncle Tom's Cabin* shared with minstrelsy was the use of vernacular speech. A contemporary London critic compared Stowe's work to a popular minstrelsy group, the Ethiopian Serenaders, and found Stowe's vernacular dialogue a welcome change: "The slang of 'Ethopian Serenaders' for once gives place to thoughts and language racy of the soil, and we need not say how refreshing it is to be separated for a season from the conventional Sambo of the modern stage."[55] Commentators then as now have praised Stowe for her skillful imitation of black speech to animate her characters. Her "innovative" use of vernacular speech made her characters vivid and emotionally engaging—maybe more engaging even than the real-life protagonists of slave autobiographies like Frederick Douglass, Josiah Henson, and Henry Bibb, who, like Richard Hildreth, used first-person narration without dialect. Douglass, Henson, and Bibb were no doubt aware of minstrelsy and its burlesque of "black speech"; perhaps they deliberately avoided the vernacular so often used in racial stereotyping.

Even Hildreth conceded that the 1854 *New York Post* critic mentioned earlier was correct in finding Stowe's book superior in "the inimitable mimicry of dialogue." But he strongly denied that this was the chief cause of her success. He may have been wrong. Without the employment of vernacular speech to distinguish class or race, Hildreth's "Cassy, Archy or Thomas," Evan Brandstadter observed, "sound[ed] much like any educated 19th century New Englander," and for him remained "lifeless stick figures."[56]

Stowe's confident use of "black dialect" goes along with her self-assured and authoritative comments about the unique qualities of African Americans, all of which display the "racial knowingness" that is part of romantic racialism.[57] If the enormous successes enjoyed by minstrelsy and *Uncle Tom's Cabin* related to their similar dramatizations of racial stereotypes and exaggerated use of "black dialect," would not the large audiences that flocked to minstrel shows also be attracted to *Uncle Tom's Cabin*? While the novel used a romanticized version of racial stereotypes to argue a case against slavery, would it not, like minstrelsy, have worked at the same time to naturalize racialism and to reinforce the idea that African Americans were irreducibly different from the "Anglo-Saxon race" and hence forever unable to assimilate fully into national life? The fact that her work continued to be published in large editions in the reactionary racial climate of the Gilded Age seems to support this view (fig. 13.2).

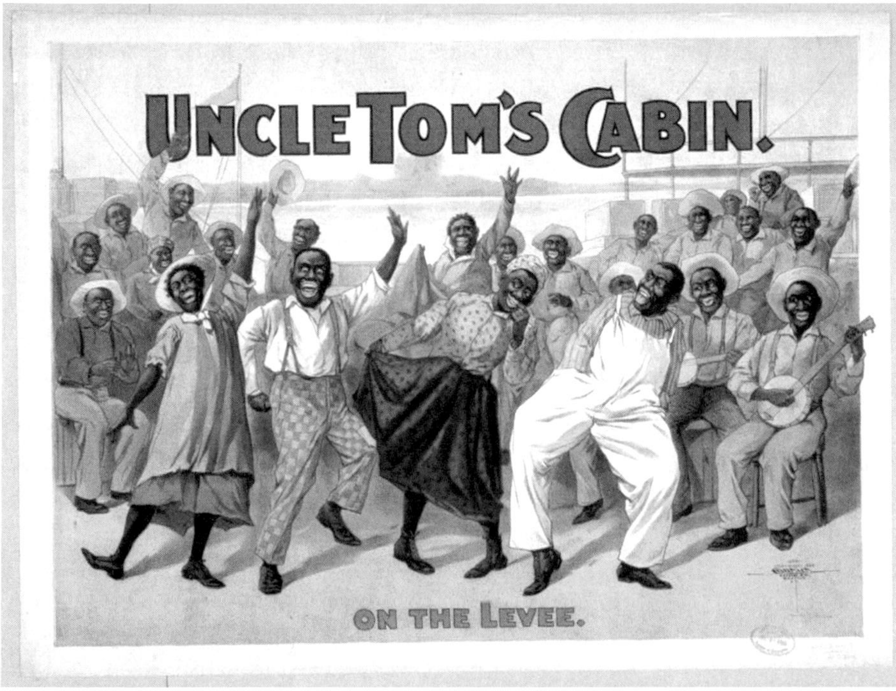


Figure 13.2 "Uncle Tom's Cabin: On the Levee," 1899. Color lithograph, 20⅞ x 28⅓ in. (52.97 x 71.96 cm). Courier Litho. Co. Online digital image.

## Melville as Counterweight

By the 1850s if not earlier, romantic racialism pervaded the pages of *Putnam's Monthly Magazine,* the New York City publisher of several of Herman Melville's short stories. In 1855 *Putnam's* published a favorable review of Stowe's *First Geography for Children,* in which she advanced her notions of racial character to young readers,[58] as well as another article praising minstrelsy. Invoking "the lightness and prevailing good humor of the negro songs . . . the character and habits of the colored race," the reviewer declared, "No hardships or troubles can destroy, even check their happiness and levity."[59] Whether or not Melville came across these reviews, he certainly could not have been unaware of the popularity of blackface minstrelsy, nor of the great commercial and critical success of *Uncle Tom's Cabin* in the face of the poor sales and unenthusiastic reviews of his own ambitious novel *Moby Dick,* which had appeared in London and New York less than a year before Stowe's.

In 1855 Melville published his novella *Benito Cereno,* unsigned and serialized, in *Putnam's Monthly;* a year later it was included in *The Piazza Tales,* a collection of several of his short works previously published in the magazine. Laden with symbols and portents, *Benito Cereno* has lent itself to any number of interpretations. I focus on it as a critical burlesque of three concerns: blackface minstrelsy, the romantic racialism displayed in *Uncle Tom's Cabin,* and the public's complacency. I argue that one of Melville's aims in *Benito Cereno* was to disturb and disrupt the public's unquestioning acceptance of racialist ideology, particularly the North's more benign romantic racialism.[60]

Melville closely based his *Benito Cereno* on chapter 18 of the real Captain Amasa Delano's *Narrative of Voyages and Travels,* published in Boston in 1817. In this purportedly true narrative, Captain Delano tells of his coming across a Spanish slave ship in distress off the coast of Chile. Delano generously gives aid to the Spanish ship, unaware that a slave rebellion has occurred, an upheaval that everyone onboard is carefully hiding from the New England captain. Delano records his impressions: "They all looked up to me as a benefactor; and as I was deceived in them, I did them every possible kindness. . . . The apparent sufferings of those about me had softened my feelings into sympathy; or, doubtless my interference with some of their transactions would have cost me my life. The Spanish captain had evidently lost much of his authority over the slaves, whom he appeared to fear, and whom he was unwilling in any case to oppose."[61] When Delano learns the truth, he rescues the ship from the slaves and restores order. After a trial held at the viceregal courts of Lima, Peru, the slave leaders are executed, their heads fixed to pikes and displayed in one of Lima's public squares.

In his reworking of Delano's narrative, Melville had only to exaggerate slightly Delano's self-promotion, his limited perceptions, his implicit racial prejudice. As in the original narrative, the fictional Delano comes across as the ideal American national type: the brave, commanding, resourceful, innocent Yankee, set against the Spanish captain Don Benito Cereno, the fey, sickly representative of the crumbling Spanish Empire (and of the decaying southern aristocracy), completely dependent on his personal slave. Like the original Delano, the fictional Delano goes about the decks misperceiving the actual life-and-death charade as if he were a mesmerized northern spectator at a minstrel show: the black rebels onboard enact the part of contented, docile slaves; Cereno plays a version of Stowe's southern aristocrat Augustine St. Clare; and Cereno's keeper Babo plays the part of the faithful, loving personal slave. Using a language similar to Stowe's, Melville described Delano's musings about the "negro":

> There is something about the negro which, in a peculiar way, fits him for avocations about one's person. Most negroes are natural valets and hair-dressers. . . . And above all is the great gift of good-humour . . . a certain easy cheerfulness, harmonious in every glance and gesture; as though God had set the whole negro

> to some pleasant turn. . . . [T]o this is added the docility arising from the unaspiring contentment of a limited mind, and that susceptibility of blind attachment sometimes inhering in indisputable inferiors, . . .[and] the African love of bright colours and fine shows.[62]

In the same passage, Melville seamlessly segued into a description of the easygoing Delano, whose "nature was not only benign, but familiarly and humorously so." In another, Delano spies his whaleboat *Rover* and thinks of home: "The sight of that household boat evoked a thousand trustful associations." In these passages and others, Melville slyly conveyed the suggestion that Delano's stereotypes of the "negro" could apply just as easily to Delano himself.[63]

Stepping back, we see that what Delano witnesses is but a minstrel show within a larger minstrel show in which he, unconsciously, and Cereno, unwillingly, are also participants. In this outer show, Delano appears as a kind of buffoon whose racialist blinkers blind him to—or condition him to reject—the reality of the slave rebellion, and to the fact that Babo now occupies the place of authority. Cereno now enacts the part of the minstrelsy dandy who affects aristocratic culture and power through pretentious manners and dress. In a further inverse of blackface minstrelsy, the slave leader Babo now plays the impersonator of white authority as the "ventriloquist" moving the "dummy" figure Captain Cereno. Similarly, Babo manipulates Delano as the stereotypical Yankee democrat. As Jason Richards has phrased it, Babo is putting on "whiteface" minstrelsy, Melville's sendup of blackface minstrelsy.[64]

If we step back further still, readers who have identified with Delano's perceptions until the charade ends also become unconscious and unwilling participants in Melville's satire. To the extent that they miss (or misread)—as Delano does—the clues to the charade that Melville craftily inserted in the text and, like Delano, willfully dismiss suspicions that things are amiss, they are also duped. One could argue that Melville lulled his readers into identifying with Delano. The seemingly omniscient narrator of *Benito Cereno* occasionally offers clues to Delano's limitations, but much of the time seems to be deferential to Delano's point of view.[65] When the deception is revealed at the end, the Yankee Delano remains unchanged by and unreflective about his experience, and readers have the choice whether or not to readjust their opinions of Delano. Up to the very end, Melville offered no authoritative direction to take. The reader is never allowed into Babo's mind, nor encouraged to sympathize with him. In Cereno's trial deposition at the end of the story, Cereno describes Babo as the cold, ruthless slave leader who would stop at nothing to secure his fellow slaves' freedom—the very opposite of the obsequious personal slave Delano so admired.[66] Babo never says a word in his own defense and remains the unbowed representative of rebellions to come: his head, "that hive of subtlety, fixed on a pole in the Plaza, met, unabashed, the gaze of the whites."[67] The aristocratic Cereno, unable to recover from his experience of slavery, dies, and thus "[does], indeed, follow his leader." The reader is left to mull over which leader Melville meant: most likely the slave owner Aranda, whom the slaves killed earlier in the insurrection and placed in a shroud at the bowsprit with the admonition scrawled underneath, "'*Seguid vuestro jefe,*' (follow your leader),"[68] but perhaps Babo, the leader of the slave rebellion. Melville left his readers uncomfortably free either to side with the dominant ideology of the Yankee Delano or to reexamine their own prior assumptions about race and American nationalism. Contemporary reviews of *The Piazza Tales* tended to be lukewarm and to favor the more romantic *Encantadas of the Enchanted Islands* over *Benito Cereno* and the other stories in the collection.[69]

Even before the reviews of *Moby Dick* came in, Melville was aware that his writing was no longer popular with publishers or with the public once he moved away from the romantic form of the travel narrative that he used with such success in his first works, *Typee* and *Omoo.* While finishing *Moby Dick,* Melville wrote to Nathaniel Hawthorne that he feared he would be remembered only for *Typee,* as "a man who lived among the cannibals! What I feel most moved to write, that is banned,—it will not pay. Yet, altogether, write the *other* way I cannot. So the product is a final hash, and all my books are botches." In the same letter he said he was a supporter of "ruthless democracy," while at the same time at odds with the democratic masses: "It seems an inconsistency to assert unconditional democracy in all things, and yet confess a dislike to all mankind—in the mass."[70] In his anonymous review of a Hawthorne work published a year earlier, Melville had written, "For in this world of lies, Truth is forced to fly like a scared white doe in the woodlands; and only by cunning glimpses will she reveal herself, as in Shakespeare and other masters of the great Art of Telling the Truth,—even though it be covertly, and by snatches."[71] Offering his ideas "only by cunning glimpses" was the strategy he adopted to reach his public on both sides of the Atlantic in the 1850s.

If Melville was increasingly pessimistic about his ability to succeed with the public, he was equally pessimistic about the world's future. Like Hildreth, he presented a slave leader of a violent insurrection, also captured and executed, and also serving as a warning of the violence to come over the slavery issue. Like Hildreth, he believed neither in fixed racial stereotypes nor in the idealized, racialized Anglo-Saxon republic. In *Redburn* he wrote, "You can not spill a drop of American blood without spilling the blood of the whole world."[72] The laboring masses of the United States, he wrote in *Moby Dick,* came from all over the world:

> Be it said, that at the present day not one in two of the many thousand men before the mast employed in the American whale fishery, are Americans born,

> though pretty nearly all the officers are. Herein it is the same with the American whale fishery as with the American army and military and merchant navies, and the engineering forces employed in the construction of the American Canals and Railroads. The same, I say, because in all these cases the native American liberally provides the brains, the rest of the world as generously supplying the muscles.[73]

Hildreth's 1852 novel ends with Archy and his family living happily in Liverpool, where his son finds a good job. Presumably Hildreth meant Liverpool to represent to American readers the shining future after the abolition of slavery in the United States. Melville had earlier toured Liverpool in 1839 as a lowly sailor and wrote up his Liverpool experiences in his novel *Redburn* (1849). In a passage Hildreth might have written, Melville observed an interracial couple strolling nonchalantly down a Liverpool street and noted Liverpool's lack of racial prejudice compared to that of New York City: "At first I was surprised that a colored man should be treated as he is in this town; but a little reflection showed that, after all, it was but recognizing his claims to humanity and normal equality; so that in some things, we Americans leave to other countries the carrying out of the principle that stands at the head of our Declaration of Independence."[74]

But Melville also noticed the condition of Liverpool's poor laborers and their squalid neighborhoods and observed the city's "landsharks, land-rats, and other vermin which make the hapless mariner their prey." He saw the farm produce and the poor laborers from starving Ireland coming through Liverpool's ports. He was also mindful of Liverpool's former infamy as a chief port of the African slave trade.[75] Unlike Hildreth, Melville was not optimistic about the future of the emancipated slave or of the free laborer. For Melville, slavery was one form of a continuum of forced labor that existed, even if more temporarily, on the ship and in the factory and office. As Ishmael rhetorically asks, "Who aint a slave?"[76]

The utilitarian and practical reformer Richard Hildreth was probably the most dedicated abolitionist and definitely the least romantic of the three writers I have been considering. As a utilitarian, he was the least critical of capitalism—or, rather, he remained optimistic about future reforms. He saw the spread of industrial capitalism and free wage labor as intrinsically progressive, something slavery was holding back. Believing in the Enlightenment notion of a universal humanity, he rejected racialism and advocated the complete assimilation of African Americans into a free capitalist society. But as a rationalist, he was unable to harness the power of sentiment or religious fervor offered by Stowe. His Thomas is the closest of his characters to a romantic hero, but he did not develop Thomas's emotional life, leaving him a consistent rational thinker but not a poetic figure who appeals to the imagination. Instead, Hildreth thought it sufficient to use the reasonable voices of Archy and those Archy encounters to convey his arguments against slavery.

Stowe was most in tune with the world of the 1850s, where the ideology of racialism, or at best romantic racialism, prevailed. She appealed to the romantic sentiment that valued feelings and faith over rationality. Whereas Hildreth advocated the complete assimilation and equality of free slaves, Stowe presented a moral end to slavery, which offered far less social and ideological upheaval and which appealed to a wide readership that was revolted by slavery but presumably shared her romantic racialism. As she proposed through her characters of Thomas and the Harrises, freed African Americans would remain docile, childlike, and subservient—like women—or they would emigrate.[77] To the public coming to grips with the new world of industrial capitalism, she expressed a romantic nostalgia for an idealized precapitalist past, providing images of home and family threatened by slavery and by industrial capitalism.

Both Stowe and Melville could be considered romantics in the sense that they both presented reactions "against the way of life of capitalist societies." Melville was in many ways the most romantic of the three in that his works offered the most thorough critique of capitalist social relations and a romantic vision that perceived "modernity as a whole whose multiple aspects are interrelated and interlocking."[78] But his revolutionary romanticism was out of tune with his times. He was close to Hildreth in his opposition to the romantic racialism and religiosity of Stowe but far apart from Hildreth in his pessimistic view of the capitalist future. As Alexander Saxton has written, Hildreth was both behind his times in his adherence to utilitarianism and ahead of his times in his racial vision.[79] Melville's critique of his times continues to provoke and to remain relevant to ours.

## NOTES

1. *New York Daily Tribune,* October 11, 1861.
2. Ibid.
3. Frank J. Klingberg, "Harriet Beecher Stowe and Social Reform in England," *American Historical Review* 43, no. 3 (April 1938): 544.
4. Stowe's visit inspired a committee of British women abolitionists, including the Duchess of Sutherland, to get half a million women to sign a petition, penned by Lord Shaftesbury, calling on American women to fight against slavery for the reasons Stowe underscored in her work. They presented Stowe with this petition, known as "The Stafford House Address." Joan D. Hedrick, *Harriet Beecher Stowe: A Life* (New York: Oxford University Press, 1994), 244; Klingberg, "Stowe and Social Reform," 547–48.
5. *Eclectic Review* (October 1856), quoted in Klingberg, "Stowe and Social Reform," 545n14.

6. Quoted in Hedrick, *Harriet Beecher Stowe,* 234.

7. Richard Hildreth, *The Slave; or, Memoirs of Archy Moore,* 2 vols. (Boston: John H. Eastburn, Printer, 1836).

8. Hedrick, *Harriet Beecher Stowe,* 223–24.

9. On the romantic critique of modernity, see Michael Löwy and Robert Sayre, *Romanticism against the Tide of Modernity,* trans. Catherine Porter (Durham: Duke University Press, 2001), 4–26.

10. The runaway slave Josiah Henson, the main model for Stowe's Uncle Tom, temporarily sought refuge in Cincinnati around 1830.

11. Daniel Aaron, *Cincinnati, Queen City of the West, 1819–1838* (Columbus: Ohio State University Press, 1992), 299–314; chap. 4, "Slavery Riots in Cincinnati," in *Life of Harriet Beecher Stowe,* ed. Charles Edward Stowe (Boston: Houghton Mifflin & Company, 1890); Wendy Jean Katz, *Regionalism and Reform: Art and Class Formation in Antebellum Cincinnati* (Columbus: Ohio State University Press, 2002), 19.

12. The "Lane Rebels" soon left the seminary and later enrolled at the nearby antislavery Oberlin College, which even today holds reenactments of the Lane Debates. On the debates, see "Resources for Studying the Lane Debates and the Oberlin Commitment to Racial Egalitarianism," www.oberlin.edu; David S. Reynolds, *Mightier Than the Sword:* Uncle Tom's Cabin *and the Battle for America* (New York: Norton, 2011), 92–93.

13. George M. Fredrickson, *The Black Image in the White Mind: The Debate on Afro-American Character and Destiny, 1817–1914* (New York: Harper & Row, 1971), 102–8.

14. Harriet Beecher Stowe, *The Annotated Uncle Tom's Cabin,* ed. with an introduction and notes by Henry Louis Gates Jr. and Hollis Robbins (New York: Norton, 2007), 189.

15. Ibid., 456.

16. Ibid., 469.

17. Henry C. Wright, "Uncle Tom's Cabin—Objectionable Characteristics," *Liberator,* July 9, 1852. Both Clay and Webster had supported legislation favorable to southern slave interests, notably the Compromise of 1850 and the Fugitive Slave Law (1850). Clay was one of founders of the American Colonization Society.

18. *The Provincial Freeman,* July 22, 1854, quoted in Benjamin Quarles, *Black Abolitionists* (New York: Oxford University Press, 1969), 220.

19. Martha Pingel, *An American Utilitarian, Richard Hildreth as a Philosopher, with Selections from His Published and Unpublished Works* (New York: Columbia University Press, 1948), 4. See also David W. Levy, "Racial Stereotypes in Antislavery Fiction," *Phylon* 31, no. 3 (Fall 1970): 265–79. Levy refers to Hildreth's characters in his discussion of racial stereotypes, but he neglects to take into account that as the first American antislavery novel, Hildreth's may have served as a prototype for the others that followed.

20. Alexander Saxton, *The Rise and Fall of the White Republic: Class Politics and Mass Culture in Nineteenth-Century America* (New York: Verso, 1990), 233.

21. Frances Milton Trollope, *The Life and Adventures of Jonathan Jefferson Whitlaw; or, Scenes on the Mississippi* (London: R. Bentley, 1836). Trollope lived for two and a half years in or near Cincinnati before returning to England in 1830—two years before Stowe moved to the city. See also Brenda Ayres, "Villino Trollope, Piazza Independenza, Florence; The Birthplace of the American Civil War: The Fanny Trollope and Harriet Beecher Stowe Connections," www.florin.ms.

22. Richard Hildreth, *The White Slave; or, Memoirs of a Fugitive* (Boston: Tappan & Whittemore, 1852); Evan Brandstadter, "Uncle Tom and Archie Moore: The Anti-slavery Novel as Ideological Symbol," *American Quarterly* 26 (May 1974): 168.

23. Richard Hildreth, "Uncle Tom, The White Slave, Ida May and the NY Evening Post," *Boston Evening Telegraph,* November 13, 1854.

24. For a more thorough comparison of the two novels, see Brandstadter, "Uncle Tom and Archie Moore," passim. Stowe may also have used ideas from Frances Trollope's antislavery novel *The Life and Adventures of Jonathan Jefferson Whitlaw.*

25. Stowe, *The Annotated Uncle Tom's Cabin,* 330.

26. Hildreth, *The Slave,* 2:72.

27. Ibid., 71–72.

28. Saxton, *Rise and Fall of the White Republic,* 239. In 1856 Stowe brought out another antislavery novel, *Dred: The Tale of Great Dismal Swamp,* which proved to be far less popular than *Uncle Tom's Cabin.* In it, her title character (actually a secondary character) is modeled more along the lines of Hildreth's Thomas, or as Stowe explained, modeled more after Vesey Denmark and Nat Turner; but again, unlike Hildreth's Thomas, Dred stops short of violent rebellion because of his religious beliefs.

29. Harriet Beecher Stowe, *The Key to Uncle Tom's Cabin; Presenting the Original Facts and Documents Upon Which the Story Is Founded, Together with Corroborative Statements Verifying the Truth of the Work* (Boston: John P. Jewett & Company, 1854), 42–44.

30. Josiah Henson, *The Life of Josiah Henson, Formerly a Slave, Now an Inhabitant of Canada, as Narrated by Himself* (Boston: Arthur D. Phelps, 1849), 24, 47–48.

31. Stowe, *The Annotated Uncle Tom's Cabin,* 104, 156, 173.

32. Saxton, *Rise and Fall of the White Republic,* 235–41; Fredrickson, *Black Image in the White Mind,* 115; Löwy and Sayre, *Romanticism against the Tide of Modernity,* 9–26.

33. Hedrick, *Harriet Beecher Stowe,* passim; Katz, *Regionalism and Reform,* 121.

34. Stowe, *The Annotated Uncle Tom's Cabin,* 118.

35. Hildreth, *The Slave,* 10.

36. Ibid., 4–5.

37. Saxton, *Rise and Fall of the White Republic,* 231; Levy, "Racial Stereotypes in Antislavery Fiction," 275–77.

38. William Wells Brown, a playwright and former slave, wrote what is considered to be the first African American novel, *Clotel; or, The President's Daughter* (London, 1853), about a fictional daughter of Thomas Jefferson.

39. Article 1 of the Virginia Bill of Rights (1776) reads, "All men are by nature equally free and independent, and have certain INHERENT RIGHTS, of which, when they enter into society, they cannot by any compact deprive or divest their posterity, namely, the enjoyment of life and liberty, with the means of acquiring and possessing property, and pursuing happiness and safety." The Virginia Bill of Rights was drafted by another Virginia slaveholder, George Mason.

40. Richard Hildreth, *Despotism in America; or, An Inquiry into the Nature and Results of the Slave-holding System in the United States* (Boston: Whipple & Damrell, 1840), 16. For pointed references to Jefferson in *The White Slave,* see 273, 320.

41. Hildreth, *Despotism in America,* 36.

42. Hildreth, *The White Slave,* 276. See also Alexis de Tocqueville, *Democracy in America,* vol. 1 (New York: J. & H. G. Langley, 1843), 408. Tocqueville, predicting a civil war over slavery, also remarked on the impracticality of colonization: it would not be possible to transport 3.5 million people fast enough to outpace population growth.

43. Hildreth, *The White Slave,* 337.

44. Ibid. In a striking passage in *Despotism in America,* Hildreth appealed to history to demonstrate the hybridity of "whites": "All the nations of Western Europe, the most civilized and enlightened communities in the world, have been formed by an intermixture of races so complicated that it is utterly impossible to trace it. Even that Saxon blood of which we boast, is far more Celtic than Teutonic, formed by the intermixture of two races, utterly diverse in their appearance, their institutions, their temper and their manners, who for centuries alternately reduced each other to slavery, and who are set down by all antiquaries and historians as being natural and irreconcilable enemies" (184).

45. Hildreth, *The White Slave,* 222, 266.

46. Arthur M. Schlesinger Jr., "The Problem of Richard Hildreth," *New England Quarterly* 13, no. 3 (June 1940): 236–38.

47. Stowe, *The Annotated Uncle Tom's Cabin,* 240–41.

48. Richard Hofstadter, *The American Political Tradition: And the Men Who Made It* (New York: Alfred A. Knopf, 1948), 88.

49. *The Times,* September 29, 1856, quoted in Klingberg, "Stowe and Social Reform," 551.

50. Hofstadter, *American Political Tradition,* 88–118; Saxton, *Rise and Fall of the White Republic,* 165; Hildreth, *Despotism in America,* passim.

51. Michael Rogin, *Blackface, White Noise: Jewish Immigrants in the Hollywood Melting Pot* (Berkley: University of California Press, 1996), 13.

52. See Eric Lott, *Love and Theft: Blackface Minstrelsy and the American Working Class* (New York: Oxford University Press, 1993), passim; Saxton, *Rise and Fall of the White Republic,* 177–78; Eric J. Sundquist, *To Wake the Nations: Race in the Making of American Literature* (Cambridge: Belknap Press of Harvard University Press, 1993), 153; Robert C. Toll, *Blacking Up: The Minstrel Show in Nineteenth-Century America* (New York: Oxford University Press, 1974), 97.

53. Stowe, *The Annotated Uncle Tom's Cabin,* 8.

54. Toll, *Blacking Up,* 78.

55. *The Times,* September 3, 1852, quoted in Hedrick, *Harriet Beecher Stowe,* 211.

56. Hildreth, "Uncle Tom, The White Slave, Ida May and the NY Evening Post"; Brandstadter, "Uncle Tom and Archie Moore," 164; cf. Hedrick, *Harriet Beecher Stowe,* 210; cf. Stowe, *The Annotated Uncle Tom's Cabin,* 28n12: "Harriet Beecher Stowe's depiction of dialogue among the slave characters is very contemporary sounding and surprisingly accurate—almost anthropological."

57. Peter Coviello, "The American in Charity: 'Benito Cereno' and Gothic Anti-sentimentality," *Studies in American Fiction* 30, no. 2 (Autumn 2002): 156.

58. Bruce A. Harvey, *American Geographics: U.S. National Narratives and the Representation of the Non-European World, 1830–1865* (Stanford: Stanford University Press, 2001), 39–40.

59. "Negro Minstrelsy—Ancient and Modern," *Putnam's Monthly* (January 1855), quoted in Sundquist, *To Wake the Nations,* 152.

60. For the connection between *Benito Cereno* and minstrelsy, see Sundquist, *To Wake the Nations,* 152–54; Jason Richards, "Melville's (Inter)national Burlesque: Whiteface, Blackface, and 'Benito Cereno,'" *American Transcendental Quarterly* 21, no. 2 (2007): 73–94, especially for his argument that *Benito Cereno* presents an inversion of minstrelsy into "whiteface." For a discussion of *Benito Cereno* being like a play, see Michael Rogin, *Subversive Genealogy: The Politics and Art of Herman Melville* (New York: Knopf, 1983), 210–15. See also Coviello, "The American in Charity," for his discussion of *Benito Cereno*'s critical relation to its readers.

61. Amasa Delano, *Narrative of Voyages and Travels in the Northern and Southern Hemispheres* (Upper Saddle River, N.J.: Gregg Press, 1970), 323.

62. Herman Melville, *Benito Cereno,* in *Herman Melville: The Piazza Tales* (New York: Modern Library, 1996), 125.

63. Ibid., 126, 115.

64. Richards, "Melville's (Inter)national Burlesque," 74–77.

65. Melville elsewhere employed narrators to disorient and provoke readers to question their accepted beliefs: for example, in *Bartleby the Scrivener* (1853), another tale of rebellion in the *Piazza Tales* collection, the narrator is also of limited perception and boundless self-justification.

66. Melville drew greatly from the lengthy trial depositions that the real Captain Delano chose to include at the end of his narrative. In the original narrative, Captain Cereno does not die a broken man but lives on to dispute energetically in his deposition and in court Captain Delano's salvage claims for half the value of his cargo—the most valuable being the slaves. Delano, *Narrative of Voyages and Travels,* 332–53.

67. Melville, *Benito Cereno,* 174.

68. Ibid., 73.

69. For two reviews mentioning *Benito Cereno,* see *New York Tribune,* June 23, 1856: "'Benito Cereno,' and 'The Encantadas,' are fresh specimens of Mr. Melville's sea romances, but cannot be regarded as improvements on his former popular productions in that kind"; and *New York Knickerbocker* (September 1856): "The tale entitled 'Benito Cereno,' is most painfully interesting, and in reading it we became nervously anxious for the solution of the mystery it involves," www.melville.org.

70. Herman Melville to Nathaniel Hawthorne, June [1?] 1851, www.melville.org.

71. Herman Melville, "Hawthorne and his Mosses," *New York Literary World* (August 17 and 24, 1850), http://xroads.virginia.edu.

72. Herman Melville, *Redburn: His First Voyage,* in *Redburn, His First Voyage; White-Jacket, or, The World in a Man-Of-War; Moby-Dick, or, The Whale* (New York: Literary Classics of the United States, 1983), 185. For a discussion of Melville's awareness of race and class in *Redburn,* see Loren Goldner, *Herman Melville: Between Charlemagne and the Antemosaic Cosmic Man;: Race, Class and the Crisis of Bourgeois Ideology in an American Renaissance Writer* (New York: Queequeg Publications, 2006), 129, 130.

73. Herman Melville, *Moby Dick, or, The Whale,* in *Redburn, His First Voyage; White-Jacket, or, The World in a Man-Of-War; Moby-Dick, or, The Whale,* 921.

74. Melville, *Redburn,* 222.

75. Ibid., 222, 152, 221, 170.
76. Melville, *Moby Dick,* 798.
77. Saxton, *Rise and Fall of the White Republic,* 241.
78. Löwy and Sayre, *Romanticism against the Tide of Modernity,* 19–21.
79. Saxton, *Rise and Fall of the White Republic,* 234–35.

# NOTES ON CONTRIBUTORS

Matthew Beaumont is a senior lecturer in English at University College London. His interests include the European *fin de siècle;* early modernism and the twentieth-century avant-gardes; utopian and dystopian literature; and Marxist and other literary and cultural theories. His book publications include *Utopia Ltd.: Ideologies of Social Dreaming in England, 1870–1900* (2nd ed., 2009); with Terry Eagleton, *The Task of the Critic: Terry Eagleton in Dialogue* (2009); and the edited volumes *A Concise Companion to Realism* (2nd ed., 2010), and with Michael Freeman, *The Railway and Modernity: Time, Space, and the Machine Ensemble* (2007).

David Bindman is a professor of history of art emeritus at University College London. His principal research interests lie in British eighteenth-century and European Romantic art, and particularly in caricature and the history of printmaking, and questions of national and racial identity. His books include *Blake as an Artist* (1977); with Malcolm Baker, *Roubiliac and the Eighteenth-Century Monument: Sculpture as Theatre* (1995); *Hogarth and His Times: Serious Comedy* (1997); and *Ape to Apollo: Aesthetics and the Idea of Race in the Eighteenth Century* (2002). Among the volumes he has edited are *John Flaxman* (1979) and *The Shadow of the Guillotine: Britain and the French Revolution* (1989).

Leo Costello is an associate professor of art history at Rice University. His research interests are primarily in British Romantic art. His book *J. M. W. Turner and the Subject of History* appeared 2012. He has also published articles and reviews in the *British Art Journal, Victorian Studies,* and *caareviewsonline,* and contributed the essay "Confronting the Sublime" and related object notes to the catalogue of the 2007 Tate Britain exhibition *J. M. W. Turner,* edited by Ian Warrell.

Wayne Franklin is a professor of English at the University of Connecticut at Storrs. His research interests cover American literature and culture, 1492–1865; American studies, especially material culture and landscape; James Fenimore Cooper; and the history of the book. His publications include *James Fenimore Cooper: The Early Years* (2007); *A Rural Carpenter's World: The Craft in a Nineteenth-Century New York Township* (1990); *The New World of James Fenimore Cooper* (1982); and *Discoverers, Explorers, Settlers: The Diligent Writers of Early America* (1989). Edited volumes include *American Voices, American Lives* (1997), and, with Michael Steiner, *Mapping American Culture* (1995). He is the founding editor of the University of Iowa Press American Land and Life series.

Nicholas Grindle is a senior teaching fellow at the Centre for Advanced Learning and Teaching at University College London. He received a Ph.D. in History of Art from the University of London in 2001 for a thesis titled "'The Wise Surveyor': Surveying and Representation in British Estate Portraiture, 1675–1715." He has taught at Birkbeck College, University of London; University College London; Imperial College, University of London; and the Open University. His articles have appeared in *Oxford Art Journal, History of Collections,* and *Res: Journal of Anthropology and Aesthetics.* He also contributed the chapter "New Ways of Seeing" to *The History of British Art,* volume 2, edited by David Bindman (2008).

Andrew Hemingway is a professor of history of art emeritus at University College London. His research interests cover aesthetics and art theory around 1800, British Romantic landscape painting, and U.S. art of the early twentieth century. His books include *Landscape Imagery and Urban Culture in Early Nineteenth-Century Britain* (1992); *Artists on the Left: American Artists and the Communist Movement, 1926–1956* (2002); and *The Mysticism of Money: Precisionist Painting and Machine Age America* (2013); as well as the edited volumes *Art in Bourgeois Society, 1790–1850* (with William Vaughan, 1998) and *Marxism and the History of Art: From William Morris to the New Left* (2006).

Janet Koenig is a New York–based artist and writer. Her work has appeared in numerous exhibitions and publications about social and political issues, including MoMA's *Committed to Print* (1988). She has participated in the artist collectives Political Art Documentation/Distribution, RepoHistory, and the catalog committee of Artists Meeting for Cultural Change that produced *An Anti-Catalog* (1977). She translated and annotated *L'enfant perdu et retrouvé; ou Pierre Cholet* by J.-B. Proulx as *Lost and Found Again, or Pierre Cholet* (2007) and *Les mots qui font peur* by Hsi Huan-Wou and Charles Reeve as *Who's Afraid of the Big Bad Words* (2013).

William Pressly is a professor of art history at the University of Maryland. His research interests lie in the field of eighteenth- and nineteenth-century European art, with an emphasis on British painting. His publications include *The Life and Art of James Barry* (1981); *James Barry: The Artist as Hero* (Tate Gallery exhibition catalogue, 1983); *A Catalogue of Paintings in the Folger Shakespeare Library* (1993); *The French Revolution as Blasphemy: Johan Zoffany's Paintings of the Massacre at Paris, August 10, 1792* (1999); and *The Artist as Original Genius: Shakespeare's "Fine Frenzy" in Late-Eighteenth-Century British Art* (2007). He contributed an essay to the exhibition catalogue *John Singleton Copley in England* (National Gallery of Art, Washington, D.C., and the Museum of Fine Arts, Houston, 1995–96).

Robert Sayre is a professor of Anglophone literature at the University Paris Est–Marne-la-Vallée. His research interests are in the sociology of literature and the history of Romanticism. His books include *Solitude in Society: A Sociological Study in French Literature* (1978); *La modernité et son autre: récit de la rencontre avec l'Indien en Amérique du Nord au XVIIIe siècle* (2008); and with Michael Löwy, *L'insurrection des "Misérables": romantisme et révolution en juin 1832* (1992), and *Révolte et mélancolie: le romantisme à contre-courant de la modernité* (1992), translated as *Romanticism against the Tide of Modernity* (2001).

William H. Truettner is a senior curator emeritus at the Smithsonian American Art Museum. His research lies primarily in eighteenth- and nineteenth-century American painting, and George Catlin and art of the American West. His books include *The Natural Man Observed: A Study of Catlin's Indian Gallery* (1979), and *Painting Indians and Building Empires in North America, 1710–1840* (2010). Truettner has organized a number of groundbreaking exhibitions including *Picturing Old New England: Image and Memory* (1999); *Thomas Cole: Landscape into History* (with Alan Wallach, 1994); and *The West as America: Reinterpreting Images of the Frontier, 1820–1920* (1991).

Dell Upton is a professor of architecture at UCLA. He works on American and world architecture and urbanism, material culture, and cross-cultural spatial formation in the postcolonial world. His publications range from pre-Revolutionary American architecture to critiques of New Urbanism and heritage tourism. They include *Another City: Urban Life and Urban Spaces in the New American Republic*

(2008); *Architecture in the United States* (1998), a volume in the Oxford History of Art series; and *Holy Things and Profane: Anglican Parish Churches in Colonial Virginia* (1986). He wrote the chief catalogue essay for the Metropolitan Museum of Art's exhibition *Art and the Empire City: New York, 1825–1861* (2000).

William Vaughan is a professor of history of art emeritus at Birkbeck College, University of London. His main research area is Romanticism, particularly British and German art around 1800. His books include, among others, *German Romantic Painting* (1980); *German Romanticism and English Art* (1979); *Romanticism and Art* (1994); and *Art in Bourgeois Society, 1790–1850* (edited with Andrew Hemingway, 1998). He has curated several exhibitions, including *Caspar David Friedrich* (Tate Gallery, 1972); *The Romantic Spirit in German Art* (Hayward Gallery, London, 1996); and *Samuel Palmer: Vision and Landscape* (British Museum, 2005).

Alan Wallach is Ralph H. Wark Professor of Art and Art History and Professor of American Studies Emeritus at the College of William and Mary. He has published over one hundred articles and reviews on the history of American art. He was co-curator with William Truettner for the 1994 exhibition *Thomas Cole: Landscape into History* and was the author of the exhibition catalogue's principal essay. His *Exhibiting Contradiction: Essays on the Art Museum in the United States* appeared in 1998. Wallach was the recipient of the College Art Association's Distinguished Teaching of Art History Award in 2007.

# INDEX